Edited by two leading analysts of postcommunist politics, this book brings together distinguished specialists on Russia and other newly independent states of the former USSR. Chapters on Belarus, Moldova, and Ukraine, plus three chapters on Russia's new political order, its political parties, and its regional politics, provide an in-depth analysis of the uneven pattern of political change in these four countries. Karen Dawisha and Bruce Parrott contribute theoretical and comparative chapters on postcommunist political development. This book will provide students and scholars with detailed analysis by leading authorities, plus the latest research data on recent political trends in each country.

Democratization and Authoritarianism in
Postcommunist Societies: 3

Democratic changes and authoritarian reactions in
Russia, Ukraine, Belarus, and Moldova

Editors

Karen Dawisha
University of Maryland at College Park

Bruce Parrott
The Paul H. Nitze School of Advanced International Studies
The Johns Hopkins University

These four volumes, edited by two leading analysts of
postcommunist politics, bring together distinguished specialists to
provide specially commissioned, up-to-date essays on the postcommunist societies of Eastern Europe and the former Soviet Union.
Each contributor analyzes both progress made toward
democratization, and the underlying social, economic, and cultural
factors that have shaped political change. All chapters contain
information on the emergence of political parties, elections,
institutional reform, and socioeconomic trends. Each volume also
contains chapters by the editors juxtaposing the overall trends in
these countries with comparable transitions and processes of
democratization elsewhere.

1. *The consolidation of democracy in East-Central Europe*

2. *Politics, power, and the struggle for democracy in*
   South-East Europe

3. *Democratic changes and authoritarian reactions in Russia,*
   Ukraine, Belarus, and Moldova

4. *Conflict, cleavage, and change in Central Asia and the*
   Caucasus

Democratic changes and authoritarian reactions in Russia, Ukraine, Belarus, and Moldova

edited by

Karen Dawisha

University of Maryland at College Park

and

Bruce Parrott

The Paul H. Nitze School of Advanced International Studies
The Johns Hopkins University

CAMBRIDGE
UNIVERSITY PRESS

PUBLISHED BY THE PRESS SYNDICATE OF THE UNIVERSITY OF CAMBRIDGE
The Pitt Building, Trumpington Street, Cambridge CB2 1RP, United Kingdom

CAMBRIDGE UNIVERSITY PRESS
The Edinburgh Building, Cambridge, CB2 2RU, United Kingdom
40 West 20th Street, New York, NY 10011-4211, USA
10 Stamford Road, Oakleigh, Melbourne 3166, Australia

First published 1997

Printed in the United Kingdom by Bell & Bain Ltd, Glasgow

Typeset in 10/12 pt, CG Times

A catalogue record for this book is available from the British Library

Library of Congress Cataloguing in Publication data applied for

ISBN 0 521 59245 3 hardback
ISBN 0 521 59732 3 paperback

FR

To Adeed, Nadia and Emile,
with love

K.D.

To Matthew,
with love

B.P.

Contents

Tables

Figures

Contributors

WILLIAM CROWTHER is Associate Professor of Political Science at the University of North Carolina in Greensboro. His publications include "Moldova After Independence," *Current History* (October 1994), and "The Politics of Ethno-National Mobilization: Nationalism and Reform in Soviet Moldavia," *The Russian Review* (April 1991). He received his Ph.D. from the University of California at Los Angeles.

KAREN DAWISHA is Professor of Government and Director of the Center for the Study of Postcommunist Societies at the University of Maryland at College Park. She graduated with degrees in Russian and politics from the University of Lancaster in England and received her Ph.D. from the London School of Economics. She has served as an advisor to the British House of Commons Foreign Affairs Committee and was a member of the policy planning staff of the US State Department. Her publications include *Russia and the New States of Eurasia: The Politics of Upheaval* (with Bruce Parrott, 1994), *Eastern Europe, Gorbachev and Reform: The Great Challenge* (1989, 2d ed., 1990), *The Kremlin and the Prague Spring* (1984), *The Soviet Union in the Middle East: Politics and Perspectives* (1982), *Soviet–East European Dilemmas: Coercion, Competition, and Consent* (1981), and *Soviet Foreign Policy Toward Egypt* (1979).

VLADIMIR GEL'MAN is a member of the Institute for Sociology of the Russian Academy of Sciences (St. Petersburg branch), and serves on the faculty of sociology and political science of the European University of St. Petersburg. His work has appeared widely in scholarly journals in the Russian Federation, as well as in the United States and Germany. He has served as associate director of the Institute for Humanities and Political Studies in Moscow.

JEFFREY W. HAHN is Professor of Political Science at Villanova University and specializes in Russian politics. He is author of *Soviet Grassroots: Citizen Participation in Local Soviet Government* (1988), editor of *Democratization in Russia: The Development of Legislative Institutions* (1996), and co-editor (with Theodore H. Friedgut) of *Local Power and Post Soviet Politics* (1994). His recent publications draw on field work conducted in Russia from 1990 to 1994. He received his Ph.D. from Duke University.

KATHLEEN MIHALISKO is Director of Management Information Systems and Communications at America's Development Foundation in Alexandria, Virginia. Formerly an analyst for Radio Free Europe/Radio Liberty providing information and prognoses to media, policymakers, and government agencies in the United States and Europe, she has published more than sixty articles in *RFE/RL Research Report* and *Report on the USSR*. Her other recent publications include "The Belarusian National Dilemma," *Demokratizatsiya* (Winter 1993/94), and "Security Policies in Ukraine and Belarus," in *Central and Eastern Europe: The Challenge of Transition* (1993). She received her M.A. in regional studies of the Soviet Union from Harvard University.

BRUCE PARROTT is Professor and Director of Russian Area and East European Studies at the Paul H. Nitze School of Advanced International Studies of The Johns Hopkins University. He is author of *Russia and the New States of Eurasia: The Politics of Upheaval* (with Karen Dawisha, 1994), *The Soviet Union and Ballistic Missile Defense* (1987), and *Politics and Technology in the Soviet Union* (1983); and editor of *The End of Empire? The Transformation of the USSR in Comparative Perspective* (with Karen Dawisha, 1996), *State Building and Military Power in Russia and the New States of Eurasia* (1995), *The Dynamics of Soviet Defense Policy* (1990), and *Trade, Technology, and Soviet-American Relations* (1985). He received his Ph.D. in political science from Columbia University.

ILYA PRIZEL is Associate Professor of Russian Area and East European Studies and Coordinator of East European Studies at the Paul H. Nitze School of Advanced International Studies of The Johns Hopkins University. His most recent work, entitled *Between Hubris and Despair: The Evolution of National Identity and Its Impact on Foreign Policy Formation in Poland, Russia, and Ukraine*, is scheduled for publication in 1997. He is also the author of *Latin America Through Soviet Eyes: The Evolution of Soviet Perceptions of Latin America During the Brezhnev Era* (1990); and co-editor with Andrew Michta of *Post-1989 Poland: Challenges of Independence* (1995), and *Post-Communist Eastern Europe: Crisis and Readjustment* (1992). He received his Ph.D. from The Johns Hopkins University.

THOMAS F. REMINGTON is Professor of Political Science at Emory University. His publications include *The Truth of Authority: Ideology and Communication in the Soviet Union* (1988), *Politics and the Soviet System* (1989), and, most recently, *Parliaments in Transition: The New Legislative Politics in the Former USSR and Eastern Europe* (1994). He is associate editor of the journal *Russian Review*. His research focuses on the development of representative political institutions in post-Soviet Russia and is supported by grants from the National Council for Soviet and East European Research and the National Science Foundation. He has spent extensive time in Moscow interviewing members of the USSR and Russian parliaments on the development of the legislative branch. He received his Ph.D. in political science from Yale University in 1978.

MICHAEL URBAN is a Professor of Politics at the University of California at Santa Cruz. He is author of *The Rebirth of Politics in Russia* (1997), *More Power to the Soviets* (1990), *An Algebra of Soviet Power* (1989), and *The Ideology of Administration* (1982), and editor of *Ideology and System Change in the USSR and East Europe* (1992). His work has also appeared in numerous scholarly journals and edited volumes. He received his Ph.D. in political science from the University of Kansas.

Preface

This study of democratization in the Russian Federation, Belarus, Moldova, and Ukraine is one of four books produced by the Project on Democratization and Political Participation in Postcommunist Societies. The project has been sponsored jointly by the School of Advanced International Studies of The Johns Hopkins University and the University of Maryland at College Park. It draws on the talents of scholars from a wide array of other universities and research institutions.

As codirectors of the project, we are grateful for material support furnished by two organizations. Principal funding for the project has been provided by the United States Department of State as part of its external research program. In addition, the intellectual planning of the project was aided at a crucial juncture by a grant from the Joint Committee on Eastern Europe of the American Council of Learned Societies. However, none of the views or conclusions contained in the book should be interpreted as representing the official opinion or policy of the Department of State or of the Joint Committee.

The three other volumes in the series deal with the countries of East-Central Europe, the countries of South-East Europe, and the countries of Central Asia and the Caucasus. Any student of contemporary international affairs knows that the delineation of "Europe" and its constituent regions frequently generates intellectual controversy about which countries belong to Europe or to "the West." We adopted our quadripartite grouping of countries to facilitate the management of a large research project and to produce books that match the curricular structure of many college and university courses devoted to the countries of the postcommunist world. Neither the grouping nor the names were chosen with any intention of suggesting that some countries are necessarily more "advanced" or "backward" politically than others. Most of the regional groups exhibit considerable internal political diversity among the member countries, and the comparative judgments presented in the volumes are based on the findings of the individual country-studies, not on preconceptions about one or another region.

In the course of this project we have received assistance from many individuals and incurred many personal obligations. We wish to thank John Parker and Susan Nelson of the Department of State for proposing the general idea of the project to us, for making helpful suggestions about how it could be carried out, and for encouraging the project participants to draw whatever conclusions the evidence supports. We are grateful to Jason Parker of the ACLS Joint Committee on Eastern Europe for his assistance. We also wish to thank several scholars for their valuable help in sorting out the basic issues at an initial planning workshop: Nancy Bermeo, Valerie Bunce, Ted Robert Gurr, Joan Nelson, and Robert Putnam. Herbert Kitschelt was likewise very helpful in this regard.

We are deeply indebted to the country-study writers for the high level of effort that they invested in writing their chapters, for their active participation in the project workshops, and for undertaking more extensive revisions than are customary in collective enterprises of this kind. We also are grateful to the four authors who served as coordinators of the workshops: Sharon Wolchik, Vladimir Tismaneanu, Ilya Prizel, and Muriel Atkin. During the organizational stage of the project we benefited from their advice, and we profited from the written comments that they made on the draft chapters presented at the workshops.

We express our special thanks to Griffin Hathaway, the Executive Director of the project, who performed a nearly endless series of administrative and intellectual tasks with exemplary efficiency; to Florence Rotz, staff person of the SAIS Russian Area and East European Studies program, who managed the production and revision of several versions of the chapters with admirable calmness and consummate skill; to Paula Smith, who proofread the manuscript; and to Steve Guenther, who helped with the logistics of the workshops. Not least, we are grateful to Murray Feshbach for generously providing demographic data for a number of the country-studies.

Finally, we express our thanks to Michael Holdsworth of Cambridge University Press for his willingness to take on this large publishing project and see it through to the end. Bruce Parrott also thanks Gordon Livingston, without whose help he could not have completed his portion of the project.

K. D.
B. P.

1 Perspectives on postcommunist democratization

Bruce Parrott

Of all the elements of the international wave of democratization that began some two decades ago, the transformation of communist political systems, once thought impervious to liberalization, is the most dramatic.[1] Since 1989, more than two dozen countries within the former Soviet bloc have officially disavowed Marxist–Leninist ideology and have dismantled, in varying degrees, the apparatus of communist dictatorship and socialist economic planning. In many cases this transformation has led to a reinvention of politics, in the sense of genuine public debate about the purposes of society and the state, and has produced significant progress toward the establishment of a liberal–democratic order.[2]

This extraordinary turn of events has evoked a surge of scholarly research and writing from specialists on the former communist countries and other social scientists. Analysts have probed the causes of the demise of communism in Eastern Europe and the former Soviet Union.[3] They have examined the communist legacies inherited by the East European and Soviet successor states and have constructed parallel narratives of early postcommunist developments in regional groupings of these states.[4] They also have produced detailed studies of recent trends in individual countries.[5] Extensive analysis and debate have likewise been devoted to the political and institutional aspects of market reform.[6]

To date, however, scholars have devoted relatively little effort to systematic cross-country comparisons of political change in the postcommunist states. With some notable exceptions, Western thinking about attempts to democratize these polities has generally been based on the experience of the countries of North America, Western and Southern Europe, and Latin America.[7] Among scholars and laypersons alike, there has been an unconscious tendency to view postcommunist political developments through interpretive lenses derived from the experiences of countries that have not undergone the historical transformations and traumas associated with

1

communism. Yet the relevance of the paradigms of democratization (and failed democratization) derived from these countries is far from self-evident. Just as some economists have challenged the applicability of models drawn from noncommunist societies to the dilemmas of economic reform in postcommunist states, some political scientists have questioned whether paradigms of democratization drawn from noncommunist countries are relevant to the study of postcommunist political change.[8] This is an issue of central importance both for social theory and for the day-to-day policies of Western governments and nongovernmental organizations.

An adequate understanding of this exceptionally complex theoretical issue, however, requires a better understanding of the nature of the political changes occurring inside the postcommunist countries themselves. Because the communist era saddled these countries with many similar political and socioeconomic dilemmas, it is logical to examine them for similar processes of political change. A strong case can be made that communist countries passed through a distinctive set of profound political and socioeconomic alterations that makes comparisons among postcommunist patterns of political development especially fruitful. On the other hand, these societies also have been shaped by dissimilar processes - witness the contrast between the Czech Republic and Turkmenistan, which today have little in common besides the fact that they were once called communist - and analysts cannot assume that they are destined to follow identical political trajectories. Controlled comparisons among postcommunist countries can help us identify the causes of the varying national outcomes that have begun to crystallize roughly a half-decade after the demise of communism.

Some valuable comparative work on postcommunist political development has already been done.[9] But the immense forces that have been unleashed and the profound questions that they raise demand much fuller exploration. Only a sustained research effort by the broad community of scholars can provide a surer baseline for evaluating recent trends and the prospects for democracy in particular postcommunist states. This long-term effort must address many aspects of each country's political life – its constitutional arrangements, the objectives of its leaders, public attitudes toward politics, ethnonational sentiments, the interplay of politics and economics, and the effects of international influences, to name only a few – and juxtapose them with comparable phenomena in other postcommunist states.

Although the project that produced this book touches on a number of these themes, the central goal has been to trace changes and continuities in elite and mass political participation in each of the postcommunist countries of Eastern Europe and the former Soviet Union.[10] By examining the major political actors and the means through which they exercise power, the project has sought to assess the extent of democratization in each country and the strength of countervailing authoritarian tendencies. In particular, we have examined the degree to which postcommunist political arrangements have fostered or inhibited an expansion of popular political participation through the introduction of competitive elections and the formation of competitive political parties. Where feasible, we also have offered preliminary assessments of the strength and orientation of the network of groups and institutions sometimes known as "civil society" – or, more generally, as political society.[11] The writers of the country-studies have necessarily approached these topics from various angles, depending on the particulars of the country being analyzed. In each instance, however, the writer has sought to clarify whether formative influences and political choices have propelled the country's postcommunist politics in a democratic or an authoritarian direction, and how durable the new constellation of power appears to be.

This approach has both intellectual advantages and limitations. The contributors to the project have harbored no illusions that we could treat all the relevant issues in the necessary depth. Separate volumes could easily have been written on particular facets of the overall comparisons we have undertaken. The value of our enterprise is that it presents a comprehensive set of carefully researched case-studies based on a common research agenda and on close interaction among the country-study writers and editors. The project provides a useful picture of each country's political development up to the mid-1990s, along with a sense of the national trends that may prevail during the next few years. In addition, it lays the groundwork for delineating and explaining alternative paths of democratic and nondemocratic change in postcommunist societies. Today, less than a decade since communist regimes began to fall, the challenge of charting these paths remains daunting. In the words of one scholar, "it is a peculiarity of political scientists that we spend much of our time explaining events that have not finished happening."[12] Identifying and explaining patterns of postcommunist political development will become easier as additional events and a longer historical perspective make those patterns more distinct; but it is not too early to begin the task.

The remainder of this chapter situates the country-studies in a general intellectual framework and highlights some of the principal themes they address. First it examines the meaning of key concepts, such as democracy and democratic transition, and sketches the types of regimes that may emerge from the wreckage of communism. Next the chapter explores the impact of the international environment and of national historical legacies on the evolution of postcommunist regimes. It then turns to a discussion of elections, party systems, and their role in the success or failure of democratization. Finally, the chapter surveys the potential effects of political culture and the intermediate groups that constitute a country's political society. In treating each theme, I draw on the chapters included in this book and the companion volumes.[13]

Democracy and the alternatives

Because the general notion of democracy has been interpreted in many different ways, it is essential to begin by discussing some of these variations and their implications for the study of postcommunist countries. After all, during their heyday Marxist–Leninist regimes claimed to be quintessentially democratic and ridiculed the "bourgeois" democracies found in other parts of the world. More to the point, proponents of liberal democracy have long disagreed among themselves about which institutional arrangements constitute the essence of a democratic system. Equally significant, some admirers of the advanced industrial democracies prefer to call such systems "polyarchies" and to treat democracy as a set of normative standards against which all political systems must be measured, in order not to gloss over the serious defects of contemporary liberal polities.[14]

For the purposes of this project, we have adopted a less stringent criterion for classifying a country as democratic. According to this standard, democracy is a political system in which the formal and actual leaders of the government are chosen within regular intervals through elections based on a comprehensive adult franchise with equally weighted voting, multiple candidacies, secret balloting, and other procedures, such as freedom of the press and assembly, that ensure real opportunities for electoral competition. Among the various attributes of democracy, competitive elections are the feature that is most easily identifiable and most widely recognized around the world. Competitive elections are arguably a precondition for the other political benefits that a democratic system may confer on its citizens, and they are a valuable yardstick for analyzing and distinguishing among postcommunist countries. One fundamental question is why some countries, such as Poland, have introduced fully competitive elections, while others, such as Uzbekistan, have not. Another question is why some postcommunist countries have continued to choose their governmental leaders through free elections, whereas other countries that initially introduced such elections, such as Armenia and Albania, have recently fallen victim to large-scale electoral fraud.

Although useful, our minimalist definition of democracy also involves potential pitfalls. Because it does not stipulate all the individual liberties that most Western observers consider an essential element of genuine democracy, it groups together the majoritarian and constitutionalist/libertarian traditions of democratic governance.[15] Under certain conditions, a competitively elected government is capable of behaving in a despotic fashion toward large numbers of its citizens or inhabitants, especially when those persons belong to a distinct ethnic or religious minority.[16] The behavior of the Croatian government toward many ethnic Serbian inhabitants of Croatia is a graphic example. Other postcommunist governments, such as those of Estonia and Latvia, have faced major dilemmas posed by the presence of sizable minorities, but they have dealt with these issues in a more humane though sometimes controversial manner. Confronted with ethnic mixes that pose less obvious risks to the state, still other governments have accorded full rights to citizens of minority extraction; Bulgaria is a case in point. In a fully functioning constitutional democracy, the rights of citizens and inhabitants are legally specified and protected by the government, no matter how sweeping a mandate it has received at the polls.

Another caveat concerns the application of the criterion of competitive elections. The project's case-studies show that in several countries postcommunist elections have been considerably more competitive than the typical stage-managed charades of the communist era, yet have not been entirely free by strict democratic standards. In the long run, however, this movement from communist-style to semidemocratic elections may constitute an important step in the process of liberalization and may lead, despite powerful resistance, to voting procedures that are fully democratic. One strand of the scholarly literature emphasizes that democracy is sometimes the unintended consequence of political struggles among antagonists who did not initially seek to create it. The political import of semi-competitive elections thus depends on whether they mark a national step forward from completely rigged elections or a regression from elections that were genuinely democratic. Semi-competitive elections in Turkmenistan would be a sign of dramatic democratic progress, whereas similar elections in the Czech Republic would not.

Care is also required in applying the notion of democratic transitions. Due to the astonishing cascade of events that brought about the collapse of communism and a Western victory in the Cold War, virtually all postcommunist leaders proclaimed their commitment to democratization – sometimes sincerely, sometimes not – and a considerable number of outside observers assumed that democracy would be the natural result of communism's demise. However, when thinking about the evolution of the postcommunist states it is important to maintain the distinction between transitions from communism and transitions to democracy. It may be true that liberal democracy has become the prevailing model of modern politics in much of the world.[17] But both historical experience and a priori reasoning suggest that a spectrum of possible postcommunist outcomes still exists. This spectrum includes variants of democracy, variants of authoritarianism, and some hybrids in between.

The consolidation of democracy is another important idea that warrants careful handling. To say that democracy has been consolidated in a country suggests, at a minimum, that the introduction of fully competitive elections has been completed and that the new political system has become stable. In this discussion, consolidation denotes the condition of a political system in which all major political actors and social groups expect that government leaders will be chosen through competitive elections and regard representative institutions and procedures as their main channel for pressing claims on the state.[18] A few scholarly critics have challenged the idea of consolidation, arguing that some democracies have demonstrated considerable staying-power without ever satisfying certain commonly accepted criteria of consolidation.[19] Nevertheless, the concept remains useful for differentiating democratic systems that have achieved internal stability from systems that have not, and for making probabilistic assessments of a particular democracy's political prospects. It calls attention to internal factors, such as fundamental divisions over national identity, constitutional structure, and criteria of citizenship, that can destroy a democratic polity. Because all systems are subject to political decay, consolidation does not guarantee that a democracy will survive, but does improve its chances. Although democratic consolidation typically required a long time in earlier eras, the contemporary ascendancy of liberal-democratic norms in many parts of the globe may accelerate the process. Since the 1970s the consolidation of new democratic systems has occurred quite quickly in some noncommunist countries, though not in others.[20]

Whether any of the postcommunist states have achieved democratic consolidation is a complex issue. A case can be made that the Czech Republic, Poland, and Lithuania have reached this political watershed, even though controversy persists over the shape of the Polish constitution. But most postcommunist states have not reached it. Some, such as Latvia and Estonia, have established representative institutions and political structures that work quite smoothly, but have not yet admitted large ethnic minorities to citizenship. Others, such as Russia, have made impressive progress in introducing competitive elections, but contain particular political parties and social groups whose loyalty to democratic principles remains highly questionable. Still others, such as Uzbekistan and Belarus, are plainly developing along authoritarian lines.

The spectrum of possible postcommunist outcomes includes such variants of democracy as parliamentary rule and presidential government. Each of these forms of government has been adopted by some postcommunist countries, and each has champions who argue that it is the least susceptible to political breakdown.[21] In addition, the spectrum of potential outcomes includes hybrid systems similar to the "delegative democracy" identified by students of comparative politics.[22] In a delegative democracy, the president is chosen through competitive elections. Once in office, however, he rules in the name of the whole nation, usually on the pretence that he transcends the petty concerns of particular parties and interest groups. Unconstrained by the legislature or the courts, the president governs without significant checks on his power, save for the constitutional requirement that regular presidential elections be held and the de facto power held by other officials, and he often seeks to change the constitution so as to prolong his time in power.[23] Several postcommunist countries, particularly some former Soviet republics, have concentrated governmental power in an executive president with the authority to issue decrees having the force of law. Depending on the future course of events, this hybrid arrangement has the potential to become either a constitutional democracy or a clear-cut form of authoritarianism.

The main potential forms of postcommunist authoritarianism are personal dictatorships, one-party states, and military regimes. The socioeconomic turmoil following the collapse of communism may make it hard to build stable versions of any of these types of authoritarianism, but oscillations among them may still preclude successful democratization. In countries where a substantial part of the population has already undergone sociopolitical mobilization, the lack of a well developed party structure makes a personal dictatorship vulnerable to sharp shifts in the public mood and to unbridled power-struggles when the dictator is incapacitated or dies.[24] Nonetheless, a few postcommunist countries are likely to come under the sway of such dictatorships. Contemporary Belarus fits this model, and Turkmenistan bears a significant resemblance to it.

Generally speaking, authoritarian states built around a single ruling party are more stable than personal dictatorships. A ramified party organization helps harness mass political participation to the leaders' objectives, reduces elite conflict, and smooths the process of succession. For postcommunist leaders set on following this path, the challenge is to create a party mechanism that can actually control mass participation and the behavior of any quasi-democratic governmental institutions that already have been set up. This stratagem is often more difficult to apply than it might seem. Once the old communist mechanisms of control have been weakened, building a stable new ruling party is a problematic undertaking, as developments in Kazakstan indicate. Success depends both on the top leader's willingness to assign high priority to building such a party and on the party's capacity to contain new socioeconomic forces within its structure. Absent these two conditions, leaders with a dictatorial bent may move toward a system of personal rule, eliminating quasi-democratic institutions and processes, such as elections, that they cannot effectively control.

As of the mid–1990s, direct military rule seemed the least likely postcommunist authoritarian outcome. Historically, one-party states have proven less susceptible to military coups than have other forms of authoritarianism.[25] Ruling communist parties exercised especially close civilian control over their military professionals, and this heritage of subordination appears to have shaped military behavior in most postcommunist countries. The rare episodes in which the armed forces have intervened collectively to affect the selection of national leaders have usually been precipitated by "demand pull" from feuding politicians eager to defeat their rivals rather than by any military desire to rule.[26] That said, it should be noted that irregular military forces and militias have played a sizable role in the politics of some postcommunist countries, especially those parts of the former Soviet Union and the former Yugoslavia that have become embroiled in warfare. In a number of countries the parlous economic and social condition of the regular military has facilitated transfers of weapons and personnel to irregular military forces. Although irregular forces have caused a change of government leadership in only a few cases, such as Georgia and Azerbaijan, they frequently have had a strong effect on the political balance inside their "host" states, whether those states are nominally democratic or authoritarian in character.[27]

The international environment and national historical legacies

The dynamics of postcommunist political change have been shaped by several major variables. One of the most important is the international environment, which includes geopolitical, institutional-normative, and cultural elements. Historically, the overall effect of the international environment on attempts to promote democratization has ranged from highly beneficial to extremely harmful.[28] By historical standards, the contemporary international setting has been relatively favorable to the creation and consolidation of new democracies, although there have been important regional variations in this respect. The generally propitious international environment has been shaped by a number of factors: the heightened Western commitment to human rights as a major aspect of interstate relations; the gradual absorption of liberal ideas into once-autarkic societies made increasingly permeable by competitive pressures from an open global economy; the decision of the Soviet leadership not to shore up communist regimes in Eastern Europe with military threats or intervention; the "gravitational pull" exerted by highly prosperous Western democracies and by multilateral institutions prepared to assist postcommunist liberalization; and the intensifying bandwagon effects exerted by leading exemplars of reform, such as Poland, on other former communist countries that initially dragged their feet.[29]

International conditions have not favored all postcommunist efforts at democratization in equal measure. The effects of the international setting have varied sharply by region and by the form of outside influence in question. For the most part, the Western powers have refused to intervene with decisive military force to suppress the savage ethnic violence that has undermined the chances for democratization in parts of the former Yugoslavia and the Transcaucasus.[30] In contrast to the situation after World War II, when the geostrategic interests of the Western Allies required the imposition of democratic institutions on the defeated Axis powers, the West has had no compelling strategic reason to impose liberal-democratic arrangements on such countries as Serbia.[31] Perhaps as significant, the West's political and economic impact on most European postcommunist states has exceeded its influence on the postcommunist states of the Transcaucasus and Central Asia. The scale of such influence is not determined solely by the receiving state's location or culture; witness the isolation of Belarus from the countries to its west. But the large cluster of established European democracies and the prospect of close political and economic ties with them have had a much stronger effect in Eastern Europe than in other postcommunist regions. In Eastern Europe, a desire to be admitted to NATO and the European Union has tempered the political conduct even of lagging states such as Romania.

Several factors account for this variation in Western influence: the greater physical and cultural distance between the West and most of the non-European postcommunist states; the lower level of Western strategic interest in these countries, coupled with a tendency to manifest less concern about their internal liberalization than about their potential as sources of energy and raw materials; the countries' greater vulnerability to pressures from a Russia preoccupied with ensuring the stability of its southern flank; and the substantial limits on the West's diplomatic leverage in Asia, where booming economies have emboldened some authoritarian regimes, such as China, to defy Western human-rights standards.[32]

In addition to being influenced by the international environment, the direction of postcommunist political development has been shaped by whether struggles over political change have taken place within the arena of a firmly established nation-state. In a handful of postcommunist countries, politics has unfolded within the boundaries and administrative framework of the old communist state. In most cases, however, the struggle over democratization has coincided with efforts to create the political scaffolding of a new state on a portion of the territory of the old communist regime. Due to the breakup of Czechoslovakia, Yugoslavia, and the Soviet Union, twenty-two of the twenty-seven postcommunist states are new sovereign entities. This is one of the main features that distinguishes postcommunist efforts to build democracy from comparable processes in Latin America and Southern Europe.[33]

The break-up of states severely complicates efforts to achieve democratization. The process frequently triggers incendiary controversies over the national identity of the new states, contested borders, and rival groups' competing claims to be the only indigenous inhabitants of their new country. In cases as diverse as Croatia, Azerbaijan, Georgia, Moldova, and

Russia, national declarations of independence from a larger communist regime have coincided with simultaneous attempts by local minorities to declare their own independence from the newly established states. Such centrifugal processes, which cannot be resolved by appealing to the principle of national self-determination, increase the probability of violent communal conflict and the emergence of ultranationalist sentiments harmful to democratization.[34] The conflicts between Serbia and Croatia and between Armenia and Azerbaijan provide examples. The collapse of an established state also accelerates the disintegration of the government bureaucracies that must function smoothly to ensure the administrative effectiveness of democratic institutions. This, in turn, may undermine the popular appeal of democracy as a political system.[35]

The creation of new states from old does not always preclude democratic development, however. The Czech Republic and Slovakia, Russia and the Baltic states, and the former Yugoslav republic of Slovenia are cases in point. Democratization is liable to fail when efforts to dismantle the old state interact with the mobilization of large internal ethnic "diasporas" and the emergence of ultranationalism in internal ethnic "homelands" to ignite large-scale violence. Democratization stands a greater chance of success when internal ethnic diasporas are small or are willing to be incorporated into successor states outside their "homeland," and when nationalist movements in the ethnic homelands are moderate rather than extremist.[36] In new, ethnically divided states, the political impact of ethnic differences depends on the actions both of the dominant group and of ethnic minorities and outside parties, as the contrasting internal political dynamics of Croatia and Estonia demonstrate.

Whether linked to the collapse of an established state or not, manifestations of nationalism and efforts to democratize can affect each other in very different ways. Careful observers have distinguished between two types of nationalism: inclusionary "civic" nationalism, which is compatible with the observance of individual rights, and exclusionary ethnic nationalism, which tends to subordinate such rights to the collectivist claims of the nation.[37] Rarely if ever do these two types of nationalism exist in pure form, but the weighting of the two tendencies in citizens' attitudes varies enormously from one country to another.[38] For example, Ukraine might be placed close to the "civic" end of the spectrum, Latvia nearer the middle, and Serbia near the "ethnic" end.[39] Before the final third of the nineteenth century, when nationhood in Europe became closely linked to ethnicity, nationalism was commonly understood to be a concomitant of democracy, and in postcommunist cases such as Poland, this connection can still be seen.[40] A modicum of nationalism is indispensable for the creation and cohesion of a modern state; without it many citizens will lack an incentive to participate actively in democratic politics, as the case of Belarus demonstrates. On the other hand, exclusionary nationalism can lead to the effective disenfranchisement of substantial segments of the population – witness the behavior of the Serbian and Croatian governments toward minorities within their borders – and undergird dictatorial practices.

In addition to examining the historical roots of national identity in each country, analysts of postcommunist political change must examine other effects of the country's precommunist political legacy. Studies of democratization in states lacking a communist past have shown that countries which have had a prior experience of democracy, even if the experience has been unsuccessful, have a better chance of democratizing successfully on their second attempt.[41] Prior democratic experience may promote current democratization in several ways. If fairly recent, it may provide "human capital" – that is, persons with a first-hand understanding of democratic institutions and practices who can help launch and maintain the new political arrangements. Even if historically remote, previous experience may provide instructive lessons in the design of democratic institutions matched to the particular features of the country in question. Finally, previous experience may help legitimize new democratic institutions by protecting them against the xenophobic charge that they are an alien cultural import.

By comparison with many democratizing countries that were never communist, the postcommunist countries have little prior democratic experience on which to draw, as Valerie Bunce has forcefully argued. This disadvantage is clearest with respect to human capital. Measured against Latin America and Southern Europe, where authoritarian and democratic rule frequently alternated with one another in the past, "Eastern Europe has no such democratic tradition. The so-called democratic experiments of the interwar period lasted less than a decade and are best understood, in any case, as authoritarian politics in democratic guise." Lacking "the 'feel' for democracy that Latin America and Southern Europe enjoyed," postcommunist states face special political obstacles.[42]

These obstacles are not insurmountable, however. Even if short-lived, a nation's previous attempts to build democracy can give reformers not only potential models for contemporary governmental arrangements but also lessons about constitutional flaws that have contributed to past democratic failures. Political learning of this kind has occurred, for example, in Estonia and Latvia. More broadly, national memories or even myths of a democratic past may facilitate popular acceptance of democratic political structures.[43] This sort of process has occurred in both the Czech Republic and Poland. Citizens of Slovakia, by contrast, tend to regard interwar Czechoslovakian history as a period of alien domination by the Czechs rather than as an integral part of their own national past, and countries such as Ukraine effectively lack any modern experience of independent statehood. But even in nations such as these, a strong popular aversion to decades of communist oppression may compensate for the absence of a "usable" democratic past. Due to the exceptional severity of most communist regimes, this kind of negative learning may be considerably stronger in postcommunist countries than in noncommunist countries that aspire to democratize.

Like the effects of the precommunist legacy, the effects of communist rule on the prospects for democratic political participation warrant careful scrutiny in each country. Exactly what constitutes political participation, it should be said, is a matter of some disagreement among Western scholars. Defining the concept narrowly, specialists on the "classic" democracies have tended to concentrate on citizen involvement in such activities as voting and contacting government officials, and have frequently excluded citizen involvement in such "unconventional" activities as peaceful protests and demonstrations.[44] This narrower definition may stem from an understandable concern, sharpened by the history of Fascism and Communism, that authoritarian elites bearing the standard of "direct democracy" can manipulate mass movements to destroy the institutions of representative democracy.[45] By contrast, scholars interested in comparative political development have tended to define participation more broadly and have sometimes classified nearly all politically motivated activities, including political violence, under this rubric.[46] Analysts also have differed over the importance of the distinction between voluntary and compulsory participation. Specialists on established democracies have generally treated the contrast between these two forms of political involvement as a key difference between democratic and non-democratic systems, whereas some students of political development have minimized its significance.[47]

Voluntary participation and compulsory participation can each be found in both authoritarian and democratic polities. However, the relative proportions of these types of participation differ dramatically in authoritarian and democratic systems and help explain the qualitative differences between the two.[48] Main-line communist regimes systematically excluded most kinds of voluntary participation – particularly competitive elections for high government office and the freedom to form independent associations – and introduced novel forms of compulsory mass participation directed from above. Mandatory participation reached its zenith in the stage of full-fledged totalitarianism. Communist totalitarianism rested on the discovery that under certain conditions the expansion of mass education and the creation of new social organizations could be joined with mass coercion to multiply rather than diminish the power of the state.[49]

The totalitarian approach to political participation was linked with a radical stance toward society. In the Stalin era, Marxist–Leninist regimes sought to create a political system that not only compelled every citizen to endorse a common sociopolitical program but excluded the very notion of a pluralist society with autonomous interests distinct from those of the ruling elite.[50] In essence, these regimes sought to obliterate the dividing-line between state and society. Although they never completely succeeded, some of them came quite close. For most of the twentieth century, communist systems remained the most stable form of dictatorship – a form so stable that their transformation into liberal polities was said by some observers to be impossible.[51]

The erosion of communism did, of course, pave the way for the expansion of autonomous political participation by citizens and groups acting outside the control of the political elite. To begin with, not all national societies went through so shattering a totalitarian experience as did the nations of the USSR, and this lent them greater political resilience. Poland, where the Catholic Church retained a substantial measure of autonomy and agriculture was never fully collectivized, is probably the best example. Moreover, although communist regimes went to unprecedented lengths to instill the official ideology, their simultaneous drive to transform the economy and raise educational levels gradually expanded the social groups whose members later found those ideological claims implausible or absurd. For example, during the early stages of Stalin's industrialization drive, citizen support for the Soviet regime was directly correlated with an individual's youth and level of education – no doubt partly because education served as an important vehicle of upward social mobility. During the next four or five decades, the stratum of persons with higher education grew dramatically, but at some point support for the regime became inversely correlated with youth and level of education.[52] In many communist countries a small group of citizens became the nucleus of a nascent civil society – that is, in the broadest sense, a society whose members insisted on a separation between state and society and on the moral primacy of societal interests – which ultimately contributed to the downfall of the political regime.[53]

Although communist regimes have generally pursued similar social and economic policies, the effects of communist rule have varied among countries and have contributed to different national patterns of postcommunist political change. At each stage in the transition from communism, the course of events has been shaped by the strength of the ruling elite *vis-à-vis* the political opposition, as well as by the relative strength within each camp of hard-line groups hostile to compromise and groups favoring compromise for the sake of peaceful change.[54] The overall disposition of the ruling communist elite for or against reform has thus had an important effect on the political development of individual countries. The dynamics of change have also been affected by the presence or absence of a vigorous dissent movement, which has sometimes exerted an indirect but powerful long-term influence on both elite and mass attitudes toward democratization. The influence of a generation of liberal Soviet dissenters on the policies of Mikhail Gorbachev contrasts strikingly with the absence of reformist currents among the intellectuals and communist party leaders of Belarus during the same period. In addition, disparate levels of social development and varying mass political cultures have affected the political evolution of individual countries. A case can be made, for instance, that Central Asia's comparatively low levels of urbanization and education have impeded efforts to democratize the states of the region. In such countries as Kyrgyzstan, these low levels have made it difficult to subordinate particularistic loyalties and local ties to a countrywide sense of political engagement and civic responsibility.

Ruling elites and opposition leaders have typically crafted their stances toward democratization with an eye to the shifting national constellation of political forces, and each group's successes and failures have been strongly influenced by its capacity to generate political power. In struggles over the postcommunist order, new forms of democratic participation, ranging from peaceful mass demonstrations to competitive elections, have frequently been pitted against antidemocratic forms of political action, ranging from attacks by hired thugs to mob violence or all-out civil war, as in Tajikistan and Georgia. Intermediate types of political action, such as organized boycotts of elections and general strikes, have been resorted to by both advocates and opponents of democracy. In cases where hostile camps of similar strength have confronted one other, the outcome has depended not only on elite objectives and tactics, but on the content of mass attitudes and the level of mass mobilization in behalf of democratic reforms.[55]

The impact of violence on struggles over the postcommunist order is complex. The prevalence of nonviolent and noncoercive forms of politics improves the chances for a democratic outcome but does not guarantee it. Under certain conditions, dictators and authoritarian parties may be voted into office and then roll back a political system's democratic features, as the example of Belarus shows. In authoritarian systems, many forms of voluntary participation regarded as normal in democratic systems are illegal, and "unconventional" forms of participation such as mass demonstrations and strikes may be indispensable for launching and sustaining the process of democratization. In these circumstances, eyeball-to-eyeball confrontations and the implicit threat of violent escalation may be a spur to reform.[56] Nor does limited violence necessarily eliminate the possibility of further democratic change; instead it may sharpen leaders' and citizens' awareness of the high risks of further violence, as it arguably did in the clash between Russian president Boris Yeltsin and his parliamentary opponents in the fall of 1993. The example of Georgia suggests that even civil war may not completely block a state's subsequent movement in a democratic direction.[57]

Nevertheless, the threshold between nonviolent and violent political action remains extremely important. Violence makes the political stakes a matter of life or death. It deepens grievances among the losers, intensifies fears of liberalization among the winners, and reduces the chances for political compromise. Often it creates armed camps that are prepared to resort to force and have a vested interest in the continued use of force to decide political conflicts, as in the countries of the Transcaucasus. Even if it sweeps away old communist structures, it may make noncommunist dictatorship more likely. Paradoxically, it also may extend the political life of established elites that are tied to the military or the security police but manage to shift the blame for past misdeeds onto the shoulders of a few fellow culprits – as the first phase of Romania's postcommunist development illustrates. The absence of violence does not guarantee a democratic outcome, but it improves the chances for substantial progress in this direction; witness the contrast between Georgia's first violence-laden years of postcommunist politics and Bulgaria's relatively peaceful transition to democracy.

Elections, parties, and political development

The introduction of competitive elections as a means of selecting a country's governmental leaders is a watershed in the transition to democracy. Because electoral rules can decisively affect the prospects for the survival of particular parties – and sometimes for the survival of an entire country – they generally become an object of intense struggle.[58] In transitions from communism, this struggle has been shaped both by the attitudes of established communist elites and by the power at the disposal of the proponents of full-fledged democratization. In a large number of cases, a combination of ideological erosion within the elite and vigorous public pressure for reform have led the elite to accept electoral procedures that are genuinely democratic by Western standards. In some instances the elite has accepted a major expansion of democratic participation partly because of doubts about the strength or reliability of the instruments of coercion needed to block it. Some major turning-points in the history of the "classic" democracies of North America and Western Europe were shaped by a similar calculus of power.[59] In contrast to most of the classic cases, however, the introduction of competitive elections at the close of the communist era generally entailed an extremely rapid expansion of voluntary political participation.[60]

Numerous postcommunist countries, of course, have experienced only a partial liberalization of electoral rules and conditions; a handful have experienced none at all. In Uzbekistan and Kazakstan, for example, where popular pressure for democratization was relatively weak, established elites managed to exert a large measure of influence over the quasi-competitive elections introduced near the close of the communist era, and thereby kept enough control over national politics to avoid comprehensive democratic reforms.[61] In lands such as Belarus, the postcommunist manipulation of electoral rules was initially more oblique, but led within a few years to flagrant violations of democratic electoral practices. Another graphic illustration of this trend is the refusal of the Serbian and Croatian regimes to recognize the victories of opposition parties in national rounds of urban elections conducted in 1995 and 1996.

In those transitions from communism in which the balance of political forces has favored the introduction of genuinely democratic elections, the choice of possible electoral systems has been wider than in most noncommunist countries. By comparison with cases of democratization in Latin America, far fewer preauthoritarian political parties have survived in the former communist states; this has reduced pressures to return to preauthoritarian electoral rules and has increased the scope for political maneuver in framing new rules.[62] Communist successor parties and nascent noncommunist parties have often altered their stance on the specifics of electoral reform according to apparent shifts in their chances under one or another electoral dispensation. However, by the mid–1990s it became clear that many of the postcommunist regimes that have introduced genuinely competitive elections have adopted rules for legislative elections that show certain broad similarities. These rules, which commonly distribute some or all legislative seats on the basis of proportional representation, have been tacitly designed to reduce the risk of extra-constitutional clashes by ensuring that all major groups will be represented in the legislature.[63]

Competitive elections have given rise to a host of postcommunist parties.[64] But just how these parties have affected the development of democracy remains an open question. Western observers have long debated the positive and negative consequences of parties for democracy and democratic values.[65] Political parties often fail to perform some functions deemed essential by democratic theorists, and in many established democracies the political salience of parties has diminished in recent decades.[66] Nonetheless, every contemporary political system that satisfies either the minimalist or a more rigorous definition of democracy has political parties. This fact indicates that the political mechanisms which enable citizens to replace governmental leaders through competitive elections cannot function effectively in the absence of parties. In this sense, parties are indispensable for the survival of democratic systems.

Party-formation in postcommunist countries has been subject to some influences that are distinctive and others that are common to postcommunist and noncommunist countries alike. As noted above, the industrial and social policies of communist regimes created many of the socioeconomic conditions – especially vastly expanded education and urbanization – that facilitate the emergence of voluntary associations and political parties. On the other hand, after seizing power communist regimes typically destroyed all noncommunist parties – with the occasional exception of one or two small "satellite" parties. Moreover, the high level of mandatory participation in communist party activities reportedly imbued the public in many countries with a distrust of parties of any kind. Also, the turbulence of postcommunist socioeconomic upheavals has hampered the efforts of voters to assess their short- and long-term interests and to pick a party that will represent those interests.[67]

Postcommunist party-formation thus appears to face an unusual array of structural obstacles. Unlike many post-authoritarian transitions in Latin America and other parts of the Third World, there are virtually no shadow-parties, independent trade unions, or other societal organizations that have roots in the pre-authoritarian period and that can quickly be reactivated to fight new elections.[68] This suggests that the rate at which postcommunist parties crystallize into reasonably stable institutions might be closer to the rates of party-formation during the nineteenth century than to the rates in other new democracies near the end of the twentieth.[69] Preliminary results of studies currently under way suggest that in several cases, postcommunist levels of electoral volatility – that is, the aggregate shift of voters among parties from one national election to the next – are unusually high by comparison with democratizing countries that lack a communist past.[70]

Other considerations, however, point in the opposite direction. Techniques of party-formation may be learned from abroad by ambitious political leaders and activists who have a large stake in party development. In addition, the proportional-representation features of the electoral systems hammered out in many postcommunist countries facilitate the formation of new parties. The sudden expansion of the scope of participation in meaningful elections also must be taken into account. In the nineteenth century, the step-by-step expansion of the franchise in most countries provided an incentive to create programmatic parties that appealed to the interests of each newly enfranchised segment of the population. By contrast, the simultaneous admission of all social strata and economic groups into postcommunist electoral systems has created an incentive to establish catch-all parties that appeal to many different constituencies.[71] Hence the low level of programmatic coherence in many postcommunist parties should not necessarily be equated with institutional weakness. Finally, the postcommunist states show major differences in the rate at which reasonably stable parties and competitive party systems are taking shape. For instance, parties in the Czech Republic and Poland appear to be fairly well institutionalized and to have established partisan attachments with a significant proportion of the citizenry. In Russia and Ukraine, by contrast, the level of party identification remains very low.[72]

In evaluating the relationship between party systems and democratization, it is important to remember that parties and party systems are overlapping but distinct concepts.[73] As used here, party system denotes all a country's politically significant parties – that is, those parties, small as well as large, whose behavior has a major impact on national politics – and the dominant characteristics of those parties taken as a constellation of political actors. Although the classification of party systems is a notoriously tricky matter, some of the relevant criteria are the number of significant parties, the strength of parties' linkages to particular social groups, the ideological range separating major parties on any given issue, and whether the strongest parties are situated near the extremes of the political spectrum or clustered near the center. Among polities lacking meaningful party competition, Giovanni Sartori has distinguished strictly one-party systems from systems dominated by a hegemonic party that permits but may not be challenged by "satellite" parties. Among polities with meaningful party competition, he has differentiated polarized multiparty systems, moderate multiparty systems, two-party systems, and systems characterized by one dominant party that is open to real electoral challenge. Sartori also has emphasized the importance of whether a particular party system promotes centripetal or centrifugal forms of competition among the parties.[74]

Scholars disagree about the effects of different types of party systems and electoral arrangements on democracy. In particular, these disagreements center on the effects of multiparty systems versus two-party systems and of proportional-representation versus winner-take-all electoral arrangements.[75] However, scholars generally agree that systems having a large number of significant parties with weak ties to a volatile electorate are harmful to democracy. They also agree that democracies with relatively strong extremist parties are vulnerable to authoritarian takeovers. Such anti-system parties may function under democratic conditions for an extended period without giving up their authoritarian orientation. This point is illustrated by the communist parties of Western Europe after World War II: most retained an anti-system orientation for many years, whereas socialist parties tended to undergo a gradual change of political ethos.[76] The largest anti-system parties, in France and Italy, appear to have been sustained by the political orientations of party activists and intellectuals, national levels of personal dissatisfaction among ordinary citizens that were unusually high by international standards, and the polarizing effects of the Cold War.[77]

Writing in 1990, Samuel Huntington observed that the international wave of democratization that began in the mid–1970s was characterized by a "virtual absence of major antidemocratic movements" that posed "an explicit authoritarian alternative" to new democratic regimes.[78] It is important to ascertain whether the same can be said of the postcommunist parties and political movements that have arisen since Huntington wrote these words. In a number of countries, such as Hungary and Lithuania, communist successor-parties have shed their hostility toward liberal democracy and accepted alternations in control of the government as the normal state of affairs. In cases such as Russia and Belarus, however, the main successor-party has not clearly disavowed its past authoritarian ethos.

As a rule, the postcommunist evolution of a party's goals and strategy depends on both elite and mass attitudes. Some observers have suggested that substantial rates of continuity between communist-era and postcommunist elites give members of the old guard a personal stake in the emerging democratic and economic system and reduce the incentive to try to restore authoritarianism. According to this analysis, extremely low or extremely high rates of elite continuity invite an antidemocratic backlash or a smothering of democratic reforms.[79] By themselves, quantitative measures of elite turnover cannot explain democratization's victories and defeats. But they may explain a great deal when combined with an analysis of elite values and the institutional structures through which elite members strive to advance their interests.[80] Taken together, these factors can help identify the point at which personal attitudes and the national political context "tip" old elites into acceptance of democratic political arrangements and practices.

Broadly speaking, the likely causes of moderating change among communist successor parties include the erosion of authoritarian ideas through the discrediting of Marxism–Leninism and generational turnover among top party leaders; a sense of "democratic inevitability" produced by shifts in the balance of organized political forces inside the country and by the seeming international triumph of liberal democracy; and widespread opportunities for personal enrichment through privatization and insider dealing.[81] In Hungary, for example, the path of political reform has been smoothed by elite opportunities for personal gain. Conversely, the factors that have facilitated the persistence of anti-democratic orientations in some successor parties include low leadership turnover; an exodus of moderate and liberal members who joined the party purely to advance their professional careers; the weakness of popular pressures for political liberalization; and a centripetal pattern of inter-party competition caused in part by deepening socioeconomic cleavages.

New anti-system parties based on ethnicity can also disrupt the process of democratization. The apparent explosion in the worldwide incidence of ethnic conflicts in the 1990s is largely a product of the increased public salience accorded such conflicts due to the end of the Cold War.[82] Still, extremist parties do pose a special danger to societies in which deep ethnic cleavages override or coincide with other socioeconomic divisions. Under these conditions, as Donald Horowitz has shown, the ethnicization of political parties and party competition for immobile blocs of ethnic supporters can lead to polarizing elections that preclude democratic alternations of government and pave the way for violence and an authoritarian seizure of power.[83] Whether postcommunist ethnic cleavages are as deep and unmitigated as the Third-World cleavages analyzed by Horowitz is a matter for careful consideration. In such countries or regions as Bosnia Herzegovina and the Transcaucasus, they often are. But in other countries, such as Kazakstan and the Baltic states, they appear to be more susceptible to political management and more compatible with democratization. Occasionally, ethnic cleavages are deeper among national elites than among ordinary citizens, and the competition to mobilize voters for electoral campaigns actually serves to reduce ethnic polarization, as in Moldova.

Anti-system parties that promote antidemocratic goals through nonviolent means should be differentiated from parties that are closely linked with paramilitary forces and are prepared to initiate large-scale violence. Although parties of both types constitute threats to democratization, the latter are probably a greater threat than the former. Nonviolent anti-system parties may gradually be coopted into the status of semi-loyal or even loyal supporters of a democratic system.[84] By contrast, parties predisposed to violence may trigger cycles of political conflict that spiral out of control. They also may precipitate military intervention in politics, either by design or as a result of the violent civil clashes that they set in motion, as some radical parties did in Latin America during the 1970s. To date, most postcommunist antidemocratic parties appear to fall in the nonviolent category. But there have been exceptions, as in Tajikistan, and under the stresses of prolonged social and economic turmoil, this broad pattern might change.[85]

A country's party system, it should be emphasized, can undercut democracy even in the absence of significant antidemocratic parties. One threat to the survival of democratic government is a widespread public perception that it is incapable of dealing with the numerous political and socioeconomic problems bequeathed by the collapse of communism. Such a perception may be fostered by feuding parliaments and inertial cabinets that seem unable to solve critical problems, or by frequent changes in governing coalitions that give the appearance of failing even to address the problems. Some types of multiparty systems are especially conducive to frequent changes of government; to the degree that they contribute to the formation of ineffectual coalition governments, they may erode the legitimacy of the whole democratic enterprise.

Such debilitating party systems may be less common than one might suppose, however. Certain types of coalition governments may last nearly as long as single-party ones, and turnover in the partisan make-up of governing coalitions does not always result in sharp changes of policy.[86] Much depends on the political longevity of individual cabinet ministers – which may considerably exceed the duration of a particular government coalition – and on the degree of public consensus or division over policy questions. Some postcommunist countries, such as Poland, Lithuania, and Hungary, have experienced several changes in the governing coalition but still have sustained quite consistent macroeconomic and social policies for several years. Moreover, a democratic government may experience several failures of performance in the economic and social realms without necessarily undermining the popular legitimacy of democratic institutions, as we shall see below.

Some postcommunist countries, of course, have remained in the grip of a single monopolistic party, or a hegemonic one. Sartori has distinguished totalitarian and authoritarian one-party systems from "one-party pragmatic systems" that have low levels of ideological intensity and are based primarily on political expediency.[87] This characterization bears a close resemblance to Turkmenistan and might become applicable to a few other postcommunist countries. The question is whether such parties have become effective instruments of authoritarian rule or have encountered serious challenges from other political forces. In addition, it is important to determine whether the satellite parties tolerated by hegemonic rulers have acquired real political influence or have become even more marginal since the cresting of pro-democratic symbolism and gestures immediately after the fall of communism. The experience of Kazakstan suggests that the role of these parties depends in part on whether elite factions seek to develop them as a means of defending their interests against attacks from other elite groups.

The effects of political culture and political society

As already noted, the political development of any postcommunist country is strongly influenced by the attitudes and strategies of elites and the character of the parties and other institutions through which they vie for power. Equally important to long-term postcommunist outcomes are the initial condition and subsequent evolution of the country's political culture and political society. Broadly speaking, a country's political culture reflects the inhabitants' basic attitudes toward such matters as the trustworthiness of their fellow citizens, the legitimacy of others citizens' rights and interests, the fashion in which conflicting interests ought to be reconciled, the ability of citizens to influence government policies, and the legitimacy of existing political institutions. A civic political culture embodies high levels of interpersonal trust, a readiness to deal with political conflict through compromise rather than coercion or violence, and acceptance of the legitimacy of democratic institutions.[88] It stands to reason that political culture affects whether citizens choose to support moderate or extreme political movements and parties, and whether they choose to engage in democratic or anti-democratic forms of political participation.[89]

Empirical evidence suggests that a country's political culture is neither fixed once and for all, nor completely malleable. It changes in response to new historical events and personal experiences, but with a considerable lag, and primarily through the generational turnover of citizens.[90] This makes political culture an important determinant of the way that political institutions evolve and operate. Over time political institutions and major sociopolitical events exert a reciprocal influence on the content of the country's political culture. But in any given period, the content of the political culture shapes the perceptions and actions of the political elite and the mass public.

A country's political culture and its political society are closely intertwined. The notion of political society is often defined broadly to include political parties, but here it is used to denote those nonparty, nongovernmental groups and associations that participate, directly or indirectly, in shaping a country's political life. The nature of these groups and associations varies widely according to the type of political society in question.[91] Civic associations, commercial enterprises, extended clans, and criminal organizations are examples of such groups. As some of these examples suggest, a political society may include a sizable number of organizational components but still not embody the values of a civic culture. In a statistical sense, social structure and the content of political culture are related; witness the widely accepted proposition that the rise of the middle class is a source of liberal democracy, and the more controversial notion that the working class is the main social basis of authoritarianism.[92] Analytically, however, social structure and political culture are distinct, and the relationship between them may vary from one country to the next. Taken in the aggregate, a country's political society generally reflects its prevailing political culture and significantly affects the operation of its governmental institutions.[93]

Civil society is a form of political society based on a dense network of nongovernmental associations and groups established for the autonomous pursuit of diverse socioeconomic interests and prepared to rebuff state efforts to seize control of these activities.[94] The components of a civil society may include such elements as independent media, religious confessions, charitable organizations, business lobbies, professional associations, labor unions, universities, and non-institutionalized movements for various social causes. The existence of a civil society depends not only on the presence of large numbers of associations and organized groups but on the spirit in which they act. The divergent fashions in which political thinkers have depicted civil society reflect the reality that relations among societal groups inevitably entail conflict as well as cooperation.[95] A society is civil only if its constituent groups demonstrate a substantial measure of self-restraint rooted in a recognition of the legitimacy of the interests of other groups – a recognition often reinforced by the existence of overlapping group memberships – and a commitment to forgo violence as means of deciding social conflicts. Because in the aggregate the structures of a civil society embody a civic culture, such a society is conducive to the consolidation of democratic governmental institutions. Under a democratic dispensation, the relationship of civil society to the state involves a large measure of cooperation as well as conflict.[96]

The application of the concepts of political culture and civil society to countries during their communist phase entails several difficulties. Until the late communist era, systematic survey data on citizens' political attitudes were generally unavailable for most communist countries; this created a risk that analysts would erroneously attempt to infer the characteristics of mass political culture from the history and structure of the regime rather than from the empirically measured values of the population.[97] Confusion also has arisen from the attribution of several disparate meanings to the concept of civil society: these range from the notion of small oppositional movements under communist regimes to the notion of the macrostructure of entire societies in noncommunist or postcommunist states.[98] Certainly the *idea* of a civil society with values and interests superior to those of the party–state apparatus was ardently embraced by many dissidents and played an important role in delegitimizing the quasi-totalitarian pretensions of a number of communist regimes. But how widely this idea was held by ordinary citizens in most countries is difficult to establish. During the communist era the notion of civil society was plainly not embodied in a ramified network of independent social organizations and associations, although elements of such a network began to crystallize during the late communist era in Poland.[99]

In addition, it is important to inquire whether all the activists who tenaciously championed the concept of civil society as a source of resistance to communism have been capable of making a postcommunist transition to tolerance and cooperation with groups whose central values and concerns differ from their own. Put differently, not all dissidents and anticommunist groups were liberals. Adamant opposition to communist rule was not necessarily equivalent to support for democracy or for compromise among conflicting societal groups, as the examples of Georgia's Zviad Gamsakhurdia and Croatia's Franjo Tudjman show. Nor do all autonomous social institutions find the transition from communism to liberal democracy easy; witness the controversies in Poland over the efforts of the Roman Catholic hierarchy to influence legislation on abortion and the curriculum of public schools.

Applying the concepts of political culture and civil society to postcommunist countries has proved easier but still entails some complexities. In many countries a wealth of survey data on popular attitudes and behavior has now become available. However, scholars have tended to disagree about the implications of political culture for postcommunist democratization.[100] Those who believe that it constitutes a serious obstacle have generally argued that the political culture which existed before the end of communism has considerable staying-power. The sources of this inertia may include enduring precommunist traditions of dictatorship and ultranationalism, as well as authoritarian attitudes absorbed by citizens from Marxist–Leninist propaganda and frequent contact with the party–state apparatus. According to this view, the content of mass political culture increases the possibility of a reversion to some form of authoritarian rule – or to its preservation in countries where the political hold of the old elite has never been broken.

Other scholars have taken a different approach that stresses the compatibility of postcommunist political culture with democratization in many countries. Research along these lines has revealed that major West European democracies and some East European countries show broad if incomplete similarities in political culture – and that some East European citizens exhibit greater acceptance of the rights of ethnic minorities than do most West Europeans.[101] Analysts of this school have often stressed the depth of the ideological erosion that occurred during the final decades of communist rule. Arguing that postcommunist political culture is more prodemocratic than Marxist–Leninist propaganda would lead one to expect, they have suggested that memories of the violence and repression experienced under communism have strengthened citizens' attachment to attitudes of tolerance and non-violence conducive to democratization.[102] Adherents of this school of thought also maintain that intergenerational turnover strongly favors democratization because younger citizens are more enthusiastic about a transition to democratic politics and market economies, partly because they can adapt more easily and have longer time-horizons in which to enjoy the personal benefits of reform.

Closely related to such issues is the question whether a particular country's postcommunist political society bears any resemblance to a civil society in the social-structural sense. Mapping the organizational density and value orientations of a whole society is an enormous intellectual task that scholars have only begun to attempt. Nonetheless, several things seem clear. Without key components of civil society, governmental structures that are formally democratic cannot be expected to operate in a fashion that is substantively democratic. This is particularly true of independent media, which serve not only as direct advocates for societal interests but as important channels through which the members of societal groups communicate with one another and voice demands on the government. In Poland, for instance, independent print and broadcast media have played a major part in the democratic process. In Serbia, by contrast, government manipulation of the media has been so extensive that opportunities for fair electoral competition at the national level have virtually been eliminated.

The character of political society varies sharply among postcommunist countries. Networks of nongovernmental organizations and voluntary associations are growing far more rapidly in states such as Poland and the Czech Republic than in states such as Belarus and Uzbekistan. But even in countries where this growth has been relatively rapid, the infrastructure of civil society has not yet approached the density and durability of such social networks in long-established democracies; in many countries the heavy dependence of the non-profit sector on funding from the state or foreign sources makes it particularly vulnerable.[103] Moreover, processes occurring after the collapse of communism may profoundly alter a country's political society and political culture – and not necessarily in a direction favorable to democracy. Of particular consequence are economic stabilization and liberalization, the privatization of state property, and changes in the levels of legality and public order.

Economic stabilization and liberalization hold out the promise of a long-term improvement in living standards, but at the cost of bruising economic hardships in the short run. When communism first collapsed, outside observers tended to adopt the pessimistic view that democratization and market reform were basically incompatible.[104] This outlook appears to have been shaped by a tendency to analyze the political behavior of economic groups schematically and to view the issue through the lens of a few dramatic but unrepresentative cases such as Chile.[105] With time it has become clear that the relationship between postcommunist democratization and economic reform varies from one phase to another and from one country to another. Economic elites and members of the working class are not monolithic blocs and do not pursue static goals. Moreover, the goals of more narrowly defined economic groups, including labor unions, encompass interests that are broadly political as well as strictly economic.[106] The citizens of many postcommunist countries do regard economic prosperity as a central feature of liberal democracy, but they seem prepared to endure material hardships so long as they believe that economic circumstances will ultimately improve.[107] On the other hand, the severe hardships inflicted on many persons by economic reform may ultimately sharpen disillusionment with democracy – especially if these hardships are accompanied by rapidly increasing disparities of income and extensive corruption.[108]

The effects of privatization on the prospects for democratization also are likely to vary. A wide distribution of private property has long been regarded by many political theorists as an essential check on the authoritarian tendencies that may arise even in popularly elected governments. In addition to this putative benefit, the privatization of state property may facilitate democratization by offering members of the old elite a means of personal aggrandizement more lucrative and far less risky than attempting to reinstate an authoritarian order. However, the insider dealings that help neutralize the former elite as a source of collective opposition also may give rise to mass sentiments that equate democracy with social injustice and rampant corruption. This is especially likely to occur if elite corruption and an equivocal elite attitude toward economic reform produce a protracted depression of popular living standards. Although national understandings of corruption and conflict of interest vary substantially from country to country, the process of economic transformation has made postcommunist countries susceptible to corruption on an unusually large scale.[109] Under these conditions, threats to democracy may come not so much from political and economic elites as from newly enfranchised citizens embittered by the emergence of a plutocracy. In Russia and several East Europe states, public disapproval of the privatization of state economic enterprises has grown substantially since 1991.[110] For most voters, political patience has thus far outweighed economic dissatisfaction, but a long-term economic downturn and an appearance of unchecked social injustice might alter their outlook.

This is one reason that changes in the level of legality and public order are significant. Economic liberalization may lead toward a civil society sustained by the growth of socioeconomic groups with a vested interest in further democratic change, predictable commercial laws, and vigorous civic associations. But the legacy of the totalitarian state may favor elements of an "uncivil" society rather than a civil one. Unless augmented by the growth of smaller civic associations, quasi-corporatist labor and industrial organizations like those in Slovakia and the Czech Republic may become the sort of large, impersonal entities that some Western political theorists view as endangering rather than embodying a civil society.[111] Similarly, deregulation of economic life in the absence of an adequate legal structure and a trustworthy state bureaucracy may lead to the domination of economic activity by predatory business and criminal groups indifferent or hostile to democracy, especially a democracy which blocks some highly profitable activities through effective laws and institutions.[112] At its worst, deregulation of this sort could generate not only citizen disillusionment with the elected leaders who set the process in motion, but also a widespread reaction against basic democratic values.

Perhaps the most fundamental question is whether most citizens in each country believe that democratization and economic reform are essential or that realistic alternatives exist. Comparing the initial phases of dual transitions – that is, the simultaneous liberalization of national political and economic systems – in selected countries of Latin America and Eastern Europe sheds light on this question. One striking difference between the two sets of countries is that elites and citizens were much more strongly convinced of the necessity for fundamental economic change in Eastern Europe than in Latin America.[113] This conviction, in turn, apparently has given greater impetus to the postcommunist drive for liberalization and has reduced the potential for a powerful political backlash against economic reforms. Evidence from some cases, such as Russia, shows that despite economic turmoil and dissatisfaction, public support for democratic political practices has grown substantially since 1991.[114]

In other words, the "deep beliefs" of the citizens of postcommunist countries – their most strongly held attitudes and values, as opposed to transient opinions about day-to-day politics – may be of decisive importance. In Western countries, disillusionment and cynicism about particular leaders and governmental institutions coexist with a continuing commitment to democratic principles.[115] The project's case studies suggest that similar split-level outlooks exist among the citizens of a number of postcommunist countries. The fact that significant proportions of citizens believe that their new governments are unresponsive or corrupt may be taken as a loss of faith in democracy. But it also may be interpreted quite differently – as an accurate assessment of current political realities, and as the social foundation for further efforts to achieve a full-fledged democratic order.

NOTES

I am grateful to Joan Nelson, Valerie Bunce, and Karen Dawisha for helpful comments on an earlier version of this chapter.

1   For a penetrating analysis of the global process of democratization, see Samuel Huntington, *The Third Wave: Democratization in the Late Twentieth Century* (Norman, OK: University of Oklahoma Press, 1991). For shifting Western views of communist systems, including the assertion that they could never be liberalized, see Abbott Gleason, *Totalitarianism: The Inner History of the Cold War* (New York: Oxford University Press, 1995), pp. 198–209.
2   The notion of the reinvention of politics is borrowed from Vladimir Tismaneanu, *Reinventing Politics: Eastern Europe from Stalin to Havel* (New York: Free Press, 1992).
3   See, among many possible examples, J. F. Brown, *Surge to Freedom: The End of Communist Rule in Eastern Europe* (Durham, NC: Duke University Press, 1991); Gale Stokes, *The Walls Came Tumbling Down: The Collapse of Communism in Eastern Europe* (New York: Oxford University Press, 1993); Sabrina Petra Ramet, *Social Currents in Eastern Europe: The Sources and Consequences of the Great Transformation*, 2d ed. (Durham, NC: Duke University Press, 1995); Tismaneanu, *Reinventing Politics*; Brendan Kiernan, *The End of Soviet Politics: Elections, Legislatures, and the Demise of the Communist Party* (Boulder, CO: Westview Press, 1993); Archie Brown, *The Gorbachev Factor* (Oxford: Oxford University Press, 1996); John Dunlop, *The Rise of Russia and*

the Fall of the Soviet Empire (Princeton: Princeton University Press, 1993); and M. Stephen Fish, *Democracy from Scratch: Opposition and Regime in the New Russian Revolution* (Princeton: Princeton University Press, 1995).

4 For example, *The Social Legacy of Communism*, ed. James R. Millar and Sharon L. Wolchik (Washington, DC and Cambridge: Woodrow Wilson Center Press and Cambridge University Press, 1994); *The Legacies of Communism in Eastern Europe*, ed. Zoltan Barany and Ivan Volgyes (Baltimore: Johns Hopkins University Press, 1995); J. F. Brown, *Hopes and Shadows: Eastern Europe after Communism* (Durham, NC: Duke University Press, 1994); Karen Dawisha and Bruce Parrott, *Russia and the New States of Eurasia: The Politics of Upheaval* (New York: Cambridge University Press, 1994); *New States, New Politics: Building the Post-Soviet Nations*, ed. Ian Bremmer and Ray Taras, 2d ed. (New York: Cambridge University Press, 1996); Anatol Lieven, *The Baltic Revolution: Estonia, Latvia, Lithuania and the Path to Independence*, 2d ed. (New Haven: Yale University Press, 1994); and *Central Asia and the Caucasus after the Soviet Union: Domestic and International Dynamics*, ed. Mohiaddin Mesbahi (Gainesville: University Press of Florida, 1994).

5 See, for instance, *Transition to Democracy in Poland*, ed. Richard F. Starr (New York: St. Martin's, 1993); Raymond Taras, *Consolidating Democracy in Poland* (Boulder, CO: Westview Press, 1995); Rudolf Tőkés, *Negotiated Revolution: Economic Reforms, Social Change, and Political Succession in Hungary, 1957–1990* (Cambridge: Cambridge University Press, 1996); Lenard J. Cohen, *Broken Bonds: Yugoslavia's Disintegration and Balkan Politics in Transition*, 2d ed. (Boulder, CO: Westview, 1995); Sabrina Petra Ramet, *Balkan Babel*, 2d ed. (Boulder, CO: Westview, 1996); Susan Woodward, *Balkan Tragedy: Chaos and Dissolution after the Cold War* (Washington, DC: Brookings Institution, 1995); Richard Sakwa, *Russian Politics and Society* (New York: Routledge, 1993); *Elections and Political Order in Russia*, ed. Peter Lentini (New York and Budapest: Central European University Press, 1995); *The New Russia: Troubled Transformation*, ed. Gail W. Lapidus (Boulder, CO: Westview Press, 1995); Stephen White, Richard Rose, and Ian McAllister, *How Russia Votes* (Chatham, NJ: Chatham House Publishers, 1997); *Independent Ukraine in the Contemporary World*, ed. Sharon Wolchik (Prague: Central European University Press, forthcoming); and Alexander Motyl, *Dilemmas of Independence: Ukraine after Totalitarianism* (New York: Council on Foreign Relations, 1993).

6 For example, Anders Åslund, *Post-Communist Economic Revolutions: How Big a Bang?* (Washington, DC: Center for Strategic and International Studies, 1992); Adam Przeworski, *Democracy and the Market: Political and Economic Reforms in Eastern Europe and Latin America* (Cambridge: Cambridge University Press, 1991); *A Precarious Balance: Democracy and Economic Reforms in Eastern Europe*, ed. Joan Nelson (Washington, DC: Overseas Development Council, 1994); Joan Nelson et al., *Intricate Links: Democratization and Market Reforms in Latin America and Eastern Europe* (Washington, DC: Overseas Development Council, 1994); *The Privatization Process in Central Europe*, ed. Roman Frydman et al. (Budapest and New York: Central European University Press, 1993); *The Privatization Process in Russia, Ukraine, and the Baltic States*, ed. Roman Frydman et al. (Budapest and New York: Central European University Press, 1993); Roman Frydman et al., *Corporate Governance in Central Europe*

and Russia, 2 vols. (Budapest and New York: Central European University Press, 1996); *Banking Reform in Central Europe and the Former Soviet Union*, ed. Jacek Rostowski (Budapest and New York: Central European University Press, 1995); Max Ernst et al., *Transforming the Core: Restructuring Industrial Enterprises in Russia and Central Europe* (Boulder, CO: Westview, 1996); and Anders Åslund, *How Russia Became a Market Economy* (Washington, DC: Brookings Institution, 1995).

7 Although the fullest coverage of democratization in the Third World has been devoted to Latin America, in the past few years more attention has been paid to democratization in other Third–World countries. See, for instance, *Politics in Developing Countries; Comparing Experiences with Democracy*, ed. Larry Diamond, Juan J. Linz, and Seymour Martin Lipset (Boulder, CO: Lynne Rienner, 1990).

8 For differing views on this question, see Kenneth Jowitt, *The New World Disorder: The Leninist Extinction* (Berkeley: University of California Press, 1992), pp. 284–305; Sarah Meiklejohn Terry, "Thinking about Post-Communist Transitions: How Different Are They?" *Slavic Review* 52, no. 2 (Summer 1993), 333–37; Philippe C. Schmitter and Terry Lynn Karl, "The Conceptual Travels of Transitologists and Consolidologists: How Far to the East Should They Attempt to Go?" *Slavic Review* 53, no. 1 (Spring 1994), 173–85; Valerie Bunce, "Should Transitologists Be Grounded?" *Slavic Review* 54, no. 1 (Spring 1995), 111–117; idem., "Comparing East and South," *Journal of Democracy* 6, no. 3 (July 1995), 87–100. See also Beverly Crawford and Arend Lijphart, "Explaining Political and Economic Change in Post-Communist Eastern Europe: Old Legacies, New Institutions, Hegemonic Norms, and International Pressures," *Comparative Political Studies* 28, no. 2 (July 1995), 171–99. The most comprehensive empirical examination of this issue is Juan J. Linz and Alfred Stepan, *Problems of Democratic Transition and Consolidation: Southern Europe, South America, and Post-Communist Europe* (Baltimore: Johns Hopkins University Press, 1996), which appeared just as this book was going to press.

9 *Developments in East European Politics*, ed. Stephen White, Judy Batt and Paul G. Lewis (Durham, NC: Duke University Press, 1993); *Developments in Russian and Post-Soviet Politics*, ed. Stephen White, Alex Pravda, and Zvi Gitelman (Durham, NC: Duke University Press, 1994); *The New Democracies in Eastern Europe: Party Systems and Political Cleavages*, 2d ed., ed. Sten Berglund and Jan Ake Dellenbrant (Brookfield, VT: Edward Elgar, 1994); *Party Formation in East-Central Europe*, ed. Gordon Wightman (Aldershot: Edward Elgar, 1995); *Public Opinion and Regime Change: The New Politics of Post-Soviet Societies*, ed. Arthur H. Miller et al. (Boulder, CO: Westview Press, 1993); *Political Culture and Civil Society in Russia and the New States of Eurasia*, ed. Vladimir Tismaneanu (Armonk, NY: M. E. Sharpe, 1995); Richard Rose, *What Is Europe?* (New York: HarperCollins, 1996); *Social Justice and Political Change: Public Opinion in Capitalist and Post-Communist States*, ed. James R. Kluegel, David S. Mason, and Bernd Wegener (New York: Aldine de Gruyter, 1995); *Stabilising Fragile Democracies: Comparing New Party Systems in Southern and Eastern Europe*, ed. G. Pridham and P. G. Lewis (London: Routledge, 1996).

10 As noted in the Preface, the term "Eastern Europe" is employed for the sake of conciseness; in this book it does not presuppose political or cultural uniformity among the countries that it encompasses.

11 The distinction between civil society and other forms of political society is discussed below.

12 Barbara Geddes, "Challenging the Conventional Wisdom," *Journal of Democracy* 5, no. 4 (October 1994), 117.

13 *The Consolidation of Democracy in East-Central Europe*, ed. Karen Dawisha and Bruce Parrott (New York: Cambridge University Press, 1997); *Politics, Power, and the Struggle for Democracy in South-East Europe*, ed. idem (New York: Cambridge University Press, 1997); and *Conflict, Cleavage, and Change in Central Asia and the Caucasus*, ed. idem (New York: Cambridge University Press, 1997).

14 See especially Robert Dahl, *Polyarchy: Participation and Opposition* (New Haven: Yale University Press, 1971), and Dahl, *Democracy and Its Critics* (New Haven: Yale University Press, 1989).

15 I am obliged to Sabrina Ramet for bringing this important point to my attention.

16 It is worth noting that such cases have not been confined to postcommunist democracies but have occurred in other democracies as well. India and Turkey, for example, have harshly suppressed some ethnic minorities among their citizens. (Samuel Huntington, "Democracy for the Long Haul," *Journal of Democracy* 7, no. 2 [April 1996], 10.)

17 Ghia Nodia, "How Different Are Postcommunist Transitions?" *Journal of Democracy* 7, no. 4 (October 1996), 15–17, 22–24.

18 This definition is derived from Joan Nelson, "How Market Reforms and Democratic Consolidation Affect Each Other," in Nelson et al., *Intricate Links*, pp. 5–6. For a similar but stricter definition designed to take direct account of military threats to democracy, see Juan J. Linz, "Transitions to Democracy," *Washington Quarterly*, 13 (1990), 156. For a more complex definition that deals also with the social and economic realms, see Juan J. Linz and Alfred Stepan, "Toward Consolidated Democracies," *Journal of Democracy* 7, no. 2 (April 1996), 34–51.

19 Guillermo O'Donnell, "Illusions about Consolidation," *Journal of Democracy* 7, no. 2 (April 1996), 38 and passim. Cf. Richard Guenther et al., "O'Donnell's 'Illusions': A Rejoinder," ibid. 7, no. 4 (October 1996), 151–59.

20 For example, a team of scholars has argued that consolidation was achieved within five years of the first democratic elections in Spain and within seven years of such elections in Greece. About a decade after the elections, elite and public acceptance of the superiority of democracy over all other forms of government in these two countries matched the average level in the countries of the European Union. By contrast, in Brazil, where the process of electoral democratization began at about the same time as in Spain, the level of elite and public acceptance of democracy remained far lower. Guenther et al., "O'Donnell's 'Illusions,'" 155-56.

21 For a sample of the Western debates over which form of democracy is more stable, see the chapters in Part II of *The Global Resurgence of Democracy*, ed. Larry Diamond and Marc F. Plattner (Baltimore: Johns Hopkins University Press, 1993).

22 Eugene Huskey discusses the applicability of this concept to Kyrgyzstan in his chapter in *Conflict, Cleavage, and Change*.
23 Guillermo O'Donnell, "Delegative Democracy," *Journal of Democracy* 5, no. 1 (1994), 59–60, 67.
24 Cf. Huntington, *Political Order in Changing Societies*, p. 177 f.
25 Huntington, *The Third Wave*, pp. 231–32.
26 On the other hand, the breakdown of communism has frequently been accompanied by a blurring of the line between civilian and military affairs and by the participation of some military men, as individuals, in civilian politics. See *State Building and Military Power in Russia and the New States of Eurasia*, ed. Bruce Parrott (Armonk, NY: M. E. Sharpe, 1995), esp. chs. 2, 8, and 13. Cf. Cohen, *Broken Bonds*, pp. 85–88, 183–88, 227–33, and Woodward, *Balkan Tragedy*, pp. 166–69, 255–62.
27 Charles Fairbanks, Jr., "The Postcommunist Wars," *Journal of Democracy* 6, no. 4 (October 1995), 18–34.
28 Assessing the character of the international environment leaves considerable room for disagreement among observers, especially where ideological and cultural currents are concerned. For example, Samuel Huntington has asserted that Marxist–Leninist regimes, Nazi Germany, and the advanced capitalist democracies shared some ultimate political values because they were all parts of the same Western civilization. In my view these three Western traditions were divided at least as fundamentally as are liberal democratic thought and the authoritarian strands of non-Western cultural traditions. See Huntington, "The Clash of Civilizations?" *Foreign Affairs* 72, no. 3 (Summer 1993), 23, 44, plus the reply from Fouad Ajami in ibid., 72, no.4 (September-October 1993), 2–9.
29 Huntington, *The Third Wave*, pp. 86–100; see also the chapters by Geoffrey Pridham, Laurence Whitehead, John Pinder, and Margot Light in *Building Democracy? The International Dimension of Democratisation in Eastern Europe*, ed. Geoffrey Pridham et al. (New York: St. Martin's Press, 1994), pp. 7–59, 119–68; and Nodia, "How Different are Postcommunist Transitions?" 15–16, 20–23.
30 Richard Ullman, "The Wars in Yugoslavia and the International System after the Cold War," and Richard Sobel, "U.S. and European Attitudes toward Intervention in the Former Yugoslavia: *Mourir pour la Bosnie?*" in *The World and Yugoslavia's Wars*, ed. Richard H. Ullman (New York: Council on Foreign Relations, 1996), pp. 9–41, 145–81.
31 During the critical early phases of the Yugoslav civil war, NATO's member-states were preoccupied with managing the consequences of the unification of Germany, other major European-security problems thrown up by the collapse of the Soviet bloc, and the Persian Gulf War. See Ullman, "The Wars in Yugoslavia and the International System after the Cold War," Stanley Hoffman, "Yugoslavia: Implications for Europe and for European Institutions," and David C. Gombert, "The United States and Yugoslavia's Wars," in *The World and Yugoslavia's Wars*, pp. 14–15, 24–31, 36, 102–18, 122–30, 136–37.
32 Samuel Huntington, *The Clash of Civilizations and the Remaking of World Order* (New York: Simon and Schuster, 1996), pp. 192–98.
33 Bunce, "Comparing East and South," 91.

34 In such instances, democratic theory provides no reliable means of determining which proposed outcome is preferable. This, in turn, often spurs the advocates of each proposed outcome to argue their case in still more vehement and uncompromising terms. See Dahl, *Democracy and Its Critics*, pp. 32–33.

35 Linz and Stepan, "Toward Consolidated Democracies," 20–21; Jacek Kochanowicz, "Reforming Weak States and Deficient Bureaucracies," in *Intricate Links*, pp. 195–96.

36 For a fuller treatment of this question, see my "Analyzing the Transformation of the Soviet Union in Comparative Perspective," in *The End of Empire? The Transformation of the USSR in Comparative Perspective*, ed. Karen Dawisha and Bruce Parrott (Armonk, NY: M. E. Sharpe, 1996), pp. 13–14, 16–20.

37 Liah Greenfeld, *Nationalism: Five Roads to Modernity* (Cambridge: Harvard University Press, 1992), pp. 8–12. Cf. John Breuilly, *Nationalism and the State*, 2d ed. (Chicago: University of Chicago Press, 1993), pp. 404–24.

38 For a penetrating discussion of this issue, see Rogers Brubaker, *Citizenship and Nationhood in France and Germany* (Cambridge: Harvard University Press, 1992).

39 One set of opinion surveys suggests considerable variation in the levels of acceptance or hostility expressed by members of several East European nations toward other ethnic groups. The levels of hostility expressed by Serbs in 1992 appear to be unusually high, although this contrast may be due partly to the fact that Serbia was at war when the survey was conducted. Mary E. McIntosh and Martha Abele MacIver, *Transition to What? Publics Confront Change in Eastern Europe*, Occasional Paper No. 38, Woodrow Wilson International Center for Scholars, Washington, DC, 1993, pp. 15–17.

40 On these linkages in the nineteenth century, see E. J. Hobsbawm, *Nations and Nationalism since 1780: Programme, Myth, Reality*, paperback ed. (New York: Cambridge University Press, 1990), ch. 1.

41 Huntington, *The Third Wave*, p. 44.

42 Bunce, "Comparing East and South," 89. Bunce grants that interwar Czechoslovakia constitutes a partial exception to this generalization.

43 Note, too, that democratic experience is a matter not simply of kind but of degree; hence scholars may apply different chronological and substantive standards to assess whether a country has had prior national experience with democracy.

44 See, for example, Sidney Verba, Norman H. Nie, and Jae-on Kim, *Participation and Political Equality: A Seven-Nation Comparison* (Chicago: The University of Chicago Press, 1978).

45 For an analogous trend in historians' treatment of American populism, see Peter Novick, *That Noble Dream: The "Objectivity Question" and the American Historical Profession* (New York: Cambridge University Press, 1988), pp. 337–41.

46 See, for example, Samuel Huntington, *Political Order in Changing Societies* (New Haven: Yale University Press, 1968), chs. 1, 3; and Samuel Huntington and Joan Nelson, *No Easy Choice: Political Participation in Developing Countries* (Cambridge: Harvard University Press, 1976), p. 13.

47 In his classic study of political development, Huntington adopts a definition that
    conflates voluntary and compulsory forms of political participation and attaches
    little explanatory significance to the differences between the two. (*Political Order
    in Changing Societies*, chs. 1, 3; cf. Theodore H. Friedgut, *Political Partici-
    pation in the USSR* [Princeton: Princeton University Press, 1979], ch. 5.) In a
    later book he and Joan Nelson do emphasize the distinction by differentiating
    "autonomous" from "mobilized" participation. (Huntington and Nelson, *No Easy
    Choice*, pp. 7–15.) In *The Third Wave*, Huntington sometimes employs the
    narrower definition favored by students of liberal democracy. For example, he
    states that one-party systems, among which he includes communist regimes, have
    "suppressed both competition and participation" (p. 111).
48 Huntington and Nelson, *No Easy Choice*, pp. 7–15.
49 In Russia, for example, the tsarist regime long feared the expansion of mass
    education as a threat to its legitimacy. The Soviet regime quickly recognized that
    the expansion of mass education would allow it to indoctrinate individuals during
    a stage of social and personal development when their capacities for abstract
    thought were weakly developed, making them highly susceptible to manipulation
    from above.
50 Gregory Grossman, "The USSR – A Solidary Society: A Philosophical Issue in
    Communist Economic Reform," in *Essays in Socialism and Planning in Honor
    of Carl Landauer*, ed. Gregory Grossman (Englewood Cliffs, NJ: Prentice Hall,
    1970); Robert F. Miller, "Civil Society in Communist Systems: An Intro-
    duction," in *The Developments of Civil Society in Communist Systems*, ed. Robert
    F. Miller (New York: Allen and Unwin, 1992), p. 5.
51 Huntington, *Political Order in Changing Societies*, emphasizes the stability of
    communist dictatorships. See also Gleason, *Totalitarianism*, pp. 198–209.
52 Brian D. Silver, "Political Beliefs and the Soviet Citizen," and Donna Bahry,
    "Politics, Generations, and Change in the USSR," in *Politics, Work, and Daily
    Life in the USSR: A Survey of Former Soviet Citizens*, ed. James Millar (New
    York: Cambridge University Press, 1987), pp. 116–121; Donna Bahry, "Society
    Transformed? Rethinking the Social Roots of Perestroika," *Slavic Review* 52, no.
    3 (Fall 1993), 514–17.
53 Miller, "Civil Society in Communist Systems: An Introduction," pp. 6–11;
    Moshe Lewin, *The Gorbachev Phenomenon* (Berkeley, CA: University of
    California Press, 1988). The concept of civil society as a separate sphere of
    social life superior to the state first emerged in the late eighteenth and early
    nineteenth centuries. See John Keane, "Introduction," and idem., "Despotism and
    Democracy," in *Civil Society and the State*, ed. John Keane (New York: Verso,
    1988), pp. 22–25, 35–71.
54 For a general discussion of these factors, see Huntington, *The Third Wave*, ch.
    3, and Guillermo O'Donnell and Philippe C. Schmitter, *Transitions from
    Authoritarian Rule: Tentative Conclusions about Uncertain Democracies*,
    paperback ed. (Baltimore: Johns Hopkins University Press, 1986), pp. 61–64.
55 For an illuminating analysis of this general issue based on noncommunist cases,
    see Sidney Tarrow, "Mass Mobilization and Regime Change: Pacts, Reform, and
    Popular Power in Italy (1918–1922) and Spain (1975–1978)," in *The Politics of
    Democratic Consolidation: Southern Europe in Comparative Perspective*, ed.

Richard Gunther et al. (Baltimore, MD: Johns Hopkins University Press, 1996), pp. 204–30.

56 For example, in the spring of 1991 the radical reform forces led by Boris Yeltsin staged a peaceful mass demonstration in Moscow, and Soviet miners launched a damaging strike that included demands for political reform and the resignation of President Mikhail Gorbachev. The sequence of events suggests that these public demonstrations of support for Yeltsin helped persuade Gorbachev to abandon his temporary reliance on conservative political forces and grant large concessions to the advocates of further reform. Brown, *The Gorbachev Factor*, pp. 283–88; Jonathan Aves, "The Russian Labour Movement, 1989–91: The Mirage of a Russian Solidarność," in Jeffrey Hosking et al., *The Road to Post-Communism: Independent Political Movements in the Soviet Union, 1985–1991*, paperback ed. (New York: St. Martin's Press, 1992), pp. 151–52.

57 In addition to the chapter by Darrell Slider in *Conflict, Cleavage, and Change*, see Jonathan Aves, *Georgia: From Chaos to Stability?* (London: Royal Institute of International Affairs, 1996).

58 In conditions of acute political tension, certain electoral rules can heighten the probability of civil war; and different electoral rules can lead to a legitimate victory of right-wing, centrist, or left-wing parties under the same distribution of popular votes. See Rein Taagepera and Matthew S. Shugart, *Seats & Votes: The Effects & Determinants of Electoral Systems* (New Haven: Yale University Press, 1989), ch. 1.

59 For example, the weakness of the US government's coercive capacities played a major role in the Federalists' reluctant decision to accept the creation of the Democratic–Republican party in the 1790s, when parties were still generally regarded as illegitimate factions harmful to democratic government. (Martin Shefter, *Political Parties and the State: The American Historical Experience*, paperback ed. [Princeton: Princeton University Press, 1994], pp. 9–10; James R. Sharp, *American Politics in the Early Republic: The New Nation in Crisis* [New Haven: Yale University Press, 1993], pp. 208–25).

60 One noteworthy historical exception is revolutionary France. For a concise historical description of the complex struggles over the scope and forms of electoral participation in several European countries, see Stein Rokkan, "Elections: Electoral Systems," *International Encyclopedia of the Social Sciences*, vol. 5 (London: Macmillan and the Free Press, 1968), pp. 7–13.

61 White et al., *How Russia Votes*, pp. 29–34; Dawisha and Parrott, *Russia and the New States of Eurasia*, pp. 148–53.

62 Barbara Geddes, "A Comparative Perspective on the Leninist Legacy in Eastern Europe," *Comparative Political Studies* 28, no. 2 (July 1995), 261–65.

63 Krzysztof Jasiewicz, "Sources of Representation," in *Developments in East European Politics*, pp. 137–46. Most of these new electoral systems also have established a minimum-vote threshold for party representation, meant to avoid a paralyzing proliferation of splinter parties in the legislature.

64 In this discussion a political party is defined as an organization that (a) is identified by an official label (b) seeks to place its representatives in government office or to change the governmental system and (c) employs methods that include mobilizing citizens and participating in free elections if the state allows such elections. This definition encompasses both political organizations that

pursue or exercise power solely through democratic methods and organizations that pursue or exercise power largely through non-democratic means. On the other hand, it excludes single-issue interest groups whose avowed purpose is not to place their representatives in government office. It also excludes organizations that pursue power solely through violent means.

65 For a brief historical account of American distrust of the impact of parties on democracy, see Alan Ware, *Citizens, Parties, and the State: A Reappraisal* (Princeton: Princeton University Press, 1987), ch. 1.

66 A list of important democratic functions includes (a) mobilizing a large proportion of the citizenry to participate in politics (b) ensuring the representation of all social groups (c) allowing citizens to select individual governmental leaders directly (d) promoting the optimal aggregation of social interests (e) ensuring that government officials fulfill their electoral promises and (f) punishing the originators of failed governmental policies. Note that not all these functions can be fulfilled simultaneously. For example, (b) and (c) are at odds, as are (b) and (d). (Ware, *Citizens, Parties, and the State*, pp. 23–29, 150–241; G. Bingham Powell, Jr., *Contemporary Democracies: Participation, Stability, and Violence*, paperback ed. [Cambridge: Harvard University Press, 1982], pp. 73–78.) The causes of party decline include such factors as media-based political campaigns, the "surrogate" effects of public opinion surveys, the displacement of some party activities by narrowly-focused interest groups, and a tendency for more citizens to regard themselves as political independents unwilling to vote automatically for any party's slate of candidates. (Robert D. Putnam, "Troubled Democracies: Trends in Citizenship in the Trilateral World," paper prepared for the planning workshop of the Project on Democratization and Political Participation in Postcommunist Societies, Washington, DC, April 1995; and Thomas Poguntke, "Explorations into a Minefield: Anti-Party Sentiment," *European Journal of Political Research* 29, no. 3 (April 1996), 319–44.)

67 Valerie Bunce, "Uncertainty in the Transition: Post-Communism in Hungary," *East European Politics and Societies* 7, no. 2 (Spring 1993), 240–75.

68 Nelson, "Introduction," in *A Precarious Balance*, pp. 4–5; Robert H. Dix, "Democratization and the Institutionalization of Latin American Political Parties," *Comparative Political Studies* 24, no. 4 (January 1992), 488–511.

69 In nineteenth-century democracies, most political parties crystallized and expanded gradually, as the suffrage was widened and as socioeconomic changes made more citizens susceptible to political mobilization. In England, for example, Liberal and Conservative elites took at least 20 years to build party structures capable of exploiting the widening of the suffrage that occurred in mid-century. Ware, *Citizens, Parties, and the State*, pp. 22–23.

70 Conference on Political Parties and Democracy, sponsored by the International Forum for Democratic Studies, National Endowment for Democracy, November 18–19, 1996, Washington, DC.

71 Geddes, "A Comparative Perspective," 253–57.

72 See the chapters by Andrew Michta and David Olson in *The Consolidation of Democracy in East-Central Europe*; the chapters by Michael Urban and Ilya Prizel in this volume; Dawisha and Parrott, *Russia and the New States of Eurasia*, p. 131; and White et al., *How Russia Votes*, p. 135.

73 The pioneering scholarly writings on parties focused solely on individual parties rather than on party systems, and a tendency to blur the distinction has persisted in some more recent scholarly analyses. (Harry Eckstein, "Parties, Political: Party Systems," *International Encyclopedia of the Social Sciences*, vol. 11, pp. 436–53.) One weakness of Huntington's seminal treatise on political development is that it assigns great weight to parties but tends to conflate parties with party systems. See Huntington, *Political Order in Changing Societies*, ch. 7.

74 Giovanni Sartori, *Parties and Party Systems: A Framework for Analysis* (New York: Cambridge University Press, 1976); Powell, *Contemporary Democracies*, pp. 74–80. For a discussion of the problems of classifying party systems, particularly by numerical criteria alone, see Eckstein, "Party Systems."

75 See especially Powell, *Contemporary Democracies*, pp. 74–80.

76 Sartori, *Parties and Party Systems*, pp. 132–42.

77 For the correlation between levels of personal dissatisfaction and the strength of extreme parties of the Left or Right in these two countries, see Ronald Inglehart, *Culture Shift in Advanced Industrial Society*, paperback ed. (Princeton: Princeton University Press), pp. 36–40.

78 Huntington, *The Third Wave*, p. 263.

79 John Higley et al., "The Persistence of Postcommunist Elites," *Journal of Democracy* 7, no. 2 (April 1996), 133–47; Michael Burton and John Higley, "Elite Settlements," *American Sociological Review* 52 (June 1987), 295–307.

80 For a critique of past elite studies and comparative survey data showing unusually deep attitudinal cleavages within the Soviet/Russian political elite during both the Gorbachev and Yeltsin eras, see David Lane, "Transition under Eltsin: The Nomenklatura and Political Elite Circulation," forthcoming in *Political Studies*.

81 For data showing that the political attitudes of former communist party members and individuals who never belonged to the communist party are quite similar in Bulgaria, Romania, and several countries of East–Central Europe, see the table in Rose, *What Is Europe?*, p. 142. (The table pools the national data sets, so that no conclusions for individual countries can be drawn from it.)

82 According to a careful study, in the past decade the number of ethnic conflicts has grown at approximately the same rate as in the 1960s and 1970s. See Ted Robert Gurr and Barbara Harff, *Ethnic Conflict in World Politics* (Boulder, CO: Westview, 1994), pp. 11, 13.

83 Horowitz, *Ethnic Groups in Conflict*, Part Three.

84 Juan Linz, *The Breakdown of Democratic Regimes: Crisis, Breakdown, & Reequilibration* (Baltimore: Johns Hopkins University Press, 1978), ch. 2.

85 For a general discussion of the connection between political parties and terrorism, see Leonard Weinberg, "Turning to Terror: The Conditions under Which Political Parties Turn to Terrorist Activities," *Comparative Politics* 23, no. 4 (July 1991), 423–38.

86 Arend Lijphart, *Democracies: Patterns of Majoritarian and Consensus Government in Twenty-One Countries*, paperback ed. (New Haven: Yale University Press, 1984), ch. 7; Powell, *Contemporary Democracies*, ch. 7.

87 Sartori, *Parties and Party Systems*, pp. 221–25.

88 My interpretation of these concepts, which have sparked vigorous scholarly debate, is derived from such works as Gabriel Almond and Sidney Verba, *The Civic Culture: Political Attitudes and Democracy in Five Nations*, paperback ed.

(Boston: Little, Brown and Co., 1965), and Inglehart, *Culture Shift in Advanced Industrial Societies*. Most of the controversial issues are well covered in *The Civic Culture Revisited*, ed. Gabriel Almond and Sidney Verba (Newbury Park, CA: Sage Publications, 1980). For reasons of space, my discussion omits several important distinctions, such as the existence of national political subcultures and differences between elite and mass political cultures.

89 However, scholars have disagreed about the particular cultural dispositions that actually support democracy. See especially Edward Muller and Mitchell Seligson, "Civic Culture and Democracy: The Question of Causal Relationships," *American Political Science Review* 88, no. 3 (September 1994), 635–52. Naturally, an important role is also played by non-cultural factors, such as the behavior of the state and major changes in citizens' socioeconomic circumstances.

90 Inglehart, *Culture Shift*, chs. 1–3. For evidence of dramatic increase in the democratic elements of German political culture and a decline in the civic elements of British and US political culture during the three decades following World War II, see the chapters by David Conradt, Dennis Kavanagh, and Alan Abramowitz in *The Civic Culture Revisited*.

91 For a discussion that relates civil society to other forms of political society, see Ernest Gellner, *Conditions of Liberty: Civil Society and Its Rivals* (New York: Allen Lane/The Penguin Press, 1994).

92 Seymour Martin Lipset, *Political Man: The Social Bases of Politics* (New York: Anchor Books, 1963), ch. 4.

93 Robert Putnam, *Making Democracy Work: Civic Traditions in Modern Italy* (Princeton: Princeton University Press, 1993). Cf. Sidney Tarrow, "Making Social Science Work Across Space and Time: A Critical Reflection on Robert Putnam's *Making Democracy Work*," *American Political Science Review* 90, no. 2 (June 1996), 389–98.

94 This paragraph is based on Dawisha and Parrott, *Russia and the New States of Eurasia*, pp. 123–25. For a nuanced discussion of the historical evolution of the concept of civil society, see Keane, "Despotism and Democracy," pp. 35–72.

95 For an exposition of these theoretical differences, which have centered especially on whether commercial organizations based on private property belong to civil society or undermine it, see Keane, "Introduction," pp. 13–14, and "Despotism and Democracy," esp. pp. 62–66. On the connection between civil society and relations within the family, see Carol Pateman, "The Fraternal Social Contract," pp. 101–28 in the same volume.

96 Larry Diamond, "Rethinking Civil Society: Toward Democratic Consolidation," *Journal of Democracy* 5, no. 3 (July 1994), 4–17.

97 For a discussion of this and other problems of analyzing political culture in the USSR and Russia, see Frederick J. Fleron, Jr., "Post-Soviet Political Culture in Russia: An Assessment of Recent Empirical Investigations," *Europe–Asia Studies* 48, no. 2 (March 1996), 225–60.

98 In keeping with prevailing usage before about 1800, the concept of civil society has sometimes been construed even more broadly to include both democratic governmental institutions and social structures conducive to democracy. However, this definition prevents analysis of the interactions between government and society that may fundamentally change the political system.

99 "Under whatever name – 'parallel*polis*,' 'independent culture,' or 'independent society' – the idea of civil society remained largely restricted to narrow circles of independent intellectuals in every East and Central European country save one. The exception . . . was Poland." Aleksander Smolar, "From Opposition to Atomization," *Journal of Democracy* 7, no. 1 (January 1996), 26.

100 Of necessity, this short excursus oversimplifies the analytical issues and omits discussion of the empirical variations among countries. For a general discussion of scholarly tendencies to explain postcommunist political development in terms of either "communist legacies" or "liberal institutional" determinants, see Crawford and Lijphart, "Explaining Political and Economic Change in Post-Communist Eastern Europe."

101 McIntosh and MacIver, *Transition to What? Publics Confront Change in Eastern Europe*, esp. pp. 6, 14.

102 For an insightful juxtaposition of survey data gathered from displaced Soviet citizens after World War II and data collected from Soviet emigrants during the late Brezhnev period, see Bahry, "Society Transformed? Rethinking the Social Roots of Perestroika." The data suggest that in the late Stalin years up to 50 percent of Soviet citizens may have favored a relaxation of intellectual controls, and that by the late Brezhnev period this percentage may have increased substantially (ibid., p. 539). On the role of authoritarian violence in strengthening the appeal of democracy, see Giuseppe di Palma, *To Craft Democracies: An Essay on Democratic Transitions*, paperback ed. (Berkeley: University of California Press, 1990), pp. 19–23, 150–51.

103 For a survey of the voluntary sector in advanced industrial democracies, see *Between States and Markets: The Voluntary Sector in Comparative Perspective*, ed. Robert Wuthnow (Princeton: Princeton University Press, 1991).

104 Geddes, "Challenging the Conventional Wisdom," 104; Jose Maria Maravall, "The Myth of the Authoritarian Advantage," *Journal of Democracy* 5, no. 4 (October 1994), 17–31; Joan Nelson, "Labor and Business Roles in Dual Transitions: Building Blocks or Stumbling Blocks?" in *Intricate Links*, p. 147. This issue was, of course, the subject of vigorous public debate in the West.

105 Geddes, "Challenging the Conventional Wisdom," 109–111.

106 In Eastern Europe, for example, labor unions have played a role in dislodging some government coalitions from power and have pressed governments to adopt their policy preferences. However, anti-democratic union violence and general strikes have been unusual and have tended to occur in countries, such as Romania, whose party systems have been least capable of representing workers' interests. Nelson, "Labor and Business Roles in Dual Transitions," pp. 154–63.

107 Linz and Stepan, "Toward Consolidated Democracies." For example, in Russia's 1996 presidential run-off, Boris Yeltsin won the votes of more than two-thirds of the persons who believed the government would solve the economy's problems in 10 years or less. By contrast, Genadii Zyuganov, the communist party candidate, won the support of 70 percent of those who thought the government would never be able to solve these problems. (*New Russia Barometer VI: After the Presidential Election*, Centre for the Study of Public Policy, University of Strathclyde, Glasgow, 1996, p. 13.) Considerable evidence also suggests that many categories of workers, though hard-hit by economic reform, have devised unofficial sources of income that are not reflected in

gloomy official estimates of declining output. See Daniel Kaufman and Aleksander Kaliberda, "Integrating the Unofficial Economy into the Dynamics of Post-Socialist Economies: A Framework of Analysis and Evidence," in *Economic Transition in Russia and the New States of Eurasia*, ed. Bartlomiej Kaminski (Armonk, NY: M. E. Sharpe, 1996), pp. 81–120.

108 In Russia and several democracies of Eastern Europe, public opinion has shifted since 1991 toward more support for government involvement in the economy, although acceptance of economic inequalities has simultaneously grown in most of the same countries. A recent survey of several postcommunist countries found that the only one in which public attitudes have moved toward greater support for egalitarianism is Russia. (James Kluegel and David S. Mason, "Social Justice in Transition? Attitudinal Change in Russia and East-Central Europe," paper presented at the annual convention of the American Association for the Advancement of Slavic Studies, Boston, November 1996.) In the early 1990s, measurable economic inequalities in postcommunist countries generally remained smaller or no larger than than those in Western democracies. (Branko Milanovic, "Poverty and Inequality in Transition Economies: What Has Actually Happened," in *Economic Transition in Russia and the New States of Eurasia*, pp. 180–81.)

109 For a discussion of national variations in the understanding of corruption, see Michael Johnston, "Historical Conflict and the Rise of Standards," in *The Global Resurgence of Democracy*, pp. 193–205.

110 Kluegel and Mason, "Justice Perceptions in Russia and Eastern Europe, 1991–1995"; Richard Dobson, "Is Russia Turning the Corner? Changing Russian Public Opinion, 1991–1996," *Research Report*, Office of Research and Media Reaction, US Information Agency, September 1996, pp. 11–13.

111 Miller, "Civil Society in Communist Systems," p. 9; Keane, "Despotism and Democracy," pp. 64–66.

112 Richard Rose, "Toward a Civil Economy," *Journal of Democracy* 3, no. 2 (1992), 13–25, and Kochanowicz, "Reforming Weak States and Deficient Bureaucracies," pp. 195–204, 214–22. The fullest account of the criminalization of economic activities in Russia is Stephen Handelman, *Comrade Criminal* (New Haven: Yale University Press, 1995).

113 Nelson, "How Market Reforms and Democratic Consolidation Affect Each Other," pp. 11–13.

114 Dobson, "Is Russia Turning the Corner?" pp. 8–9.

115 For example, surveys of citizens in the European Community's member-countries show that the average percentage of respondents saying they were "very satisfied" or "fairly satisfied" with the way democracy works ranged between 66 and 41 percent in 1985–1993. Leonardo Morlino and Jose R. Montero, "Legitimacy and Democracy in Southern Europe," in *The Politics of Democratic Consolidation: Southern Europe in Comparative Perspective*, p. 239.

2   Democratization and political participation: research concepts and methodologies

Karen Dawisha

The primary objectives of the Project on Democratization and Political Participation have been to gauge the prospects for democratization in Eastern Europe and the former Soviet Union by systematically examining and comparing trends in the organized political activities of society in each country and to contribute to the theoretical discussion about the determinants of these trends. This chapter has several objectives. It begins with an discussion of how the concepts of democracy, democratization, and democratic consolidation are defined and operationalized in this project. Three sections then follow in which the research questions which have guided the project are discussed (the questions themselves are presented in the Appendix), along with propositions and hypotheses derived from the existing literature on democratization. The sections substantively address three disparate parts of the democratization process: two sections on inputs to the process, namely factors influencing the formation of political groups and parties, and the political evolution of society, and one section on outcomes, namely the factors affecting the possible emergence of party systems in postcommunist states.

Conceptualizing democracy and democratization

What is meant by democracy, and how is the process of democratization understood in this project? In line with recent research,[1] a procedural or minimalist conception of democracy was employed. Democracy is defined as a political system in which the formal and actual leaders of the government are chosen through regular elections based on multiple candidacies and secret balloting, with the right of all adult citizens to vote. It is assumed that leaders chosen via free and fair elections, using universal adult suffrage, will be induced to modify their behavior to be more responsive to popular wishes and demands than leaders in authoritarian states.

There remains, however, the crucial task of making the transition from the conceptual level to the empirical-observational level. Even if the features of the conception can be elaborated, how does one determine their presence or their absence over time, within individual countries or across the postcommunist world? Simply put, how does one know when the level of democracy is high, or when it is low or non-existent? Over the past thirty years or so, there have been numerous attempts at objectively measuring democracies.[2] Some of the more recent efforts such as those of Kenneth Bollen have, arguably, resulted in more finely calibrated instruments.[3] These measures are most useful as indicators of the extent to which democracy exists in a country at a specific time. In and of themselves, they are not useful for explaining democratic change. As noted recently, "with these scores, one can only estimate the extent to which democracy has advanced or regressed in that given country over a very long period of time or compare the country with others similarly scored."[4] Indeed most analysts who draw up such indicators would be the first to recognize that their contribution has been in measuring democracy, not explaining its underlying dynamics.

Civil liberties and political rights can be viewed as two distinct conceptual dimensions of democracy. The dimension of political rights can be, more or less, directly observed. The degree to which adult suffrage is universal, elections are fairly conducted, and all persons are eligible for public office can be directly observed through objective analysis of electoral laws and practices. The degree to which leaders freely compete for votes can be ascertained in a similar manner. An analysis of political rights allows one to draw conclusions about the level of democracy, since it can reasonably be hypothesized that the higher the number of rights universally enjoyed by the population, the greater will be the level of democratization.

Democracy is also dependent upon the provision of civil liberties, specifically: (1) freedom to form and join organizations; (2) freedom of expression; and (3) access to multiple and competing sources of information. Empirical data can be garnered to support a judgment about the extent to which the three components of civil liberties exist. It is assumed that the more the number and level of civil liberties enjoyed by a country's population, the greater will be the level of democratization. Thus, political rights and civil liberties serve as indicators of democracy and both must be present in order for a country to be classified as democratic. Through the assignment of numerical values to the empirical properties representing political rights and civil liberties, according to consistent rules, one could draw up a representation of the level of democracy existing within a country at any given time.

Such a measure, however, would not necessarily allow one to conclude that any given democracy was likely to be both stable and durable. Indeed, the free and unfettered exercise of political rights and liberties has been seen on occasions as negatively affecting the durability of democracies, sometimes obliging leaders and populations to accept various trade-offs which would limit the degree of representation of societal groups in return for sustaining democratic institutions over time. A good example is the tendency of democracies to introduce measures which effectively limit the number of parties that can be represented in the legislature to those which gain above a certain percentage threshold of the popular vote, so as to lessen the impact of minority opinion and of groups at the left and right of the political spectrum and magnify the influence of majoritarian views and centrist groups. Such measures, while in fact denying some voters the right to have their votes have an equal impact upon outcomes, are justified by reference to the universal interests of all voters in ensuring the long-term durability of democratic institutions.

Equally, democracies vary in their protection of civil liberties such as freedom of speech and assembly. Many established democracies curtail the rights of groups which have in the past shown their intent to overthrow the democratically elected order. These actions, too, are justified by reference to the right of the state to limit the liberties of some in the short term in order to ensure the liberty of all in the long-term.

Finally, one must distinguish between democracy and democratization. To a certain extent, all states, even those that call themselves, and are recognized by others as, democratic are still evolving, either towards or away from more democracy. The perennial debates in even the most stable democracies about justice, liberty, equity, rights, and governability reflect this continuing concern. But more problematic is drawing the line between an authoritarian polity which is breaking down and a democratic entity which is emerging. When can one say that the process of democratization actually begins? For the purposes of this project, democratization is said to begin when the first set of free and fair elections for national-level office takes place. This first set of elections must be accompanied in short order by the granting of civil liberties and political rights and the establishment of both state institutions that operate according to the rule of law and intermediate organizations that mediate between the citizen and the state. If these events do not take place, then it is likely that the process of democratization will not be fully consolidated.

Measuring democratic consolidation

Unlike the numerous efforts to measure democracy systematically, relatively few attempts have been made to measure democratic consolidation. Central to this notion is acceptance that not all states that start out on the road to democracy will complete the transition. Some will fall back into authoritarianism, others might regress into civil war, others will maintain a low equilibrium democracy for decades, verging constantly on the brink of collapse.[5] And all transitions will differ, combining as they do on the one hand individual historical legacies, leaders, socioeconomic foundations and international interactions and on the other hand the policies pursued by elites and their varied impact on individual societies at any given time.

A consolidated democracy is one in which most major social groups expect that government leaders will be chosen through competitive elections and regard representative institutions and procedures as their main channel for processing claims on the state. One way of measuring consolidation is to apply a "two-turnover test," in which a democracy "may be viewed as consolidated if the party or group that takes power in the initial election at the time of the transition loses a subsequent election and turns over power to those election winners, and if those election winners then peacefully turn over power to winners of a later election.[6] Thus, for example, when communism fell, a first round of elections was held. Typically two to four years later, a second round was held: if the group in power since the fall of communism was displaced, this would count as the first turnover. Only after this group or party was displaced by a second round of elections could one then speak of a country having passed the 'two turn-over test.' Of the postcommunist states, only postcommunist Lithuania had by the end of 1996 passed such a test: the Lithuanian Democratic Labor Party, the renamed Communist Party, took power from the conservative Sajudis led by Vytautas Landsbergis in 1992, and then surrendered it back to Landsbergis' party (the renamed Homeland Union) when they lost parliamentary elections in November 1996. However, such a test has been criticized on the grounds that it would fail to classify either interwar Eastern Europe or postwar Italy or Japan as democracies. Moreover, if used alone, it does not provide levels of calibration and gradation adequate for the comparative scope of the project. Also while a determination could be made if a democracy were consolidated or not using a two-turnover test, it would not be possible to answer the questions "why?" or "why not?" using the test.

In measuring democratic consolidation over time within a given country or across nations, it may prove more theoretically informative to treat it as a continuum, rather than a two-step process. There are at least four distinct conceptual aspects of democratic consolidation, each of which could be observed by various measures: the two-turnover test, low public support for anti-system parties or groups, high public commitment to the fundamental values and procedural norms of democratic politics, and elite consensus about the desirability of institutionizing and legitimizing democratic norms and values.[7]

An index could be constructed by combining the latter three indicators if the criteria for the two-turnover test are not met. This would serve at least three purposes. First, several variables relating to democratic consolidation could be represented by a single score, thereby reducing the complexity of the data and facilitating comparison. Second, such an index could provide a quantitative measure of democratic consolidation amenable to statistical manipulation. Finally, because it measures several properties, the index is inherently more reliable than a measure based on a single factor.

Clearly, democratic consolidation is still a goal in almost all of the postcommunist countries, yet significant strides have been made. Autonomous societal action has largely replaced communist dictatorship in most countries; and the notions of choice, competition, and tolerance are increasingly salient. As emphasized in the working definition of democracy, elections should be based on multiple candidacies that ensure real opportunities for electoral competition. Informal alliances rapidly evolved into political parties in the wake of the communist collapse: these parties are gradually becoming rooted and stable. The following section examines some of the factors influencing the formation of political groups and parties across the countries under investigation. In each of the following sections, the research questions (as presented in the Appendix) which were given to the authors are used as the basis for deriving hypotheses and propositions, and a consideration is made of the range of results which might be expected from the various hypotheses. This section is followed by sections on the political evolution of society and on the emergence of political parties and party systems.

Factors influencing the formation of parties

Authors were presented with a number of questions, listed in the Appendix, which addressed the factors influential in forming the political groups and parties, considered as a cornerstone in any country's move toward democracy. The comparative literature is deeply divided over the relative influence of historical, ethnic, social, cultural, institutional, and economic factors in determining the success of a country's move toward democracy. This section was intended to elicit the panel's responses to these various issues.

In the literature on transitions, it is generally assumed that those countries which have to establish a national identity before going on to build the institutions of the state and inculcate civic virtues in the populace will face the greatest challenge.[8] In doing so they will have to replace other national identities which may command popular support if the new state was carved out of old ones and strive to surpass and mobilize the other nested identities of family, clan, region, and ethnicity in the service of a new civic mindedness.

Authors were asked to elaborate the key elements of the precommunist historical legacy of each country. They were additionally asked to focus on any precommunist experience of democracy, and whether elements of the postcommunist polity, such as particular government structures, intermediary associations, and political parties have been modeled on precommunist patterns.

The literature would appear to support three interrelated hypotheses: polities with a strong, unified national identity based on a precommunist legacy of independence will be able to make the most rapid and peaceful transition to sovereign independence; those polities with a precommunist tradition of exclusivist nationalism will have more difficulty in making the transition to democracy; and those polities with a precommunist tradition of competitive multiparty systems are most likely to be successful in establishing stable multiparty democracies.

It could reasonably be assumed that those countries which are being "reborn" after a period of communist suppression would have an enormous advantage over states being established for the first time. One would expect a shorter time in putting basic institutions in place, in passing a constitution and other basic laws, and in regularizing state-society relations on the basis of a national accord. States coming into existence for the first time are not able to operate on the basis of historical trust or on a shared remembrance of the role the state played in the past in forging a partnership between state and society to nourish and sustain the nation. On the contrary, given the role of the state in the communist period in suppressing both nation and society (although to be sure the nation was often harnessed to the needs of the state during times of crisis in all the communist states and was symbiotically allied to the state in Yugoslavia, Hungary, and Romania in particular), any state without a precommunist legacy of trust might reasonably be expected to falter in the project of legitimization.

There are, however, two related dilemmas: first, countries that are resurrecting states which, in the precommunist era, had an authoritarian character may have more difficulty overcoming the burden of this legacy than countries that are creating state institutions anew. Secondly, while a regeneration of a previous national identity is expected to facilitate the process of state-building, if the national identity was exclusivist, then its renaissance might promote state-building but impede democratization. This tendency is underscored by Beverly Crawford and Arendt Lijphart, who address the problem that unlike in France or England, where nationalism had its origins in the Enlightenment, in Eastern Europe and the former Soviet Union, it had its roots "in the Russian and German tradition of *Volk*, blood, *narod*, and race as the basis for membership in the nation."[9] To be sure, the distinctions between the historical origins of the national identities of the Germans and Russians on the one hand and the British and the French on the other are clear. Yet this view does not account sufficiently for the fact that even in England, the process of transforming narrow English identity centered in the Home Counties into a greater United Kingdom entailed the forcible suppression of independent national aspirations in Wales and Scotland, as we;; asa lengthy and continuing struggle with Northern Ireland. And despite this, democratization proceeded apace in Great Britain, suggesting that the connections between a state's formative national identity and the identity which underpins its institutions is not fixed for all time.

It is also posited in the transitions literature that those states with precommunist traditions of multiparty elections and capitalist development are more likely to be able to reestablish these institutions. There are two reasons: one is that to the extent that a state had already adopted a multiparty system and/or capitalism in the past, protracted and often divisive national debates on paths of development could be avoided. Additionally many of the actual laws governing political and economic life can be resuscitated with only minor amendments. Of course, given the number of ultra-nationalist parties that inhabited the landscape of interwar Eastern Europe, the resuscitation of these parties has not necessarily promoted simultaneous liberalization.

Postcommunist states have had to sift through, resurrect, and overcome elements not only of their precommunist heritage, but also of their communist past. Authors were asked to identify key elements of the legacy of the communist era. In addition, they were asked to speculate on how the political and social evolution of each country in the late communist era (e.g., the emergence or nonemergence of a significant dissent movement) affected the postcommunist formation of societal interest groups and parties.

Prevalent in the field are two core assumptions that require some systematic elaboration: first, the assumption that the more and the longer a country was subjected to the antidemocratic and totalitarian features of Stalinism, the less likely will be the chances of democracy succeeding, and secondly, if there is a prior history of democracy and civil society, and a communist legacy of reform and openness, then the chances of a successful transition to democracy will be greater and the speed of transition will be quicker.

The literature on the legacy of the communist era is vast, growing, and divided. Most would agree that communism left a "poisonous residue"[10] on virtually all aspects of society, but whether that residue can easily be washed away is open to controversy. Those who subscribe to the view that the legacy of communism will be significant and abiding look at its effect in several areas.[11] Politically, the fact that there essentially were no public politics in the communist era is presumed to have left a deep legacy: there were no self-governing institutions, no interest groups or rival parties operating independent of the state, and no competing sources of information. At the same time, Soviet systems were characterized by a single elite which, while capable of being split into factions, did not regularly or routinely circulate into and out of power. These elites, it was assumed by some, would resist the construction of new institutions which would limit the reach of their authority.[12] Some would see these features as a significant barrier to the emergence of democracy and civil society.[13] Other authors also assume that the Soviet-era largely succeeded in one of its aims, namely to destroy the pre-Leninist past, thus robbing these societies of their ability to resurrect precommunist identities, parties, and institutions.[14]

Soviet-style systems, in addition, were command economies controlled from the center, without private ownership of the means of production or market relations. As the sector ideologically most suited to the Stalinist world view and economically most capable of thriving under command conditions, the military-industrial complex grew to become not only the dominant sector of the economy but also the only sector which functioned more or less according to plan. The performance of this sector in most communist countries (most notably the USSR, Yugoslavia, and the Slovak sector of Czechoslovakia) not only gave central planning whatever credibility it enjoyed but also was designed to form the protective outer shell for the entire system, leading analysts inside and outside the country to attribute far more capability to the economy and the system as a whole than ultimately it possessed.[15] This sector bequeathed to the successor states industries which could produce high quality goods but which required both continued subsidies and a Cold War-style mission concomitant with its size and orientation. Additionally, it is believed by some that sectors of the military-industrial complex in Russia, in support of like-minded groups within the Ministry of Interior, the revamped KGB, and the Ministry of Defense, have been a major buttress of a strong but not necessarily democratic or non-imperial state.[16]

Underneath this strong outer shell resided the light industrial and consumer sectors of the economy which were denied funds, resources, initiative, and personnel – virtually everything except planning targets; and after de-Stalinization ended the use of terror to force compliance, these could be met only by bribery, corruption, distortion, and the formation of informal and illegal production networks. The fact that such a high percentage of total state economic interactions took place outside the plan meant that whatever performance the economy achieved was bought at the expense of the integrity of the planning mechanism of the state and the trust, loyalty, and ultimately the compliance of the population. These socioeconomic and political failures weakened central control, but also left a legacy of cynicism and disrespect for the state, to say nothing of the vast array of informal economic networks which fell out of the state and beyond the law when the regimes collapsed.[17] In *New World Disorder*, Ken Jowitt predicted that the combined legacy of bureaucracy, corruption, and interpersonal distrust would hinder the implementation of democratic reforms, although it is unclear from his analysis whether and why this legacy might vary across countries and whether and why it might be relatively transient.[18]

The great difficulty of establishing political and economic institutions from the bottom up cannot be overstated: Samuel Huntington found that twenty-three of the twenty-nine countries that democratized during the so-called "third wave" (between 1974 and 1990) had previous democratic experience. Equally, those that had not democratized by 1990 had no democratic past. So while states are not condemned necessarily to relive their past, clearly the results of Huntington's study would support the thesis that all other factors being equal, previous democratic experience greatly facilitates the transition to democracy.[19]

The hypotheses generated in the remainder of the section are designed to address not the legacy of the precommunist or communist era, but the nature of the transition and the actual social situation inherited by the first postcommunist leaders. In particular, questions focus on the possibility of overcoming the Leninist legacy through what Crawford and Lijphart call "the imperatives of liberalization." As they state, this approach "suggests that new institutions can be crafted and new international pressures can be brought to bear that shut out the negative influences of the past."[20] Even those authors like Samuel Huntington who favor a strong political cultural argument are supportive of the view that the success of one country or region in introducing democratic reforms can have a snowballing effect in encouraging democratization elsewhere. The economic, political, and cultural policies pursued by actors in the external environment also are seen as extremely consequential for stimulating and supporting movement toward liberalization, particularly in an era when communication is global and international norms favor human rights and democracy.[21]

From this discussion and the literature on transition, it is possible to generate a number of propositions and hypotheses: the following are among the most salient. In those countries whose transition was non-violent and pacted between the elites and the opposition, a party system is most likely to be quickly established.[22] In those countries whose transition was non-violent and pacted between different groups of elites, the ruling party or group will be most able to maintain their elite status, if not their monopoly.[23] In those countries where the new elites moved most quickly to impose rapid liberalization, privatization, and democratization, extremist opposition parties will be less likely to gain a foothold amongst the populace.[24] In those transitions marked by violence, the elites are most likely to attempt to preempt the emergence of independent associations and parties.[25]

Another crucial aspect of transition is the assertion of civilian control over violent coercion in society. Many theorists, most notably Robert Dahl, have underlined the civilian control of the military as a crucial requirement for successful democratization,[26] leading one to suppose that it should be possible to demonstrate the validity of the following propositions: the greater the popular support for democracy as opposed to other political systems or of democratic values as opposed to other political ends (for example, stability, social justice, and so forth), the lower the levels of military intervention in domestic politics;[27] the greater the participation of the citizenry in electoral politics, the lower the levels of military intervention in politics;[28] and the greater the tradition of civilian control of the military within a country, the less will be the tendency of the military to intervene in politics.[29]

Also of concern is the need to analyze the impact on democratization of the political balances among the transitional groups, since much has been made by Adam Przeworski, Mancur Olson, and others of the likelihood that transitional elites would attempt to shape new institutions to maximize their interests. Thus it could be hypothesized that the more that the transition is coopted by hard-liners on the ruling side and radical factions amongst the opponents, the greater will be the prospect for failure of talks to produce a workable and democratic electoral system.[30] And conversely, the more evenly balanced the power amongst diverse elite groups at the time of transition, the more will be the tendency to design electoral legislation which does not favor any particular electoral constituency.[31]

Social and ethnic cleavages suppressed under communism are likely to emerge in the transition and are often intensified by economic changes and political and personal uncertainty. The challenge facing authors is both to identify these cleavages and to analyze the extent to which they have shaped the formation of parties and other political groups. The literature suggests the following relationships exist between social and ethnic cleavages and the prospects for democratization: the more that societies are characterized by spatial distances between mutually reinforcing and exclusivist ethnic, social, economic, and religious groups, the greater will be the tendency for parties to be formed reflecting these divisions;[32] the larger the size of ethnic minorities as a proportion of the total population, the greater is the probability that democratization using majoritarian formulas will fail to contain communal violence if it breaks out;[33] as long as no group has a monopoly over control of resources, then social divisions and unequal access to those resources can be mitigated within a democratic regime;[34] and to the extent that parties and associations promote and facilitate social mobility and civic awareness, then their aggregative function will assist democratization.

The pattern and pace of postcommunist economic change is another independent variable seen as having an impact on democratic outcomes, affecting the emergence of political parties, and increasing the stakes of winning and losing in the political arena. On the whole, it is accepted that the pattern and pace of economic change is a function of the political will of the ruling elites, but that both elites and social groups interact to maximize their access to resources. Thus, political elites will structure economic reforms to maximize their political and economic interests, while setting the pace of change in order to minimize the chances of systematic and widespread social unrest.[35]

Among the greatest challenges to successful democratization is the existence of violent conflict either inside the country or with other states. Indeed, it would appear that the greater the level of violent conflict within a society, the more democratic institutions will be undermined.[36] But its actual impact, upon observation, is diverse, depending on the level and direction of conflict, elite reaction, state capacity to terminate, suppress, resolve, or withstand the violence, and the impact of the violence on the attitude of core social groups toward the process of democratization. Violence may weaken existing institutions in an emerging democracy, but it can also increase pressure toward the adoption of changed institutional arrangements which maintain democracy, ranging from the introduction of nonmajoritarian consociational arrangements to widen the representation of marginalized and alienated minorities[37] to the adoption of corporatist forms of democracy in which large interest-based groups mediate between the state and the citizenry, to a certain degree suppressing citizens' direct involvement in policy making and aggregating overlapping and pluralistic intermediate groups into larger and more monopolistic associations.[38]

The political evolution of society

Central to the questions in this section is the assumption that citizens' attitudes matter. Gabriel Almond and Sidney Verba's theory of civic culture[39] postulates that the viability of democratic institutions is significantly affected by attitudes such as belief in one's ability to influence political decisions, feelings of positive affect for the political system, and the belief that fellow citizens are trustworthy. Challenges to political culture theory have taken place primarily on two levels and have emerged from two intellectual camps.

One challenge emerged in the 1960s and lasted throughout the 1970s as radical scholars polemicized against political culture theory. These scholars, many of them Marxist or neo-Marxist, argued that the dominant political culture in any society was a necessary reflection of the relationships between the ruling and subordinate classes. As Almond later wrote, political culture theory, in particular, "was challenged on the grounds that political and social attitudes were reflections of class and/or ethnic status or else were the 'false consciousness' implanted by such institutions as schools, universities and media."[40]

Also in the 1960s another challenge to political culture theory emerged with the ascension of rational choice models, which asserted that all individuals and institutions in a political system – whether ordinary members of society or politicians or parties, coalitions, intermediate organizations, and governmental institutions comprised of or representing those individuals – would act efficiently to maximize interests, often defined in economic terms.[41] By the late 1960s models based on rational choice and game theoretic approaches had become a dominant mode of social analysis. This emergence of "rational choice," "public choice," and "positive political theory" challenged the very premise of political culture theory. From within this perspective, examining political culture amounted to little more than a superfluous exercise. It was widely held that sufficient explanatory power could be generated by assuming self-interested, short-run rationality. Contributing to the ascension of this mode of analysis, especially within comparative political science, were the availability of economic data and the lack of sufficient cross-national data on political attitudes.

This paucity of aggregate data or large-N studies that would allow researchers to go beyond individual country or region case-studies and draw broader conclusions about factors outside the economic realm hampered efforts by those interested in political culture to reach generalizable conclusions. However, by 1988, Ronald Inglehart[42] had compiled data on attitudes of the general public for a sample of countries large enough to permit multivariate statistical analysis of the relative influence of mass political attitudes as compared with macro-socioeconomic variables on democratization. The accumulation of cross-national data on attitudes of the general public combined with the collapse of Marxism as an alternative explanatory system and the reorientation of some public choice theorists toward a "new institutionalism" has led to a resurgence of interest in political culture as an explanatory variable.

It is now more generally accepted that democracy requires a supportive culture, even if it is agreed that this culture can be strongly shaped both by transient and short-term factors including economic performance and by more underlying variables, including the institutional setting in which this culture is set. Democratic institutions both promote and are promoted by a democratic political culture. In a democracy, popular support for the creation of an independent civil society embodying intermediate groups and associations which feed into the political process and aggregate different societal interests is also required. Because freedom of speech, media, religion, assembly and the right to form independent groups and opposition parties were all suppressed in the communist era, the norms associated with a civic culture cannot be expected to emerge overnight. The legacy of mistrust must first be overcome in order for a previously atomized society to establish the basic level of tolerance and civic responsibility required to sustain even the most basic levels of freedom.[43] Even then, clearly, underlying cultural factors independent of the communist legacy could accelerate or impede the emergence of the kind of civil society associated with liberal democracy.[44]

When examining the emergence of political associations in early transitional societies, authors were asked to collect data on the types of political associations or actors that have become most prominent in each country's political life, that is, political parties, state sector managerial lobbies, trade unions, business organizations, professional associations, religious organizations, clans, paramilitary units, criminal groups, and so forth. In addition, data was collected on how the public perception of political parties and what they claim to represent has affected citizens' attitudes to the political system. Authors were asked to comment on the relative importance of parties as vehicles for new elites intent on accumulating political power and wealth, as opposed to alternative vehicles, such as associations, informal groupings, and the like.

The assumptions in the comparative politics literature that underlie the section on the emergence of political parties are several, including: the higher the level of citizen distrust of political institutions, the greater will be the difficulty of establishing a viable party system; parties will gain preeminence as intermediary institutions only if elections are regular, free, and fair; and the holding of regular, and free and fair elections will increase civic trust over time.[45]

Also central to an understanding of the evolution of societies in transition is the extent to which attempted marketization and privatization have affected the political strength and behavior of various economic groups in society. Operating at the level of abstraction, one could envision distinct responses from economic groups along a continuum ranging from strategies of intransigent resistance to reforms which directly (and in the short-term, negatively) impact their respective economic interests to strategies of ready accommodation with the reforms based on the assumption that these individuals are, or could easily become, aware of the long-term benefits of marketization and privatization which are readily observable throughout the West. With this continuum in mind, authors were asked to analyze the extent to which attempted marketization and privatization have affected the political strength and behavior of business and managerial groups, agricultural groups, and organized industrial labor. Authors were asked to gather information on whether these groups had formed or formally affiliated themselves with political parties and what role they had assumed in the financing of elections and the control of the media.

Monitoring of the emergence of new economic strata in transitional polities is important because of the assumptions about the relationship between marketization and democratization which underpin the literature. The transition to democracy has previously been thought to occur as a result of a long period of capitalist development in which previously subordinate classes – the middle class, most notably, but also the urban working class and small and medium-sized farming interests – evolved an economic interest in the promotion of democracy as a way of balancing class power. Thus, a strong middle class allied with commercial and industrial elites in the private sector is generally seen as a necessary but not sufficient condition for successful democratization.[46] Economic winners are thought to support democracy to the extent they feel it legitimizes and sustains their dominant economic position, whereas economic losers are seen as supporting democracy to the extent they feel the existence of democratic state autonomous of dominant economic classes erodes economic inequality.[47]

This obviously raises the question of whether an economy which liberalizes before the rule of law is in place can prevent the rise of organized criminal activity which in turn can disrupt, impede, and even capture the process of democratization itself. Authors were asked to analyze the political impact of organized criminal groups in the respective countries under review and to discuss the extent to which associations or political parties have become linked with organized crime. In general, it can be assumed that the emergence of organized crime will not be welcomed by the population, and authors were asked to gather data on how the public perception of the role of organized crime has affected citizens' attitudes toward the political system. But studies done in economic theory suggest that to the extent that organized crime provides stability and economic security and benefits, the population will be more likely to acquiesce in its existence.[48] And further, it is postulated that the existence of widespread random criminality will predispose the population to allow organized crime to establish rules and norms over geographic regions.[49] The public's predisposition to prefer organized criminal activity to large-scale inchoate activity does not necessarily translate into greater support for democracy, however, and indeed one could suppose that the existence of connections between elected officials and organized crime would erode public confidence in democracy and increase public support for a "strong hand" to end corruption, even if democracy is put on hold for a time.[50]

The redistribution of wealth, the emergence of political parties tied to diverse societal interests, the struggle to control marketization – all have an impact on citizen attitudes toward the democratic process. The collapse of communism has allowed researchers to conduct public opinion surveys and collect data on the changes over time in the level of public support for democratization. Many of these countries have had declines in economic performance which have matched or even exceeded rates seen in the West during the Great Depression, a depression in which democracy endured the test in most of Western Europe and North America, but was wiped out in Germany, Austria, and Italy by the rise of fascism. Based on past trends, it can obviously be expected that the impact of poor economic performance can and will erode support for government leaders, but it is not clear that such performance will necessarily also diminish popular support for democracy as a whole; and authors were asked to collect data on this where it exists.[51]

Surveys also exist which measure a number of factors – such as attitudes toward specific institutions, levels of tolerance in the society, the likelihood of participation in elections, and membership in political parties and intermediary associations – as among different sectors of the society: specifically, authors were asked to gather data which surveyed attitudes by various groups. As with other democratic countries, one would expect attitudes toward democratization to vary across generations, ethnic identification, region, class, and gender.[52]

Popular attitudes are in constant interaction with a free media, which both reflects those attitudes and helps to shape them. What is at stake in postcommunist countries is the establishment of a media which is a channel for the expression of a range of societal interests independent of the preferences of the government. And while the media in all countries are subject to some regulation, what is vital to examine is whether control of the media has affected the conduct of elections and other forms of political participation. It can generally be assumed that the greater the independence and pluralism of the media from the outset of the democratization process, the greater will be the level of civic trust and civic involvement.

Political parties and the party system

With the political evolution of society and increases both in levels of tolerance and in civic involvement, it is assumed in a democracy that a system which promotes parties' sustained competition and pluralism over time will enhance the possibility that political parties will develop and become rooted. Clearly, the comparative literature supports the proposition that a strong civil society is a necessary but not sufficient condition for a strong party system, and it is difficult to find examples where party systems have been established in states with weak civic cultures.[53] Authors were presented with a number of questions addressing the actual emergence of party systems in postcommunist states. They were asked to assess the strength and durability of political parties and the impact of electoral laws, electoral competition, and the type of government on the development of a party system. Particular attention was paid to the renamed communist parties and extremist anti-democratic parties and social movements. Finally, the effect of the party system on the strength of government itself was studied.

Literature in the field traditionally has been divided over the prerequisites for the creation of a strong party system between those who assess the strength of political parties by reference to their intrinsic qualities (internal structure, leadership, platform) and those who emphasize their strength in terms of their ability to perform effectively as a channel for, and reinforcement of, citizens' interests. The former view minimizes the relationship between civil society and political parties; the latter sees that relationship as intrinsic to, and the *raison d'etre* for, a party system. Thus, the former would see a strong party system existing without civic engagement as unproblematic for democracy: the latter would see such a situation as inimicable to the very aims of democracy.

Authors were also asked to comment on the type of electoral system introduced in the postcommunist states and the results. Electoral laws provide the method for the conversion of votes into the selection of leaders for electoral office. There are two major types of electoral systems – majoritarian and proportional representation (or PR). Plurality and majority systems reflect a majoritarian philosophy – the candidate who garners the largest number of votes wins. These formulas can be used to elect both individual leaders, as with presidential elections, and multimember bodies, as with parliaments and legislatures. The PR model, which can be used only for multimember bodies, provides proportional allocation of seats according to the percentage of votes parties received. These differences in electoral systems have an impact on party evolution, with parties in majoritarian systems tending to move toward the center of the political spectrum (median voter theorem), and parties in PR systems likely to be more diverse and more extreme in their approach.[54] The desire to favor majoritarian rule while not disenfranchising minorities has also produced a large number of mixed systems, including in the postcommunist states. Mixed systems typically utilize a version of PR to elect the legislature, and one of several majoritarian formulas to select the chief executive, thereby balancing the benefit of governability produced by majoritarian results with the value of representativeness exhibited by PR formulas.[55]

The strength and structure of the party system is also affected by the structure of government, especially whether the system is parliamentary or presidential. Studying the failures of presidential regimes in Latin America, Juan Linz has concluded that parliamentarism imparts greater flexibility to the political process, promotes consensus-building, and reconciles the interests of multiple political parties. Presidentialism, by focusing on the election of a single individual to an all-powerful post, diminishes the influence of the party system. Political parties tend to be less cohesive in presidential than in parliamentary systems. Presidential systems foster the creation of a two-party or two-bloc system.[56] It has also been shown that presidentialism favors the emergence of two large parties and reduces their distinctiveness and internal cohesion. Party discipline is stronger in parliamentary systems where the prime minister or chancellor belongs to the legislative branch and depends on disciplined and cohesive parties for the survival of government. It is possible for presidential systems to maintain a strong party system and better represent minorities by encouraging federalism and separation of powers, but one cannot ignore findings which point to the tendency of presidentialism to overrepresent the majority, thereby increasing the chance that an alienated and mobilized minority might drop out of party life and pursue political objectives by other, often violent, means.[57]

The attitudes and activities of extremist and communist parties and movements are central to an analysis of the future stability and cohesiveness of party systems in postcommunist countries. The impact of all these parties will depend on their leadership, the institutional and legal setting, constituency, and organization. But postcommunist regimes are challenged to build consensus at the center at the same time they are trying to overcome the institutional and bureaucratic inheritance of a one-party system which still has many well-organized adherents at the political extreme. Trying to construct an electoral and legal system which favors a shift to the center while these groups remain powerful is, therefore, a significant and indeed unprecedented challenge.

Turning to parties of the left and the right, authors were asked to examine the extent to which the renamed communist parties have actually changed (a) their attitudes toward liberal democracy (b) their political leadership, and (c) the interests that they represent as a result of their experience in the emerging democracies. On the other side of the political spectrum, anti-democratic parties and social movements based on clericalism, fascistic traditions, or radical nationalism have arisen in some countries, and authors were asked to determine, among other things, the number and importance of such parties, their willingness to endorse political violence, and their links with paramilitary forces. The literature is split between those who maintain that when electoral systems provide the possibility of coming to power by legal means, the tendency of communist and extremist parties to support the overthrow of the current elected government will subside and those who assert that extremist parties become most destructive to the democratic process when they win elections. These two views are reconciled by the notion that extremist groups will become less extreme through participation in the democratic process, that they will lose their authoritarian and anti-democratic impulse and cease to be a threat to the democratic order. This assumption works best when there is a strong and stable center, fairly good economic conditions, and low levels of social mobilization. However, as the example of Weimar Germany demonstrated, both the Nazis and the Communists won seats in the legislature; and the violent fighting between them paralysed the body in the face of Hitler's rise to power. Concern about the possibility of a repeat of the Weimar example has been widespread in postcommunist countries, most notably Russia, with many analysts concerned about the growth of extremist groups. It is assumed that such groups have the best chance of coming to power without a significant moderation of their political platform when poverty is on the rise, when elected officials are perceived as unable or unwilling to take steps to ameliorate the situation, and when the electoral system is so structured in favor of a pure PR formula as to give parties little incentive to moderate their stand.[58]

Authors were asked to assess the strength of the countries' political parties and party system, including whether emerging party systems are characterized only by the creation of ephemeral parties, or by more stable parties, as indicated by patterns of leadership, electoral results, and survey data. Studies have shown that the more a party exhibits a stable constituency, a consistent party platform, and internal consensus, the greater its durability over time.[59] In looking at parties, authors were also asked to speculate on how the structure and durability of political parties has been affected by any laws on campaign finance and by the timing of elections – including regional versus countrywide elections. Additionally, the literature suggests many propositions which deserve analysis in light of results from postcommunist elections: that the number of coalitions amongst parties will be lower in countries with a proportional representation system than in a majoritarian electoral system; that parties representing women and minorities will fare better in proportional representation systems than in majoritarian systems; that voter turnout will be less among women and minorities in majoritarian systems; that majoritarian systems produce moderate parties, weak in ideological and social class definition, whereas proportional representation systems encourage parties defined along class, ethnic, and regional lines, including extreme right-wing and left-wing parties. All of these propositions can be tested in the new

environment provided by postcommunist transitions. Elsewhere, it has been
shown that even in a mixed presidential/parliamentary system with proportional representation used for the legislative elections, the large parties which
are favored in a winner-take-all presidential election continue to be favored
in elections to the legislature, particularly if they are held at the same time,
thereby reducing the bias of proportional representation toward greater
inclusion of minorities, regional elites, and women.[60]

The party system as it has emerged in postcommunist countries has
sometimes facilitated and sometimes obstructed the creation of governments
able to formulate and carry through reasonably coherent policies. And
conversely the capacity of postcommunist regimes to formulate and
implement policies has affected citizen support of democratization and
marketization processes. This interaction and essential circularity makes the
identification and isolation of variables responsible for shaping the process of
democratization difficult. Yet the reasons for undertaking the attempt go
beyond the normal intellectual curiosity of academe: never before have so
many countries which cover such a large percentage of the world's surface
started at the same time along the path of transition from one single kind of
regime to another; never before have populations embarking upon a
democratic path been so educated, urban, and mobile; and never before has
the international system been so clear and unequivocal (if not unanimous) in
its support for democracy and marketization as the dominant paradigm. This
unique opportunity essentially to control for so many variables makes it all
the more likely that observers will be able to judge whether differential
strategies for democratic development will also have predictable outcomes.
Democracy may be the "only game in town" but as with any game there can
be winners and losers, and the winners will be those countries where social,
economic, and institutional engineering has received the most attention by
elites, parties, and citizens alike.

NOTES

For their generous and insightful comments on an earlier draft of the chapter,
the author wishes to thank Valerie Bunce, Joan Nelson, Bruce Parrott, Darya
Pushkina, Melissa Rosser, and DelGreco Wilson.

1 *Politics in Developing Countries: Comparing Experiences with Democracy*, ed.
Larry Diamond, Juan Linz, and Seymour M. Lipset (Boulder, CO: Lynne
Rienner, 1990); *Elites and Democratic Consolidation in Latin America and
Southern Europe*, ed. John Higley and Richard Gunther (Cambridge: Cambridge
University Press, 1992); Samuel Huntington, *The Third Wave: Democratization
in the Late Twentieth Century* (Norman, OK: University of Oklahoma Press,
1992); Stephanie Lawson, "Conceptual Issues in the Comparative Study of Regime

Change and Democratization," *Comparative Politics* 25 (January 1993), 88–92; Scott Mainwaring, "Transition to Democracy and Democratic Consolidation: Theoretical and Comparative Issues," in *Issues in Democratic Consolidation*, ed. Scott Mainwaring, Guillermo O'Donnell, and J. Samuel Valenzuela (Notre Dame, IN: University of Notre Dame Press, 1992).

2 Among the more pioneering works are Daniel Lerner, *The Passing of Traditional Society* (Glencoe, NY: Free Press, 1958); Seymour M. Lipset, "The Social Requisites of Democracy," *American Political Science Review* 53 (1959), 69–105; James P. Coleman, "Conclusion: The Political Systems of the Developing Areas," in *The Politics of Developing Areas*, ed. Gabriel A. Almond and J. S. Coleman (Princeton: Princeton University Press, 1960); Phillips Cutright, "National Political Development: Its Measures and Analysis," *American Sociological Review* 28 (1963), 253–64; *On Measuring Democracy*, ed. Alex Inkeles (New Brunswick, NJ: Transaction Publisher, 1991); and Arthur S. Banks and R. B. Textor, *A Cross Polity Survey* (Cambridge, MA: MIT Press, 1963).

3 For example, see Kenneth Bollen, "Issues in the Comparative Measurement of Political Democracy," *American Sociological Review* 45 (1980), 370–90; Kenneth Bollen, "Political Democracy: Validity and Method Factors in Cross-National Measures," *American Journal of Political Science* 37 (November 1993), 1207–30; Raymond D. Gastil and Freedom House, *Freedom in the World* (New York: Freedom House, annual); and Ted Robert Gurr, et al., Polity I, II and III data sets, Inter-University Consortium for Political and Social Research.

4 Doh Chull Shin, "On the Third Wave of Democratization," *World Politics* 47 (October 1994), 148.

5 See Valerie Bunce, "It's the Economy, Stupid . . . Or Is It?" Paper presented for the Workshop on Economic Transformation, Institutional Change and Social Sector Reform, National Academy of Sciences/National Research Council, Task Force on Economies in Transition, Washington, DC, September 19-20, 1996.

6 Huntington, *The Third Wave*, 266–67.

7 Peter McDonough, Samuel Barnes, and Antonio Lopez Pina, "The Growth of Democratic Legitimacy in Spain," *American Political Science Review* 80, no. 3 (September 1986), 735–60. While focusing on the prerequisites and indicators of democratic legitimacy they nevertheless are concerned with consolidation more broadly. Also see *Transitions from Authoritarian Rule: Prospects for Democracy*, ed. Guillermo O'Donnell, Philippe C. Schmitter, and Laurence Whitehead (Baltimore, MD: Johns Hopkins University Press, 1986).

8 For a classic statement of this view and the corollary that factors other than a country's level of economic development were crucial to the explanation of why some countries embarked upon democratization and others did not, see Dankwart Rustow, "Transitions to Democracy," *Comparative Politics* 2 (April 1970), 337–63.

9 Beverly Crawford and Arend Lijphart, "Explaining Political and Economic Change in Post-Communist Eastern Europe: Old Legacies, New Institutions, Hegemonic Norms, and International Pressures," *Comparative Political Studies* 28, no. 2 (1995), 187.

10 Tina Rosenberg, "Overcoming the Legacies of Dictatorship," *Foreign Affairs* 74, no. 3 (May–June 1995), 134.

11 There are many articles and books in the literature, but one which approaches the subject thematically is *The Legacies of Communism in Eastern Europe*, ed. Ivan Volgyes (Baltimore, MD: Johns Hopkins University Press, 1995).

12 The best case is made by Ken Jowitt, *New World Disorder: The Leninist Extinction* (Berkeley, CA: University of California Press, 1992).

13 See Jacques Rupnik, *The Other Europe: The Rise and Fall of Communism in East Central Europe* (London: Pantheon, 1989); Roy Medvedev, *Let History Judge: The Origins and Consequences of Stalinism* (Oxford: Oxford University Press, 1989); Jeffrey Goldfarb, *After the Fall: The Pursuit of Democracy in Central Europe* (New York: Basic Books, 1992); Timothy Garton Ash, *The Uses of Adversity: Essays on the Fate of Central Europe* (New York: Vintage Books, 1989); Milovan Djilas, *The New Class: An Analysis of the Communist System* (New York: Praeger, 1957); and Vladimir Tismaneanu, *Reinventing Politics: Eastern Europe from Stalin to Havel* (New York: The Free Press, 1992).

14 Richard Rose in doing cross-national surveys found support for the hypothesis that "if the common historical experience of Sovietization has had a decisive influence, generational differences in attitudes should be similar from one former Communist country to another." "Generational Effects on Attitudes to Communist Regimes: A Comparative Analysis," *Post-Soviet Affairs* 11, no. 1 (January–March 1995), 37. Also see Ellen Comisso, "Legacies of the Past or New Institutions?" *Comparative Political Studies* 28, no. 2 (July 1995), 200–38; and Barbara Geddes, "A Comparative Perspective on the Leninist Legacy in Eastern Europe," ibid., 239–74. Both maintain that the Soviet era destroyed popular support for pre-Leninist parties and traditions in most countries.

15 See, for example, Anders Åslund, *Gorbachev's Struggle for Economic Reform* (Ithaca, NY: Cornell University Press, 1989); and Ed A. Hewett, *Reforming the Soviet Economy* (Washington, DC: Brookings Institution Press, 1988).

16 The varied political views and splits within the military/security services are discussed in Karen Dawisha and Bruce Parrott, *Russia and the New States of Eurasia* (Cambridge: Cambridge University Press, 1993), ch. 6. Although she is dealing only with the security service, the role and political attitudes of this service are discussed by Amy Knight, *Spies without Cloaks* (Princeton, NJ: Princeton University Press, 1996).

17 Janos Kornai, *The Socialist System: The Political Economy of Communism* (Princeton, NJ: Princeton University Press, 1992). See also Peter Wiles, *The Political Economy of Communism* (Cambridge, MA: Harvard University Press, 1962).

18 Jowitt, *New World Disorder*. Also see Sten Berglund and Jan Dellenbrant, "Prospects for the New Democracies in Eastern Europe," in *The New Democracies in Eastern Europe*, ed. Sten Berglund and Jan Dellenbrant (Brookfield, VT: Edward Elgar Publishing Company, 1991).

19 Huntington, *The Third Wave*, pp. 40–6; also see Valerie Bunce and Maria Csanadi, "Uncertainty in the Transition: Post-Communism in Hungary," *East European Politics and Societies* 7 (Spring 1993), 240–75.

20 Crawford and Lijphart, "Explaining Political and Economic Change," p. 172.

21 Huntington, *The Third Wave*, pp. 85–108.

22 For a consideration of the impact of previous regime type on transition success and of transition type on prospects for consolidation, see Juan J. Linz and Alfred Stepan, *Problems of Democratic Transition and Consolidation: Southern Europe, South America, and Post-Communist Europe* (Baltimore, MD: Johns Hopkins University Press, 1996), ch. 4.

23 For a discussion of pacted transitions, see Arend Lijphart, *Democracy in Plural Societies: A Comparative Perspective* (New Haven: Yale University Press, 1977); and in the Arab world, see *Democracy without Democrats? The Renewal of Politics in the Muslim World*, ed. Ghassan Salame (New York: I. B. Taurus, 1994).

24 This hypothesis is drawn from Joan Nelson, "How Market Reforms and Democratic Consolidation Affect Each Other," in *Intricate Links*, ed. Joan Nelson (New Brunswick, NJ: Transaction Publishers, 1994).

25 See Alfred Stepan, "Paths toward Redemocratization: Theoretical and Comparative Considerations," in *Transitions from Authoritarian Rule*, ed. O'Donnell, Schmitter, and Whitehead, pp. 79–81.

26 Robert A. Dahl, *Democracy and Its Critics* (New Haven: Yale University Press, 1989).

27 The idea that a state's movement toward democracy is conditioned by its ability to exercise civilian control of violent coercion is most fully developed by Dahl in *Democracy and Its Critics*.

28 See, for example, Jendayi Frazer, "Conceptualizing Civil–Military Relations during Democratic Transition," in *Africa Today*, Quarters 1 & 2 (1995), 39–48; Philippe Schmitter, "Dangers and Dilemmas of Democracy," *Journal of Democracy* 5, no. 2 (April 1994); and *Civil–Military Relations in the Soviet and Yugoslav Successor States*, ed. Constantine Danopoulos and Daniel Zirker (Boulder, CO: Westview, 1996).

29 S. E. Finer, *The Man on Horseback: The Role of the Military in Politics*, 2d ed. (Boulder, CO: Westview Press, 1988); and Morris Janowitz, *The Military in the Political Development of New Nations* (Chicago: University of Chicago Press, 1964).

30 This proposition is derived from Adam Przeworski, *Democracy and the Market: Political and Economic Reforms in Eastern Europe and Latin America* (Cambridge: Cambridge University Press, 1991). It largely coalesces with the view promoted by rational choice theorists such as Douglass C. North, *Institutions, Institutional Change, and Economic Performance* (Cambridge: Cambridge University Press, 1990); Anthony Downs, *An Economic Theory of Democracy* (New York: Harper and Row, 1957); and Mancur Olson, "Dictatorship, Democracy, and Development," *American Political Science Review* 87 (September 1993), 567–76.

31 G. Bingham Powell, Jr., *Contemporary Democracies: Participation, Stability and Violence* (Cambridge, MA: Harvard University Press, 1982); Larry Diamond and Marc F. Plattner, *The Global Resurgence of Democracy* (Baltimore, MD: Johns Hopkins University Press, 1993).

32 See, for example, Phillippe C. Schmitter, "The Consolidation of Democracy and Representation of Social Groups," *American Behavioral Scientist* 35 (March–June 1992), 422–49.

33 See Ted Robert Gurr, *Minorities at Risk: A Global View of Ethnopolitical Conflict* (Washington, DC: US Institute of Peace, 1993). Also Linz and Stepan, *Problems of Democratic Transition and Consolidation: Southern Europe, South America and Post-Communist Europe.*

34 This problematic relationship between capitalism and democracy is most fully explored in Przeworski, *Democracy and the Market.*

35 The debate over whether shock therapy or gradualism is the best policy is extensive and is well analyzed in *The Postcommunist Economic Transformation: Essays in Honor of Gregory Grossman*, ed. Robert W. Campbell (Boulder, CO: Westview Press, 1994); and in articles by Anders Åslund and Bela Kadar in *Overcoming the Transformation Crisis: Lessons for the Successor States of the Soviet Union* (Tubingen, 1993). Public choice literature has contributed most to a discussion of rational calculations in polities which are already established, not in those being formed, so its contribution has been more limited, but is discussed in Dennis Mueller, "Public Choice: A Survey," in *The Public Choice Approach to Politics*, ed. Dennis Mueller (Brookfield, VT: Edward Elgar, 1993), pp. 447–89.

36 Donald L. Horowitz, *Ethnic Groups in Conflict* (Berkeley, CA: University of California Press, 1985); Juan Linz, *The Breakdown of Democratic Regimes: Crisis, Breakdown, and Reequilibration* (Baltimore, MD: Johns Hopkins University Press, 1978).

37 See especially Arendt Lijphart, "Consociational Democracy," *World Politics* 21 (January 1969), 207–25.

38 Charles Tilly, *Coercion, Capital, and European States*, rev. ed. (Oxford: Blackwell, 1992); Harry Eckstein, ed., *Internal War: Problems and Approaches* (Glencoe, IL: Free Press, 1963); and *Organizing Interests in Western Europe: Pluralism, Corporatism, and the Transformation of Politics*, ed. Suzanne Berger (Cambridge University Press, 1981).

39 Gabriel Almond and Sidney Verba, *The Civic Culture: Political Attitudes and Democracy in Five Nations* (Princeton: Princeton University Press, 1963).

40 Gabriel Almond, "Foreword: The Return to Political Culture," in *Political Culture and Democracy in Developing Countries*, ed. Larry Diamond, ix–xii. Among the more important critiques lodged against mainstream comparative politics during this era were the following: Mark Kesselman, "Order or Movement? The Literature of Political Development as Ideology," *World Politics* 26, no. 1 (1973); Fernando H. Cardoso and Enzo Faleto, *Dependency and Development in Latin America* (Berkeley: University of California Press, 1979); and André Gunder Frank, *Latin America: Underdevelopment or Revolution* (New York: Monthly Review Press, 1969).

41 Among the seminal works are Downs, *Economic Theory of Democracy*, and William Riker, *The Theory of Political Coalitions* (New Haven: Yale University Press, 1962).

42 Ronald Inglehart, "The Renaissance of Political Culture," *American Political Science Review* 82, no. 4 (December 1988), 1203–30; and idem., *Culture Shift in Advanced Industrial Society* (Princeton: Princeton University Press, 1990).

43 This requirement is explored most fully by Ernest Gellner, *Conditions of Liberty: Civil Society and Its Rivals* (New York: Allen Lane, The Penguin Press, 1994).

44 The debate about this possibility was begun by the publication of Samuel P.
   Huntington, "The Clash of Civilizations," *Foreign Affairs* 72 (Summer 1993),
   22–49.
45 See Seymour M. Lipset, "The Social Requisites of Democracy Revisited,"
   American Sociological Review 59 (February 1994), 1–22; Inglehart, "The
   Renaissance of Political Culture"; and Inglehart, *Culture Shift in Advanced
   Industrial Society*; Almond and Verba, *The Civic Culture*. The dilemma of how
   to build trust in societies where the state had systematically gone about its
   destruction is deftly argued in Richard Rose, "Postcommunism and the Problem
   of Trust," in Diamond and Plattner, *The Global Resurgence of Democracy*, 2d
   ed., pp. 251–63.
46 Barrington Moore, *Social Origins of Dictatorship and Democracy* (Boston: Beacon
   Press, 1966); and Charles Lindblom, *Politics and Markets: The World's Political-
   Economic Systems* (New York: Basic Books, 1977). They were among the first
   to assert the connection between a strong bourgeoisie and democracy. This view
   has been challenged only rarely, including by Dietrich Reuschemeyer, Evelyne
   Huber Stephens, and John D. Stephens in *Capitalist Development and Democracy*
   (Chicago, IL: University of Chicago Press, 1993) who argued that it was the
   working class that had proved over time to have been the greatest supporter of
   democracy.
47 Mancur Olson, "Dictatorship, Democracy, and Development," *American Political
   Science Review* 87, no. 3 (September 1993), 567–76; Rueschemeyer, Stephens,
   and Stephens, *Capitalist Development and Democracy*; and Edward N. Muller,
   "Democracy, Economic Development and Income Inequality," *American
   Sociological Review* 53 (1988), 50–68.
48 Louise Shelley, "The Internalization of Crime: The Changing Relationship
   Between Crime and Development," in *Essays on Crime and Development*, ed.
   Ugljesa Zvekic (Rome: UN Interregional Crime and Justice Research Institute,
   1990); J. S. Nye, "Corruption and Political Development: A Cost-benefit
   Analysis," *American Political Science Review* 61, no. 2 (1967), 417–27.
49 This is a central tenet of Olson, "Dictatorship, Democracy and Development."
50 James Walston, *The Mafia and Clientism* (London: Routledge, 1988); Rensselaer
   W. Lee III, *The White Labyrinth* (New Brunswick, NJ: Transaction Publishers,
   1989).
51 Studies done in six Central European countries suggest that respondents continue
   to have a very positive perception of the political benefits of democracy even as
   they hold a very negative perception of the economic benefits of marketization.
   See Richard Rose and Christian Haerpfer, "New Democracies Barometer III:
   Learning from What is Happening," *Studies in Public Policy* 230 (1994),
   questions 26,35,36,39,40,42, as presented in Linz and Stepan, *Problems in
   Democratic Transition and Consolidation*, 443.
52 The first attempt to see democracy as strongly affected by culture was Almond
   and Verba, *The Civic Culture*. Page and Shapiro have argued that irrespective of
   cleavages within public opinion, overall the public in aggregate is able to make
   rational and informed judgments (Benjamin Page and Robert Shapiro, *The
   Rational Public: Fifty Years of Trends in Americans' Policy Preferences* [Chicago:
   University of Chicago Press, 1992]). One of the first attempts to gauge public
   opinion and attitudinal shifts in the Soviet Union was Ada W. Finitfer and Ellen

Mickiewicz, "Redefining the Political System of the USSR: Mass Support for Political Change," *American Political Science Review* 86 (1992), 857–74. More recently, a wide array of authors have examined changes in public opinion and political culture in postcommunist states: see, for example, James L. Gibson, "The Resilience of Mass Support for Democratic Institutions and Processes in the Nascent Russian and Ukrainian Democracies," and Jeffrey W. Hahn, "Changes in Contemporary Political Culture," in *Political Culture and Civil Society in Russia and the New States of Eurasia*, ed. Vladimir Tismaneanu (Armonk, NY: M. E. Sharpe, 1995).

53   In *Making Democracy Work: Civic Traditions in Modern Italy* (Princeton, NJ: Princeton University Press, 1993), Robert Putnam argues that a strong party system can operate within a weak civic culture; also see Robert Putnam, "Troubled Democracies," paper prepared for the University of Maryland/Johns Hopkins University Workshop on Democratization and Political Participation in Postcommunist Societies, US Department of State, May 1995; and Robert Putnam, "Bowling Alone: America's Declining Social Capital," in Diamond and Plattner, *The Global Resurgence of Democracy*, 2d ed., pp. 290–307.

54   Connections between electoral laws and political parties are the subject of many works, of which some of the best are Arend Lijphart, *Democracies* (New Haven, CN: Yale University Press, 1984); Arend Lijphart, *Electoral Systems and Party Systems: A Study of Twenty-seven Democracies, 1945–1990* (Oxford: Oxford University Press, 1994); Richard S. Katz, *A Theory of Parties and Electoral Systems* (Baltimore, MD: Johns Hopkins University Press, 1980); and *Electoral Laws and Their Political Consequences*, ed. Bernard Grofman and Arend Lijphart (New York: Agathon Press, Inc., 1986). Also see Part II of Dennis Mueller, *The Public Choice Approach to Politics* (Brookfield, VT: Edward Elgar, 1993).

55   On the effects of different varieties of electoral systems, see Douglas W. Rae, *The Political Consequences of Electoral Laws*, 2d ed. (New Haven: Yale University Press, 1971); and Rein Taagapera and Matthew Soberg Shugart, *Seats and Votes: The Effects and Determinants of Electoral Systems* (New Haven: Yale University Press, 1989).

56   See Juan Linz and Arturo Valenzuela, *The Failure of Presidential Democracy* (Baltimore, MD: Johns Hopkins University Press, 1994), for an argument in support of this hypothesis. By contrast, see Donald Horowitz, *A Democratic South Africa? Constitutional Engineering in a Divided Society* (Berkeley: University of California Press, 1991), who finds no necessary link, and W. H. Riker, who theorizes that all party systems converge to two coalitions of equal size (*The Theory of Political Coalitions* [New Haven, CN: Yale University Press, 1962]).

57   Juan Linz, "Presidential or Parliamentary Democracy: Does it Make a Difference?" in Linz and Valenzuela, *The Failure of Presidential Democracy: Comparative Perspectives*, 3–91; and Arend Lijphart, "Democracy in Plural Societies: A Comparative Exploration," in *The Failure of Presidential Democracy*, 91–105. Also see Vladimir Tismaneanu, *Fantasies of Salvation: Post-Communist Political Mythologies* (Princeton, NJ: Princeton University Press, forthcoming).

58   Quentin L. Quade examines the impact of an unmodified proportional representation system on the potential for takeover by extremist groups in "PR and Democratic Statecraft," in Diamond and Plattner, *The Global Resurgence of*

Democracy, 2d ed., pp. 181–7. The case for the likely rise in extremist politics was first and most forcefully made in Jowitt, *The New World Disorder*.

59 Giovanni Sartori, *Parties and Party Systems* (Cambridge: Cambridge University Press, 1976), 6; and Lijphart, *Democracies;* in opposition to Robert Michels (*Political Parties* [Glencoe, IL: The Free Press, 1958]) who dismissed the need for constituency support, focusing instead on the centrality of elites and their ability to instill beliefs in the masses. On the need for a party to show internal consensus, see Katz, *A Theory of Parties and Electoral Systems*.

60 The seminal work on the relationship between party and electoral systems is Maurice Duverger, *Political Parties: Their Organization and Activity in the Modern State* (New York: Wiley, 1954); see also Douglas J. Amy, *Real Choices/New Voices: The Case for Proportional Representation in the United States* (New York: Columbia University Press, 1993); and Michel L. Balinski and H. Peyton Young, *Fair Representation: Meeting the Ideal of One Man, One Vote* (New Haven, CN: Yale University Press, 1982).

The Russian Federation

3   Democratization and the new political order in Russia

Thomas F. Remington

Introduction: political conflict and institutional change

Russia's contemporary political order is the product of a series of radical changes in the institutional framework of the Soviet and Russian state since the late 1980s. Considering the stakes involved, these changes have been surprisingly peaceful. Even the violent constitutional crises of 1991 and 1993 are modest in comparison with the terrible convulsions of 1917. Compared with Central Europe, however, Russia's postcommunist political evolution has been both turbulent and inconclusive. After events such as October 1993, when the army shelled the parliament building, and the war in Chechnia, few would claim that the advances which have been made in transforming Russia's political life in the direction of democracy are either decisive or irreversible. It may be the case that Russia will become a democracy only after it has passed through a period of authoritarianism, which would allow durable structures of social power to form and check the power of the state.[1]

This chapter is addressed to the question of Russia's postcommunist political evolution. It attempts to determine whether Russia's constitutional framework is becoming consolidated, such that the main contending forces in Russian politics are generally observing the rules set by constitution and law, rather than seeking to subvert or ignore those rules.[2] In order to answer this question, I will describe the political institutions established by the Yeltsin constitution of 1993 and discuss the steps that led to them. I will focus particularly on the 1994–95 period, a time of relatively stability, and seek to assess the political strategies of the major actors.

In the second section, after considering some of the wrenching social and economic changes which have occurred since 1991, I will survey several sets of old and new social groups and elites, including state enterprise managers, private business, organized labor, the military, and the church. The question underlying the section is how social change has affected the distribution of political power. I will argue that the economic transformation of society and elimination of many of the previous political controls exercised by the state and party have brought about significant social changes, weakening the cohesiveness of some inherited organized groups while creating new latent interests. Many of the divisions and alignments commonly assumed to shape Russian politics have in fact broken down due to the force of changed economic and political circumstances. Inequality, criminality and corruption have risen, but so have pluralist tendencies in the articulation and aggregation of demands. To a large extent, organized political forces have proven their willingness to abide by constitutional rules of competition. But because of the concentration of power in the presidency, control of it is the ultimate prize in Russian politics: a peaceful transfer of power from one president to another following a free and fair election is therefore a critical condition for a democratic outcome in Russia.

Origins and structure of Russia's political institutions

The Soviet transition

In some important ways, the postcommunist transition in Russia and other former Soviet states differed from the paths taken by Central European countries. In Russia the dismantling of the communist system occurred in the absence of a negotiated agreement between outgoing and challenger elites over new rules of the game: the Soviet leadership never considered itself forced to surrender to or share power with an organized popular opposition. No "pact" was signed which provided for the democratization of political institutions. The successive constitutional schemes devised by Gorbachev and Yeltsin between 1988 and 1993 were instruments designed to enable them to achieve their policy goals by giving constitutional status to an existing power base. Not surprisingly, these arrangements were not accepted by their opponents and proved unstable. In their rivalry, Gorbachev and Yeltsin followed somewhat parallel strategies, employing electoral democracy to mobilize mass support in the 1989 and 1990 elections as a counterweight to the communist party apparatus, then transferring their base of operations to an executive presidency.[3] In this game Yeltsin held the advantage, first by seeking and winning office in direct electoral contests in three races in three successive years, culminating in his landmark victory in the popular election to the Russian presidency in 1991, and second by virtue of the fact that Russia was a political community with a national identity and national culture whereas the Soviet Union was not: the democratic opening ultimately destroyed the Soviet Union as a state but made Russia's post-Soviet statehood possible.

Therefore, rather than following a roundtable agreement between regime and opposition on new electoral rules, Russia's elections of 1989, 1990, 1991 and 1993 were held at the initiative of the leader of the day seeking a popular electoral base for his power. Although these elections had profound consequences for the mobilization of new political forces, old elite groups whose power was vested in the old state and party bureaucracy had no stake in the success of these arrangements and finally rejected their authority in coup attempts of 1991 and 1993. Neither democrats nor opposition made a "credible commitment" to abide by the decisions reached under the new democratic order.[4] Like the Provisional Government of 1917, the provisional USSR and RSFSR constitutional regimes of 1989–93 had few defenders when they were dismantled. These precedents offer little encouragement to those appraising the prospects for consolidation of the current, post–1993 constitutional system.

A brief review of the sequence of steps leading to the adoption of Russia's 1993 constitution helps explain the configuration of the current political system.

The rise of partisan politics

Glasnost in the late 1980s and the succession of elections under Gorbachev and Yeltsin powerfully affected the formation of new political movements.[5] As Michael Urban and Vladimir Gel'man point out in their contribution to this volume, some of the contemporary parties arose out of the "informal organizations" that formed in the late 1980s. Glasnost, and the accompanying widening of political rights that allowed autonomous groups to organize, stimulated the formation of a broad popular opposition movement devoted to liberalizing economic and political reform. In turn, the 1989 and 1990 elections of USSR and Russian deputies, much as in several Central European countries, tended to result in the rise of a polarized alignment pattern in which insurgent anti-communists won dramatic electoral victories by opposing the communist establishment. Nationalist elements were divided in this period, some joining in the cause of political and economic liberalism, others allying with the communists around the defense of state and imperial values.

The polarized ideological cleavage between conservative defenders of state socialism and anti-communist insurgents was most evident in the 1990 electoral campaign. In Russia, the March 1990 election races of deputies prompted reformers to coalesce in a movement called "Democratic Russia." It claimed about 40 percent of the seats in the new Russian Congress, and some major local city soviet victories in Moscow, St. Petersburg (then still Leningrad), and Ekaterinburg (still Sverdlovsk) but it soon splintered and declined as a movement. Nonetheless, thanks in part to its parliamentary base of operations, it bequeathed leaders and regional organizations to a variety of successor groups, much as its formation in 1990 had been aided by the nucleus of democratic deputies in the USSR Congress. Some of Democratic Russia's off-spring groups were active in the 1993 parliamentary elections in the form of reform-oriented parties such as Russia's Democratic Choice, Yabloko and a variety of smaller political groups. In turn, these groups gave rise to yet other political movements, often highly personalistic, which ran party lists in the 1995 parliamentary election. By 1995 fragmentation of democratic forces reached the point that it scattered votes across a half dozen pro-reform parties, none of which except for Yabloko then crossed the 5 percent threshold needed to receive parliamentary mandates.

Likewise, the conservative forces which mobilized in 1989 and 1990 formed parties and movements of their own. The communists divided into a relatively moderate Communist Party of the Russian Federation, the more narrowly focused Agrarian Party of Russia, and a large number of smaller and more radical Marxist groups. Likewise, especially after 1990, nationalist movements began to split off, some from the democratic movement and others from the communists, and form their own organizations. Among these are the Congress of Russian Communities, Vladimir Zhirinovsky's quirky, extremist Liberal Democratic Party of Russia, former Vice President Rutskoi's movement "Derzhava" ("Great Power"), the Russian Assembly (*russkii sobor*, headed by retired KGB general Aleksandr Sterligov), and a diverse collection of other defenders of ethnic, statist, monarchical, Orthodox, and communal national causes. Among reform, communist, and nationalist movements, the mobilization of political energies around ideological causes during glasnost soon turned to electoral mobilization under the influence of the 1989 and 1990 electional campaigns. The proto-parties of 1990–93 then chose, for the most part, to enter the races for elections to the State Duma in the fall of 1993, and the eight electoral associations which won party list seats then proceeded to form parliamentary factions.

These parliamentary factions, and others which formed over the 1994–95 period, as well as political groups outside parliament, in turn formed new electoral blocs and associations to contest the 1995 parliamentary elections. The rapid sequence of elections – 1993 and 1995 – and the employment both times of electoral rules which allocate half the seats in the Duma (225 of 450) to list candidates whose parties won at least 5 percent of the vote in the nation-wide electoral district, have strongly affected the development of Russian parties. First, they tended to focus parties' energies on creating national electoral organizations, if only, in many cases, as the personal followings of a particular leader. Second, they have tended to reward a few strong partisan organizations – the communists, Yabloko, and Zhirinovsky's Liberal Democrats especially – which exceeded the 5 percent threshold in both elections. This trio of parties (which, with Prime Minister Chernomyrdin's centrist bloc "Our Home is Russia," were the only ones of the forty-three blocs running to win party list seats in the Duma in 1995) represents the three major ideological camps that emerged during glasnost: communist, liberal democratic, and nationalist.

Yeltsin and the presidency

Boris Yeltsin chose not to affiliate himself with any organized political movement, although for the most part he identified himself as a radical democrat, particularly in the fall of 1991 when he provided political backing for the radical economic stabilization program led by his acting prime minister, Egor Gaidar. Moreover, his strategy concentrated on transforming the constitutional setting in such a way as to secure complete autonomy for Russia within the union and, for himself, to expand his own control of Russian policy.

Yeltsin's remarkable success in Russian politics in 1989–91 – he won three successive popular elections in three successive years[6] – can only be explained by the fact that he had the support of a unique coalition of forces. He was the champion simultaneously of radical economic reform and of radical democratization. He also advocated populist egalitarian policies, such as stripping the nomenklatura of its power and privileges. Finally, he supported political and economic autonomy for Russia *vis-à-vis* the union. This latter cause had a strongly nationalist appeal, and enjoyed the support of many conservative elements in the Russian-republic level branches of the union state and party hierarchies who saw autonomy as a way to gain direct power over Russia's vast economic resources. It is owing to this diverse base of support that he was finally and narrowly elected chairman of the Supreme Soviet by the deputies at the First Congress of People's Deputies of the Russian Republic in June 1990.

Gorbachev's political resources were distinctly inferior to Yeltsin's at this time, given the fact that Russia accounted for three-quarters of the territory of the union, half its population, and the vast bulk of its natural resource wealth. There simply could be no union without Russia. By mobilizing a broad political movement in Russia, therefore, Yeltsin forced Gorbachev to accept his terms – but not before their struggle reached a violent climax.

Gorbachev of course resisted Yeltsin's demands for political autonomy for Russia and executive power for himself as president. Gorbachev in the 1990–91 period allied himself with the orthodox conservative forces represented by the union-level KGB, Ministry of Internal Affairs (MVD), communist party apparatus and economic administrative bureaucracy.

Gorbachev's clumsy attempt to intimidate the Russian deputies as they met in their extraordinary Third Congress in late March 1991 probably had an effect opposite from that intended, for even though the reformers lacked a firm majority, the Congress fully approved Yeltsin's constitutional and policy proposals. Yeltsin held several trump cards. Yeltsin's presidential scheme had already received overwhelming popular support in the March 1991 referendum. Popular sentiment in Russia in the spring of 1991 was hugely favorable to Yeltsin, a fact which Yeltsin skilfully exploited. Massive popular demonstrations in March endorsed Yeltsin against Gorbachev, and a new rolling wave of miners' strikes in March and April were only resolved when Yeltsin promised to put the mines under the control of the Russian government. Finally, in April, Gorbachev gave in, and called for negotiations with Yeltsin and the other union republic leaders on a new treaty of union.

Gorbachev's defeat had substantial repercussions. Both Gorbachev and Yeltsin represented a particular coalition of political forces; when Gorbachev was defeated, both moderate and hard-line supporters of a reformed union lost power. Gorbachev found that the only terms on which republic leaders were willing to negotiate a new treaty of union conceded almost total sovereignty to the republics. As Gorbachev's ability to preserve union power declined in the spring and summer of 1991, his conservative flank sought to rid itself of him. A conspiratorial committee of hard-line bureaucratic and security elements struck preemptively in the 1991 August coup, attempting to remove Gorbachev from power and restore the old union regime by force. However, as we know, the junta collapsed ignominiously within three days when the army refused to give it its full support. The political structures governing the union were fatally weakened by this action as well as by the fear on the part of other republican leaders that in the resulting vacuum, Russia would acquire a hegemonic position *vis-à-vis* the other republics. The popular support in Moscow, St. Petersburg and other large cities for the cause of Russian sovereignty, anti-communism, and radical democratization which rallied to oppose the coup provided Yeltsin with a considerable political boost for his policy and constitutional goals. Through the fall of 1991, as the already-attenuated structures of union power grew exiguous, Yeltsin sought and won approval for his program of radical economic reform and decree powers from the Russian Congress of People's Deputies. Had he at the same time sought to consolidate his position by calling new parliamentary elections, the 1993 coup attempt might possibly have been avoided.

This second coup attempt grew from the struggle for power between President Yeltsin and the irreconcilable communist opposition based in the Russian Congress. His own vice president, Alexander Rutskoi, and the chairman of the Supreme Soviet, Ruslan Khasbulatov, became the leaders of this opposition.[7] Initially, in the fall of 1991, the Congress granted Yeltsin the extraordinary powers he demanded to carry out radical reform but stipulated that these powers expired after one year's time. Yeltsin, however, demanded to keep them. The Congress, increasingly dominated by a communist-led coalition, refused to grant him the authority he demanded or to submit the constitutional question to a popular referendum.[8] In March 1993 it nearly passed a motion for his removal by the required two-thirds majority. Ultimately Yeltsin resolved the conflict by force. In a series of decrees in September and October 1993 he dissolved parliament, annulled the parliamentary mandates of its members, called new elections, decreed that a new draft constitution was to be put to a referendum for ratification, suspended the Constitutional Court, removed its chairman from the chairmanship, dissolved all lower soviets (except those in the national republics) and called for new elections to new local representative bodies.

The opposition forces refused to comply. Barricading themselves inside the the Russian "White House" where parliament met, they called a rump session of the Congress, elected Rutskoi president, and defied Yeltsin. After a ten-day stand-off, paramilitary forces loyal to the anti-Yeltsin opposition broke through the cordon surrounding the White House and moved to take over the Moscow mayor's office building next door, as well as the Ostankino television tower. Evidently they calculated that their actions would trigger a general uprising against Yeltsin: Rutskoi went so far as to call on his followers to seize the Kremlin. After initial vacillation, however, the army supported Yeltsin and suppressed the uprising, and for the most part the public reaction was one of indifference. After arresting the leaders, the army proceeded to lob artillery shells at the White House, killing around 150 people. The "events of October" then cast a long shadow over the legitimacy of the elections to the new parliamentary bodies designed by Yeltsin and his advisors and the national referendum to ratify the constitution Yeltsin proposed.

Outcomes of the Russian transition

Despite the bloodshed which accompanied its establishment, the new constitutional order which took effect after the elections and referendum proved to be surprisingly stable. Politics at the national level over 1994–95 was no longer dominated by the polarizing struggle between communists and democrats. Nonetheless, as the elections both in 1993 and 1995 indicate, the search for electoral success by staking out a centrist position has been surprisingly ineffective.[9] In the next section we will discuss the new institutional architecture in more detail and analyze its influence on the behavior of the major political forces. To begin with, though, let us sum up the conclusions from this review of the formation of the present constitutional regime.

Firstly, parties and party-like groups in Russia today arose out of the social and intellectual ferment created by Gorbachev's glasnost policy, which brought to the surface the major ideological under-currents present in Russian society. Their particular forms and identities have been largely shaped by the rapid succession of national electoral contests which resulted from leaders' attempts to mobilize popular support to their side in their struggles against their opponents. These elections include the 1989 USSR elections, the 1990 republican elections, the March 1991 referendum, the June 1991 presidential race, the April 1993 referendum, the December 1993 parliamentary elections and constitutional referendum, and the December 1995 Duma election. In view of rapid change in social interests and identities, a powerful popular antipathy to party identification, a highly personalized and fragmented spectrum of organized political forces, and the absence of a recent historical experience with multi-party politics, these elections have contributed to giving form and definition to the main partisan tendencies in Russian society. Leaders' use of the device of calling parliamentary elections to bid for popular support against their enemies has thus usually had quite unintended results: under Gorbachev elections tended to mobilize radical national and democratic forces, and under Yeltsin elections after 1991 resulted in major victories for nationalists and communists strongly antagonistic to his policies.

Secondly, the current constitutional arrangements reflect Yeltsin's success in creating a strong presidency. In 1991 the presidency enabled him to concentrate power in his struggle against Gorbachev and the conservative union bureaucracy; in 1992 it allowed him to give his government enough autonomy to launch radical economic reform. His strategy of winning autonomy for Russia from the union was supported by a coalition of conservative state and party bureaucrats who saw opportunities for greater power if Russia were freed from the supervening control of the union, as well as on the part of radical democrats and liberals who believed that the replacement of communist with demoratic and market institutions was only possible by defeating the conservative hold of union-level power interests. Later, however, Yeltsin's use of the powers of the presidency provoked strong resistance, especially from among communist opponents of radical market reform, as well as forces sympathetic to a restoration of the old union. Over the concerted opposition of the communist-nationalist alliance, he succeeded in winning ratification of his ideal constitutional framework in the December 1993 vote. Both in 1991 and 1993, extra-constitutional force decided the outcome of a struggle over Russia's constitutional forms.

However, the powerful presidential office that Yeltsin and his allies created in this way has since become the chief prize for political competition among all the organized political forces in the country. An institution created by one coalition of forces at one particular time for one particular set of purposes has outlived its origins and now shapes the strategies of both the political friends and foes of President Yeltsin.

The constitutional setting

Russia's current constitution was ratified in a national referendum held simultaneously with parliamentary elections on December 12, 1993. Suspicion lingers that the results of the referendum were falsified, and that the required 50 percent turnout of the population was not in fact achieved, making the results invalid under the rules Yeltsin himself decreed into force.[10] Still, a majority of those who voted approved the constitution, and democrats, communists and nationalists alike have accepted the validity of the constitution's ratification.

For the most part the constitution can be regarded as the handiwork of Yeltsin's own administration. The constitution establishes a system of separation of powers in place of the older model of soviet power, under which executive and representative power were said to be fused. However, the constitution is a hybrid of presidential and parliamentary forms. In the widely-used typology proposed by Matthew Shugart and John Carey, Russia's is a "presidential-parliamentary" regime, in which the president has wide law-making powers and authority over the cabinet, while the government must also maintain the confidence of the parliament.[11] As they point out, such a system is fraught with the potential for instability because of the difficulty for the president of maintaining a partisan majority in parliament. Moreover, under the electoral rules for president and parliament in Russia, elections will not be concurrent even though the deputies and the president all have four-year terms. Shugart has recently argued that non-concurrence of elections by itself helps account for the instability for presidential regimes.[12] Little about Russia's political arrangements or recent history offers much evidence to think that Juan Linz's case for the weakness and instability of presidentialism for new democracies should not apply to Russia.[13] Still, we should remember that many believed that France's Fifth Republic was also bound to fail. As Linz reminds us, contextual factors such as the president's personality, the historical setting and the nature of the party system are crucial in determining the viability of a particular constitutional system.[14]

Presidential power

Yeltsin's model for the post-Soviet Russian state was that of a "presidential republic." Accordingly, the presidency is the dominant political institution. The president is the head of state, the commander in chief of the armed forces, and the chairman of the Security Council. He can declare a state of war or state of emergency on Russian territory subject to the requirement that he immediately notify parliament (he cannot declare war on another state on his own authority, however). He is given responsibility for directing foreign policy and protecting national security, and overall responsibility for both domestic and foreign policy. He appoints the prime minister subject to the consent of the State Duma, the popular chamber of parliament; he appoints the deputy prime ministers and other ministers at the initiative of the prime minister although the Duma can vote no confidence in the government. He also appoints a number of other government officials, among them the chairman of the central bank, the general procurator, and the members of the three highest judicial bodies, the Constitutional Court, the Supreme Court, and the Court of Arbitration. Again, however, in each case, his appointments are subject to parliamentary consent. He needs no parliamentary consent to appoint the top military commanders, the presidential administration, regional presidential representatives, and the members of the Security Council. And he possesses the power to enact binding decrees without parliamentary consent and thus to make law.

In this power, however, he faces an important but ambiguous limitation. His edicts may not contradict existing law or the constitution. In November 1995, however, the Constitutional Court ruled that parliament had no authority directly to block a presidential decree. In other decisions as well, the Court has shown little inclination to challenge the president. In the first major test of presidential power that the Court ruled on, it found that the president had not exceeded his constitutional authority in launching military operations in Chechnia by decrees. Certainly more challenges to the president's decree power are likely and the court's rulings in themselves will test the willingness of Russian political elites to abide by constitutional norms.

The president also has wide nominal powers over lower tiers of government. Under the constitution, for example, he can countermand actions of lower executive bodies pending final decision by a court. He exercises a power – which Yeltsin asserted by decree – under which he can appoint the heads of government in subjects of the federation other than national republics unless he authorizes an election to fill the position. The great majority of "governors" (as the regional administrative chiefs are usually called) continued to be Yeltsin's appointees through 1995. Yeltsin's power over the chief executives of the regions vitiates some of the promise of federalism in the constitution. His actual power over regional governments is strongly limited, however. Parliament passed and Yeltsin reluctantly signed a law under which members of the upper chamber cannot be removed from their jobs except with the consent of the chamber. In effect this provided a guarantee of job security for those deputies of the Federation Council who were Yeltsin appointees and diminished Yeltsin's hold over them. For another, the means of control Yeltsin has had at his disposal over regional administrators are attenuated by the difficulty of exercising direct power in a weakly institutionalized setting over long distances amid an overloaded agenda. Yeltsin's influence at the regional level is certainly lower than was the corresponding power of the Central Committee Secretariat over the obkom secretaries in the communist period and may be closer to the degree of power that the tsar could exercise over the gubernatory before the revolution. Gubernatorial elections will further increase the political autonomy of the governors.

As Jeffrey Hahn's chapter observes, Yeltsin's decrees of September–October 1993 abolished soviet power in Russia. That is, not only did he disband the Congress of People's Deputies and Supreme Soviet at the central level, but he also decreed the dissolution of local soviets and the election of new representative bodies in regions and towns. Note that in the twenty-one ethnic republics, however, President Yeltsin lacks the constitutional power to determine their form of state power. They are able to write their own constitutions and laws so long as their decisions do not contradict federal law or constitution. Ten republics have instituted presidencies. Here even the attenuated control that President Yeltsin exercises in other regions is absent, and the center exercises its power through a combination of sticks and carrots, particularly in the form of federal fiscal policy.

The president's powers could be reduced by constitutional amendment. The procedure the constitution provides for amendment poses major obstacles, though, since success would require that one political camp hold a sizeable majority in both chambers of parliament and in two thirds of the constituent territories of the federation, and the presidency as well. Should that happen, however, the incentive for that camp to weaken the single most important lever of power it possessed would quickly evaporate. More probable than a successful amendment reducing presidential power is the tacit limitation of presidential power through the accumulation of precedent and decisions by the Constitutional Court interpreting the sense of the constitution. The evolution of constitutional practice in the French Fifth Republic suggests that a rather wide range of alternatives in the scope of presidential power is possible in a hybrid system depending on the political balance of forces and the personality of the president.[15]

These constitutional provisions, then, and the hurdles the constitution erects to changing them, appear to give the Russian president enormous policy making power. Both constitutionally and practically, however, his power faces important limitations. The president may not constitutionally ignore the decisions of parliament or the Constitutional Court, both of which can overrule him: parliament can override a presidential veto of a bill by a two-thirds vote of each chamber, and the Court can decide that a presidential "normative act" is unconstitutional. Through 1995 the Constitutional Court did not issue any decisions restricting Yeltsin's freedom of action in any important ways. The present court has, however, two important predecessor bodies, whose success in limiting presidential power may serve as precedents in the future.

The first was the "Committee for Constitutional Oversight" proposed by Gorbachev as part of his great political reform package of 1988. In one of its first decisions, in September 1990, it found unconstitutional a decree Gorbachev had issued unilaterally claiming for himself as president the power to approve or prohibit demonstrations within the city of Moscow. Gorbachev chose not to challenge the ruling, thus tacitly acknowledging its validity.

While this USSR-level body was not itself a court, the Russian Republic established a Constitutional Court by constitutional amendment in July 1991; one of its first rulings in early 1992 also found a presidential action unconstitutional. The court struck down President Yeltsin's decree merging two ministries into one. He too complied with the ruling, again accepting the principle that the court had jurisdiction to adjudicate constitutional disputes to which he was a party. To be sure, since then, Yeltsin has taken several baldly unconstitutional steps, among them the dissolution of parliament and suspension of the Constitutional Court itself in September 1993. Yeltsin's 1993 constitution preserved the institution of Constitutional Court. Since the new constitution came into force, his actions have generally complied with the provisions of the constitution, if we can accept the Constitutional Court's finding about the legality of his decision to launch full-scale combat operations in Chechnia. However great the temptation must be for Yeltsin to ignore the restrictions on his powers set by the constitution, he must calculate that not only would he jeopardize substantial Western aid and goodwill by stepping outside the limits of his constitutional powers, but he would also provide his successors with strong reasons to do so as well and thus to reverse many of the changes he has brought about. The more that the opposing forces adhere to constitutional procedures in settling their differences, the costlier it is for any one side to be the first to violate it. In this way a self-enforcing agreement on the institutional framework can acquire binding force. Having accepted the Constitutional Court's decision that his Chechen decrees were constitutionally permissible, Yeltsin would increase the risks to his power and political legacy if he chose to ignore the court in a future decision that went against him.

Similarly, the president's powers *vis-à-vis* parliament are great but should not be exaggerated. Certainly the constitution makes it extremely difficult for the parliament to remove the president. As in the United States, the legislature's sole device for forcing out the president is the drastic means of impeachment (the word impeachment is used in the constitution to refer to the actual removal from office, rather than, as in the United States, to the "indictment" enacted by the House of Representatives preparatory to Senate action). The Russian procedure is even more cumbersome than the American.[16] Parliament's power to check the president has little to do with the threat of impeachment, however. Rather it stems from two more immediate considerations: the need for the parliament's approval of any piece of legislation, and the constitutional requirement of parliamentary confidence in the government. A president who ruled by decree could not be certain that the government would comply with his directives; this consideration appears to have moved Yeltsin to use his decree power rather sparingly, to invite parliament to pass its own legislation on some matters, and even in certain cases to amend decrees to satisfy parliamentary objections.[17] Of course there are large swaths of executive power where the parliament's influence is diminished because they are directly overseen by the president. In his capacity as guarantor of national security, chief of the armed forces, and architect of the main directions of foreign policy, the president is directly responsible for the "power ministries" (defense, interior, foreign affairs, and the successor agencies to the KGB), which former acting Prime Minister Gaidar has called the "presidential ministries." Parliament has nothing to say about the decisions or even composition of the Security Council although the constitution specifies that parliament is to adopt a law regulating its powers and formation. So far, however, parliament has not adopted such a law and the Security Council's composition and activity have been regulated by presidential decrees.

Nonetheless, the Russian president's ability to make policy in contravention of parliament's will faces certain constraints even in foreign and defense policy domains. This is because parliament, by rejecting a candidate for prime minister three times or denying a government its confidence twice within three months, can force the president to choose whether to dissolve the government or dissolve the parliament and call new elections. The president must therefore calculate whether by dissolving parliament and holding new elections he will wind up with a friendlier or more hostile parliament. Over 1994–95 President Yeltsin evinced little desire to invoke this procedure. Moreover, he is constitutionally prohibited from doing so within one year of a parliament's election, within six months of a new presidential election, or if the Duma has (by the required two-thirds vote) approved a motion calling for the removal of the president through impeachment. Thus the balance of power, while asymmetrical, is by no means as one-sidedly tilted in favor of the president as is often thought.

Parliamentary institutions

Let us first review the basic features of the Federal Assembly, as the new parliament is called.[18] The new constitution established a bicameral parliament called the Federal Assembly. The Federal Assembly replaced the Supreme Soviet and Congress of People's Deputies, which Yeltsin had dissolved in September, 1993. The Federal Assembly's lower house is the State Duma, and the upper chamber the Council of the Federation. The State Duma has 450 seats. Half are filled on the basis of proportional representation in a single, federal-wide district, and half are elected in 225 single-member districts. The 178-seat Council of the Federation comprises two deputies from each of the 89 constituent regions of the Russian Federation (known as subjects of the federation – that is, the republics, oblasts, krais, and two cities of like status into which Russia is divided).

Except for certain categories of legislation for which the constitution assigns unique jurisdiction to one of the chambers, bills originate in the Duma and upon passage are sent to the Council of the Federation.[19] If the Council of the Federation approves the legislation or fails to examine it within fourteen days, the legislation is deemed enacted, subject to the president's signature. If the Council of the Federation rejects the legislation, the two houses may form a conciliation commission to resolve differences. Any compromise legislation must be approved by the Duma. With or without a conciliation commission, the Duma may enact legislation after Federal Council rejection with a two-thirds majority vote. Passage of laws in each chamber requires a majority of the total number of deputies of that chamber. Within five days of final action by the Federal Assembly, legislation is sent to the president, who then has fourteen days to sign or veto the legislation. A veto can be overridden only by a two-thirds majority vote in both chambers, that is, two-thirds of the total number of deputies in each chamber.

The new constitution specified that in the future both the president and deputies of the Duma would have four-year terms; the president could serve a maximum of two consecutive terms but deputies are not restricted in the number of terms they can serve. The transitional articles of the 1993 constitution provided, however, that the first wave of deputies in both chambers would serve only a two-year term, after which new elections would be held.

The electoral system used in the December, 1993, elections was established by presidential decree while the 1995 elections of deputies of the State Duma proceeded under a new election law enacted in 1995 after protracted debate.[20] Both elections employed a mixed system of proportional representation and single-member districts. Half of the 450 seats were allocated proportionately to registered parties that received at least 5 percent of the vote. The other half were filled through a single-stage plurality election in single-member districts. The new 1995 law on parliamentary elections preserved the most important features of the 1993 electoral system but added a new requirement that parties must divide their national lists into regional sub-lists.[21] After the twelve seats on the party's central list were filled, seats were filled by candidates running on the regional sub-lists according to the share of the vote received for the party in each region.

The new Standing Orders provided that the Duma was to be steered by a council on which each faction had a single vote. Thus, unlike the old presidium of the Supreme Soviet, where committee chairs comprised the membership, parties would organize the major decisions about agenda and would have the opportunity to hammer out agreements on the shape of legislation. Deputies outside particular factions would therefore be unrepresented on the governing council. Moreover, the new rules diminished the powers of the chairman, turning some of the powers enjoyed in the past over to a committee on organizational matters, and others to the new Council of the State Duma. The new Duma was therefore considerably less centralized than the old Congress and Supreme Soviet system and gave a substantial advantage to political parties to organize decision-making processes. This institutional change proved critically important in parliamentary law-making and relations with the president in 1994–95.[22]

The 1993 parliamentary elections gave no one political party or camp a clear victory. A simple way of characterizing the distribution of party and factional strength would be to say that reform oriented deputies occupied about a third of the seats in the new parliament; centrist forces about a quarter; and opposition deputies about 40 percent.[23] Majority coalitions normally required the support of so-called centrist forces, and the most frequently occurring combination was one we might characterize as "left-centrist" – that is, an alliance of communists, agrarians, the centrist "Women of Russia" group and, nearly as often, Zhirinovsky's Liberal Democrats and Glaz'ev's Democratic Party of Russia. An analyst working for parliament calculated a set of agreement scores for the major factions for spring 1995 (January through May) and found that, on issues where they took a definite stand, the communists were joined about 80 percent of the time by the agrarians, about 73 percent of the time by the Women of Russia, about 58 percent of the time by the LDPR, about 56 percent of the time by the

Democratic Party of Russia, and only 28 percent by Russia's Choice and PRES. How often these alliance partners defined the majority may be judged by a separate count of a set of fifty-five substantive issues voted on in February and March 1995. Here Russia's Choice voted on the winning side less than any other major faction, while the agrarians, communists and Women of Russia voted with the majority at least 60 percent of the time, with the agrarians most likely to vote on the majority side.[24] Thus, although there was no one stable majority coalition in the Duma, there was a tendency for a center-left coalition to define the winning position most of the time. It was such a coalition, in fact, that succeeded in winning a narrow victory for its candidate, Ivan Rybkin, as chairman of the Duma. Formerly a leader of the communist faction in the old Congress/Supreme Soviet, Rybkin had run on the Agrarian Party list and remained a nominal member of the agrarian faction. His reputation, however, was that of a straightforward, rather pragmatic figure, and he was therefore acceptable to many centrist and some democratic deputies. Since then, his position evolved; he consistently steered the Duma in the direction of compromise with the president.[25]

The 1995 elections changed the balance of political forces in the State Duma. The Communist Party of the Russian Federation was most successful and did well both in the party list ballotting and in district races. Its 22 percent share of the popular list vote converted to about twice that percentage of seats because votes cast for parties failing to win 5 percent were redistributed to those four which did, and half the voters cast votes for parties that failed to cross the threshold. Accordingly, it received almost 100 list seats and more than 50 district seats. With one third of the seats, therefore, it acquired substantially more influence than any party had in the 1994–95 Duma.

The Council of the Federation is organized very differently from the Duma. Conceived as a body through which the interests of regional governments may be represented in national policy-making, partisan factions are not recognized and for all practical purposes do not exist. Nor is there any central executive committee, although in practice the chairman has met regularly with committee chairs to discuss the agenda and other housekeeping issues. The Council of the Federation also has been in session much less than the Duma, and has tended to leave the day-to-day work to its chairman and staff.[26]

As a result of the changes in parliamentary organization brought about through the new constitution of 1993 and the elections to parliament held at that time, power in parliament grew more decentralized than in the past, while the articulation of conflict within the Duma, between the two chambers of parliament, and between parliament and the executive, became more structured. Parliament and government used procedures established by the

Standing Rules and the constitution to identify and resolve their differences. Nearly every major issue on which parliament – either or both of its chambers – and the executive (either government or presidency) differed over 1994–95 was resolved by a compromise. To a surprising degree, therefore, the actors on both sides of the system found it advantageous to compose their differences through compromise. Even in the case of the parliament's early vote in favor of an amnesty for those jailed as a result of the 1991 and 1993 coup attempts, when the president threatened to refuse to comply, he quickly abandoned his opposition to it and allowed the order to be carried out. To be sure, the political elite well remembered how close Russia came to civil war in October 1993 and evidently desired to avoid another such episode: no side felt itself strong enough to win in such a mutually destructive confrontation. But for this reason, they created a set of institutional arrangements conducive to negotiated agreements on policy differences. These spared Russia a repetition of the constant brinkmanship and crisis prevalent in 1992–93 in the relations between executive and parliament. Rather than use presidential decrees to enact measures on controversial matters, representatives of the president and government usually worked with parliament in joint commissions to find mutually acceptable solutions. The 1994, 1995, and 1996 budgets all passed after long negotiations between representatives of the major Duma factions and the government. So did other important and divisive pieces of legislation, such as the first and second parts of the Civil Code; the Land Code; the law on local self-government; the law on elections of the Duma; the law on formation of the Council of the Federation; and the law on sharing of production (*razdel produktsii*). (An exception was the program for the second, cash, phase of privatization, where a greatly-modified bill acceptable to the government failed by a small margin in the Duma). In each case compromises were hammered out by commissions representing the major factions and the executive branch, permitting passage of the measures in parliament and presidential approval. This was possible on parliament's side because major political decisions were made in camera by faction leaders, who were reasonably sure of being able to deliver enough votes to attain their desired outcomes on the floor.

The Federal Assembly, then, is divided into a party-oriented, full-time lower chamber and a generally non-partisan, part-time, upper chamber. Since a competitive party system is still weakly developed, and the constitution mixes elements of separation-of-powers and parliamentary government, it is not surprising that the Cabinet of Ministers lacked a distinct partisan identity in the 1994–95 period. It included both reformist and anti-reformist elements as well as figures defining themselves as centrists and pragmatists. The composition of government was modified, however, to align itself more closely with the dominant coalition in parliament, by including two high-

86   *Thomas F. Remington*

ranking agrarians to handle agricultural policy, a communist to serve as justice minister, and Nikolai Travkin to serve as minister without portfolio. These later additions served politically to offset the presence of such figures as Anatolii Chubais (first deputy prime minister in charge of economic policy) and Andrei Kozyrev, the foreign minister, both of whom were affiliated with reformist factions. Co-optation of opposition deputies into the government showed the president and government's reluctance to face a direct showdown with parliament over a vote of confidence. So did many of the policy measures taken by the government, particularly its habit of dividing the agrarians from the communists by pumping resources into the agro-industrial sector to win the votes of the agrarians for the budget. The government's ability to win over moderate opponents and parliament's ability to structure outcomes resulted in the failure of the opposition's attempts to remove it in October 1994 and June–July 1995 through the no confidence mechanism.

Toward checks and balances

Let us sum up the discussion so far by offering two observations about the ways in which the constitutional landscape structured elite politics in Russia over the 1994–95 period.

First, no single seat of power or ideological camp dominated the political arena. The semi-presidential or "presidential-parliamentary" character of the regime gave the presidency a dominant position but not exclusive power over policy making. Executive power was divided between presidency and government, and checked by the Constitutional Court and and parliament. Parliament itself was decentralized through bicameralism and the dispersion of power in the lower chamber across an an array of left, centrist, and liberal partisan factions, each of which had a share of power in decision-making. Neither parliament nor government was firmly in the hands of a majority party or coalition. Parliamentary majorities were constructed out of broad coalitions that usually included large numbers of centrist deputies. The government was internally diverse. It often took positions in a rather non-ideological, *ad hoc* way, staking out a centrist position to win the support, depending on the issue at hand, either of opponents or proponents of liberal reform. Its pragmatic strategy allowed it over and over to reach compromises with parliament, enabling the passage of legislative acts and the avoidance of a showdown with its parliamentary opponents.

Second, the major political actors made policy decisions using constitutional procedures of legislative deliberation and majority decision, requiring compromise with other players, rather than by going outside the constitutional rules. Even the president avoided provoking a confrontation with parliament by bypassing the legislative process or exercising his decree powers beyond the limits of parliamentary tolerance. On a number of occasions the president accepted parliamentary decisions that he opposed, or settled for compromise agreements both in policy and personnel. As in the French Fifth Republic, contextual factors appeared to influence the distribution of power between president, government and parliament a good deal. Perhaps it is fair to conclude that the structure of incentives built into the institutional framework contributed to overcoming the destabilizing polarization between supporters and opponents of liberal reform which brought down the failed provisional regimes of the 1989–91 USSR and 1990–93 RSFSR constitutions.

By the same token, these features of Russian politics made national policy fuzzy and incoherent. This frustrates anyone who would prefer government to exercise power more decisively, whether for or against reform. Some critics claim that the government was the captive of various powerful bureaucratic interests and uninterested in making more than cosmetic attempts to place the economy on a real market footing. Indeed many would go so far as to argue that the constitutionally prescribed political processes that we have outlined simply masked the real play behind the scenes by criminal and bureaucratic power centers. In the next section, we examine how the distribution of social and political power has changed over the last several years in order to determine to what degree policy processes take place outside the rules prescribed by law and constitution.

Social change and political pluralism

The dismantling of many of the old political and economic controls in Russian society since 1989 has substantially changed the organization and expression of social interests. In this section I shall begin by cataloguing a few of the political and economic changes that have affected social interests, as well as outlining elements of continuity with the Soviet regime in the organization of social power. Then we will proceed to a closer examination of the way economic changes have affected groups in Russian society in order to understand better the base of support for different sorts of organized associations. I shall argue that some seemingly strong organizations are weak in fact because of internal divisions arising from the changed economic environment while other organized and latent groups with cohesive interests are more effective in pursuing their goals. I conclude the section with a discussion of two contextual problems affecting the stabilization of the political system around a democratic order: the weakness of state authority in enforcing the law and the high level of alienation on the part of Russian citizens toward the post-Soviet regime.

Dimensions of social change

Political freedom and civic associations. Since 1989 the state's control over society has receded significantly. Citizens have gained the freedom to form political associations and to articulate demands. Hundreds of political parties have registered; the Central Electoral Commission stated that as of August 1995, some 259 political associations were registered with the Justice Ministry and eligible to participate in the 1995 electoral campaign. Many thousands of civic associations have formed: according to a report put out by Freedom House, "there are over 3500 groups registered in Moscow, but thousands more exist around the country."[27] Civil freedoms have benefitted religious organizations, both Orthodox and non-Orthodox, as the state has turned buildings over to churches and citizens are no longer pressured to reject religion. Private schools have formed. Towns and regions are more autonomous in setting policy. When government, whether central or sub-central, violates these rights, citizens have few means of redress, however. They have few means to counter repressive acts by dictatorial regional governors or to stay the massive bombardment of civilian residences in Chechnia by federal armed forces. Nonetheless, political liberties have expanded substantially.

Mass media. Government control over the mass media continues to be strong but by no means as all-encompassing as in the Soviet era. Much of its control derives from the financial dependence of both print and broadcast media on government subsidies. Government also uses its monopoly over state television to promote positive images of state leaders and policies. But pluralism in the mass media enjoys certain legal and financial protections. NTV, an independent, commercially-backed television firm, offers alternative news and opinion programming which is widely consumed by the political, intellectual and commercial elite. A diverse range of newspapers is published. The greater freedom for the mass media is offset, however, by the financial difficulties they face as the costs of newsprint and distribution services have soared. Still, while the government's own tolerance of independent media is insecure, as the short-lived effort by the government to censor the press after October 1993 uprising and the July 1995 initiation of a legal case against NTV for its weekly program of political satire, "*Kukly*" (Puppets) show, the press has generally been able to defend its freedom. The censor-ship efforts in October 1993 quickly ended, and the procuracy dropped its case against *Kukly* a few months later.

A crucial test of the press's ability to defend its political independence occurred over the question of its coverage of the fighting in Chechnia. Television correspondents from NTV and press journalists on the ground were able to show that the government was flatly lying when it claimed that it had refrained from carrying out massive destruction of civilian areas. The government nonetheless did not impose any censorship on the media in response. In their relationship to the state, the Russian mass media illustrate a common difficulty impeding the emergence of an autonomous civil society. The expansion of press freedom has been accompanied by enormous financial pressure because state subsidies have not kept pace with fast-rising production and distribution costs. The press has therefore been in the paradoxical but characteristic position of simultaneously demanding political independence and more subsidies. Prices have risen sharply, with a corresponding effect on subscriptions and sales: according to a report in summer 1995, subscriptions to newspapers and periodicals had declined to 7 percent of their 1990 level.[28] Other problems are affecting the press as well. The old dominance of the central tier of media organizations is giving way to a greater role for regional and local newspapers, magazines, radio and television in the media consumption of the public. But regional media organizations frequently depend on the goodwill of local authorities for their operations and must therefore cleave closely to the interests of the local government.[29] Finally, the dominant position of television in the media system has grown as the print media have declined. Control of state television is therefore an increasingly critical instrument of power (a fact mitigated somewhat by the proliferation of local and regional television programming and by the existence of independent, non-state television).

Therefore the ability of the press to stand outside state power and hold government answerable to the populace is compromised by its dependence on subsidies, exemptions, goodwill and facilities that government, central and regional, still controls. Like other would-be components of civil society, the press is quick to seek the state's protection from the harsh post-Soviet environment. Nonetheless, the press has managed to perform a watchdog function, to voice a wide range of ideological perspectives, and to provide citizens and elites with access to a vastly expanded pool of factual information that would have been closely guarded under the old regime. Therefore the press, for all its limitations, has tended to check government power.

Economic transformation

The end of state planning. Profound changes have occurred in the ownership and control of economic resources. For one, the system of centralized economic planning and administration has been dismantled. Since 1991, state planning, and the system of "state orders" which Gorbachev vainly hoped would replace it, has disappeared. The state planning commission, Gosplan, now exists as the Ministry of the Economy, and performs forecasting and coordination functions. Many of the administrative bodies, such as ministries, which ran productive enterprises in the past have now been reorganized as parastatal firms conducting profitable commercial activity (often benefitting from their monopoly status in a particular field). An important but less often noticed aspect of the elimination of the planning system is the independence of enterprises from the ministries. Gorbachev's economic reforms failed in their attempt to ally with enterprise managers in the cause of market reform against the state economic bureaucracy through the 1987 Law on the State Enterprise and later reforms. As a result, state enterprise managers have divided between those favoring a more open and competitive economic environment and those pressing for a return to a protected, autarkic and state-controlled economy. A conflict has opened between export-oriented branches and enterprises, which seek a cheaper ruble and a more open foreign trade regime, and those branches and enterprises demanding high tariff barriers and a high-priced ruble.

Rising poverty and inequality. For individuals, the economic reforms of 1992–93 have had mixed effects. In 1992, when most prices were decontrolled, the consumer price index rose by a factor of 26 while the incomes of the population rose by a factor of only 8.5.[30] Gradually the rise in prices has slowed while real earnings have risen at a faster pace. In 1995 real income per capita was on average 60 to 70 percent of the pre-reform level.[31] Breaking down the aggregate figures, however, reveals a pattern of widening inequality between rich and poor. Figures on these politically sensitive subjects are not always reliable, but most estimates agree that the ratio of the average per capita income of the richest 10 percent of the population to that of the poorest 10 percent rose from 5.4:1 in 1991 to almost 11:1 at the end of 1993 and 13:1 at the end of 1995.[32] In 1994, average real incomes began to rise again and savings increased, but in 1995 real incomes appear to have slipped again. Poverty has also continued to grow. In May 1995, the state statistical committee reported that between January and April, 30 percent of the population, or 44 million people, had monthly incomes below the subsistence minimum of 385,000 rubles, or $45 US.[33] The Russian government's own Working Center for Economic Reform, however, estimated that by September 1995, the proportion of the population living in poverty had declined to 34 million, or 23 percent.[34] Another estimate, by Branko Milanovic of the World Bank, gives the proportion of the population living in poverty in 1993 as 21 percent, as compared with 2 percent in 1987–88. Milanovic estimates aggregate inequality in Russia to be slightly less that in the United Kingdom, but higher by 50 percent than the Russian level in 1987–88.[35]

Table 3.1 *Ruble exchange rate against the US dollar, 1990–95*

	Rubles per dollar
December 1990	25
December 1991	170
December 1992	415
December 1993	1,240
December 1994	3,500
December 1995	4,650

Source: Rates calculated by author.

Table 3.2 *Monthly inflation rates in Russia, 1992–95 (percent change over previous month)*

	1992	1993	1994	1995
January	245.0	26.0	21.0	17.8
February	38.3	25.0	10.0	11.0
March	29.8	20.0	9.0	8.9
April	21.6	19.0	10.0	8.5
May	12.0	18.0	8.0	7.9
June	18.6	20.0	5.0	6.7
July	11.0	22.0	5.0	5.4
August	9.0	26.0	4.0	4.6
September	12.0	23.0	8.0	4.5
October	23.0	20.0	15.0	4.7
November	26.0	16.0	14.0	4.5
December	25.0	13.0	16.4	3.2

Note: The figures measure month-to-month change in the consumer prices index.
Sources: The figures for 1992 and 1993 are reported by Joshua Chadajo, "The Independence of the Central Bank of Russia," *RFE/RL Research Report* 3, no. 27 (8 July 1994), p. 28; the figures for 1994 and 1995 are from reports of the State Statistics Committee.

Inflation has been a persistent problem. Although the rate of inflation has fallen, it still poses a severe hardship, particularly for individuals living on fixed incomes (see tables 3.1–3.3). Many fear that the government's policy for fighting inflation has been by the expedient of not paying wages. According to a survey by Richard Rose, more than half of Russian workers report that they were not paid on time or at all for at least one month in 1994.[36]

Table 3.3 *Annual inflation rates in Russia, 1991–95*

1991	1992	1993	1994	1995[a]
144	2,318	841	203	145

Notes: Rates calculated as percentage change of end-year retail/consumer price index over previous year. [a]Estimate.
Source: European Bank for Reconstruction and Development, *Transition Report 1995: Investment and Enterprise Development* (London: EBRD, 1995), p. 186.

Privatization. A third major feature of economic transformation has been the shift to private ownership of productive resources through a program of privatization of state assets and the start-up of new business enterprises.[37] By the middle of 1994, when the first phase of mass privatization ended, 70 percent of large and medium-sized industrial firms had been privatized, as had 80 percent of small firms. Private entrepreneurship was growing as well: as of the middle of 1994, some 10 percent of the population were self-employed, and their numbers had risen by 25 percent since the beginning of the year.[38] Around one million small and medium-sized private businesses were legally registered as of mid-1994, and they employed around 12 million people.[39] It is possible that at least two or three million more exist off-book.[40] The results of privatization have been mixed. Market forces now play a far greater role than in the past, but control over real economic assets of factories and farms often remains in the hands of the same managers and officials who held them in the past, with the difference that now they have acquired legal title.[41] Privatization has scarcely touched agriculture; virtually all collective and state farms have been legally reorganized, for example as closed stock companies; but real control tends to remain with the same administration as before, and they continue to operate in an environment which is almost entirely protected from commercial competition. Barriers to entry are particularly high in agriculture: fewer than 300,000 private farms existed as of the end of 1994.[42] A Freedom House report states that as of the end of 1993, for every 100 new private farms that formed, 52 folded.[43] Over 90 percent of agricultural land is still held by state and collective farms, a figure which did not change appreciably between 1993 and the end of 1995.[44] As will be argued below, the managers of state and collective farms form a powerful political lobby which has successfully resisted establishment of a competitive market in land or produce.

Nonetheless, although its effects have been uneven across sectors, privatization has launched an enormous struggle for control over state assets, one of the most powerful underlying forces driving postcommunist politics.

Table 3.4 *Production and investment in Russia, 1989–95 (percentage change over previous year)*

	1989	1990	1991	1992	1993	1994	1995[a]	Cumul
Real GDP		-4.0	-13.0	-19.0	-12.0	-15.0	-3.0	-51
Investment (constant prices)	4.1	0.1	-11.0	-45.0	-15.0	-27.0	-10.0	
Industrial production	1.4	-0.1	-8.0	-18.8	-16.0	-21.0	-6.0	

Note: [a]Estimate.
Source: European Bank for Reconstruction and Development, *Transition Report 1995: Investment and Enterprise Development* (London: EBRD, 1995), p. 185, 205.

Declining output. Finally, economic activity suffered a deep decline over 1992–94 as a result of the government's efforts at fiscal and monetary discipline. Russian official figures showed that GDP had fallen 39 percent from the end of 1991 to the start of 1995, with industrial production dropping by half, and agricultural output by a quarter.[45] Table 3.4 provides some indication of the decline in production. It also suggests that industrial growth is likely to be hampered for years to come by the severe fall in capital formation.

The decrease in economic activity brought some enterprises to a standstill and forced many to lay off workers or place them on short time. Unemployment figures are extremely unreliable, but perhaps 10 to 12 percent of the workforce is laid off, on enforced vacation, or working limited hours.[46] These figures probably overstate the problem. For instance, official unemployment figures fail to report how many nominally unemployed workers are actually working off-book. Surveys of the population by VtsIOM find that 24 percent of the unemployed are earning outside incomes; 11 percent are earning three times or more the average wage.[47]

The decline in economic activity is also overstated in official figures. For one thing, electricity consumption has declined far less than has industrial production, yet consumption of electricity per unit output does not appear to have grown sufficiently to explain the gap. The EBRD estimates that while GDP in Russia declined 49 percent between 1989 and 1994, power consumption dropped only 21 percent.[48]

One of the most dramatic changes in the structure of the Russian economy, and a significant factor in the underestimation of national income, is that the private sector now accounts for a much greater share of output. Table 3.5 indicates how rapid the change has been.

Table 3.5 *Private sector share in GDP and employment in Russia, 1989–94*

	1989	1990	1991	1992	1993	1994
Pure private sector in GDP	5.3	6.0	10.1	14.0	21.0	25.0
Non-state sector in GDP	–	–	–	25.0	52.0	62.0
Pure private sector in employment	1.6	2.6	4.8	18.3	28.1	31.0
Non-state sector in employment	–	18.0	25.0	31.0	46.0	51.0

Source: European Bank for Reconstruction and Development, *Transition Report 1995: Investment and Enterprise Development* (London: EBRD, 1995), p. 30.

Another reason that the figures on declining national output are overstated is that traditional measures of output – and not only in a Soviet-type economy where physical output (*val*) was so heavily emphasized – perform poorly in capturing economic activity in services. However, services have now replaced manufactured goods as the largest source of value-added in the economy. For example, the share of value-added produced by non-state firms rose from 53 percent in January–August 1993 to 58 percent in the same period of 1994, according to Egor Gaidar's Institute for the Economy in Transition.

In addition, a great deal of economic activity in Russia is off-book, not always because it is illegal, but often to escape taxation. A conservative estimate of the scale of the output of unrecorded, untaxed goods and services is 20 percent of GDP, but of course it could well be higher.[49] Tatiana Zaslavskaia's surveys of household incomes find that about 25 percent of the average earnings of households comes in the form of in-kind goods and services from auxiliary garden plots or the output of enterprises paid in lieu of cash wages. Another 16 percent of income is unreported in household surveys but is observed in aggregate flows of regional incomes. A very large portion of the Russian economy, therefore, both in cash and in kind, is unrecorded.

Finally, the decline in economic activity appears to be slowing. In May 1995, for the first time since radical reform began, economic production showed an increase. In June, GDP rose 3 percent, and industrial output 2 percent, over May.[50] Some branches of the economy have been growing steadily, among them parts of the construction industry.

Overall, the results of economic reform have been highly uneven: a minority of the population is better off, and a larger part of the population is either more insecure, poorer, or both, compared with Soviet times. A large share of the population resorts to various means outside the recorded economy to get by or earn additional income. A profound liquidity crisis continues to depress the economy. A great deal of entrepreneurial activity is occurring, both on the part of new start-up firms and former state enterprises, but the economy as a whole has not yet recovered from the shock of the 1992 stabilization program. As a result, a substantial part of the population is sympathetic to platforms of political opposition to the Yeltsin-Chernomyrdin government.

Institutional adaptation

Some powerful interests formed under the old regime retain at least a part of their former influence. A prime example is the security police. Despite a succession of reorganizations, the old KGB continues to exercise many of its former powers. Having reviewed several dozen functions performed by the KGB in the past to determine whether they were still being performed by its successor organs, Michael Waller observed that: "Continuities vastly outnumber the changes both qualitatively and quantitatively. The KGB was disbanded in name only after the August 1991 putsch and preserved in smaller functional and territorial components endowed with similar powers."[51] The Russian journalist Evgeniia Albats reached a similar conclusion: "the events of the last three years [1991–94] have demonstrated the KGB's fantastic capacity for regeneration and revival."[52] It has remained the case that not one person has been held legally accountable for acts of repression committed under the communist regime. To the contrary, many individuals who have been close to the security organs or have made their careers in them hold positions of high responsibility.

Still, changes in the status of the several state bodies responsible for national security are observable. The armed forces has suffered a significant loss in corporate power as well as open internal divisions: general officers have openly disobeyed orders with impunity (General Lebed' over the withdrawal of the 14th Army from Moldova, General Vorob'ev over the operation in Chechnia, both of whom went on on to win seats in parliament). Several top army officers have openly called for the resignation of the defense minister, General Pavel Grachev. Armed Force commanders have demanded, in vain, that severe budget cuts be reversed, although pressure from the military was successful in obtaining parliamentary passage of a law ending student deferments from conscription. Perhaps most significantly, the military has failed to gain approval for its demand to unify all armed forces under a single command. Some reports indicate that MVD (Ministry of Internal Affairs) troops now outnumber those of the armed forces as a result of successful recruitment of forces withdrawn from Eastern Europe. Certainly the Interior Ministry and the Federal Security Service (FSB, the successor body to the KGB in the area of domestic security and intelligence) provide officers with considerably better living standards than can the armed forces.[53] The armed forces, moreover, compete with the defense industries over arms export policy. All these circumstances create divisions within and among the multiple competing security forces of Russia.[54]

In some respects, the early post-Soviet period has reinforced the power of older, prerevolutionary attachments; these are especially visible in the case of organizations appealing to ethnic and religious identity. Foremost among these is the resurgent status of the Russian Orthodox Church in state and society. The Church has benefited from two trends in the late 1980s and early 1990s: first, a change in state policy which has given it new legal rights and a considerable measure of political prestige; and second, the surge in religious affiliation on the part of Russian citizens. Not only does the Church now have the right of legal personhood, entitling it to own property and enter into contractual agreements, it also has benefited from the eagerness of the political elite to associate itself with the Church. Beginning with Gorbachev's celebration of the millenium of Russian Christianity in 1988 and continuing with President Yeltsin's attendance at major church events and Moscow Mayor Luzhkov's forceful drive to rebuild the Cathedral of Christ the Savior, torn down under Stalin, numerous Russian political leaders have found it expedient to embrace the Church as a symbol of Russian national unity, continuity, and statehood. The Church, for its part, has not been reluctant to take advantage of its newly privileged status.[55] Certainly the Church's new vitality owes also to the the increased popularity of religion among the Russian population. On the other hand, not all of the newly religious have chosen to affiliate themselves with the Russian Orthodox Church; many have gravitated to Protestant and other churches. The Orthodox Church has lobbied to protect itself from the influence of competing churches and in 1993 succeeded in persuading parliament to pass a law prohibiting missionary activity by foreigners except with the express permission of government authorities. President Yeltsin then vetoed the law.[56] The Church has also labored to preserve its control over Orthodox faith in the newly independent states.

Finally, as we have noted, there are substantial continuities in the way politically powerful interests of the Soviet era have converted their administrative privileges into profitable commercial activity. Elements of the communist party, the KGB, and, especially, Komsomol, were among the first groups to form banks and trading companies. The Menatep bank was created with a substantial infusion of Komsomol resources, for example. Other illustrations are the powerful sectoral interests of the military-industrial complex, the agro-industrial complex, and the fuel-energy complex (VPK, APK, and TEK, as they are commonly known in Russia). Although, as I shall argue, not all of these are cohesive interests, the organizations they represent are all direct descendants of Soviet-era administrative bodies rather than of new entrepreneurial capital.

In important ways, therefore, the structure of social influence today is an outgrowth of Soviet-era institutional arrangements, which enabled some strategically placed elites to convert productive, ideological and administrative resources into assets in post-Soviet society when economic and political controls were relaxed. In the case of the Church, an older organization has gained a great deal of new power. For bureaucratic structures such as the security organs, proliferation and reorganization have led to internal divisions and competition for influence. In the case of the great industrial bureaucracies, new daughter firms have formed, often becoming powerful players in world markets.

Often it is claimed that the old political elite has held on to power at the center and in the regions.[57] To a large extent this is undoubtedly so, but the old political elite has adapted itself to a large degree to the new economic conditions. A large section of it has gone into business, while another part strenuously opposes the market. We can see this division in the politics of the former communist party, the largest part of which, the Communist Party of the Russian Federation has moved toward acknowledging the the market (many of its supporters are business people) while most of the other communist splinter groups adhere to orthodox Marxism–Leninism. Many powerful interests which have profited from the partial opening to a market economy demand protections and exemptions that would effectively shut the door to competition from domestic and international rivals, allowing them to collect rents from their monopolistic and monopsonistic positions rather than to raise productivity.[58]

Social change and collective interests. These contradictory economic trends have created an array of new social cleavages. They have divided social groups that previously had relatively homogeneous interests and intensified competition between winners and losers in economic reform. An illustration is the situation of state industrial managers. Although they are a powerful latent force where their interests converge, the contradictory stakes that they hold in the outcome of market reform has made it impossible to unite them as a common political movement. The well-known organization, Civic Union, is a good case in point. Its history demonstrates the difficulty for organizations of remaining united at a time when economic conditions in the country are changing so deeply and quickly that their membership divides over programmatic goals.[59]

Civic Union and the state industrial directors. During the Gorbachev period, an association of the heads of state enterprises called the "Scientific-Industrial Union" was created. Its leader, Arkadii Vol'skii, had made his career in the party apparatus, where he headed the Central Committee department overseeing industrial machine-building, and later became an aide to Yuri Andropov during Andropov's brief tenure as party General Secretary. He was known as capable administrator with strong ties to state industrial directors; his reputation was that of a competent, pragmatic, and influential insider. The Scientific-Indutrial Union was formed to preserve economic ties among enterprises to offset the breakdown of the old system of central planning. After the dissolution of the Soviet Union, the organization reformed as the Russian Union of Industrialists and Entrepreneurs. Although the RUIE professed to have no explicit political goals, it did seek to defend the interests of state industry – including their interest in obtaining credits and production orders – as well as to maintain lines of supply and trade in the face of economic upheavals. Like other interest groups, Vol'skii's organization was inevitably drawn into more direct political activity. In spring 1992, Vol'skii entered politics directly, first forming a political arm of the RUIE, then allying it with other parties and political groups in a coalition called Civic Union. Civic Union insisted that its outlook was "centrist" and indeed sought to stake out the center ground in politics as opposing lines were hardening over the radical Yeltsin/Gaidar stabilization program. Centrism, for the Civic Union, meant ending the "shock therapy" program which sharply cut back government subsidies to state enterprises and opening up the country's borders to free trade. But Civic Union also claimed to back a gradual transition to a market system even though it allied itself with some nationalist groups whose opposition to the Gaidar program was far more extreme.

Many observers thought that the Civic Union was a major force with which Yeltsin and Gaidar had to contend, and for a time, it probably was. A direct test of the clout of the Civic Union came in December 1992 during the Seventh Congress of People's Deputies. Yeltsin had signalled his intent to reach an accommodation with the parliament by offering to modify his government's economic program. In a speech to the Supreme Soviet in November, he referred favorably to Civic Union.[60] But if Yeltsin thought that a tactical feint in the direction of the Civic Union could buy him time and avert a confrontation with the Congress of People's Deputies, he was mistaken. Despite consultation between Yeltsin and the Civic Union on a modified economic program, Civic Union proved unable to carry a majority at the Congress or broker a deal between the deputies and the president. Civic Union's leaders divided over whether Gaidar was acceptable to them as prime minister – some considered him an unrepentant champion of shock therapy who must be removed, while others thought that by ensuring a majority for his confirmation, they could acquire a decisive say over his future policy program. Yeltsin concluded that the Civic Union was a paper tiger that he did not need to appease any longer. Calling the organization's power "mythical," Yeltsin's press spokesman explained that there was no need any longer to bargain with it since it could not swing a majority of the congress to back a compromise program.[61] Yeltsin proceeded to nominate Egor Gaidar as prime minister anyway despite indications that the nomination would fail. When it did, he proposed Viktor Chernomyrdin, a much more agreeable figure from the standpoint of the industrial lobby. Chernomyrdin's nomination was confirmed by the congress, and Chernomyrdin went on to begin an unexpectedly long term of service as head of government.[62] Initially considered a faithful member of the state industrial lobby, Chernomyrdin committed the government to a line of moderate fiscal discipline and free trade. Again, the evidence is consistent with an explanation that Yeltsin conceded to the demands of a powerful *latent* interest group – the state industrial directors' lobby – but that the *manifest* interest association, the Civic Union, had failed in a critical test of its power.

A second test of the strength of the Civic Union came one year later when parliamentary elections were held. Earlier in 1993, part of the Civic Union coalition had split off. Vol'skii reorganized what remained into a new political party called the Civic Union for Stability, Justice, and Progress which put forward a list of candidates on the PR portion of the December 1993 parliamentary election. Civic Union campaigned as the party of moderation, gradualism and experience. It received 1.93 percent of the vote, however, well below the 5 percent threshold required for representation of its party list candidates in parliament. Once again, but now in an electoral contest rather than pressure group politics, Civic Union was unable to demonstrate actual strength.

Finally, Vol'skii reorganized the Civic Union as the Russian United Industrialists' Party under the leadership of Vladimir Shcherbakov. This party then formed an electoral alliance for the December 1995 elections with the main state trade union federation as a bloc called "Trade Unions and Industrialists of Russia: Union of Labor." Despite the ostensibly vast reach of this bloc (the membership of trade union federation numbers over 50 million workers), it performed even worse than had Civic Union in 1993, receiving only 1.63 percent of the national list vote.

Why did Civic Union turn out to be so weak when it had appeared so strong? The reason seems to be that Civic Union was deeply divided internally. When forced to commit itself to a positive program it was unable to speak with a common voice. Some of its members were closely allied with hard-line opponents of the market-oriented, pro-Western, liberal policies of the Yeltsin/ Gaidar government, while others were far more positive toward market reform. This division reflects the fundamental divergence of interests among the enterprises that formed the backbone of Civic Union: some, especially those that were more competitive on the marketplace, came to oppose government protectionist policies that simply fueled inflation and cushioned inefficient enterprises. These favored a more open, internationalist trade policy, and the reduction of state subsidies and credits which interfered with the marketplace. Other enterprises, especially those which were least ready to adapt themselves to the pressures of competition (and these included a sizeable share of defense-related plants), supported a more conservative, backward-looking program. There simply was less and less common ground between those enterprise directors who were operating in a competitive and commercial environment, and those who still were tied to the system of state life support.

Moreover, Civic Union, founded on the premise that state industry shared a common stake in the outcome of change, has had to operate in an environment grown increasingly pluralistic. State industrial managers now may choose among several competing interest associations. For instance, military industry is represented by a lobby which has stayed away from partisan politics, the League in Support of Defense Enterprises, headed by Aleksei Shulunov. According to Julian Cooper, it is little more than an information network linking state and privatized defense plants, but it effectively speaks for their common interests, enjoys their support, and is consulted by government.[63]

The case of Civic Union illustrates the difficulty for an interest organization in aggregating the demands of its members when they are severely divided over policy goals. At the same time, when they share a common *latent* interest, the state industrial directors have been extremely strong even without a unified political organization because the government anticipates their preferences and modifies policy accordingly. Their common interest in retaining control over their enterprises as the privatization process unfolds has been well served. For example, almost no enterprises have been allowed to go bankrupt, despite the fact that many are highly inefficient. By allowing directors a strategic role in its economic program, the government has weakened the industrial ministries which had been an essential prop of the communist regime. It has also ensured that the massive de-nationalization of state property has met with virtually no resistance. This is a key to understanding why the extraordinary transformation of Russia from the communist regime towards liberal democracy has been accomplished without bloodshed. Thus, even though the directors appear to be divided over the degree to which they are prepared to embrace the market economy, the government has modified its economic policy in recognition of their collective power and preeminent stake in control over industrial assets, an issue over which they share a latent interest.

Industrial sectors

The articulation of new cleavages in response to market pressures and opportunities affects industrial sectors differently: some have remained relatively cohesive while others have divided between those well positioned to take advantage of market openings and those demanding protection from the state. For several decades, strong complementarity of interests within three sectors made them particularly powerful voices in state policy-making. These three are the Fuel-Energy Complex (TEK, or Toplivo-Energeticheskii Kompleks); the Agro-Industrial Complex (APK, or Agro-Promyshlennyi Kompleks); and Military-Industrial Complex (VPK, or Voenno-Promyshlenny Kompleks). Social change in the post-Soviet era has affected their cohesiveness and influence in varying ways. Let us briefly summarize these changes.

The Fuel-Energy Complex. Enormous differences between market winners and losers have opened up among the three fuel branches forming this complex: oil, gas and coal. The uncompetitiveness of coal has become a severe political problem; the oil industry is divided into multiple firms hungry for investment; and gas is organized as a vast, wealthy and powerful empire which is one of the largest energy corporations in the world.[64] The gas industry has not experienced the crisis that most of the rest of Russian industry has undergone in the past few years; output has hardly declined and it is a major export industry. Because of the nature of the product – gas cannot be readily divided up into discrete units – it forms a natural monopoly, represented by the firm Gazprom, which is the lineal successor of the old Ministry of the Gas Industry. A vertically integrated firm, it owns its own extraction facilities, pipelines, and trading company. Generally speaking, it has sought a political environment conducive to exports, and has not pressed hard for price deregulation. The fact that Prime Minister Chernomyrdin, prior to being made deputy prime minister in spring 1992, was head of Gazprom, has undoubtedly benefited Gazprom. Nonetheless, there are indications that Chernomyrdin's decision to raise excise taxes on gas exports was strenuously opposed by the industry.

The oil industry, however, has experienced a sharp decline in output; its 1994 production was 44 percent lower than in 1988. The industry is organized very differently from gas: there are some thirty extracting firms and nearly as many refining facilities and petrochemical factories, as well as numerous independent pipeline transport companies, and wholesale and retail trading companies. Around ten oil firms are vertically integrated and economically autonomous, and some of these are powerful political actors in the national and international arena. LUKoil, for instance, is participating in the consortium deal to develop new Caspian Sea reserves, and is a major source of financing for the government budget through the "loans for shares" auctions that the government launched in 1995.

The coal industry is the most troubled energy sector: not only has production declined (by 34 percent in 1994 over 1988), but it loses money and absorbs a large share of the state budget for subsidies. Employment has been falling and some mines have been closed, but, as government officials recognize, more will still need to be closed. The obstacles to further cost-cutting in the industry are both political and economic; the coal miners are well organized and strongly dissatisfied already (around half the workers in the Kuzbas fields voted for the communists in 1995, after having been a staunch bastion of loyalty to Yeltsin in the past). Moreover, closings are expensive in the short run, costing more than annual subsidies. Therefore the industry will be a net drain on state resources for the foreseeable future.

The situation of these three components of the fuel-energy complex, in short, differs so sharply one from another that little is gained by using the traditional concept of a "complex." Rather, it is necessary to disaggregate these industries and even particular firms within them, and to examine the different effects on them that the opening to the world market has had.

The agro-industrial complex. The same cannot be said of the agro-industrial complex. This sector has been able to resist nearly all significant market-oriented change and to lobby for high levels of subsidies and tariff protection. A revealing pattern of political alignments has emerged here as well, however. The political arm of the state and collective farms is the Agrarian Party of Russia, although the farm lobby was already an organized and sizeable political faction among the members of the USSR Congress of People's Deputies; and they formed a large faction as well among the deputies at the counterpart RSFSR Congress. The leaders of this faction, the Agrarian Union, organized the party in 1992 together with leaders of the Communist Party of the Russian Federation.[65] When Yeltsin banned the Communist Party following the August 1991 coup attempt, a number of communist party members and organizers entered the Agrarian Party of Russia; the Agrarian Party then served as a refuge for the communist party until the Communist Party of the Russian Federation was allowed to operate legally again in 1993. Even then, some communists chose to run for the Duma on the agrarian party ticket and one, Ivan Rybkin, was elected Chairman of the State Duma.

The Agrarian Party's voting record in the Duma suggests a greater degree of pragmatism than one would have suspected from its history of alignment with the communists. By concentrating its energies on two principal goals – preventing the legalization of a market in agricultural lands and securing generous subsidies to the agro-industrial sector – the party was highly effective.[66] Its alignment patterns reveal its single-issue orientation: the party allied itself with the communists against the government to block land reform, and with the government against the communists to win passage of government budgets granting generous credits and loans to agriculture. It also won from the government a promise to raise tariffs on imported food over the strenuous objections of city mayors and government reformers. Two members of the parliamentary faction were in the Chernomyrdin government, one as deputy prime minister in charge of agricultural affairs, and one as minister of agriculture,[67] yet on a variety of issues it voted with the communist faction, even to the extent that many of the agrarians supported the votes of no confidence in the government in June and July 1995.

Its ambiguous political stance may have won the agrarian lobby substantial policy benefits, but did not seem to benefit it electorally. Despite predictions that it would hold its share of votes because of its firm grip on the impoverished and dependent rural population, the Agrarian Party suffered a significant defeat at the polls in December 1995, winning only 3.78 percent of the party list vote (as opposed to 8 percent in 1993). Still, it formed a parliamentary faction again on the strength of the twenty APR deputies elected in single-member districts and some communist deputies who were "lent" to it by the communist party to enable it to meet the thirty-five member threshold established for parliamentary factions under the Duma's Standing Rules.[68]

The military-industrial complex. The opportunity to earn foreign exchange by exporting Russian arms has generated intense competition among enterprises, trading corporations, banks, and regions for the right to represent the arms industry abroad. In the process, new alliances between private and state bodies have formed, as, for example, between defense plants manufacturing attractive export commodities and the financial, transportation, insurance and trade services firms that work with them.[69] Fissures between the defense ministry and defense industries have widened over issues such as procurement, mobilization planning, and the restructuring of defense production.[70] Moreover, defense plants themselves compete for scarce subsidies and orders. Generally, Julian Cooper argues, "a true Russian 'military-industrial complex' has yet to emerge."[71] The strongest evidence for this, he points out, is the military's inability to prevent sharp reductions in the military budget. "In the face of tough lobbying," he observes, "the government and Yeltsin stood firm. The voting patterns on the budget were revealing: the Communist Party of the Russian Federation, the Agrarian Party, and even some supporters of Vladimir Zhirinovsky were not prepared to back a larger defense budget."[72]

I have argued that political and economic changes have divided formerly united interests, created new alliances, and led to a more pluralistic and competitive environment for the articulation of preferences. Old interest associations inherited from the Soviet era are weak when they attempt to unite groups whose interests have diverged as a result of economic change. By the same token, the government anticipates the preferences of some important latent interests even when these are not organized as interest groups, and responds to pressure from well organized groups. Interest representation remains fluid and fragmented, however, with multiple associations competing to represent the same interests. These points apply to labor as well as to capital.

Organized labor. Industrial workers are threatened by several effects of the economic transformation of the country: frequent long delays in receiving their monthly pay; widespread lay-offs and forced leave; price inflation; the privatization of many previously subsidized or state-provided services, such as education, children's day-care, health care and vacations; and the heavy burden of uncertainty about their own and the country's future. The arrangement that once had been termed a tacit "social contract" between regime and working class, under which the regime guaranteed certain social benefits such as secure employment to the workers in return for their acceptance of the regime, has largely vanished.[73]

How has organized labor responded to this enormous social change? To date, there has been surprisingly little collective action on the part of workers. Attempts by the leadership of the Federation of Independent Trade Unions of Russia (often called by its Russian initials, FNPR), the main umbrella organization of trade unions, to call a general strike in October 1993 failed utterly. Workers themselves, when polled, seem to oppose strikes as a means of articulating grievances. Strikes in the first part of 1992 actually declined, despite the rapid rise in prices, compared with 1991.[74] In summer 1992, after the initial effects of the "shock therapy" program had begun to be felt, only 10 percent of workers surveyed by the FNPR said that they would support a strike against the Gaidar government program, although 86 percent said that they were willing to participate in other forms of protest, such as rallies and demonstrations.[75] Strikes by coal miners and industrial workers are frequent, although short-lived, and in December 1995, for the first time, school-teachers struck in many regions. The principal grievance motivating these strikes is non-payment of wages.

Yet what impresses an observer is not that there have been frequent strikes, but that strikes have not been even more widespread despite the severe hardships of living conditions. By November 1995, total wage arrears had mounted to 10 trillion rubles, or $2.2 billion.[76] Yet no branch-wide or region-wide strikes have been organized, let alone general strikes. Why has there not been more labor unrest?

One reason for the reluctance of workers to support strike calls is their close ties to the enterprises where they work for a variety of social benefits, administered through the enterprise – often these include basic subsistence needs, such as food and housing.[77] A survey found that in 1992, two-thirds of urban workers received fringe benefits, usually in the form of paid vacations, medical care, and child care.[78] The change in the economic environment has, in many cases, deepened this dependency, as directors gain greater autonomy *vis-à-vis* their enterprises.[79] It becomes more difficult to organize workers of a single industry across enterprises, as individual enterprises are positioned differently with respect to their sources of supply and sales revenues. Evidence for this is found in the fact that at different enterprises, workers choose to affiliate with any of a number competing labor unions and federations.[80] Again, where the collective interests of formerly homogeneous social categories diverge as a result of social change, interest associations based on older lines of organization are likely to decline in effectiveness.

As is the case with associations representing the state industrial directors, pluralism has resulted not only from the new divisions of interest brought about by economic reform, but also from splits and rivalries within organizations, often brought about by the tactical manoevers of their leaders. Independent trade unions split off from the state trade union movement over economic and political issues, but both state and independent union associations have subsequently splintered and reformed as well. As a result, Russia has several competing labor union federations: besides the largest, the FNPR, there are Sotsprof (the Union of Socialist Trade Unions); the All-Russian Confederation of Labor; the Confederation of Labor of Russia; the Congress of Trade Unions of Russia; and various unaffiliated branch unions.

The FNPR is the successor to what used to be the single, monopolistic former trade union federation under the Soviet regime (VTsSPS, or All-Union Central Council of Trade Unions). Its membership is by far the largest of any of the union federations; it claims around 50 million members, or 95 percent of Russia's organized workers, as compared with a total of at most 5 million for all the rest. Until September 1993, FNPR had the right to collect workers' contributions to the state social insurance fund. This fund allowed the official unions to distribute benefits such as disability pay and sick pay, but it also was used to pay union dues. Control of this fund enabled the official trade unions to acquire enormous income-producing property over the years, including hotels and resorts. These assets give officials of the official unions enormous advantages in competing for members. But the FNPR lacks the degree of centralized control over its regional and branch

members that it once had, as is evidenced by the failure of member unions
to heed the leadership's strike calls in the fall of 1993. Many of the member
organizations of the FNPR considered the central leadership too closely allied
with the anti-Yeltsin opposition and preferred a strategy that concentrated on
bread-and-butter material issues.[81]   Mikhail Shmakov, chairman of FNPR,
does dispose of substantial financial resources, but cannot speak for his
organization: regional and branch union organizations are politically
autonomous. In the 1993 and 1995 elections, for example, they freely formed
their own political alliances. FNPR's coalition with Vol'skii's industrial
association clearly brought no dividends to either side, as both turned out to
have negligible influence over their members' partisan choices.

The independent trade unions arose out of the waves of miners' strikes
in 1989 and 1991. In April 1995 seven indepedent unions – those representing miners, dockers, air traffic controllers and others – formed the
Confederation of Labor of Russia (KTR). It took the position that unions
should not have have management as members, as was the traditional practice
in the Soviet-era "industrial"-style unions, and they should remain independent of the state. However, the chairman of the Independent Trade Union of
Miners of Russia (NPGR), disagreed, and broke with the KTR, joining with
Sotsprof to form the All-Russian Confederation of Labor (VKT) in August
1995. Each group then sought its own political alliance for the December
1995 elections. Moreover, both compete with the FNPR for seats on the
Tripartite Commission which, with representatives of management and
government, sets annual wage rates and decides other social policy questions.[82]

The operation of quasi-corporatist consultative mechanism of the
Tripartite Commission is probably another reason for the relatively low level
of strike activity. Through it, since 1992, the government has met with
representatives of organized labor and managers organized labor and
employers to discuss general wage levels and working conditions, giving
unions at least a nominal voice in social policy. This institution has had little
influence over government economic policy, but has demonstrated that labor
unions have more to gain by joining enterprise directors in seeking state
support for industry than by taking a position opposed to management.
Government has agreed to grant substantial wage increases and other social
benefits under the annual "General Agreement" reached among the three
sides. Under the first such agreement, signed in March 1992 by representatives of government, trade unions, and various employers' associations,
each side made commitments. The government promised to create safety nets
for workers such as unemployment benefits and retraining programs; the
employers promised not to slash workforces, and the unions agreed not to
call strikes. To some extent, each side made good on its part of the bargain;

the catch is that there is no way the agreements can be enforced. Yet each year the three sides meet and sign an annual General Agreement, and perhaps the bargaining process itself enables each side to ensure that certain of its interests are met. Alliance patterns on the Tripartite Commission are difficult to discern; certainly they have little to do with the classic division between capital and labor which corporatist structures in Europe seek to mediate. More often, it appears, state industry and official unions join to pressure government to increase state credits and orders to keep enterprises afloat.[83]

Despite the government's half-hearted effort to devise neo-corporatist arrangements such as the Tripartite Commission to solve problems of social conflict, interest representation and mediation in Russia have little in common with corporatism. Apart from the fact that government itself seems not to take such mechanisms seriously in making policy, the fragmented, fluid character of interest representation makes corporatist institutions ineffective. As Elizabeth Teague points out, "corporatism is a system that works best in circumstances in which there is strong social consensus and shared values. In the Russian Federation today, such consensus is largely lacking."[84] In corporatism interest associations are inclusive, comprehensive, monopolistic, and hierarchically ordered; although several of the statist interest associations of the Soviet regime possessed these characteristics, they have subsequently dissolved or splintered, or faced new rivals, under the pressure of social change. In each case we have examined, it appears that when members' interests are growing differentiated, organizations formed to articulate demands under the old Soviet regime find it hard to take act cohesively. Overall, therefore, interest representation has shifted from a statist to a pluralist pattern. Except perhaps for the collective and state farm sector, where the alliance of the agrarian party, trade union of farm employees, and farm directors has succeeded in retaining a rather unified and effective voice, other formerly cohesive economic sectors and public assocations have had to learn to operate in a far more competitive and pluralistic environment. Moreover, the pressure of new opportunities and threats has prompted the formation of a number of new types of associations representing interests that had never been organized in the past.

Regional associations. Among the new types of associations are those defending particular regions and groups of regions, as well as particular levels of government. An example of the latter is the Union of Governors, an association of the chiefs of administration in the oblasts and krais. Generally the governors have been willing to support Yeltsin in national politics, but at the price of demanding substantial autonomy in their own territories, which their union seeks to protect. First formed in 1992, they meet periodically to discuss issues of center-regional relations, such as the legal status of regional and local government.

Organizations representing the interests of groups of contiguous provinces have become another important form of association. Among these are organizations such as "Black Earth," which voices the demands of Voronezh, Lipetsk, Kursk, Belgorod, Tambov and Orel oblasts – where agriculture is vital to the economy. Other associations include the "Urals Interregional Association," "Central Russia," "Northwest," "Siberian Accord," and "Great Volga." These regional associations have become a significant political force. Representatives of the associations meet regularly with the government and parliament to press for the needs of their areas. Moscow views the rise of strong regional associations as a useful way in which the interests of regions can be aggregated and channeled to policy-makers, while checking some of the more radical aspirations of individual territories.

Issue and occupational associations. The range of new interest organizations is wide. One rapidly growing type of organization is women's groups, hundreds of which have sprung up in recent years. Some run health care and maternity centers, family planning centers, or foundations for the care of abused women and children. Others operate charitable institutions for indigents or for the families of discharged servicemen. Still others promote the development of small businesses owned by women. Newspapers, research and public policy centers, and professional associations oriented principally to women's concerns have formed. In the city of Novosibirsk, a group called the "Disabled Parents' Association," most of whose members are women, created a program to lobby for social services for disabled people and to enable them to discuss common problems.[85] Most of the new women's organizations are based in particular cities, most of them Moscow. Unlike the Soviet Women's Committee or the "women's soviets" that were a visible feature of the statist system of public organizations under the old regime, however, they are autonomous of the state and can focus their attention on the issues with which they are most concerned. And, in sharp contrast to the past, now many of the new autonomous organizations have established direct ties with counterpart groups abroad.

Some groups have formed to protest injustices resulting from the rapacious, unregulated free-for-all that post-Soviet Russian capitalism has often exhibited. An example is the "deceived investors'" movement. Lacking clear understanding of the risks attendant upon investment in dubious get-rich-quick schemes, unprotected by any effective legal requirements of disclosure of records, and operating in a fast-moving, often bewildering, new commercial environment, many Russians invested their privatization vouchers and their money in banks, mutual funds, stock companies and other financial vehicles which collapsed. Some were simply ponzi schemes. Depositors and investors have had almost no recourse to the courts, so, as has so often been the case with groups in the private sector, they have turned to political action.

Two associations representing the interests of deceived investors have formed, the United Congress of Investors and Shareholders, and the All-Russian Movement of Investors, both of which were founded in October 1995, and both of which demanded that the government find ways to compensate citizens who were defrauded. Evidently in response to their demands, President Yeltsin decreed in November 1995 that the government must find a way to compensate deceived investors.[86]

Similarly, a large number of the electoral associations which attempted to run party lists in the December 1995 election were interest groups or amalgams of interest groups, rather than parties.

Together, these groups received a total of just over 1 percent of the vote. It is striking that the leaders of these groups should have considered it more useful to organize separate electoral organizations than to put their resources behind supporting existing parties or lobbying government for their interests. What explains the tendency for associational groups to behave as if they were political parties, seeking to acquire a share of state power rather than remaining outside the sphere of state power? Perhaps the reason that in the transitional environment, in which state still monopolizes control over a range of crucial scarce resources needed to preserve organizational cohesion, organizations can only solve their own collective action problems by capturing a share of state power; they cannot acquire needed resources through the market or by pooling the resources of private citizens. Merely winning the abstract freedom to organize may not suffice to allow civic associations to operate effectively. In the absence of a market for such basic material necessities as meeting and office space and communications equipment, many groups – particularly outside the capital cities – depend upon the state to obtain what they need through official allocations.

Clearly, the degree of associational pluralism today is incontestably greater than in the late Soviet period. The evidence reviewed here, however, suggests two characteristic patterns of the new system of interest representation: the preoccupation of associations with capturing shares of state power even to the extent of forming their own electoral blocs; and second, the fragmentation among them, so that many interests are represented by two, three, or more rival associations. The record also suggests that in several important policy domains, the pattern of influence of interest groups on policy making is pluralistic rather than statist or corporatist.

In cases ranging from the military's intense pressure for greater budget allocations, the Church's demands for protectionist policies against foreign missionaries, the agrarians' constant needs for new credits and tariffs, the regions' desires to limit central power and increase their own, the defense industry's demands to increase arms exports, the coal industry's need for heavy subsidies, and countless more cases that we have not considered, lobbies make demands on the budget. The process of budget approval has come under parliament's control, requiring that interests press their case not only in the corridors of executive power, but openly in parliamentary debate. The politics of budgetary policy making has produced some unexpected coalitions, but, most significantly, it has required open deliberation on setting national policy priorities. Neither corporatist nor statist channels of influence are always adequate in securing the interests of the wealthy and powerful. The zero-sum politics of the budgetary game has produced a more pluralistic policy making process.

Dilemmas of stabilization

The soft state. A grave problem in Russia's young post-Soviet political order is government's inability to enforce its will. The point may appear paradoxical given President Yeltsin's efforts to wield centralized presidential power over central and regional government. Yet, as in previous Soviet and tsarist regimes, hyper-centralization results in dissipated control. Precisely for this reason, in fact, Gorbachev launched his strategy of glasnost, hoping to increase his ability to enforce policy by expanding the transparency of the behavior of lower levels of the bureaucracy to higher levels. Democratic reformers also believed that glasnost would make government more democratic by raising the accountability of officials to the public.[87] The problem of over-centralization and under-institutionalization certainly is a characteristic dilemma of states in which an ambitious government lacks the institutional means to exercise its authority.[88] Yeltsin's Russia today displays all the pathologies of a soft state: government cannot ensure policy is carried out, or even guarantee the timely payment of wages to employees; announcements about new state agencies and programs are made and soon forgotten, and a crisis in law enforcement is manifested by the enormous rise in organized crime, deep government corruption, and lax fiscal control. Elites and the public alike tend to assume that the answer to a breakdown of the legal order is more state power: *stateness* is confused with *law*. Frequently, as a result, the authorities grant law enforcement bodies wide extra-legal powers while restricting the civic rights of citizens. This in turn undermines respect for the law still further.[89] Legal anarchy and uncertainty encourage the varieties of anti-social, beggar-thy-neighbor behavior in society that prevent the consolidation of democratic and capitalist institutions. Let us look at a few of these problems more closely.

Organized crime. The problem of organized crime has been discussed extensively in the Western and Russian press but reliable indicators of its scale are elusive.[90] By all accounts, however, organized crime is deeply entrenched and broad in scope. A series of articles in *Izvestiia* in October

1994 observed that in a majority of regions of the country, the local authorities grant licenses to new businesses only with the consent of local crime bosses. "'Godfathers' of the mafia exist in many countries," the authors point out:

> but there for the most part they control illegal business, such as narcotics, gambling, thieves' hang-outs. Here they have established total control over ordinary commerce. As a result we pay for our daily bread, for our basket of consumer goods, around 20–30 percent more. In the farmers' markets exotic fruits cost less than tomatoes and cucumbers – because of the tribute to the mafia that is paid. Thus the population is supporting two states with its money – the legitimate government and the criminal one – that exist in parallel. Or rather, the legal state more and more depends on the power of the criminal one.[91]

Organized crime makes frequent use of contract killings of prominent figures to enforce its interersts. On October 17, 1994, a bomb planted in a briefcase carried by a young journalist working for a Moscow newspaper exploded, killing him and destroying many of the documents he had gathered. Since he had been collecting evidence about high-level corruption in the armed forces, many believe that his murder was the work of those who wanted to put an end to his investigations. His death was one of a number of attacks on journalists whose investigations threatened powerful interests. The most shocking such attempt occurred on March 1, 1995, when Vladislav List'ev, a prominent television journalist, was killed. The most probable reason for the murder was his support of an effort to clean up corrupt practices in state television under which millions of dollars worth of advertising revenues were being skimmed off by organized crime.

Another target of contract killings by organized crime has been bankers. According to the Russian news agency, between 1992 and mid-1995, attempts on the lives of eighty-three bankers were made, of whom forty-six were killed. For example, Ivan Kivelidi, president of Rosbiznesbank and head of a major business interest association, the Russian Business Roundtable, and his secretary, were murdered by poison in August 1995. His was one of two murders of prominent bankers in a little over a week.

Public outrage over the scale of organized crime prompted President Yeltsin to issue a decree in June 1994 granting the procuracy and police extraordinary powers of search and seizure, "including access to normally confidential business and financial documents, and the right to hold suspects for thirty days without charge" solely on the authority of the procurator rather than a judge.[92] Many legal specialists protested the decree on the grounds that by authorizing official violation of the Constitution and of existing law, it would only increase lawlessness in the country. In any event it was only one more in a series of anti-crime campaigns in 1993 and 1994 which had been aimed at fighting organized crime, all ineffective in making any headway against it.[93]

Government corruption. One reason government laws and decrees have done so little to reduce organized crime is that the law enforcement organs themselves are deeply corrupted. A widely-cited anecdotal indication of the severity of police corruption was the story by the Interior Minister, Anatolii Kulikov, that upon his appointment to the position in summer 1995, he had sent a truck carrying a cargo of vodka on a 700–kilometer trip across southern Russia. Out of the twenty-four times that police stopped the truck, they had demanded bribes twenty-two times.[94] As a result of his investigations, General Kulikov declared that he had fired a number of senior police officials, including four generals. One official fired was the deputy chief of police of Moscow.[95]

The chairman of the Duma Committee on Security, Viktor Iliukhin, declared in April 1994 that in 1993, some 1,500 officials were investigated or arrested in connection with corruption charges. About 50 percent of them were high ranking employees of the executive branch, and 27 percent were officers in law enforcement agencies.[96] Corruption pervades government more generally. Stephen Handelman observes that "In 1993, more than 46,000 officials from all levels of government in Russia were brought to trial on charges relating to corruption and abuse of office, according to Acting Procurator Aleksei Ilyushenko."[97] Moreover, the view is widespread that under the "so-called democrats," corruption grew worse.

Perceptions that the new post-Soviet elite is more corrupt than the old communist elite are reinforced by the enormous growth of opportunities to use public office for private gain and the weakness of enforcement of those rules which exist. Public scrutiny of official behavior is weakly developed and many scandals unearthed by the press peter out with no action taken. Many gray areas exist where the standards of legal conduct are unclear or unwritten, allowing practices to flourish that would be illegal on conflict-of-interest grounds in other societies. Public officials commonly hold gainful positions as share-holders, board members, consultants or employees of private firms with which they have close working ties. Members of parliament write laws affecting organizations in which they have a personal financial stake. Members of the government maintain close relations with the executives in state industry. Senior government officials demand large "fees" for meetings with western businessmen. In the atmosphere of unregulated and cozy ties between business and government, suspicion is rampant, and many officials are reluctant to play a sucker's game by not taking advantage of opportunities for self-enrichment which, they assume, everyone else is enjoying.

Lax budgetary practices. Budget practices unfortunately encourage the exercise of unaccountable influence over the allocation of resources. Particularly vulnerable to abuse is the practice of creating special-purpose off-budget funds in order to shelter state revenues from legislative scrutiny. These can serve, in effect, as huge slush funds for public officials. This device has become particularly popular as the development of private property has created huge opportunities for quick profits through favorable government licensing, privatization, taxing and other policies. Now and then an indication of the scale of the problem is revealed. At the federal level the two major categories of protected funds are those for social support, and those under ministry control. Local governments also sometimes create their own off-budget funds as well.

Vast streams of revenue are removed from outside scrutiny this way. A sum equal to almost two-thirds of the state budget goes into social funds such as the pension fund, the employment fund, and the medical insurance fund. They are channeled not through the state treasury (where, their protectors insist, they would be cannibalized by the government for more immediate spending needs) but are often held in commercial banks, often at well-below-market rates of interest. This fact, plus the fact that they are not subject to regular audits by parliament or the government's own controllers, renders them susceptible to misallocation. Recently a rare audit of the Pension Fund by the parliament's Budget Committee discovered three billion rubles that had not been accounted for. A bill which would require all off-budget funds to be approved by the Duma, ensure that they were kept in the state treasury rather than commercial banks, and be subject to regular audits, was recently proposed in parliament, but failed to pass even on first reading.[98]

The bill would also have abolished the other major type of extra-budget funds, those under branch control. Branch funds are formed by requiring enterprises to pay deductions into a special ministerial kitty used for research and development or other purposes. No taxes are paid on these funds and, like social funds, they stay outside the regular tax system and are held in banks. One of the largest was that of Gazprom, which realized revenues of ten trillion rubles in 1994 (or approximately US $3 billion). Insulated from parliamentary and even government scrutiny, such a fund could readily lend itself to becoming a war-chest for supporting the political campaign of a politician who headed a major electoral bloc.

Popular alienation. The pathologies of the soft state described here have affected public opinion and electoral behavior in Russia. The popular wave of enthusiasm for democratic and market reform that propelled a new generation of political elites into power in 1989–91 has been spent. It has been followed by a wave of disillusionment with the initial results of change, and expressed by voter support for the communist and nationalist opposition.

Vladimir Zhirinovsky's Liberal Democratic Party and Gennadii Ziuganov's Communist Party of the Russian Federation have been highly successful in appealing to popular discontent with their radical opposition platforms.[99] The issues that helped to bring democrats into power in 1989–91 – radical anti-establishment egalitarianism, political freedom, economic opportunity – no longer move voters. Instead, in 1995, on a number of issues voters cared about most, including the economy and crime, it was the communists who were best able to capture the support of Russian voters.[100]

Probably of greater importance than the surge in electoral support for communists and radical nationalists, however, is the rise in disaffection with democratic institutions more generally. Recent survey data shows that public opinon in Russia is increasingly inclined to evaluate the old Soviet regime favorably and the current regime negatively, and that pessimism about future change is rising.[101] Mistrust of official institutions is very high. As has been the case in polls for the past few years, the Church and the army have the highest levels of popular confidence (51 percent and 41 percent respectively, in Richard Rose's 1994 survey). Representative political institutions are actively distrusted by very high proportions of the populace. Rose found that 83 percent of the public mistrusted political parties and 72 percent parliament. His surveys also show that confidence in the president is declining.[102] Something of the old dilemma of the "dual Russia" – where state and society are divided by a gap of mutual misunderstanding and mistrust[103] – seems to have returned. Rose found that two-thirds of his 1995 respondents felt that the central government had little or no influence on their everyday lives.[104]

Among East European postcommunist states, indeed, Russia stands out in the high levels of popular alienation from government. A large scale, cross-national survey of popular attitudes about politics and the economy conducted by Geoffrey Evans and Stephen Whitefield in 1993 reveals very low ratings of their current national political institutions by Russians, much lower, in most cases, than those of Bulgarians, Estonians, Hungarians, Lithuanians, Poles, and Romanians. Russian disaffection with government is exceeded only by the Ukrainian level. Asked whether government acts for the benefit of the majority of society, 76 percent of Russians answered in the negative, more than did so in any of the other sampled cases. The same proportion agreed that "elected officials don't care much what people like me think." Equivalent shares expressed alienation on other items as well.[105] Overall, asked to provide a general assessment of the "actual practice of democracy" in Russia, only 19 percent gave a favorable answer while 57 percent answered negatively, the highest level of any country in the study.[106]

Evans and Whitefield argue that it is experience with political institutions rather than with the performance of the economy which tends to influence individuals' commitment to democratic values. They show that in the case of several East European postcommunist democracies, this is encouraging from the standpoint of a normative interest in democracy: the new democracies' political performance tends to be rated more highly than do their economies, suggesting that democracy calls upon a more robust core of reserve support than would be true if it were evaluated mainly in terms of its contribution to economic well-being. This is well since Russians' evaluations of the market economy's performance are even lower than are evaluations of the political system (14 percent positive, 70 percent negative). But what do such negative evaluations of both political and economic experience bode for the prospects of democratic consolidation in Russia?

The evidence from public opinion surveys in fact is ambiguous. As negatively as Russians evaluate the present political arrangement, they continue to express high levels of support in the abstract for liberal freedoms, with elites tending to be still more inclined to support democratic values than ordinary citizens.[107] The great majority of Russians consider themselves to have more political freedom than they did under the old regime. Two thirds and more of Russians surveyed in 1993 report themselves to be freer to say what they think than they were in the past, freer to join any organization they wish, and to practice any religion.[108] High proportions of the public continue to express support for certain general principles of democracy, such as freedom of speech and a free media.[109] At least in the short run, moreover, support for democratic principles appear to be more stable than support for the institutions of a market economy.[110] To be sure, as Raymond Duch points out, people tend to express much higher levels of support for abstract political principles, such as free elections and the desirability of party competition, than they do on more concrete issues such as the willingness to tolerate freedom for those whose views are considered threatening to social order.[111] As William Reisinger et al. observe, confirming the findings of other researchers, individual civic rights are widely valued in Russia, but tend to be accompanied by a strong desire for political order.[112] Thus while there is evidence of severe disillusionment, distrust, and alienation on the part of citizens toward the present regime, there is also evidence of abstract support for democratic principles.

How is this pattern of frustration and disillusionment expressed in the political arena? Have stable party attachments begun to form? A lively discussion in the scholarly literature has begun over what, if any, is the likely direction that the formation of a postcommunist Russian party system will take.[113] Analyses of Russian electoral behavior suggest that cleavage lines are beginning to form and that party development will be strongly influenced by the social divisions, for example between those favoring and opposing market reforms, and those favoring and opposing communist principles.[114]

As we know, the formation of a party system will also be influenced by a variety of other institutional and contextual factors, such as the electoral and constitutional rules of the game. Certainly the party system changed substantially between the 1993 and 1995 parliamentary elections. It changed: but many elements remained the same. The four parties which received more than 5 percent of the vote each on the party list vote in 1995 all did so in 1993. They represented the major ideological tendencies of the society: communist, nationalist, centrist, and reform.

At the beginning of the paper I noted that Russian representative institutions face not only obstacles created by the inheritance of the old regime, but also are struggling to establish links of communication and accountability to voters at a time when mass communications technologies have begun to replace older face-to-face forms of organization and participation. These trends are evident in Western democracies as well. They tend to personalize politics, to replace the substance of policy differences with appeals to personal attractiveness and emotion-laden imagery. It is not only in Russia that observers fear that parties are becoming vehicles for advancing the political careers of ambitious politicians rather than for keeping government responsive to the policy preferences of popular majorities. It is easy, therefore, to overstate the fluidity of Russian politics, and to overlook the faint lines of partisan differentiation that are forming. As Gennadii Burbulis has pointed out, many Russian citizens may not be able to articulate their interests programmatically, but can identify individual political leaders as embodiments of their own political preferences. Thus, while it may be highly personalized and centered on leaders, the nascent political system is developing a more structured character.[115] There are grounds for believing, therefore, that along with the emergence of a more competitive and pluralistic environment for social interests, the foundations for a competitive party system are being formed.

Toward democratic pluralism?

It is common to ascribe the pathologies of the postcommunist order to factors specific to Russia's communist past and path of transition. Russian writers and post-Sovietologists tend to focus their attention on the "legacy" of the Soviet and pre-revolutionary past, and to the effects of "shock therapy" or its absence.[116] We should not forget the prevalence of those same pathologies elsewhere, however, where there has been neither a communist past nor a wrenching economic transition. Are rampant organized crime, the confusion of private and public interests, the use of creative budget practices for political and personal advantage of politicians, or public cynicism about politics greater in Russia than in countries such as Indonesia, Japan, Southern

Italy, Mexico or Brazil? We have no good way of measuring fragmentation and disorder comparatively. If there is a certain background level of political pathologies in many societies, what is the share of them in Russia that is caused by factors unique to Russia's communist past or transitional present? Applying a comparative perspective makes it harder to exaggerate the importance of the degree of fragmentation and disorder which we observe. Certainly skepticism about the health of organizational pluralism in Russia today is justified. The evidence we have cited here suggests that the deep economic and political changes have transformed the way social interests are organized and expressed. Groups have organized to defend collective interests, many of them seeking to confirm and widen property rights, others attempting to prevent true market competition for economic resources. Characteristic of group life, we observed, were fragmentation and politicization; but we noted that many groups have a stake in the preservation of political and economic rights. These rights are also widely valued by the public despite the high level of disaffection expressed by the populace toward the present regime.

The condition most likely to favor the establishment self-enforcing rules of democratic political competition is one in which no single powerful group or actor can dominate political processes and control their outcomes.[117] The evidence we have reviewed in this chapter shows that politics has grown competitive, and outcomes uncertain. Over 1994–95, groups have generally competed according to the constitution and the law. Deep uncertainty hangs over the future because the power and centrality of the presidency tempts many actors to step outside the constitutional order. Social power has become sufficiently plural, however, that few groups can be sure that they would succeed if they bid to seize power by force: both the 1991 and 1993 coup attempts failed. Many organized political actors are therefore likely to calculate that they are better off playing by the rules in the hopes of improving their positions for the future. After enough rounds, their behavior would become mutually self-reinforcing.

Therefore a gradual increase in political order through democratic pluralism is possible over the long run. Institutional change can be a powerful impetus to a self-sustaining democratic equilibrium. Where once it was assumed that social modernization tended to drive the development of political regimes, now scholars are inclined to believe that well-constructed institutions can provide elites with sufficient incentives to resolve their differences and achieve their goals by democratic means. Much depends on the players' time horizons and expectations of the future. Where time horizons are short because people do not expect a stable future, they tend to seek short-term rewards. They avoid investing much material or political capital into a setting where their rewards are uncertain or subject to a high probability of being confiscated. A society where people believe that they must take advantage of others before others take advantage of them can become a self-perpetuating equilibrium and last for centuries. There is no iron sociological logic according to which society must advance to higher levels of social trust and cooperation, economic growth, and democratic self-rule. But where people begin to reinforce one another's expectations that they are able to cooperate in common endeavors without relying upon a harsh, dictatorial central authority, a "virtuous cycle" results in which more complex and effective organizational forms evolve.[118]

What would set such a developmental sequence into motion in Russia? The preceding discussion has suggested that Russia stands poised between two alternative paths. The disintegrating forces of repressiveness, crime, corruption, and popular alienation may take the upper hand and lead to a new form of authoritarianism, or the integrating forces of a pluralistic and law-regulated order may gradually grow stronger. In this delicate state of equipoise, the behavior of central political elites could tip the balance: in particular, their behavior during and after the 1996 presidential election. Recall Samuel Huntington's "two-turnovers" rule in judging the degree to which democracy is consolidated in a post-authoritarian regime.[119] If following the collapse of an authoritarian regime, the incumbents lose the first election and give up power peacefully, and then, following the second election, their successors do the same, we may say that democracy is well established. Although Russia's parliamentary election of 1995 was the first in which a free election was held on schedule since the October Revolution, the most important test of a peaceful transfer of state power is the presidential election: 1996 will be the first; 2000 would be the second. If incumbents lose twice and exit willingly, their behavior will be crucial in setting examples for other political leaders at all levels of government.

By itself, the very fact of the 1996 presidential election, in defiance of widespread expectations that it would be cancelled, postponed, or overturned, will be an important signal. To the extent that the elections are generally judged to be free and fair, the result will command that much more acceptance. Beyond the electoral process is the question of the transfer of power. A peaceful transfer of power from an incumbent to a democratically elected challenger would be an extraordinary – and, in Russia's thousand-year history, unprecedented – signal that an era of the rule of law had begun. Finally, if the opposition wins the election, assumes power peacefully, and then uses presidential power in such a way as to reinforce rather than overturn the democratic institutional fabric of Russia's postcommunist political order, this will contribute powerfully to the odds that the next, and the next, electoral turnover will also proceed by the rules.

These are strong conditions, but less so than the commonly offered theory that democracy in Russia can succeed only if a congruent cultural, social, civic and economic foundation is created first. The behavior of political elites, interacting and monitoring one another's willingness to comply with democratic rules of procedure, can itself launch Russia onto either the democratic or the autocratic path. While it is still too early to tell whether Russia in its post-Soviet, postcommunist phase will succumb to a lengthy phase of self-reinforcing demands for authoritarian rule, or whether the culture and institutions of pluralist democracy will ultimately triumph, it is fair to say that democracy remains a *possible* outcome.

Appendix: Additional demographic, social, and economic indicators

Table 3.6 *Population of Russia, 1985–94*

	1985	1990	1993	1994
Total (in thousands)	143,528	148,164	147,997	147,938
Males (%)	46.4	46.9	46.9	n.a.
Females (%)	53.6	53.1	53.1	n.a.
Urban (%)	72.2	73.8	73.0	72.9
Rural (%)	27.8	26.2	27.0	27.1

Source: The World Bank, Studies of Economies in Transformation, *Statistical Handbook 1995: States of the Former USSR* (Washington, DC: International Bank for Reconstruction and Development, 1995), p. 418.

Table 3.7 *Selected social indicators for Russia, 1993*

Indicator	
PPP-GNP per capita ($US)[a]	5,050
Primary school enrollment (%)	94.2
Secondary school enrollment (%)	71.7
Male life expectancy at birth (years)	58.2
Female life expectancy at birth (years)	71.4
Infant mortality rate (%)	15.7

Note: [a]PPP stands for purchasing power parity. It is calculated by dividing GNP per capita, at nominal rates, by "purchasing power parity," meaning the number of rubles needed in Russia to purchase the same amount of goods and services on the domestic market as one US dollar would buy in the United States. (See EBRD, *Transition Report 1995: Investment and Enterprise Development* [London: EBRD, 1995], p. 21, n. 1).

Source: EBRD, *Transition Report 1995*, p. 21.

Table 3.8 *Educational attainments of adults in Russia, 1989*

Educational level of adult population[a]	Percentage
Complete higher	11.3
Incomplete higher	17.0
Specialized secondary	19.2
General secondary	27.4
Incomplete secondary	21.0

Note: [a]Age fifteen and above.
Source: *Rossiiskii statisticheskii ezhegodnik. 1994: Statisticheskii sbornik* (Moscow: Goskomstat Rossii, 1994), p. 57.

Table 3.9 *Educational attainments of employed population in Russia, 1993*

Percentage of employees with:	Total	Men	Women
Full higher education	17.2	15.6	18.5
Secondary specialized or secondary education	65.1	63.1	67.3
Lower than complete secondary	17.7	21.3	14.2

Source: *Rossiiskii statisticheskii ezhegodnik. 1994*, p. 66.

Table 3.10 *Population of major ethnic groups of the Russian Federation, 1970-89 (in thousands)*

Ethnic group	1970	1979	1989
Russians	107,748	113,522	119,866
Tatars	4,755	5,006	5,522
Crimean Tatars[a]	3	5	21
Ukrainians	3,346	3,658	4,363
Chuvash	1,637	1,690	1,774
Bashkirs	1,181	1,291	1,345
Belorussians	964	1,052	1,206
Mordva	1,177	1,111	1,073
Chechens	572	712	899
Germans	762	791	842
Udmurts	678	686	715
Mari	581	600	644
Kazak	478	518	636
Avar	362	438	544
Jews	792	692	537
Peoples of the north	168	170	199
Total	130,079	137,410	147,022

Note: [a]Crimean Tatars are enumerated as a separate ethnic group from Volga Tatars.
Source: *Rossiiskii statisticheskii ezhegodnik. 1994*, p. 30.

NOTES

Research for this paper has been supported by funding from the National Council for Soviet and East European Research, which, however, bears no responsibility for the content or conclusions reported here.

1 Andranik Migranyan, "Dolgii put' k evropeiskomu domu," *Novyi mir*, no. 7 (July 1989), 166–84.
2 Douglass C. North, *Institutions, Institutional Change and Economic Performance* (Cambridge: Cambridge University Press, 1990), pp. 72–83; Douglass C. North, "Institutions and Credible Commitment," *Journal of Institutional and Theoretical Economics* 149, no. 1 (1993), 13.
3 Thomas F. Remington, "Representative Power and the Russian State," in *Developments in Russian and Post-Soviet Politics*, 3rd ed., ed. Stephen White, Alex Pravda, and Zvi Gitelman (London: Macmillan, 1994), pp. 63–75.
4 North, "Institutions and Credible Commitment," pp. 11–23; Barry R. Weingast, "Constitutions as Governance Structures: The Political Foundations of Secure Markets," *Journal of Institutional and Theoretical Economics* 149, no. 1 (1993), 286–311; Elinor Ostrom, *Governing the Commons: The Evolution of Institutions for Collective Action* (Cambridge: Cambridge University Press, 1990).

5 On glasnost and the rise of political movements and parties, see Thomas F. Remington, "Socialist Pluralism of Opinions: Glasnost' and Policy-Making under Gorbachev," *Russian Review* 48, no. 3 (1989), 271–304; Marcia A. Weigle, "Political Participation and Party Formation in Russia, 1985–1992: Institutionalizing Democracy?" *Russian Review* 53 (1994), 240–70; M. Steven Fish, *Democracy from Scratch: Opposition and Regime in the New Russian Revolution* (Princeton: Princeton University Press, 1995); Yitzhak M. Brudny, "The Dynamics of 'Democratic Russia,' 1990–1993," *Post-Soviet Affairs* 9 (1993), 141–70.

6 He won his race for USSR deputy from the at-large Moscow district in March 1989 with 90 percent of the popular vote. He won his race for Russian Republic deputy from Sverdlovsk in March 1990 with 80 percent of the vote. And he won his race for president in June 1991 with 58 percent of the vote. Gorbachev, it will be remembered, never ran in any popular electoral contest until 1996.

7 For more on the 1990–93 period and the confrontation between president and parliament, see Thomas F. Remington, "Menage à Trois: The End of Soviet Parliamentarism," in *Democratization in Russia: The Development of Legislative Institutions*, ed. Jeffrey W. Hahn (Armonk, NY: M. E. Sharpe, 1996), pp. 106–39.

8 Yeltsin and the Congress were then able to compromise on a referendum on four questions concerning voter approval for Yeltsin and his government, as well as whether new parliamentary and presidential elections should be held. The outcome of the April 1993 referendum gave the Yeltsin forces a strong political victory although the vote favoring new parliamentary elections fell short of the total needed to have binding force.

9 Michael Urban, "State, Property, and Political Society in Postcommunist Russia: In Search of a Political Center," in *In Search of Pluralism: Soviet and Post-Soviet Politics*, ed. Carol R. Saivetz and Anthony Jones (Boulder, CO: Westview Press, 1994), pp. 125–50.

10 For the argument that the reported turnout in the December 1993 referendum and elections was falsified, see V. Vyzhutovich, "Tsentrizbirkom prevrashchaetsia v politicheskoe vedomstvo," *Izvestiia*, 4 May 1994 and Mikhail Myagkov and Alexandr Sobyanin, "Irregularities in the 1993 Russian Elections: Preliminary Analysis," unpublished paper. A comprehensive collection of Sobyanin's analyses of voting irregularities since 1991 is A. A. Sobianin and V. G. Sukhovol'skii, *Demokratiia, ogranichennaia fal'sifikatsiiami: vybory i referendumy v Rossii v 1991–1993 gg.* (Moscow: Proektnaia gruppa po pravam cheloveka, 1995).

11 Matthew S. Shugart and John M. Carey, *Presidents and Assemblies: Constitutional Design and Electoral Dynamics* (Cambridge: Cambridge University Press, 1992).

12 Matthew S. Shugart, "The Electoral Cycle and Institutional Sources of Divided Presidential Government," *American Political Science Review* 89, no. 2 (June 1995), 327–43.

13 Juan Linz, "Presidential or Parliamentary Democracy: Does It Make a Difference?" in *The Failure of Presidential Democracy*, ed. Juan J. Linz and Arturo Valenzuela (Baltimore and London: Johns Hopkins University Press, 1994), pp. 3–87.

14 Ibid., pp. 52–54.

15 Ezra N. Suleiman, "Presidentialism and Political Stability in France," in *The Failure of Presidential Democracy*, pp. 137–62.

16 The constitution provides that the president can be removed only in case of serious crime or high treason and specifies the sequence of procedures required: one third of the members of the Duma must initiate the process; the decision must be considered by a special commission of the Duma; the Duma must approve the action by a two-thirds vote; the Supreme Court must issue a ruling finding that the president's actions constituted a grave crime or act of treason; the Constitutional Court must find that the parliament acted properly; and the Federation Council must finally approve removal by a two-thirds vote.

17 Over 1994–95, the Duma passed 461 laws, and of them 282 were signed by the president. Around 100 of the latter were major regulatory or distributive policy acts in areas such as budget appropriations, social welfare, reform of state political institutions, and reform of law enforcement and the judicial system (*Segodnia*, 23 December 1995). Over the same period, the president issued approximately 4,000 decrees (*ukazy*), most of them of minor significance – such as appointments of individuals to state positions or the awarding of honors for merit. A few, however, were highly important because they attempted to shape major national policy. These included the terms of privatization of shares of the state television and radio company, the powers that law enforcement bodies would have to prosecute organized crime, and decisions on which enterprises were subject to privatization in the current cash phase of the privatization program. In the case of the cash privatization program, the president's decree was modified to accommodate some of parliament's concerns, and in the case of the decree on fighting organized crime, the president invited parliament to pass its own more sweeping crime-fighting legislation.

18 See Thomas F. Remington and and Steven S. Smith, "The Early Legislative Process in the Russian Federal Assembly," *Journal of Legislative Studies* 2, no. 1 (Spring 1996), 161–92.

19 The Council of the Federation is granted the right of approval of the use of Russian military forces outside of the Russian Federation and confirmation of presidential appointees to high courts. In addition to confidence votes, the unique jurisdiction of the Duma includes confirmation of the president's nominee for prime minister. The Constitution obligates the Council of the Federation to act on Duma-passed legislation concerning budget, taxes, financial policy, treaties, customs, and war.

20 Thomas F. Remington and Steven S. Smith, "Political Goals, Institutional Context, and the Choice of an Electoral System: The Russian Parliamentary Election Law," *American Journal of Political Science* 40, no. 4 (November 1996), 1253–1279.

21 Parties were free to choose how to divide the country into electoral regions, so that the divisions differed substantially among the forty-three parties which ran candidates on lists. The major purpose of this provision was to induce parties to place representatives of the regions onto their lists, thus checking the ostensibly Moscow-centric tendencies of the parties.

22 Thomas F. Remington and Steven S. Smith, "The Development of Parliamentary Parties in Russia," *Legislative Studies Quarterly* 20 (November 1995), 457–90.

23 As of April 1994, Russia's Choice, PRES, Yabloko and the December 12 faction deputies held 157 seats, or 35 percent. Deputies from the Democratic Party of Russia, Women of Russia, and New Regional Policy factions had 104 or 23 percent of the seats. The agrarians, communists, Liberal Democrats (Zhirinovsky) and Russia's Way group had 178 seats, or 40 percent. Analysis of the voting records finds that while the agrarians and communists tend to vote very similarly, the Liberal Democrats are somewhat less predictable in their voting.

24 Analiticheskii tsentr Federal'nogo sobraniia-parlament Rossiiskoi Federatsii. *Gosudarstvennaia Duma: Informatsionnyi biulleten'*, no. 4 (24 April–24 May 1995), pp. 3 ff.; ibid., no. 2 (23 February–22 March 1995), p. 7. Of course these figures need to be used with some caution: they are affected by the structure of the agenda over the time period chosen and by the method for determining what a faction's position was: this is a particularly slippery issue given that many members choose not to vote rather than to cast a "nay" vote and it is necessary therefore to determine how to treat missing votes.

25 Rybkin has written a memoir about the first year of the State Duma: I. P. Rybkin, *Gosudarstvennaia Duma: piataia popytka* (Moscow: Znamia, 1994).

26 The Council of the Federation which was in existence in 1994–95 was formed by election in December 1993. Most of its members worked full-time as regional government or enterprise administrators, but some were full-time parliamentarians. According to the new law on the chamber, however, all its members beginning with the new term in January 1996 are heads of executive and legislative branches in the subjects of the federation. None, therefore, are full-time parliamentarians.

27 *Nations in Transit: Civil Society, Democracy and Markets in East Central Europe and the Newly Independent States* (Washington, DC: Freedom House, 1995), p. 115.

28 OMRI Daily Digest, 6 July 1995.

29 Ibid., 7 December 1995.

30 Tat'iana Zaslavskaia, "Rossiiskoe naselenie postepenno snizhaet svoi zhiznennye standarty," *Segodnia*, 2 August 1995, p. 3.

31 Ibid.

32 On 1995, see the summary figures provided by Economics Minister Evgenii Yasin in an Interfax report cited by the OMRI Daily Digest of 5 January 1996.

33 OMRI Daily Digest, 17 May 1995.

34 Cited in OMRI Economic Report, 2 November 1995.

35 Branko Milanovic, "Poverty and Inequality in Transition Economies: What Has Actually Happened," in *Economic Transition in Russia and the New States of Eurasia*, ed. Bartlomiej Kaminski (Armonk, NY: M. E. Sharpe, 1996), table 8.1, pp. 180–81. His measure of aggregate inequality, a Gini coefficient, is estimated at 36 for Russia in 1993 and 24 in 1987–88. For the United Kingdom in 1993 it is 37; for the three Baltic states and the Central Asian states it is 34.

36 Richard Rose, "Russia as an Hour-Glass Society: A Constitution without Citizens," *East European Constitutional Review* 4, no. 3 (Summer 1995), 37.

37 On privatization, see Lynn D. Nelson and Irina Y. Kuzes, *Property to the People: The Struggle for Radical Economic Reform in Russia* (Armonk, NY: M. E. Sharpe, 1994), and Pekka Sutela, "Insider Privatization in Russia: Speculations on Systemic Changes," *Europe-Asia Studies* 46, no. 3 (1994), 417–35.

38 Russian Statistical Committee figures cited in the newspaper *Segodnia*, 9 August 1994.
39 *Segodnia*, 1 September 1994.
40 European Bank for Reconstruction and Development, *Transition Report 1995: Investment and Enterprise Development* (London: EBRD, 1995), p. 55.
41 Peter Rutland, "The Economy: The Rocky Road from Plan to Market," in *Developments in Russian and Post-Soviet Politics*, ed. White et al., p. 161.
42 EBRD, *Transition Report 1995*, p. 55.
43 *Nations in Transit*, p. 120.
44 Centre for Economic Reform, Government of the Russian Federation, *Russian Economic Trends 1993* 2, no. 3 (1993), 62; EBRD, Transition Report 1995, p. 55.
45 See OMRI Daily Digests for 18 January, 17 February and 13 March 1995.
46 Ibid., 8 August 1995.
47 Ekaterina Khibovskaia, "Rossiiane stali bol'she opasat'sia poteriat' rabotu," *Segodnia*, 26 July 1995.
48 EBRD, *Transition Report 1995*, pp. 181–82.
49 OMRI Daily Digests for 20 April and 30 May 1995.
50 Ibid., 13 July 1995.
51 J. Michael Waller, *Secret Empire: The KGB in Russia Today* (Boulder, CO: Westview, 1994), p. 284.
52 Yevgeniya Albats, *The State within a State: The KGB and Its Hold on Russia – Past, Present, and Future*, trans. Catherine A. Fitzpatrick (New York: Farrar, Straus and Giroux, 1994), p. 358.
53 Mikhail Tsypkin, "The Politics of Russian Security Policy," in *State Building and Military Power in Russia and the New States of Eurasia*, ed. Bruce Parrott (Armonk, NY: M. E. Sharpe, 1995), p. 19.
54 Besides the armed forces, the MVD, and the FSB, all of which possess armed formations, the Border Troops and Construction Troops also have their own militarized units. Mikhail Tsypkin argues that the military have been more preoccupied with defending their own corporate interests than with influencing, still less assuming responsibility for, the government of the state more generally. He portrays a military establishment gravely threatened by contemporary economic and political trends, and divided across multiple cleavages. Tsypkin, "The Politics of Russian Security Policy," pp. 11–43.
55 On the politics of the Church, see John Dunlop, "The Russian Orthodox Church as an 'Empire-Saving' Institution," in *The Politics of Religion in Russia and the New States of Eurasia*, ed. Michael Bourdeaux (Armonk, NY: M. E. Sharpe, 1995), pp. 15–40; and Dimitry V. Pospielovsky, "The Russian Orthodox Church in the Postcommunist CIS," in ibid., pp. 41–74. Dunlop and Pospielovsky differ in their interpretation of the political line taken by the Church's Patriarch, Aleksii II. Dunlop considers him sympathetic to the hard-line nationalist opposition, while Pospielovsky portrays him as a moderate seeking to preserve a measure of autonomy from the state while not aligning the Church too closely with extremist opponents of the Yeltsin administration.
56 Pospielovsky, "The Russian Orthodox Church," p. 64.

57 A good empirical analysis of the former communist nomenklatura's adaptation to the new circumstances is an article by Boris Golovachev, Larisa Kosova, and Liudmila Khakhulina, "'Novaia' rossiiskaia elita: starye igroki na novom pole?" *Segodnia*, 14 February 1996. This is a report from a study conducted by the Russian survey institute VTsIOM in 1993–94 as part of an international project on political elites.

58 Anders Åslund, *How Russia Became a Market Economy* (Washington, DC: Brookings Institution, 1995), pp. 300–9.

59 Information on the Civic Union may be found in Stephen White, Graeme Gill and Darrell Slider, *The Politics of Transition: Shaping a Post-Soviet Future* (Cambridge: Cambridge University, 1993), pp. 166–69. A more detailed study is Peter Rutland, "Business Elites and Russian Economic Policy" (London: Royal Institute of International Affairs, 1992). See also Michael McFaul, "Russian Centrism and Revolutionary Transitions," *Post-Soviet Affairs* 9, no. 3 (July/September 1993), pp. 196–222. Wendy Slater, "The Diminishing Center of Russian Parliamentary Politics," *RFE/RL Research Report* 3, no. 17 (29 April 1994), discusses the fate of the Civic Union through the 1993 elections.

60 Quoted in Nelson and Kuzes, *Property to the People*, p. 77.

61 RFE/RL Daily Report, 7 December 1992.

62 On Chernomyrdin's tenure as prime minister, see Anders Åslund, "Russia's Success Story," *Foreign Affairs* 73, no. 5 (September/October 1994), 58–71.

63 Julian Cooper, "Defense Industries in Russia and the Other Post-Soviet States," in *State Building and Military Power in Russia and the New States of Eurasia*, ed. Parrott, p. 76.

64 The following discussion relies heavily on the account provided by Yakov Pappe, a senior associate of the Institute of Economic Forecasting of the Academy of Sciences, in the newspaper *Segodnia*, "Kakaia Rossiia nuzhna otechestvennomu toplivno-energeticheskomu kompleksu," 15 August 1995.

65 Sources differ as to the founding date of the Agrarian Party of Russia. The information provided here is taken from A. Ostapchuk, E. Krasnikov and M. Meier, *Spravochnik: Politicheskie partii, dvizheniia i bloki sovremennoi Rossii* (Leta: Novgorod, 1993), pp. 17–18. Mikhail Lapshin, who became chairman of the Board of the Council of the Agrarian Party, was also at the time the chairman of the Agrarian Union faction in the Russian parliament, and simultaneously the deputy chairman of the Central Executive Commitee of the CPRF. There was thus a close overlap between the agrarian and communist parties, especially in 1992 when the communists were still outlawed.

66 Michael McFaul and Nikolai Petrov, *Previewing Russia's 1995 Parliamentary Elections* (Moscow: Carnegie Endowment for International Peace Carnegie Moscow Center, 1995), p. 63.

67 In January 1996 Yeltsin sacked his minister of agriculture, Alexander Nazarchuk, ostensibly for failing to prevent an extremely poor 1995 harvest, and made Deputy Prime Minister Alexander Zaveryukha acting minister of agriculture.

68 OMRI Daily Digest, 11 January 1996.

69 Tsypkin, "The Politics of Russian Security Policy," p. 28.

70 Cooper, "Defense Industries," pp. 71–2.

71 Ibid., p. 77.

72 Ibid.

73 Linda J. Cook, *The Soviet 'Social Contract' and Why It Failed: Welfare Policy and Workers' Politics from Brezhnev to Yeltsin* (Cambridge: Harvard University Press, 1993); and Cook, "Russia's Labor Relations: Consolidation or Disintegration?" in Douglas W. Blum, *Russia's Future: Consolidation or Disintegration?* (Boulder, CO: Westview, 1994), pp. 69–90.
74 Elizabeth Teague, "Russian Government Seeks 'Social Partnership,'" *RFE/RL Research Report*, 2 June 1992.
75 RFE/RL Daily Report, 19 August 1992.
76 Interfax, 3 November 1995, as reported in the OMRI Economic Digest, 9 November 1995.
77 Stephen Crowley, "Barriers to Collective Action: Steelworkers and Mutual Dependence in the Former Soviet Union," *World Politics* 46, no. 4 (July 1994), 589–615.
78 Richard Rose, "The Value of Fringe Benefits in Russia," *RFE/RL Research Report* 3, no. 15 (15 April 1994), p. 19.
79 Michael Burawoy and Pavel Krotov, "The Rise of Merchant Capital: Monopoly, Barter, and Enterprise Politics in the Vorkuta Coal Industry," *Harriman Institute Forum* 6, no. 4 (December 1992).
80 Dmitrii Semenov and Vladimir Gribanov, "Grozit li nam proletarskaia revoliutsiia?" *Nezavisimaia gazeta*, 21 August 1993; the authors are officials of Sotsprof. Viktor Khamraev, "Byvshaia shkola 'kommunizma' v novom politicheskom kontekste, *Segodnia*, 26 October 1995.
81 *RFE/RL Daily Report*, 28 October 1993.
82 Khamraev, "Byvshaia 'shkola kommunizma,'" and Viktor Khamraev, "Profbossy ne dogovorilis' o proportsiiakh v 'tripartizme,'" *Segodnia*, 20 December 1995.
83 On the Tripartite Commission, see Elizabeth Teague, "Pluralism versus Corporatism: Government, Labor, and Business in the Russian Federation," in *In Search of Pluralism: Soviet and Post-Soviet Politics*, ed. Carol R. Saivetz and Anthony Jones (Boulder, CO: Westview Press, 1994), pp. 109–24.
84 Ibid., p. 119.
85 Marc Krizack, "Disabled Women Form Coalition for Change in Novosibirsk," *Initiatives in the New Independent States*, World Learning, Inc., Issues II & III (Spring/Summer 1994), p. 15. This publication is a valuable source of information on women's organizations in the former Soviet republics and their contacts with organizations in the United States.
86 OMRI Daily Digest, 11 October and 10 November 1995.
87 Thomas F. Remington, "Gorbachev and the Strategy of Glasnost'," in *Politics and the Soviet System: Essays in Honour of Frederick C. Barghoorn*, ed. Thomas F. Remington (London: Macmillan Press, 1989), pp. 56–82.
88 Samuel P. Huntington, *Political Order in Changing Societies* (New Haven: Yale University Press, 1968).
89 Peter H. Solomon, Jr., "The Limits of Legal Order in Post-Soviet Russia," *Post-Soviet Affairs* 11, no. 2 (April-June 1995), 107–8.
90 One useful recent source is Stephen Handelman, *Comrade Criminal: Russia's New Mafiya* (New Haven: Yale University Press, 1995).
91 "Neizvestnaia voina . . . s korruptsiei," *Izvestiia*, 22 October 1994.
92 Solomon, "The Limits of Legal Order," p. 101.
93 Handelman, *Comrade Criminal*, pp. 285–93.

94   OMRI Daily Digest, 23 August 1995.
95   OMRI Daily Digest, 30 November 1995.
96   These figures are cited from RFE/RL Daily Reports and OMRI Daily Digests, including those of 27 April 1994; and 2 March, 30 March, 11 April, and 7 August 1995.
97   Handelman, *Comrade Criminal*, p. 285.
98   Details on the extra-budgetary funds are drawn from articles in *Izvestiia*, 6 June 1995, *Segodnia*, 8 June 1995, and interviews in Moscow.
99   See the Urban/Gel'man chapter in this volume.
100 Sarah Oates, "Vying for Votes on a Crowded Campaign Trail," *Transition* 2, no. 4 (23 February 1996), 26-9.
101 Rose, "Russia as an Hour-Glass Society," p. 40.
102 Ibid., p. 40.
103 Robert C. Tucker, "The Image of Dual Russia," in *The Soviet Political Mind*, revised ed. (New York: Norton, 1971), pp. 121–42.
104 Rose, "Russia as an Hour-Glass Society," p. 41.
105 "People like me have no say in what government does," with which 68 percent agreed, and "everyone has an influence on the election of the government," with which 73 percent disagreed.
106 Geoffrey Evans and Stephen Whitefield, "The Politics and Economics of Democratic Commitment: Support for Democracy in Transition Societies," *British Journal of Political Science* 25, no. 4 (October 1995), 485–514; data taken from table 4 on p. 497.
107 William Zimmerman, "Markets, Democracy and Russian Foreign Policy," *Post-Soviet Affairs* 10, no. 2 (April–June 1994), 103–26; and Zimmerman, "Synoptic Thinking and Political Culture in Post-Soviet Russia," *Slavic Review* 54, no. 3 (Fall 1995), 630–41.
108 Richard Rose, "Getting By Without Government: Everyday Life in Russia," *Daedalus* 123, no. 3 (Summer 1994), 52.
109 James L. Gibson, Raymond M. Duch, and Kent L. Tedin, "Democratic Values and the Transformation of the Soviet Union," *Journal of Politics* 54, no. 2 (May 1992), 329–71.
110 James L. Gibson, "A Mile Wide But an Inch Deep (?): The Structure of Democratic Commitments in the Former USSR," paper presented to the 1994 Annual Meeting of the American Political Science Association, New York, September 1994.
111 Raymond M. Duch, "Tolerating Economic Reform: Popular Support for Transition to a Free Market in the Former Soviet Union," *American Political Science Review* 87, no. 3 (September 1994), 599.
112 William M. Reisinger, Arthur H. Miller, Vicki L. Hesli, and Kristen Hill Maher, "Political Values in Russia, Ukraine and Lithuania: Sources and Implications for Democracy," *British Journal of Political Science* 24 (1994), 211.
113 Ian McAllister and Stephen White, "Democracy, Political Parties and Party Formation in Postcommunist Russia," *Party Politics* no. 1 (1995), 49–72; Matthew Wyman, Stephen White, Bill Miller, and Paul Heywood, "Public Opinion, Parties and Voters in the December 1993 Russian Elections," *Europe-Asia Studies* 47, no. 4 (1995), 591–614; Evans and Whitefield, "The Politics

and Economics of Democratic Commitment"; Herbert Kitschelt, "Formation of Party Cleavages in Post-Communist Democracies," *Party Politics* 1, no. 4 (October 1995), 447–72; Peter McDonough, "Identities, Ideologies, and Interests: Democratization and the Culture of Mass Politics in Spain and Eastern Europe," *Journal of Politics* 57, no. 3 (August 1995), 649–76.

114 McAllister and White, "Democracy, Political Parties, and Party Formation in Postcommunist Russia," pp. 66–67.

115 Based on comments made at a workshop on "parties and electoral systems" sponsored by the East–West Parliamentary Practice Project, 18–19 September 1995, Izhevsk, Udmurtia, Russia.

116 A discussion of the distinction between "legacy" and "aftermath" in this connection is found in James R. Millar and Sharon L. Wolchik, "Introduction: The Social Legacies and the Aftermath of Communism," in James R. Millar and Sharon L. Wolchik, *The Social Legacy of Communism* (Washington, DC: Woodrow Wilson Center Press, 1994), pp. 1–30.

117 Adam Przeworski, *Democracy and the Market: Political and Economic Reforms in Eastern Europe and Latin America* (Cambridge: Cambridge University Press, 1991), pp. 1–99; Dankwart Rustow, "Transitions to Democracy: Toward a Dynamic Model," *Comparative Politics*, no. 2 (1970), 337–64.

118 Robert D. Putnam with Robert Leonardi and Raffaella Y. Nanetti, *Making Democracy Work: Civic Traditions in Modern Italy* (Princeton: Princeton University Press, 1993).

119 Samuel Huntington, *The Third Wave: Democratization in the Late Twentieth Century* (Norman and London: University of Oklahoma Press, 1991), pp. 266–67.

4 Democratization and political participation in Russia's regions

Jeffrey W. Hahn

The problem: regional politics and democratization in Russia

Broadly speaking, the literature on transitions to democracy suggests three phases: the breakdown of the old authoritarian regime, the introduction of transitional democratic institutions, and a period of democratic consolidation.[1] However, the level of analysis used almost exclusively in this literature is the national state or comparisons between states. Such analysis rarely deals with how transitions are realized at the sub-national level of politics. Yet it is hard to imagine a successful transition to democracy taking place only at the national level. Indeed, it seems more reasonable to argue that the democratization of national political institutions without corresponding changes taking place locally would be a prescription for political instability. What this chapter proposes to do is to examine how the phases of transition noted here have been implemented in Russian regional politics and to draw some conclusions about the underlying factors that will help determine whether Russia will become a stable democracy.

What do we mean by regional politics? According to the Constitution adopted in December 1993, Russia is formally a federation comprised of eighty-nine sub-national members (in Russian, *sub"ekty*). Among these members are forty-nine oblasts, twenty-one republics, ten okrugs (national districts), six krais (territories), two large cities (Moscow and St. Petersburg) and the Jewish autonomous oblast. The term "regional" is most accurately used to refer to politics and government in the oblasts, krais and two largest cities of the Russian Federation (all of which have the administrative status of an oblast), although it is commonly extended to cover the republics as well. The republics, as well as okrugs and the Jewish autonomous oblast, are defined with reference to their ethnic composition and have special rights as a result. In this chapter, the term regional politics is used broadly to refer to politics at levels of government below the national level.[2]

A stable federal system can contribute to democracy where legitimate and effectively functioning regional governments can act to limit central power; its absence creates greater opportunity for abuse of central power. Unfortunately, in Russia, relations between the central government and the regions are still very much in flux; a stable balance of power between Moscow and the regions has not yet been achieved. Two reasons for this state of affairs are worth noting; both relate directly to the issue of democratization. One is that although governors in all the oblasts are supposed to be popularly elected, by the end of 1995 most held their positions by presidential appointment, partly because Yeltsin feared the election of those opposed to him and partly because he wanted oblast executives dependent on him until after the presidential elections scheduled for June 1996. By contrast, chief executives in the republics have all been elected. Secondly, although the Constitution establishes that all members are "equal" in status, the reality is that fiscal relationships with Moscow vary greatly from one region to the next. The ensuing struggle over fiscal policy has greatly contributed to the lack of clarity and stability in center–regional relations. In particular, republics have been able to negotiate separate deals with Moscow, allowing them to pay far less in taxes than many of the oblasts while enjoying greater discretion in the uses of local resources.[3]

The first part of this chapter will address the question: Has Russian regional politics become more democratic? Certainly, sub-national Russian politics has undergone major changes in the period since Gorbachev introduced perestroika in 1985. These changes correspond to the phases of democratic transitions already identified. So, for the sake of comparison over time this section will look first at how the old soviets worked prior to the reforms of 1990 and why they failed; then at the introduction of democratic institutions, including competitive elections, in 1990–93; and finally at the difficulties of consolidating democracy at the local level since then. In each phase we will first analyze changes in political participation, focusing on elections and on the formation of political parties, and then examine how democratically the institutions that emerged from them functioned. Because any transition to democracy arguably requires popular support for democratic institutions and values, the question of Russian political culture will also be considered. This section of the chapter will draw heavily on field work which the author has conducted in Yaroslavl, Russia to demonstrate how the changes worked out in practice.[4]

At the conclusion of the first part of the chapter some generalizations will be presented about whether regional Russian politics has become more democratic. At that point, the chapter will also review some of the recent legislation related to local government in Russia and analyze what it may mean for future democratization at the local level. However, because any generalizations may fail to reveal important regional differences, the second part of the chapter will address the question: Are some regions more democratic than others? In this section we will first compare the differences in democratization between oblasts and republics. Then we will look at macroregional differences and review the literature that attempts to sketch a sort of regional political geography for Russia. By providing tentative answers to the two questions put forth here, we hope to contribute not only to a better assessment of whether a stable democracy will emerge in Russia, but also to our understanding of what engenders (or impedes) the process by which other formerly communist countries become democratic.

Has Russian regional politics become more democratic?

Authoritarian breakdown: the system until 1990

Local political institutions in Russia prior to 1990 did not differ significantly across regions or by level of government.[5] In theory, it was a system based on the primacy of local legislative institutions called "soviets." The word soviet, which can be translated innocuously as "council," came to denote a system of local government peculiar to Leninist communist systems. By official count, deputies to the soviets everywhere were elected directly by 99.9 percent of the eligible voters every two and a half years in what Soviet propaganda called the most democratic elections in the world, but which lacked any element of competition. On the average, about 250 deputies were elected to oblast soviets and 100-200 to city and district soviets.[6] At the first session after their election, deputies elected an executive committee, known in Russian as an *ispolkom*. The ispolkom was in charge of the daily administration of local government. Because the ispolkom was elected by the deputies and legally accountable to them, legislative primacy was, in theory at least, assured.

The reality was quite the opposite. In practice, the deputies met in session four times a year for a few hours each session to unanimously approve whatever items were placed on the agenda by the organizational-instructional department of the ispolkom. This same department was responsible for all other matters of business before the deputies, as well. No detail was left to chance, not even the deputies' speeches which were often scripted before-hand. Although deputies may have had some marginal opportunity to influence policy in the standing committees of the soviet and could act as something of an "ombudsman" for their constituents in their dealings with the administration their impact on local politics was minimal at best.[7] Real political power did not rest with any governmental institution, but with the Communist Party of the Soviet Union (CPSU). At the top of the local party organization was the oblast committee (*obkom*) first secretary whose control over appointments and political recruitment ensured virtually unlimited authority within the region.[8]

Central to the party's ability to control local government was its control over the nomination of candidates to the local soviets. In the old system, all nominations were made at the place of work and no one was nominated without the support of the secretary of its party committee (*partkom*), a person whose job depended on the obkom first secretary. In single candidate elections, therefore, the party was assured that only those compliant with its policies would be elected. By controlling elections to the soviets, the party also controlled the composition of the executive committee. At the first "organizational" session of the soviet, the deputies voted unanimously for the slate of candidates to the ispolkom that was put before it, also subject to party approval. Unlike the composition of the deputies as a whole (which was broadly representative demographically and typically included more than 50 percent non-communists) the composition of the executive committee was almost exclusively made up of party members, usually drawn from the upper ranks of the party organization.

In this way, regional Russian politics prior to 1990 mirrored the authoritarianism of the old regime at the national level. The reforms of local government which were first proposed by Gorbachev to the Nineteenth Conference of the CPSU in June 1988, struck at the heart of this old order.[9] In the first place, Gorbachev's proposal for holding competitive elections to a national Congress of People's Deputies in 1989 was accompanied by the recommendation that similarly competitive elections be held to the republican and local soviets in 1990. The introduction of competitive elections at the local level struck at the Achilles heal of the "soviet" system because it ended party control over the political recruitment process. Moreover, Gorbachev called for giving real authority to the legislative branch and separating its powers from those of the executive. Finally, he insisted that the party get out of the business of day to day governing, locally, as well as nationally. It is the implementation of these reforms in 1990–1991 more than any other factor that led to the breakdown of the old system.

Democratic construction: reforming the Soviets, 1990–93

Political participation. As indicated, the most important step in the break-down of the authoritarian system in the government of the USSR was the introduction of competitive elections. In Russia these "founding elections" took place at the national level and locally in March 1990. Were they "open, free, and fair?"[10] The election law adopted by the RSFSR Supreme Soviet on October 27, 1989 provided for direct elections to all local soviets on the basis of equal and universal adult suffrage and by secret ballot. No seats were automatically allocated to the CPSU and its allied "public organizations" and there was no requirement that candidates be approved at pre-election meetings of district election commissions as had been the case in the 1989 elections to the USSR Congress of Peoples' Deputies (CPD). Candidates could be nominated not only at the work place, as under the old system, but by officially registered public organizations, or at places of residence. Even so, electoral competition was not guaranteed: According to the election law, the number of candidates per single-member district was "unlimited" thus making uncontested seats possible.[11]

To be elected a candidate had to receive more than 50 percent of the votes cast, with no fewer than 50 percent of the eligible electorate turning out to vote. Because it was entirely possible, even likely, that no one would emerge victorious in a district with several candidates, provisions had to be made for runoffs (where three or more candidates were running) and for repeat elections (where one or two ran and did not get 50 percent of the vote). As a result, the election law for the 1990 local elections was cumbersome, to say the least. By not allowing the winner to take all and by requiring that 50 percent of those eligible vote, it created the possibility for virtually endless elections; from the standpoint of the average voter, the process was unnecessarily complicated. A simple majority without a required level of turnout would have been equally democratic. Despite its many shortcomings, however, the Law provided a legal basis for comparatively democratic elections.

How did these elections work out in practice? The first round of elections held on March 4, 1990 in Yaroslavl provides a useful case study. The number of seats in the new city and oblast soviets each numbered 200. Runoff elections were held two weeks later on March 18 and repeat elections on April 22. Did they meet the requirements of a free election? *Quantitatively*, there should be at least two candidates for each position. Generally, this was the case in Yaroslavl. In the city soviet, there were 565 candidates were registered for the 200 seats; for the 200 seats available in the oblast soviet, there were 597 candidates. However, although twenty of the city districts had between five and seven candidates, in forty-seven of them there was only one. In oblast races, there were as many as nine candidates per district; twenty-seven seats were uncontested. Running unopposed, however, did not guarantee election. In seven of the city districts, and in at least three of the oblast districts, more than 50 percent of those voting defeated single candidates by crossing their name off the ballot; among those defeated in this fashion were the first and second secretaries of Yaroslavl'Yaroslavls city Party Committee.

As this last point suggests, the local elections in Yaroslavl provided some degree of meaningful choice in a *qualitative* sense as well. In the first place, voters could voice their opinions on the old party-state apparatus by voting them out of office. To a considerable extent, this happened.[12] But there was also a second way in which the voter's choice was meaningful qualitatively. For those opposed to the continued political domination of members of the Party organization (*apparat*), the Yaroslavl Popular Front (YPF) represented an alternative which people could vote *for*.[13] The YPF supported sixty-seven candidates in the city elections winning twenty-two seats to the first session of the soviet which was convened on May 10, 1990. Because enough other deputies were elected who were sufficiently sympathetic to the YPF they formed a voting bloc of forty-four deputies called "Democratic Yaroslavl" which, in coalition with two other reform-minded deputy groups, easily controlled the election of the chair and vice-chair of the city soviet. The YPF did not fare as well on the oblast level although they won more seats (thirty-three). The reason for this is that in the oblast soviet only 85 of the 200 possible seats were located in the city of Yaroslavl. Rural voters proved to be far more likely to vote for those associated with the old order, especially collective farm chairs. Along with enterprise directors, these chairs had been subject to appointment by the obkom first secretary.[14] As a result, the forty-seven members elected from among the apparat formed a working majority within the new oblast soviet together with deputies who were enterprise managers or collective farm chairs.

Despite its limited success and limited resources, the YPF acted like a proto-party. Not only did it recruit and support candidates, it organized mass demonstrations on February 25 and on March 17. It disseminated information to the public by maintaining a kiosk in the center of town next to the city bus terminal. Although not always efficiently, the leadership provided a measure of internal discipline. At an organizational meeting attended by the author on the eve of the March 4 elections, much of the discussion turned on getting out the vote, giving out telephone contact numbers, going over the mechanics of voting, reading telegrams of support from "Democratic Russia" leaders Yeltsin and Gavriil Popov – in short, the sort of precinct politics familiar to anyone who has participated in an election in the United States.[15]

How democratic were these "founding elections?" What were their implications for future democratization of Russian regional politics? Clearly by comparison with the old system they were a step in the right direction. First of all, there was an unprecedented degree of competition. This was true not only in Yaroslavl, but elsewhere in Russia as well. In Moscow and Leningrad the "democratic" opposition actually won a majority of seats to their soviets.[16] Although this was not the case in other parts of Russia, active opposition minorities were formed in most local legislatures. Generally speaking, the pattern found in Yaroslavl held in other Russian regions: "democratic movement" candidates did comparatively well in cities; representatives of old elites dominated oblast soviets. Secondly, there was a high level of popular participation. Interest in the elections was high, as was turnout, and engendered active campaigning including public meetings and demonstrations. Approximately 70 percent of the eligible electorate took part in the elections in Yaroslavl which was close to the 77 percent for Russia as a whole. Thirdly, it appears that despite scattered cases of fraud, proper registration and counting procedures were followed to insure an honest election. To some extent, the legitimacy of an election is in the eyes of the voters. Voters' attitudes on this question were measured in the survey conducted by the author in Yaroslavl in 1990. The results showed that nearly 70 percent of the electorate felt that the March 4 elections had been fair; only 16 percent thought they had not been.

At the same time this "founding election" cannot be said to have fully met the requirements of free elections. In large part this is because of the absence of a multiparty system. The only hint of partisan identification was whether the candidate was a member of the CPSU. If not, they were identified as "non-party" (*bezpartiinyi*). Because most candidates in 1990 were party members, including many supported by the democratic movement, these labels had little meaning. The absence of legislation by which alternative parties could register and identify their candidates meant that voters had to rely on word of mouth and on other forms of mass communication to know which candidates stood for what. Moreover, it is not clear that those contending for office had the equal opportunity to persuade the voters, largely because they lacked resources to do so. According to the election law, campaign expenses were paid by the state and they were severely limited. In practice this meant that local Party officials had an overwhelming advantage in resources: they commanded a fleet of cars, telephones, finances, offices, and the main means of mass communication, including access to radio, TV and the press. And, of course, they had an effective organization. In sum, the election law of 1990 resulted in too many candidates running for too many seats in too many different election stages without parties to structure the voters choice. Nevertheless, the results counted: deputies elected in 1990 remained in office until the soviets were abolished in October 1993. It was they who determined how the next stages of reform would play out.

Political institutions. The elections to the soviets of March 1990 played a defining role in the development of regional as well as national Russian political institutions in the period 1990–93. In many ways the struggle between the national legislative and executive branches which ended in the destruction of the former is traceable to them. Nonetheless, initially at least, the fault lines that would lead to this explosion were hardly visible. In many respects, the new institutions that emerged were functionally far more democratic than their predecessors, but in form they were not. The new soviets, like the old ones, were essentially parliamentary systems, that is the executive branch was formed by the legislature from among its own members.[17] What was different, of course, was that the choice of the members of the executive committee (ispolkom) was no longer a formality in which the deputies unanimously voted for a slate of candidates approved in advance by the obkom first secretary. Now the choice about who would head the government was made among several candidates and by secret ballot. The fact that the 1990 elections had been truly competitive insured that in most cases the vote would be divided. Bruce Parrott has pointed out that "parliamentary systems generally increase the incentives for the creation of cohesive parties."[18] However such cohesion proved elusive largely because political parties had not been the basis on which deputies were elected. Except for the choice of leaders, during which deputies did coalesce around candidates favored by either the Popular Front or the apparat, most deputies most of the time went their own way.

The personnel decisions in the new soviets, as in the old, were made at the first (or "organizational") sessions of the local soviets which in most cases were held in May–June 1990. The organizational sessions held in Yaroslavl represented a major departure from past practice. In a meeting of the 179 deputies elected to the city soviet (twenty-one seats had not been filled by the first session), four candidates for chair of the soviet were nominated including the first secretary of the CPSU city committee. After it became clear he could not win, he withdrew and Lev Kruglikov, a candidate supported by the democratic forces, won easily among the remaining nominees. The chair of the executive committee was then chosen. One of the nominees, Viktor Volunchunas, had been chair of the previous ispolkom and so was a prominent member of old party–state apparat. He was elected, but only because the new chair of the soviet endorsed him on the grounds of his experience and personal integrity.

At the oblast level, the political composition of the deputies was more favorable to the old elite for reasons already discussed. Still, elections here were also competitive for the first time and here, too, the obkom first secretary was unable to gain election as chair of the oblast legislature. Instead, the head of one of the city party organizations outside of the oblast capitol was chosen. Together with the election of yet another leading member of the apparat to the position of executive chair, the continued dominance of candidates from the old party appointed elite (the so-called "nomenklatura") in the new oblast legislature was assured, although not without vocal opposition.

In principle, Gorbachev's reforms of local government had been intended to "democratize" the soviets by making the executive branch genuinely accountable before the peoples' representatives. Because members of the executive now understood that they owed their positions to the deputies and not to the party, a major step in the direction of a asserting legislative authority was achieved. Moreover, enabling legislation (*reglamenty*) of the soviets made it clear that the soviets had the right to overrule executive decisions. Even so, in practice, despite the new institutional arrangements, the balance of power between the two branches still favored the executive. Interviews with members of the Yaroslavl soviet in 1990–91 suggest that the executive branch continued to dominate the governing of Yaroslavl, not because of its total control over the organization of the work of the deputies as before, but because of the expertise and experience of its leaders in running the government.

In this context, it is significant in understanding the evolution of executive-legislative relations in the first two years of the new system that those chosen to exercise *executive* authority in both the oblast and the city were often drawn from those who had exercised it previously. This merits further explanation. One of the major institutional changes that occurred during this initial period of reform was the decline of CPSU influence over local politics. Even before the CPSU was abolished in the wake of the August 1991 coup attempt, party membership including those in the party organization had greatly diminished. Party discipline in the soviets was so poor that although 70 percent or so of the deputies were nominally party members, they could not elect either the city or oblast party secretary to positions of leadership in local government. As the power of the local party organization began to wane many party professionals left and found positions in the ispolkoms, especially at the oblast level where deputies drawn from the former "nomenklatura" formed a working majority. As members of the ispolkom they could use their experience running local affairs and their personal connections to their advantage. In this way, by transferring their base of power from the party organization to the executive branch of local government, some members of the old communist elite managed to survive the institutional changes aimed at reducing their influence. Many even claimed conversion to the new order, if not before then after August 1991.

The tendency toward executive dominance was accelerated in the period following the failed coup attempt of August 19, 1991. Yeltsin used support for the coup by some executive officials as an excuse to remove from office those executives whom he regarded as opponents and replace them with allies many of whom were drawn from the ranks of reformers in parliament. But the most visible assertion of executive authority in the wake of the coup was the appointment of "presidential representatives" in virtually all the oblasts of Russia. Although Yeltsin intended to establish this position even before the coup attempt, the events of August 19, 1991 gave added urgency to the move and on August 31 Yeltsin signed a "temporary" regulation defining their role.[19] As originally conceived presidential representatives were to act as a link between the President and local authorities. They were to oversee the implementation of the acts of the federal government and to make recommendations about removing local executives from office if they violated federal acts.

In practice, not surprisingly, presidential representatives were Yeltsin political supporters, most being deputies to the Russian parliament affiliated with the "Democratic Russia" political movement despite the legal proscription that they not belong to a political party. Also not surprisingly, given their political character and their authority to oversee local legislation, they were the target of growing opposition by the regional soviets, and by the Russian parliament, which demanded their abolition as early as the Sixth Congress of the Russian CPD of April 1992.[20] When the position of the representatives became the subject of continuing skirmishes between Yeltsin and parliament, Yeltsin proposed giving them permanent legal status in his version of the draft constitution presented in the summer of 1993. The skirmishes were conclusively ended only with the demise of parliament in October 1993. The presidential representatives, of course, have remained in place.

The other major way in which executive authority was strengthened was through the establishment of the office of chief of administration (*glava administratsii*). This new institution represented a fundamental change in the institutional balance which existed previously because it removed the leadership of the executive branch of government from the control of the legislature. As conceived, heads of administration were to be popularly elected. At the oblast level they would be known as governor (*gubernator*) and at the city level they would be called mayor (*meyr*). They, and not the local legislature, would be responsible for appointing other members of the "administration." This new body would replace the old ispolkom in the day-to-day running of government. The functions of the soviets were to be limited to making policy and representing constituents, not directing the work of the executive branch. In effect, the new system would replace the parliamentary structure of the soviets with a semi-presidential one.[21]

Prior to attempted coup it was expected that elections for heads of administration would be held in December, 1991. But, because of the strength of the old communist "nomenklatura" outside of Moscow, especially in the oblast soviets, it had became increasingly clear to everyone, above all to Yeltsin, that his opponents stood a good chance of winning these elections. Consequently, he asked the fifth session of the Russian CPD in October 1991 to declare a moratorium on them for one year and they agreed. Surprisingly, given the increasingly bitter hostility of parliament toward the President during the course of 1992, the moratorium on elections of chief administrators was not lifted after one year. Instead, at the seventh session of the CPD, parliament compromised by ruling that such elections would held only if oblast soviets insisted on it. In April 1993, a few such elections occurred.[22] By the end of 1993, of course, Yeltsin had abolished parliament and the local soviets promising a new constitution and elections to a new federal parliament in December 1993. Elections to new local legislatures were scheduled for early 1994. In the interim, the administration of local government was placed in the hands of the governors all but a handful of whom were Yeltsin appointees and who, on the whole, have proven to be politically loyal.[23]

As already noted, the balance of power between the legislative and executive branches at the local level favored the latter even before the strengthening of local executive control in 1992–93. That this imbalance grew after the coup attempt was certainly due in part to the introduction of presidential representatives and chief administrators, but it also had to do with the shortcomings of the soviets themselves. Generally speaking, the soviets proved to be ineffective legislative institutions. In large part this is a residual of the communist period. Like their predecessors, the soviets were too large. Two hundred deputies can function if no real debate takes place and all votes are unanimous, but the same number of deputies, lacking the discipline that party ties might have given them and lacking any real experience in local government, can hardly be expected to produce coherent legislation. Chaos rather than calm deliberation often characterized the sessions of local soviets attended by the author in this period. To respond to this problem, "small soviets" numbering about twenty were elected from among the body of deputies as a whole in the winter of 1991–92. But they too were for the most part political amateurs only a few of whom occupied their positions on a full-time basis. Lacking sufficient professional staff, the leaders of these "small soviets" were no match for the executive branch. In many respects, the executive branch took real power in Russia's regions by default; someone, after all, had to govern.

The development of regional politics in Russia after 1992 was also very much effected by the growing struggle for power nationally. The 1991 amendments to the Russian Constitution grafted a presidential system of government on to what was, structurally, a parliamentary one. As we have seen, in the Fall of 1991 Yeltsin extended this institutional miscegenation to the local level by creating strong chief executives who were no longer directly accountable to local legislators for their positions. His decision clearly was made to counteract what he viewed as opposition to his reforms among the "conservative" soviets. Locally as well as nationally he and his aides demonized the soviets as opponents of reform who would return Russia to its authoritarian past. In doing so he polarized Russian politics, creating a standoff which would ultimately be resolved by the forced abolition of all the soviets in October 1993.

Yeltsin's depiction of the soviets as bastions of anti-democratic sentiment is hard to sustain. As Josephine Andrews and Kathryn Stoner-Weiss point out, far from all the deputies in the regional legislatures were loath to support political and economic reforms.[24] Moreover, arguably the new soviets were far more democratic than the old: competitively elected deputies engaged in vigorous dissent from government positions; members of the executive branch were for the first time truly accountable before the people's representatives; almost all votes were divided unlike the unanimous voting that characterized the old soviets. Above all, perhaps, the Communist Party's monolithic control over the soviets no longer existed. Democratic institutions had been introduced into Russian local government in 1990–93 and they functioned, however imperfectly.

1994 and beyond: democratic consolidation?

Much was learned in the period 1990–93 which could contribute to the future democratization of Russian regional politics. To what extent has this knowledge been useful in creating new political institutions in Russia's regions since 1993? When Yeltsin abolished the soviets in the course of the "Second October Revolution," he promised that a referendum would be held on December 12, 1993 for a new Russian Constitution along with elections to a new national parliamentary body called the Federal Assembly. With respect to the local soviets, on October 9 Yeltsin decreed that they were to be replaced by new bodies consisting of between fifteen and fifty deputies whose initial term of office was to be two years. All deputies were to serve full-time although this was later reduced to two-fifths of the deputies when Yeltsin realized that those working as administrators would be barred from running unless they gave up their posts.[25] More details regarding the new legislatures were forthcoming in the President's decree of October 22, 1993, "On Basic Principles of Organizing State Power in the Members of the Federation." Elections to the new local legislatures were to be held between December 1993 and March 1994. Only in Moscow were they required to be held on December 12. Following the example of the new constitution, the balance of executive-legislative power was clearly tilted in favor of the executive branch. Among other provisions, the legislatures would have to muster a two-thirds vote of their membership as a whole to override a governor's veto. Yet another decree issued on October 27 established general rules for the elections. Unlike the 1990 elections with their complicated procedures for run-offs and repeat elections, winners were decided by a simple plurality with a minimum 25 percent of the eligible electorate voting. On the basis of these decrees electoral commissions were created to organize new local elections to legislative bodies that, in most cases, would be called either assemblies (*sobranie*) or dumas although the choice of name was not specified.[26] The fact that members of these commissions were nominated by the regional administration and required approval by the Central Election Commission gave the executive branch an advantage and was the subject of protest by political groups not affiliated with the parties in power.[27]

Elections to the new legislatures began with those held in five oblasts (including the city of Moscow) and in three republics on December 12, 1993. They were to have been completed by the end of March, but in fact continued to be held throughout Russia during the rest of 1994. By early April they had taken place in sixty-seven of the eighty-nine members of the Federation.[28] The process was completed in all oblasts except Ulianovsk only by early 1995. Typically the new bodies formed three to seven standing committees including: committees on budgets and taxes; on social policies; on economic policy, property and the environment; on relations with lower level governments; and a mandate committee. Future relations between legislative and executive branches were to be defined in "charters" (*ustavy*) adopted by the new duma or assembly, but until the new structures were in place oblast governors continued to exercise a veto over decisions of the legislature by virtue of the presidential decree issued on October 22, 1993.[29]

The results of the elections to the new oblast legislatures varied considerably from one region to the next. However, some generalizations can be made. In the first place, although elections were less complicated than in 1990, turnout was generally much lower. In many districts, predominantly urban ones, election turnout failed to reach the 25 percent threshold of eligible voters required in each district and repeat elections had to be organized. As a result some new legislatures (including St. Petersburg, Orenburg, Murmansk, Kamchatka, and Novosibirsk) lacked the required two-thirds needed to constitute a quorum and were consequently unable to begin work for months. Because turnout was not as severe a problem in rural areas most of those seats were filled. This in turn gave deputies from rural districts an advantage at the initial organizing sessions of those legislatures that did meet and which made important decisions regarding personnel. Even in districts where the threshold was met, however, turnout rarely exceeded 40 percent.[30]

A second generalization to be made is that the pattern of voter participation observed in 1990 continued: Rural voters were more likely to vote than urbanites. Although overall turnout in both rural and urban areas was down the districts that failed to clear the 25 percent threshold generally were urban, not rural. What explains this pattern? Donna Bahry and Lucan Way suggest that it is a residual of the Soviet period when there was universal mobilization of the masses to vote. They found that voters from higher socio-economic levels would engage in more complex forms of political activism, but were less likely to vote; for lower levels it was just the opposite.[31] Russian analyst Leonid Smirniagin suggests it is an urban protest vote against a time when voting was meaningless, but mandatory. The attitude of urban voters, he argues, is that "it is Moscow's task to curb the local bosses, not the local voters."[32] Although there is probably some merit to the argument that the Soviet practice of ritualized mass voting alienated the educated voter, but retained its influence on rural (and elderly) voters, there are other possible explanations. For one, rural voters may be more dependent on the local boss for wages and benefits and therefore more open to manipulation of rewards; the potential costs of <u>not</u> voting aren't worth it. Another rational voter argument holds that rural voters are especially vulnerable to the loss of agricultural subsidies and, except for a few, lack resources to take advantage of land privatization. Voting for Communists and voting in numbers become a matter of self-interest.[33]

Finally, it is clear that party labels did not play a significant role in the 1994 regional legislative elections, except in cases of candidates associated with "democratic" parties, where it was a liability, and for communists, who did well in southern, more rural oblasts (Orlov, Penza, Smolensk, Lipetsk, and Bryansk).[34] Data reported by Darrell Slider indicate that less than 14 percent of those elected had a party affiliation. Of these 46 percent were affiliated with the Communist Party of Russian Federation (CPRF), 11 percent with the Agrarian Party, 10 percent with Russia's Choice, 4 percent with Nikolai Travkin's Democratic Party of Russia, and 2 percent with Sergei Shakrai's Party of Russian Unity and Accord (PRUA). Vladimir Zhirinovsky's Liberal Democratic Party (LDPR) elected very few deputies in Russia's regional elections despite his nationwide success in December 1993. Only in Krasnodar Krai in Russia's far south did the LDPR do well. Together with the nationalist party, "Otechestvo," candidates supported by the LDPR won half the seats. As Slider also points out, the real winners in the 1994 regional legislative elections were those who already held positions of power either as members or chiefs of local administration, as directors in industry, or as collective farm chairs. Taken together they accounted for about half of those elected.[35]

A closer examination of how these elections were carried out in Yaroslavl provides a more nuanced basis for comparing the regional legislative elections of 1994 with those of 1990. For the better, the electoral laws for the February 27, 1994 elections to both the oblast duma and the city council (in Yaroslavl called the "municipalitet") were based on a winner-take-all principle in which whoever got the greatest number of votes won regardless of how many candidates there were. Furthermore, only 25 percent of the eligible electorate had to take part for elections to be valid, not 50 percent.[36] As in 1990 there were many more candidates than seats available. In all, 211 candidates competed for twenty-three seats to the oblast duma (an average of nine per district); 123 ran for twenty-two seats in the city municipalitet (for an average of six per district). The candidates were mostly middle-aged males with higher education. Compared to 1990 the level of voter participation was much lower. Overall, 33 percent of those eligible voted in the oblast duma election; only 26 percent took part in the election to the city council. The higher percent of turnout for the duma elections reflects the pattern noted earlier regarding greater voting in rural districts. Of the twenty-three seats in the oblast duma, thirteen are located in rural districts and in those districts turnout was heavier. Overall, in six of the oblast districts (all in urban areas) and seven of the city council districts, less than the necessary 25 percent of the electorate came out to vote and new elections in those districts were scheduled for April 24.

How important were political parties in the 1994 elections in Yaroslavl? In 1990, of course, there were no parties. By 1994, however, there were some fifty-five parties and political movements with a national affiliation registered in Yaroslavl including all the major national parties. Although in reality most of these groups exist on paper only, both Russia's Choice and the Communist Party of Russia of the Russian Federation (CPRF) were active in the 1994 elections. The local Communist Party, in particular, is easily the best organized in Yaroslavl.[37] Yet the political composition of those elected was, if anything, less partisan in 1994 than in 1990 when the Yaroslavl Popular Front challenged candidates supported by the CPSU organization. Few candidates in 1994 ran as representatives of a party or were publicly supported by a party. Nearly all the candidates who won ran as "independents" and were enterprise directors, heads of administration, or professionals (doctors or educators).[38] Only one member of the oblast duma is a member of the Agrarian party; two others are regarded as members of the CPRF. What this suggests is that although partisanship may be salient for voters in Yaroslavl in national elections, it is not so locally, or at least not yet.

How are we to explain the apparent lack of partisanship in regional Russian politics? The unimportance of parties in local elections is especially remarkable because parties had played an important role in elections to the national Duma only two months earlier. The allocation of half the seats in that body on the basis of party lists contributed to a sense of party identification on the part of Russian voters.[39] Moreover, survey research conducted in the city of Yaroslavl in December 1994 found that 70 percent of the respondents expressed support for a national party; only 30 percent did not. This contrasted significantly with data gathered in May, 1993 indicating that 78 percent supported no party. It seems reasonable to attribute the difference to the fact that half of the deputies to the State Duma elected in December, 1993 were elected on the basis of party lists.[40] But, if voting for party lists in national elections contributes to a sense of party identification, why did parties play such a negligible role locally? One argument suggests that a general antipathy towards parties prevails throughout Russia, perhaps reflecting experience with the CPSU, the only party most Russians had known until after 1990. Yet most polls show support for a multiparty system among Russians, and in any case this view seems to runs counter to the evidence just cited of growing party identification nationally. It may simply be that although party list voting does foster greater partisanship, voting in regional elections in 1994 was organized with very few exceptions on the basis of single member districts and in these races candidates ran on their own merits.[41] Whether the development of greater partisanship in national elections will eventually lead to an increased role for political parties locally is uncertain; if it does, the 1994 elections suggest that it won't be soon.

It is tempting to explain the lower levels of electoral participation in the 1994 elections to regional legislatures by suggesting that the novelty of competitive elections which existed in 1990 had worn off and that voters were sick of politics. Although this explanation may have some merit, survey research conducted in Yaroslavl in 1991, 1993 and 1995 suggests another: Voters surveyed in 1991 and 1993 felt that their local legislature had somewhat more influence in resolving problems in Yaroslavl than the executive branch, but by 1995 this view was reversed by about 2:1. Among deputies themselves it was 4:1 in favor of the executive branch.[42] It may well be that voters showed less interest in the 1994 regional legislative elections because they realized that real power had passed to the executive branch. After all, there were good grounds for such a conclusion. For one thing, Yeltsin had shown his contempt for legislative opposition to his programs by abolishing the soviets in October 1993, the members of which had been chosen in the freest elections in Russian history. For another, the new Russian Constitution adopted on December 12, 1993 (under controversial circumstances) established a strong presidential system, one which greatly reduced legislative authority.

The constitutional establishment of strong executive authority at the top set a precedent for the development of regional politics in Russia in 1994–95. The tendency toward greater executive control over local affairs which had begun before the events of October 1993 was accelerated in this period. To begin with the position of the presidential representatives has been strengthened. Yeltsin's intention to give them a permanent legal basis found expression in article 83 of the new constitution according to which the President "appoints authorized representatives of the President of the Russian Federation and relieves them of their duties." In June 1994, presidential decree No. 1186 established that presidential representatives are to be regarded as plenipotentiaries of the president in all the sub-national members of the Federation.[43] How important a role these representatives actually play varies regionally, but they can "vet" decisions of local executives for consistency with presidential decrees and make personnel recommendations. What they may not do, according to the presidential representative in Yaroslavl, is to interfere with the running of government by the governor.[44] There is some evidence that by 1995 those among them associated with the democratic movement had become unhappy with what they see as backsliding on reform and may be replaced.[45] But, on the whole, the longevity of these people in office is pretty high. Through mid–1994, 53 of the 61 representatives appointed with six months after August, 1991 were still in place.[46]

The importance of the oblast chief of administration or governor has also grown since October 1993. As already discussed, even before the abolition of the soviets at that time, oblast governors had become the most significant actors in local Russian government, if only because they possessed greater expertise and experience; the destruction of the local soviets could not but make them stronger still. During 1994 their position became even more dominant for at least two reasons. Firstly, whereas the old Soviet Constitution gave significant power to the legislative branch, the Russian Constitution of 1993 which replaced it provides for an extremely strong executive who can dissolve parliament in certain cases and who can rule by decrees that are not unconstitutional or in violation of federal law. This imbalance in favor of executive power is also manifest locally. Local dumas can do little to thwart the purposes of a determined executive, especially one that enjoys the favor of the President. Secondly, a Presidential decree issued on October 3, 1994, tightened Yeltsin's hold over the governors. Pending the adoption of a law on their status, all appointments, punishments and dismissals related to that post were to be handled by the president. Significantly, the scheduling of elections for chief administrators during the "transitional period" was also placed under the President's exclusive jurisdiction.[47] Moreover, according to presidential decree No. 2093 of November 22, 1994, executives at the municipal level are appointed by those at the oblast level. In short, by the end of 1994 and continuing through 1995, all real local power in Russia resided with the governors, and the great majority of governors owed their jobs not the electorate, but to Yeltsin.[48]

Legally, and in accordance with article 77 of the Russian Constitution, relations between the executive and legislative branches of government in the regions are defined by charters (ustavy) adopted by the legislature. In the republics, they are defined by constitutions of which there were fifteen by the end of 1994. In the oblasts, ten charters had been adopted by April 18, 1995 and thirty more were in the draft stage. Generally speaking, the regional legislature can adopt either a parliamentary or a presidential system of local government; which one is selected varies considerably from one region to the next. As Vladimir Lysenko points out, the variant chosen depends on "whatever relations are like at the time between the chief administrator and the oblast duma in a given region."[49] Executive-legislative relations in Yaroslavl are defined by a charter adopted, after six months of debate, by the oblast duma on May 23, 1995. It establishes a strong presidential system which has been likened by the journalist Alexander Tsvetkov, who is also a deputy to both the Yaroslavl oblast and city legislatures, to a "mini-presidency."[50] It calls for a directly elected governor who has immunity, may veto the duma's legislation, appoints a government and its chair, and can dismiss the duma and hold new elections if they fail three times to approve his nominee to chair the government.

Why, it may be asked, would a legislative body voluntarily give so much power to the executive branch? As Lysenko suggests, the answer lies in the political composition of the duma. It will be recalled that most of those elected were directors of regional enterprises or were members of administrations elsewhere in the oblast. Indeed, five of the twenty-three elected were themselves chief administrators. One of these is Yaroslavl city mayor, Viktor Volunchunas, whose election to the oblast legislature (along with that of Valentina Istomina, the city's chief financial officer) insures that the city's interests are protected. As a result, the overwhelming majority of those elected, including the mayor, are more or less directly dependent on the good will of the governor, Anatolii Lisitsyn, who enjoys Yeltsin's patronage and as a result is unquestionably the most powerful figure in Yaroslavl politics.[51] It is for this reason that Tsvetkov calls the composition of the oblast duma "scandalous." As a professional journalist, he attributes the growth in executive power locally at least in part to the lack of truly independent local media. In Yaroslavl, the two main local television stations are run by the governor and by the mayor; local newspapers are unable to publish without government subsidies.[52] The chair of the duma, Valentin Melekhin, was himself a former administrator from the city of Rybinsk whose election as chair was unanimous. Fifty-nine years of age and in poor health, Melekhin is not a strong political figure and certainly is no match for the governor which is apparently why he was chosen. The main point to be made here is that relations between legislative and executive branches in Yaroslavl were defined by a legislature that was largely composed of those with a stake in continued dominance by executive authority. By the end of 1995, government in Yaroslavl had become something of an oligopoly.

Before turning to the problem of comparing politics across regions, it may be appropriate at this point to offer a generalization regarding the question of whether regional politics in Russia have become more democratic. The analysis of the development of local government in Russia presented here tends to support the conclusion that at least since the coup attempt of August 1991 there has been a growing tendency toward virtually unlimited rule by local executive officials, a tendency which has accelerated since the abolition of the soviets in October 1993. By the end of 1995 this tendency reached the point where power had become so concentrated in the chief executive at the oblast level (the governor) that it is possible to speak of a new "Russian prefect" similar in stature to the obkom first secretaries of the Soviet period.[53] William Clark has made the case that Yeltsin sought a "suitable substitute" for the old regional party organization; just as the soviets were marginalized under that system, so too are the new dumas and assemblies in their relationship with the governors.[54] Moreover, as was normally the case with obkom first secretaries, turnover among the governors has been infrequent. Until December 17, 1995 only nine of the sixty-eight holding office were elected; of the sixty-eight, fifty-three were appointed by Yeltsin in the six months or so after August, 1991. As a result of Yeltsin's decrees of October 3 and November 22, 1994 the President gained the exclusive right to appoint, punish and dismiss governors (and indirectly, lower level executives) apparently whether they are elected or not. Yeltsin has been reluctant to use the power he has over governors, perhaps because he needs them as much (and in the case of popular governors, probably more) than they need him. Nevertheless the current situation is reminiscent of the obkom first secretary's subordination to the CPSU General Secretary.[55]

One can describe oblast governors as "new prefects," however, only if they continue to be appointed and not elected. Until September 18, 1995 there was no mention of electing governors except, as noted, in Sverdlovsk where such an election was held in August 1995 by way of special presidential exemption. On September 18, 1995, however, Yeltsin issued decree No. 951 "On Elections to the Bodies of State Power and to the Bodies of Local Self Government in the Members of the Federation." In accordance with this decree, all oblast level legislative elections are to be postponed until December 1997. The decree also puts off elections to bodies of local self-government until December 1996 despite article 58 of the "Law on Local Self Government" which was signed into law by Yeltsin on August 28, 1995 and which established that elections to legislatures throughout Russia at the city level and below would be held within six months.[56] With respect to gubernatorial elections, the decree postponed them until December 1996 with the exception of Nizhny Novgorod, Moscow, and Omsk oblasts which were allowed to hold them on December 17, 1995, the same day as elections to the

State Duma.[57] There would appear to be at least two reasons for Yeltsin's decision to delay the elections of governors. For one thing, he wanted to keep people in these positions who could be expected to be more supportive of him during the presidential elections scheduled for June 1996. For another, if elections of governors were held simultaneously with those to the Federal Assembly the likely result would be a Federation Council composed of far more members hostile to him.

Elections of governors and mayors would clearly be an important step toward greater regional democracy in Russia when and if they are held. Such elections would make the most important local decision makers accountable to the local electorate rather than to the president. And there is evidence of widespread popular support for such elections with two-thirds to three-fourths favoring direct election.[58] For this reason, elections for local executives would be likely to stimulate popular political participation and mobilize broader support for democracy. Moreover, popular accountability would make local executives more attentive to local needs and demands and therefore more independent from the center.[59] This would create a natural check on the abuse of federal power by Moscow, surely a prerequisite for the emergence of genuine federalism in Russia. In fact, as regional charters were adopted in 1994–95 specifying rules for selecting executives, there was growing pressure on Yeltsin to hold such elections and on October 15, 1995 he allowed governors to be elected in an additional nine oblasts simultaneously with the December elections to the Russian State Duma. However, in most of these cases, incumbents were expected to win (and did), ensuring that Yeltsin's dominance over most chief regional executives would remain intact.[60] Thus, the net impact of Yeltsin's decision to suspend gubernatorial elections was to continue executive dominance at the regional level for at least another year.

Some observers would argue that a return to strong executive authority is congruent with the authoritarian traditions of Russian political culture: What the Russian people want is not democracy but a leader who will rule with a "strong hand." According to this view, there is a lack of support among Russians for democratic values and institutions resulting from an underlying continuity of Russia's authoritarian political culture. In the words of Walter Lacqueur, "Basic instincts do not easily change; the Russians never respected and loved democracy as they respected and loved autocracy."[61] An authoritarian political culture persists in Russia, it is claimed, because there were no democratic traditions in that country either before or after the Bolshevik revolution of 1917. The autocratic rule of the Tsar was reincarnated in the authoritarian rule of the CPSU especially under Stalin. Lacking democratic traditions, most Russians supported the system at least passively. "Stalinism," writes Robert V. Daniels, "may be comprehended in part as an expression of the enduring features of Russian political culture."[62] Such a view raises serious doubts about whether a transition to democracy is possible in Russia: How, after all, can such a transition take place if there is no popular support for it? The electoral success of Vladimir Zhirinovsky in December 1993 is sometimes cited as evidence that Russians are reverting to the "natural" preference for authoritarianism.[63]

The thesis that democratization in Russia is rendered futile by the persistence of an authoritarian political culture is not universally shared by students of Russian politics. For one thing, not all observers agree that pre-revolutionary Russian political culture was antithetical to democratic values. S. Frederick Starr find elements of liberalism in what he calls Russia's "usable past," including elements of civil society, a rule of law and guaranteed individual rights.[64] Nicolai Petro also rejects the idea that Russian political culture is fundamentally undemocratic placing the blame on the misapplication of "mainstream" political culture theories to Russia. Instead he argues that there are historically rooted strands of what he calls Russia's "alternative political culture" which can become a basis for the "rebirth of Russian democracy."[65] Alongside arguments that not all Russian political history was undemocratic are findings based on survey research in contemporary Russia which flatly contradict the contention that Russian political culture is antithetical to democracy. Such research was prohibited under the old regime and consequently our ability to empirically test the cultural continuity thesis was limited. After 1989, however, this ceased to be the case and access has been unprecedented.[66]

What have we learned from survey research about Russian political culture? Although the foci of this research varied from one study to another, after five years of such research carried out by different teams of researchers all working independently, something like a consensus seems to be emerging. Not all researchers would subscribe to all of them, but the following broad generalizations can be offered.[67] Firstly, there is far more support for democratic values and institutions among inhabitants of the former communist countries, including Russia, than the cultural continuity thesis would have led us to expect. Secondly, the one value relevant to democratic political culture which does not appear strong is tolerance of minority rights, although some studies suggest that political tolerance is equally low in some West European democracies. Thirdly, and perhaps surprisingly, support for democratic values has remained relatively stable over time despite poor economic performance. Replicate surveys of Yaroslavl voters conducted in 1990 and 1993 (a period of great economic dislocation) showed only a modest decline in measures of political efficacy, political trust, support for democratic elections, and political participation (see tables 4.1–4.4). Political interest declined somewhat more substantially, but 1990 levels may have been especially high because it was the first time truly competitive elections had been tried in Russia. Fourth, support for democratic values and institutions varies with socio-economic variables in ways similar to what we find in western democracies, especially with respect to levels of education (see table 4.5). Finally, the concept of democracy in these countries comes closer to the ideal of social democracy found in continental Europe than to what we find in the United States. That is to say, there is an expectation of a strong social welfare component. Taken together, the picture that emerges from this research is of political cultures in the former European communist countries generally, and for our purposes, Russia in particular, which are sufficiently hospitable to the emergence and maintenance of democratic institutions. If these findings are valid, efforts to restore strong executive rule in Russia or return to the authoritarianism of the past will come about not because of popular support for such institutions, but in spite of it.

Are some regions in Russia more democratic than others?

Republics versus oblasts?

According to Article 5 of the Russian Constitution, the Russian Federation consists of eighty-nine sub-national members "all of which are *equal* members of the Russian Federation (emphasis added)."[68] Yet, how "equal" are they? Article 66 establishes that the status of republics is defined by their own constitutions, but oblast affairs are governed by "charters" adopted by their legislatures. Further, Article 68, section 2 gives republics the right to establish their own state language. But these are not serious discrepancies.[69] There are, however, more serious ways in which the republics enjoy rights that oblasts do not. Politically, the heads of oblast governments have been, with few exceptions, appointed by Yeltsin while the republics have formed their own systems of government and in fifteen cases elected their heads of government including thirteen Presidents. As Julia Wishnevsky points out, this is regarded as a form of discrimination by many living in the oblasts.[70]

Another way in which the republics have gained preferential treatment is through the signing of "bilateral treaties" with the federal government. The first of these was signed on February 15, 1994 and ended a standoff between Tatarstan and Moscow over the question of whether Tatarstan was a member of the Russian Federation.[71] This treaty was intended to be a model for relations with other republics seeking greater autonomy, and indeed as of January 1996 eight more similar treaties had been signed, some with better terms for the given republic than the model one.[72] Aside from granting the republics greater control than oblasts over their natural resources, the principal way in which the treaties unequally benefit the republics is by

Table 4.1 *Comparative political efficacy measures for local and national government in Yaroslavl, 1990 and 1993 (in percent)*

	Yaroslavl 1990[a] (n=975)	Yaroslavl 1993[a] (n=1,019)
Political efficacy: national		
1. People like me don't have much to say about what government does.		
Agree	84.8	89.0
Disagree	9.0	6.3
Don't know[b]	6.3	4.7
2. I don't think public officials care much what people like me think.		
Agree	55.9	72.5
Disagree	29.4	15.4
Don't know	14.7	12.1
3. Sometimes government seems so complicated that people like me can't really understand what's going on.		
Agree	69.4	70.9
Disagree	23.2	20.8
Don't know	7.5	8.4
4. Generally speaking, those we elect lose touch with the people quickly.		
Agree	61.0	87.4
Disagree	16.3	3.5
Don't know	22.6	9.0
Political efficacy: local		
5. People like me don't have anything to say about what the local government does.		
Agree	83.3	83.6
Disagree	10.4	8.5
Don't know	6.0	7.9
6. Sometimes local government seems so complicated that a person like me can't really understand what is going on.		
Agree	59.7	62.9
Disagree	30.6	23.8
Don't know	9.7	13.2

Notes: [a]Column may not total 100 due to rounding.[b]The "don't know" response was noticeably more frequent among Russian respondents than among Western respondents. This could be interpreted as reflecting greater passivity or lack of interest in matters political. However, a contrary interpretation is also possible. The "don't know" response may represent a particularly thoughtful and interested opinion; e.g., upon reflection, the respondent really "doesn't know" whether "the government cares what people think," etc.

Source: Surveys conducted by the author in 1990 and 1993.

Table 4.2 *Comparative measures of political trust in local and national government in Yaroslavl, 1990 and 1993 (in percent)*

	Yaroslavl 1990[a] (n=975)	Yaroslavl 1993[a] (n=1,019)
Political trust: national		
1. How much of the time do you think government makes the right decisions?		
Almost always	18.3	6.4
Half the time	39.2	38.6
Rarely or never	26.3	32.4
Don't know	16.2	22.7
2. Would you say that government, when it makes decisions, takes care for the well-being of all the people or only for a few?		
Benefits all	36.3	14.3
Sometimes all	26.2	23.7
Benefits few	29.6	53.2
Don't know	7.9	8.8
3. Do you feel that a majority of those running the government are capable or do you think only a few are?		
A majority	24.7	13.0
About half	24.9	22.9
A minority	37.0	46.2
Don't know	13.2	18.0
Political trust: local		
4. How much of the time do you think your city government makes the right decisions?		
Almost always	6.3	12.2
Half the time	23.1	38.4
Rarely or never	36.3	19.5
Don't know	34.3	29.9
5. Would you say that your local government when it makes decisions takes care for the well-being of all people or only for a few?		
Benefits all	15.2	17.0
Sometimes all	23.3	31.2
Benefits few	46.3	38.7
Don't know	15.3	13.2

Note: [a]Column may not total 100 due to rounding.
Source: Surveys conducted by the author in 1990 and 1993.

Table 4.3 *Comparative levels of popular support for elections in Yarolavl, 1990 and 1993*
      (in percent)

		Yaroslavl 1990 (n=975)	Yaroslavl 1993[a] (n=1,019)
1.	A good many local elections aren't important enough to bother with.		
	Agree	14.0	27.1
	Disagree	82.5	62.0
	Don't know	3.5	10.8
2.	If a person doesn't care how an election comes out, then that person shouldn't vote.		
	Agree	44.2	51.2
	Disagree	50.8	37.5
	Don't know	5.0	10.8
3.	So many other people vote in national elections that it doesn't matter much whether I vote or not.		
	Agree	27.5	39.3
	Disagree	68.3	53.7
	Don't know	4.2	7.1
4.	It isn't so important to vote when you know your candidate doesn't have a chance to win.		
	Agree	28.2	37.2
	Disagree	62.0	52.2
	Don't know	9.8	10.6

Note: [a]Column may not total 100 due to rounding.
Source: Surveys conducted by the author in 1990 and 1993.

Table 4.4 *Political participation levels in Yaroslavl, 1990 and 1993 (rank order, percent)*

		1990	1993
1	Voted in the previous elections for deputy to Russian Congress of People's Deputies	99.0[a]	81.9
2	Voted in the previous elections to local soviets	99.0[a]	78.0
3	Discussed political issues in meeting of work collectives	63.3	55.1
4	Attended pre-election meetings	44.0	35.5
5	Participated in election work	30.1	32.7
6	Took part in political demonstrations	13.2	12.8
7	Attended meeting of constituents with deputy	23.4	12.4
8	Wrote to deputy about political opinion	6.7	7.0
9	Met with deputy in reception hours	7.6	6.4
10	Met with deputy on personal problem at another time	7.8	5.5
11	Met with deputy on a matter of public concern at another time	5.4	4.5
12	Made formal complaints to deputy to bring to city government	4.2	2.7
13	Expressed political opinion in media	4.4	2.7

Note: [a]Estimates. Voter turnout for elections prior to 1990 was 99 percent as was customary in old-style Soviet elections.
Source: Surveys conducted by the author in 1990 and 1993.

Table 4.5 *Correlates of political culture in Yaroslavl, 1993 and 1990*[a]

	1 Education	2 Occupation	3 Income	4 Socio-economic status	5 Age	6 Gender (M/F)	7 Birthplace	8 Material well-being
Political participation	.25 (.20)	.20 (n.s.)	n.s.	.25	.11 (.09)	n.s. (n.s.)	n.s. (n.s.)	n.s.
Political efficacy	.30 (.26)	.24 (.15)	.10	.26	n.s. (.11)	-.12 (-.09)	.13 (n.s.)	.14
Political trust	n.s. (-.12)	n.s. (.13)	n.s.	n.s.	.14 (.13)	n.s. (n.s.)	n.s. (-.16)	.13
Support for elections	.15 (.09)	.12 (.10)	n.s.	.11	n.s. (.15)	n.s. (.10)	n.s. (n.s.)	n.s.
Political interest	.10 (.24)	n.s. (.12)	n.s.	.06	.09 (n.s.)	-.08 (-.13)	n.s. (n.s.)	n.s.
Multi-party system	.30 (.16)	.22 (.11)	.11	.26	.10 (.10)	-.09 (-.16)	.10 (n.s.)	n.s.

Notes: [a] A Pearson's R correlation coefficient is reported in all cases. A .05 level of probability or lower was the standard for statistical significance. Since ordinal or interval levels of measurement were used for all variables, the direction of the association is always positive, that is, as predicted by the hypothesis (e.g., less education is correlated with lower levels of participation, but at -.12 greater education is associated with lower levels of trust). Where comparable data from 1990 are available they are reported in parentheses. The approach used here and the large number of missing data probably underestimate the correlation.

Source: Surveys conducted by the author in 1990 and 1993.

giving them tax breaks. Both of these inequalities are deeply resented in the oblasts and have encouraged demands by their leaders for similar treatment. In fact, by January 31, 1996 such treaties had been signed with four *oblasts* risking what one analyst has suggested could become a "bidding war among the regions."[73]

Who governs in the oblasts and republics? As we have already seen, in the oblasts at least until December 1995 forty-five out of forty-nine governors were appointed by Yeltsin, most (thirty-nine) in first few months after the August 1991 coup attempt, and they have generally proven to be politically loyal to him. Many were supporters of the democratic movement in the Russian parliament. The exceptions to this are found in oblasts where elections were held in April 1993 and in a few other districts. Executive leadership in the republics is quite another matter. By the end of 1993, sixteen of the republics had used their right to form their own governments to create presidential systems and had elected presidents, ten of them by the end of 1991. The other five republics retained a soviet style parliamentary system in which the parliamentary body elects a council of ministers to govern. Significantly, three of these kept the name "Supreme Soviet," including Mordovia which had opted for a presidential system and then switched back. With respect to comparing democratization in the republics and the oblasts, it is clear that the choice of presidential systems created strong executive authority in most of the republics. Even before Yeltsin abolished the soviets in October 1993, parliaments in the republics had less ability to exert legislative authority than did the soviets in the oblasts. His abolition of the soviets further eroded whatever independence they enjoyed. Paradoxically, however, by further strengthening the control of executives in the republics Yeltsin may have given even greater power to his opponents.[74]

Aside from the fact that most have been elected rather than appointed leaders in the republics also differ greatly from those in the oblasts in their political backgrounds: fifteen of them were high-ranking party officials, usually obkom first secretaries; one was the chair of an oblast ispolkom. Two (the presidents of Chechnya and Ingushetia) come from the military; one (Chuvashia) had a judicial background and one (Bashkiria) was director of an oil refinery. The President of Kalmykia, Kirsan Iliumzhinov, is a thirty-two year old millionaire entrepreneur who was previously expelled from the CPSU for promoting drug use. Iliumzhinov, who has expressed his desire to eventually restore a Kalmyk khanate in the Russia Federation, runs his republic like an autocrat and scheduled an election to "President for Life" on October 15, 1995.[75] In generalizing about whether democratization has proceeded more rapidly in the republics or in the oblasts, it is undeniably true that most republican leaders were popularly elected while those in the oblasts were not. Yet ironically, most of the elites in the republics were high ranking members of the old nomenklatura; this is not the case in the oblasts where most of the leadership was appointed from the ranks of the democratic movement. On the whole candidates supported by reformist parties have not done well in the republics. One exception was B. Guslianikov, the President of Mordovia and the candidate of "Democratic Russia" who was elected in December 1991 only to have his post abolished in the wake of scandal in 1993. The December 12, 1993 election in Kalmykia was more typical: Iliumzhinov got 75 percent of the vote while the candidate of Russia's Choice could only muster 19 percent.[76]

Why have the members of the old party-state apparat done so well, comparatively speaking, in the republics? The answer has a lot to do with the political composition of voters in these areas. Data from the December 1993 elections to the 225 seats in the Russian State Duma based on party lists tell us something about partisan preferences in the republics.[77] Republics giving relatively high levels of support for reformist parties in 1993 included Tuva, Karelia, Kabardino-Balkaria, Gorno-Altai and Komi.[78] However, this relatively high level of support was because Sergei Shakrai's Party of Russian Unity and Accord (PRUA) did well in these republics. Shakrai had campaigned heavily on greater autonomy for the regions and the preservation of favorable treatment in the ethnic republics. Only in Karelia did Russia's Choice win a plurality of votes (22 percent). In contrast, among those regions giving the highest relative support to the Communist and Agrarian parties were the republics of Dagestan, Karachai-Cherksass, North Ossetia, Bashkortostan (formerly Bashkiria), Adygeia, Kabardino-Balkaria, Chuvashia, and Mordovia. Only in Karelia did the "anti-reform" parties fail to do well. Not surprisingly, given his emphasis on Russian nationalism and the need to end special treatment of the republics, Zhirinovsky's Liberal Democratic Party of Russia (LPDR) did badly in the republics.[79] In attempting to explain why, except for Karelia, democratic parties did poorly and communists did well in the republics, two reasons suggest themselves: first, the republics are comparatively more rural than urban and the communists do better in rural areas; second, the old communist elites are at the forefront of the struggle against Yeltsin and the "center" which separatist-minded voters in the republics see as the enemy, as a force for control by Moscow.

Macroregional analysis

So far in this chapter attention has been focused on individual units of analysis in Russia's regions, especially oblasts and republics. But what if political results from these units are aggregated? After all, since the beginning of 1989 there have been no less than four federal campaigns, three national referenda and two sets of local elections. Are there political patterns that emerge which can contribute to answering whether some Russian regions are more democratic? One of the first attempts to apply macroregional analysis appeared after in the 1989 elections to the USSR Congress of People's Deputies. The authors of the study found a clear division between voting patterns in the north and south of the USSR bisected by the fifty-fifth parallel. "The fifty-fifth parallel stood out in the 1989 elections to the CPD. It was striking that communist party leaders were defeated in nearly all the regions north of that parallel while in the regions to the south of it, nearly all of them were elected."[80]

Using results from the presidential election of 1991 and the referendum of April 1993, a team of researchers led by Aleksandr Sobyanin confirmed this general finding of a north-south division for Russian elections. The 1991 and 1993 elections both centered on support or opposition to Yeltsin and his reforms. In general he received support in: Moscow and St. Petersburg and the industrial regions between them; the northern regions of the country; most regions in western Siberia; and the far east. He was opposed in: the central economic regions (oblasts) south and east of Moscow including the Volga economic region; the republics of the north caucasus; the republics of the middle Volga region (except Tatarstan); and three oblasts in the southern Urals plus Novosibirsk. Overall, with very few exceptions, the regions in which support for Yeltsin was lowest all fell between the forty-ninth and fifty-fifth parallels of southern Russia.[81]

Why is there this split between a politically "progressive" north and a "conservative" south? Using data from all elections from 1989–95, Nikolai Petrov argues that we can speak of a well developed "electoral landscape" today in Russia. The key to understanding this landscape is voter turnout. Comparing data on levels of turnout for these elections by region over time leads Petrov to two conclusions. First, the more politically active and involved the population is, the more likely it is to turn away from electoral participation which is associated with the totalitarian past. In practice, this means lower voter turnout in urban areas where there are more well educated (and more democratic) voters and higher turnout in rural areas (which are more likely to support communist and nationalist candidates). As Petrov observes, "Moscow and St. Petersburg, undoubtedly leaders when it comes to political liberalization in the country, demonstrated minimal interest in electoral participation. Maximal interest was found in the agrarian central and southern countryside (*glubinka*)."[82] The political differences between the cites and countryside can be seen in data analyzed by Petrov from thirteen Russian regions for the December 1993 party list elections to the state Duma. In Moscow and St. Petersburg, candidates from "democratic" parties (Russia's Choice, Yabloko and the RDDR) got 55 percent of the vote with communists (CPRF and Agrarians) getting 11 percent and nationalists 15 percent. In oblast capitals, the corresponding figures were: democrats, 38 percent; communists, 12 percent; nationalists, 20 percent. But in the rural districts (raions) the outcome was reversed: democrats, 19 percent; communists, 30 percent, nationalists, 27 percent.

Petrov's second conclusion is that this urban-rural distribution of voting patterns by region is "stable, continuous and predictable" though it cannot be used to predict the outcome of given elections. These conclusions lead Petrov to modify the north-south political dichotomy somewhat. Below the fifty-fifth parallel he sees regional subdivisions: a "revanchist-communist southwest"; a more moderate European south; a "staunchly conservative" northern Caucasus; and southern Siberia. Above in the north, he sees a progressive non-agricultural belt stretching from St. Petersburg through to the oil-producing districts of Siberia. In between he posits an "interstitial strip" varying in its political sympathies. The point is this: Rural voters are as likely to vote more heavily and to vote "conservatively" in the north as in the south, but because there are far more rural areas in the south, the pattern of southern conservatism emerges more clearly there. Moreover, because rural voters vote in greater numbers and proportionately more for nationalist and communist candidates, Petrov foresees what he calls the "progressively growing ruralization" of Russian political life. Implicit in his assessment is the possibility that regional Russian politics may become less democratic, not more.

Data from the party list voting to the December 1993 State Duma were analyzed regionally by Darrell Slider and his colleagues and reveal yet another perspective on political preferences in Russia's regions. Agreeing that the dichotomization of the Russian political spectrum between communists and anti-communists worked well before these elections, the authors argue that post-Soviet Russian reality is more complex. Factor analysis of voting for parties in eighty-seven regions yields two dimensions: economic liberalism vs. state control over the economy define one of these; support for strong regions vs. support for a strong center defines the other. Plotting one dimension on a vertical axis and the other horizontally yields four quadrants in which each of the eighty-seven regions can be located. Doing so enables the authors to tease out regional differences in support for Zhirinovsky's anti-democratic LDPR on the one hand, and the Democratic Party of Russia (Travkin) and PRUA (Shakrai) on the other. Thus although all three were located near the center of the of the economic dimension, LDPR supporters were on the opposite side of the spectrum defined by a strong center vs. regionalism. This approach allows for a more precise identification of the regional basis for Zhirinovsky's support, all of which (with the exception of Mordovia) cluster in one quadrant: ethnically Russian border areas.[83] The study concludes with the prediction that the LDPR would not do well in future regional elections, but that candidates from the old communist nomenklatura would leading the authors to warn that "future attempts by Moscow to carry out reforms could meet insurmountable opposition when local administrations and legislatures are legitimately controlled by communist and agrarian anti-reformers."[84]

Conclusions

A minimalist definition of democracy describes it as "a political system in which the formal and actual leaders of the government are chosen within predictable intervals through a set of elections based on multiple candidacies, secret balloting and other procedures that ensure real opportunities for competition."[85] To what extent can regional politics in Russia in 1995 be regarded as democratic? Certainly, if the standard of comparison is the old Soviet system, then a great deal of progress has been made in that direction. For one thing there is real electoral competition. Unlike elections before 1990, when only one candidate ran for each seat, multiple candidacies are now the rule. Moreover, in place of the inflated figure of 99.9 percent turnout claimed by the old system, popular participation in these elections is no longer mandatory, but genuine. There are other reasons for optimism about the development of regional democracy in Russia. Studies of Russian political culture, regionally, as well as nationally, suggest that there is far more support for democratic values and institutions in Russia than those anticipating a persistence of authoritarianism among Russians would have predicted. Moreover, these attitudes have remained fairly stable despite the Russian government's flawed economic performance.[86] There has also been some institutional improvement. Legislatures openly, and often critically, debate the policies of local executive officials. Election laws have become simpler, replacing complicated procedures which left voters confused with simple majority election requiring 25 percent participation by the eligible electorate instead of 50 percent. Finally, there is now legislation enabling political parties to register and compete, thus opening up the possibility that voter choices can be more meaningfully structured.

Alongside these positive developments, however, there are some real problems with democracy in Russia's regions. If the stage of democratic construction can be said to have proceeded with some success, the stage of democratic consolidation has proven less so. To begin with, political parties have been slow to develop on the regional level. Bruce Parrott states: "To the degree that parties structure social forces and channel them into peaceful political competition, a party system based on well-institutionalized parties seems indispensable to the consolidation of democracy."[87] But as he also points out not all multiparty systems are conducive to democratic consolidation. The one clearly antidemocratic party in Russia today, the LDPR, has not so far made major inroads in the regions, but this may be due more to a lack of organization than a lack of potential supporters. The only parties which do have effective organization in the regions are the communist parties, but their electoral success has been largely limited to the rural south. Parties favoring political and economic reform are not well organized and there is little broad support for them in the regions. What success they have enjoyed has been in Moscow and St. Petersburg and to a lesser degree in oblast capitals. Disturbingly, however, it is in the cities, where those most likely to support democracy and democratic parties are found, that electoral participation is lowest. In the rural areas participation is much greater, but the voters there are much more apt to vote for communists or nationalists. One other problem with democracy in the regions is the continued growth of executive authority at the expense of the legislatures, which are, after all, the institutions intended to represent the popular will. In democracies, government should be limited by a system of checks and balances. In Russia's regions today the trend has been in exactly the opposite direction.

In some ways, democratization in Russia may have proceeded more rapidly on the national level than locally. For one thing, the use of party list voting to elect half of the State Duma in 1993 provided a basis for the emergence of real national parties. For another, there is evidence to suggest that the State Duma has operated far more effectively as a legislature than anybody predicted it would at the time of the election.[88] Will regional Russian politics "catch up" with these trends? As the definition of democracy cited earlier suggests, much depends on the nature of upcoming elections. The elections to the State Duma of December 17, 1995 may accelerate the development of partisan competition locally. As data from Yaroslavl cited in the chapter suggest, there may now be a basis for partisan support for candidates that did not exist before the 1993 Duma election. Data from Yaroslavl also suggest that although turnout for local elections in 1994 was a feeble 26 percent, the figure for those reportedly willing to participate regularly in local elections is around 40 percent, similar to what one finds in the United States. In the December 1995 elections to the State Duma, turnout in Yaroslavl reached 66 percent. Almost certainly, however, the most important election as far as the further development of regional democracy in Russia is concerned will be the elections for governor scheduled for December 1996. If these elections take place, they will mark a major step forward in consolidating democracy in Russia's regions.

NOTES

This chapter is a revised version of a paper prepared for the Workshop on Postcommunist Democratization and Political Participation in Russia, Ukraine, Belarus, and Moldova, which was held on November 16–17, 1995 at The Johns Hopkins School of Advanced International Relations in Washington, DC. The author is very grateful to Bruce Parrott, Karen Dawisha, and Ilya Prizel for their careful reading of the first draft and for their many helpful suggestions about how it might be improved. He would also like to thank the Carnegie Corporation of New York, IREX, and the National Council for Soviet and East European Research for financial support over the last several years which made possible the research on which this chapter is based.

1 Among others in a vast literature, see Dankwart Rustow, "Transitions to Democracy: Towards a Dynamic Model," *Comparative Politics* (April 1970); Juan J. Linz, "Transitions to Democracy," *Washington Quarterly* (Summer 1990); Philippe C. Schmitter and Terry Lynn Karl, "The Conceptual Travels of Transitologists and Consolidologists," *Slavic Review* (Spring 1994); and Larry Diamond, "Toward Democratic Consolidation," *Journal of Democracy* (July 1994). The definitions of these phases used in this paper generally conform to those offered in the "Revised Research Guidelines for Country Study Writers" provided to participants in the Democratization Project in a letter dated 18 May 1995.

2 This includes not only government at the oblast and republic level (called institutions of "state power"), but at the city and district level (officially referred to as local self-government) as well. When differentiating levels of government is necessary, the appropriate terminology will be used. Although most of the paper focuses on regional politics in the oblasts, differences between republican and oblast politics are also addressed.

3 For a detailed analysis of how the intergovernmental fiscal system works in Russia, see Christine I. Wallich, "Russia and the Challenge of Fiscal Federalism" (Washington, DC: The World Bank, 1995).

4 Yaroslavl oblast is located in central Russia and has a population of about 1.5 million. Its capital, Yaroslavl, is an industrial city of about 650,000 people located about 200 miles northeast of Moscow on what is known as the "Golden Ring," referring to ancient Russian political and religious centers surrounding Moscow. To what extent Yaroslavl is representative of other regions of Russia is difficult to say. However, Yaroslavl is overwhelmingly Russian (95 percent) and there is no *a priori* reason to believe that it is so far out of the mainstream of Russian regions as to constitute a unique case. On the contrary, by such measures as size, education, age, percent of the population engaged in industry and other indicators commonly used in determining comparability, Yaroslavl appears to be similar to other regions of central Russia. In any case, the author's purpose in focusing on Yaroslavl is to show how the reforms of regional politics worked out in practice and to generate hypotheses which may be tested later for other regions.

5 For this reason this paper does not dwell separately on what politics in Yaroslavl were like prior to 1990. This information can be found in the author's chapter, "The Evolution of Local Legislatures in Russia: The Case of Yaroslavl," in *Democratization in Russia: the Development of Legislative Institutions*, ed. Jeffrey W. Hahn (Armonk, NY: M. E. Sharpe, 1996).

6 Jeffrey W. Hahn, *Soviet Grassroots: Citizen Participation in Local Soviet Government* (Princeton, NJ: Princeton University Press, 1988), p. 86. In addition to this treatment of the old soviets, see Theodore H. Friedgut, *Political Participation in the USSR* (Princeton, NJ: Princeton University Press, 1979). The description of local government under the old regime is taken from these sources.

7 Hahn, *Soviet Grassroots*, p. 194.

8 For more on the role and powers of the obkom first secretary, see Jerry Hough, *The Soviet Prefects* (Cambridge, MA: Harvard University Press, 1969). Fedor I. Loshchenkov, the obkom first secretary in Yaroslavl from 1964–86, was widely, if discreetly, known as "Tsar Fedor." Nothing of significance was done in Yaroslavl without his approval.

9 A more detailed analysis of these reforms can be found in Jeffrey W. Hahn, "Power to the Soviets?" *Problems of Communism* 38, no. 1 (1989).

10 According to Gerald Pomper, *Elections in America* (New York: Dodd, Mead, 1968), pp. 262–66, at least six requirements need to be met before an election can be regarded as truly free: meaningful choices; the freedom to know and discuss the choices; a manageable number of clear choices; the equal weighting of votes; free registration of choices (a secret ballot); and accurate registration, counting, and reporting.

11 Zakon RSFSR, "O vyborakh narodnykh deputatov mestnykh sovetov narodnykh deputov RSFSR," 27 October 1989.

12 In city elections, sixty-five members of the old party–state apparat were on the ballot on 4 March 1990; only twenty-seven of the 179 seated for the first organizational session of the city soviet which met on 10 May were from this group. In oblast elections, apparatchiki competed in 102 districts, and although thirty-one of them lost in the first round, in the end they did rather better than in the city, electing forty-seven by the time of the first session. Overall, however, some voters do appear to have exercised a degree of choice by voting *against* candidates from the old elite.

13 The YPF originated as a protest movement against the election of obkom first secretary Loshchenkov to the Nineteenth CPSU Conference in the summer of 1988 (*Izvestiia*, 18 June 1988). Although the movement was initiated mostly by those in the Party committed to Gorbachev's policies of perestroika, it became radicalized over time and by the time of the local elections, it was openly campaigning against the local Party establishment, even though four of its five co-chairs were Party members (*Izvestiia*, 10 January 1990). Although splintered by the emergence of a more radical group called The Movement for Popular Rule, the YPF had managed to elect Boris Shamshev to the USSR Congress of People's Deputies and had become broadly affiliated with the Inter-regional Group of Deputies (of which Shamshev was a member) and the national democratic movement, "Democratic Russia."

14 See Gavin Helf and Jeffrey Hahn, "Old Dogs and New Tricks: Party Elites in the Russian Regional Elections of 1990," *Slavic Review* 51, no. 3 (November 1992), 518.

15 The other three requirements for free elections identified by Pomper – equal weighting of votes, free registration of choices, and accurate registration, counting and reporting of ballots – appear to have been largely fulfilled in Yaroslavl.

16 For Moscow, see Timothy J. Colton, "The Politics of Democratization: The Moscow Elections of 1990," *Soviet Economy* 6, no. 4 (1990); on Leningrad, see Josephine Andrews and Alexandra Vacroux, "Political Change in Leningrad: The Elections of 1990," in *Local Power and Post-Soviet Politics*, ed. Theodore H. Friedgut and Jeffrey W. Hahn (Armonk, NY: M. E. Sharpe, 1994).

17 Unlike the old soviets, however, the new soviets elected their own leadership, including a chair and vice chair, and had their own staff. Because chairs of the executive were also elected, the result was that there were effectively two local leaders. The potential for conflict between the two was one of the reasons cited by Yeltsin for abolishing the soviets and replacing them with a directly elected executive.

18 See his workshop paper, "Parties, Political Participation, and Postcommunist Democratization," prepared for the Workshop on Comparative Analysis of Postcommunist Democratization and Political Participation (unpublished manuscript, 9 May 1995), p. 4.

19 The office was "temporary" in that it was supposed to last only until Yeltsin completed his economic reform, something which he was given a year to do by decree at the fifth Russian Congress of People's Deputies held in Fall 1991.

20 Yeltsin's response to parliament took the form of a decree issued 15 July 1992, strengthening the institution by placing it directly under his authority, by increasing its staff and financial base, and by promising to give it permanent legal status.

21 The concept of the "glava administratsii" (chief of administration) was legislatively introduced first at the municipal level of government (cities and below) in the "Law on Local Self-Government of the RSFSR" (Zakon o mestnom samoupravlenii v RSFSR) adopted on June 6, 1991. This law remained in effect until September 1, 1995, when it was replaced by the Russian Federation "Law on General Principles of the Organization of Local Self-Government in the Russian Federation" ("Zakon ob obshchikh printsipakh organizatsii mestnogo samoupravleniia v RF," *Rossiiskaia gazeta*, 1 September 1995, pp. 4–6). The only legislation to the end of 1995 defining the role of the "glava administratsii" at the oblast level appears to be presidential decree No. 75, issued on 22 August 1991 (see *Vedomosti RSFSR*, no. 34, item 1146, pp. 1422–24). Although this has since been amended (see especially presidential decree No. 1723 of 22 October 1993), the relations it establishes between the executive and legislative branches is patterned after that found in the Law on Local Self-Government.

22 See Julia Wishnevsky, "Problems of Russian Regional Leadership," *RFE/RL Research Report*, 13 May 1994, p. 8. Wishnevsky argues that the compromise was undertaken because of "pressure" from regional governors who sought to complete their terms of office and that parliament wanted to at least "neutralize" them, if not enlist their support. This may have been a miscalculation on

parliament's part, however, because in the few regions where elections *were* held (in April 1993), Yeltsin's opponents did rather well, electing governors in the southern "red-brown" oblasts of Orel, Cheliabinsk, Bryansk, Penza and Lipetsk, and in Krasnoyarsk Krai. Nation-wide elections for governors might have produced greater regional support for parliament in its struggle with the president.

23 See Elizabeth Teague, "Yeltsin Disbands the Soviets," *RFE/RL Research Report*, 29 October 1993, p. 1; and, by the same author, "North-South Divide: Yeltsin and Russia's Provincial Leaders" *RFE/RL Research Report*, 26 November 1993, pp. 10–11.

24 Josephine Andrews and Kathryn Stoner-Weiss, "Regionalism and Reform: Evidence from the Russian Provinces," *Post-Soviet Affairs* 11, no. 4 (October–December 1995). The authors argue that regional elites who support both economic reform and object to how the center implements it are merely reflecting the views of their constituents. Additional data from oblast and city deputies in five regions of central Russia on this question are reported in Jeffrey W. Hahn, "Attitudes Toward Reform Among Provincial Russian Politicians," *Post-Soviet Affairs* 9, no. 1 (1993). On p. 84, the author concluded that "there seems to be more support than not among the deputies for market and democratic reforms."

25 The discussion here is largely limited to politics in all the federal subdivisions except republics which were not required to take action in accordance with these decrees. Political institutions in the twenty-one republics differ significantly from those in the oblasts. For example, the size of republic legislatures varies from 32 to 148. These differences are discussed later in this chapter.

26 For further discussion of the legislative basis for the new local governments see Elizabeth Teague, "Russia's Local Elections Begin," *RFE/RL Research Report*, 18 February 1994, pp. 1–4, and Darrell Slider, "Elections in Russia's Regions," a paper presented at the Annual Meeting of the American Association for the Advancement of Slavic Studies (AAASS), Washington, DC, 28 October 1995. As both authors note, some variation in how the elections were actually conducted was allowed.

27 On this point see Julia Wishnevsky, "Moscow's Policy Towards the Regions in View of the Forthcoming Federal Elections," a paper presented at the Annual Meeting of the AAASS, Washington, DC, 28 October 1995. See also Slider, "Elections in Russia's Regions," p. 4.

28 Central Election Commission Report of 7 April 1994 as noted in Slider, "Elections in Russia's Regions," p. 3.

29 The 22 October 1993 decree, "Regulations Governing the Basic Principles of Organizing the Bodies of State Power Among the Members of the Russian Federation," was published in *Rossiiskie vesti*, 26 October 1993. See also the discussion in Aleksei Glubotsky, Aleksei Markhin, and Nikita Tiukov, *Organy vlasti sub"ektov Rossiiskoi Federatsii* (Moscow: Panorama, 1995), p. 9.

30 These generalizations are based on reports in *Izvestiia*, 2 February 1994, p. 1 and 3 February 1994, p. 1; *Segodnia*, 22 March 1994, p. 2 and 26 November 1994, p. 2; and also Slider, "Russia's Regional Elections." See also Julia Wishnevsky, "Problems of Russian Regional Leadership," *RFE/RL Research Report*, 13 May 1994, pp. 6–13 and Robert W. Orttung, "A Government Divided Against Itself," *Transition*, 13 May 1995, pp. 48–51.

31 Donna Bahry and Lucan Way, "Citizen Activism in the Russian Transition," *Post-Soviet Affairs* 10 (1994), pp. 350–52.

32 See Leonid Smirniagin's analysis of the elections in *Izvestiia*, 23 March 1994, p. 1–2.

33 The author thanks Ilya Prizel for sharing these observations in a written memo. Professor Prizel makes the point that many big city mayors, and especially Moscow Mayor Luzhkov, purchase large quantities of imported food, further impoverishing the countryside and aggravating the rural bias in favor of the communists. As Jerry Hough has argued, however, we really don't know very much about the conservative views of rural voters because we lack good research. See Jerry Hough, "The Russian Election of 1993: Public Attitudes Towards Economic Reform and Democratization," *Post-Soviet Affairs* 10, no. 1 (1994), p. 26.

34 Typical in this regard was the legislative election in Penza (held 1 February 1994, one of the earliest), in which forty of forty-five seats went to the former nomenklatura candidates. See Elizabeth Teague, "Russia's Local Elections Begin," pp. 1–2. In Orlov oblast (in one of the last elections, held 26 February 1995) candidates of the Communist Party took ten of eleven seats in the legislative assembly. The oblast governor, Yegor Stroyev, was formerly the obkom first secretary. See Yelena Tregubova's article in *Segodnia*, 28 February 1995, p. 2. Stroyev was one of the few governors elected in April 1993. In January 1996 he was chosen chair of the Russian Council of the Federation.

35 See Slider, "Elections in Russia's Regions," pp. 6–8. He cites the figures of 29 percent for administrators and 24 percent for directors. Similar figures (31 percent and 21 percent, respectively) are reported by Lawrence R. Robertson based on data gathered somewhat later. See Lawrence R. Robertson, "Unstable Regions or Center: Separatism and Centrism in the Russian Federation, 1991–93," a paper presented to the Annual Meeting of the AAASS, Washington, DC, 28 October 1995, p. 23.

36 The statute (*polozhenie*) on elections, "O vyborakh deputatov gosudarstvennoi dumy Yaroslavskoi oblasti," was published in the regional newspaper, *Zolotoe kol'tso*, on 21 January 1994. A similar statute for the city was amended to incorporate these provisions. *Zolotoe kol'tso*, 25 January 1994. The Yaroslavl elections were organized in accordance with Yeltsin's decree of 27 October 1993 establishing rules to be used throughout Russia. Some regional variation, however, was permitted. Thus, in a few oblasts multi-member rather than single member districts were used (Penza, Sverdlovsk, Tambov, Kamchatka, Krasnodar, Krasnoyarsk). Some, including St. Petersburg, held runoff elections and a very few employed party list voting for some of the deputies (Saratov, the Republic of Tuva). Slider, "Elections in Russia's Regions," p. 4–5.

37 The Communist Party, although the best organized, enjoys support of only about 13 percent of the population, the percentage of the vote the Communists got in the 1993 party list elections to the Federal Duma. In an interview with the author on 15 June 1994 the leader of the Ziuganov faction of the Communist Party in Yaroslavl, V. A. Gordeev, claimed 4,000 members and organizations in each of the districts in the oblast. According to him they hold regular meetings and collect 1 percent of members' salaries as dues. He acknowledged that many of the Party's supporters came from among pensioners attached to the old communist

party, but claimed that many younger persons had also joined. He insisted that his party was not interested in restoring the old Soviet order and expressed nothing but contempt for Zhirinovsky and his followers among the nationalist right. Confirmation for this view of the Communist Party in Yaroslavl came from others, including the journalist Alexander Tsvetkov, who indicated in an interview on 17 June 1995 that the Communist Party is indeed well organized and active, attracting about 4,000 supporters to a public meeting in May 1995. The "democratic" parties, by comparison, were very weak. Tsvetkov, who holds seats in the city and oblast legislatures, thought that the party was split between what he regarded as "new" communists who support Ziuganov and the more "anti-system" variety who identify with Viktor Anpilov.

38 Among those elected were: enterprise directors (seven in the oblast; six in the city); heads of administration from elsewhere in the region (five in the oblast; one in the city); and professionals from medicine or education (two in the oblast; ten in the city). There was also one journalist and one Father Superior. The author thanks Brian Sloyer, a graduate student in political science at Villanova University, for his help in analyzing the 1994 election data from Yaroslavl.

39 Research conducted by a team of British and Russian specialists before and after the 1993 elections showed that those willing to identify with a party had grown from about one in five to one in three. As the authors of this study note, "While not high by Western standards, this level of party identification represents significant progress from the situation before the elections." Matthew Wyman et al., "Public Opinion, Parties and Voters in the December 1993 Russian Elections," *Europe–Asia Studies* 47, no. 4 (1995), 604. This tendency towards the development of party attachments may have been strengthened by the elections to the Duma in December 1995, when four rather than eight parties exceeded the required 5 percent threshold in party list voting.

40 Research conducted in the city of Yaroslavl in December 1994 by the Yaroslavl Center for the Study of Public Opinion and Sociological Research showed the following levels of support for national parties: Yabloko, 31 percent; Russia's Choice, 20 percent; the Communist Party of Russia, 13 percent; the Democratic Party of Russia, 10 percent; Zhirinovsky's Liberal Democratic Party, 9 percent, and Shakrai's "PRUA" party, 5 percent. Data were published in a report dated May 1995 and entitled "Mnenie naseleniia gorod Yaroslavlia i Yaroslavlskoi oblasti po obshchestvenno-politicheskim i sotsial'no-ekonomicheskim problemam v dinamike (1990–95)."

The 1993 figure comes from a fully representative sample survey of Yaroslavl voters conducted by the author in 1993. It is worth noting that in the same survey 54 percent of the respondents thought a multiparty system was needed (24 percent thought it was not). Obviously there appears to be a difference for Russian voters between supporting a multiparty system and supporting a party. Part of the explanation probably lies with the fact that until December 1993, elections in Russia had not been held on a partisanship basis. The drop in the course of a year or so from 78 percent to 30 percent among those not supporting a party in turn suggests that the 1993 elections to the Russian Duma may have marked an important turning point in the development of a multiparty system in Russia.

41 The author thanks Bruce Parrott for this insight. As he correctly points out in his reviewer notes, there was a lower level of partisanship in races for the single member district portion of the seats in the State Duma.

42 These data were provided to the author by Tatiana P. Rumiantseva, Director of the Yaroslavl Center for the Study of Public Opinion and Sociological Research during a visit to Yaroslavl in June 1995.

43 Decree No. 1186, "On the Powers of the Representatives of the Russian Federation President in the Russian Federation Members," *Rossiiskie vesti*, 16 June 1994, p. 2. By the beginning of 1995, there were presidential representatives in sixty-eight of eighty-nine member units of the Russian Federation.

44 The new presidential representative, Yurii Afanasevich Zaramenskii, replaced Vladimir G. Varukhin, who was relieved of his duties by Yeltsin on 29 December 1994. Varukhin had apparently accused some key members of the governor's staff of impropriety and lost the ensuing power struggle with him. Zaramenskii was interviewed by the author on 14 June 1995.

45 See for example, the letter of resignation by the presidential representative in Tambov, V. Davituliani, in *Izvestiia*, 5 February 1994, p. 2. In it he notes that Yeltsin's chief of staff, Sergei Filatov, in a conference of regional presidential representatives on 31 January 1994, told the representatives that they were "forbidden" to publicly criticize local executives. In Yaroslavl, similar tensions led to the removal of that oblast's presidential representative, Vladimir Varukhin, by presidential decree on 29 December 1994. Varukhin had been a member of parliament with close ties to "Democratic Russia."

46 William A. Clark, "Central Authority and Local Governance in Post-Communist Russia," unpublished paper presented at the twenty-sixth Annual Meeting of the AAASS, Philadelphia, PA, 17–20 November 1994, p. 18.

47 The immediate cause of this decree appears to have been a meeting of the Union of Governors in Yaroslavl in September 1994 at which the holding of elections in 1996 (when their terms expire) was advocated. At least one of the governors – Evgeni Nazdratenko of Primorsky Krai – planned to go ahead even earlier. The elections were canceled on Yeltsin's orders a few days before they were to be held. See the article by Natalia Gorodetskaia and Elena Tregubova in *Segodnia*, 5 October 1994, p. 2.

The only exception to this decree prior to 17 December 1995 was the election for governor held in Sverdlovsk oblast on 21 August by way of an exception from the president. It was won by the chair of oblast duma, Eduard Rossel, who beat the candidate supported by "Our Home is Russia," Prime Minister Chernomyrdin's "party of power." See *Segodnia*, 22 and 23 August 1995, also translated in the *Current Digest of the Post-Soviet Press* (hereafter *CDPSP*) 47, no. 34 (1995), pp. 14–16. On 18 September 1995 a presidential decree further postponing gubernatorial elections was announced. It will be discussed below.

48 This was presumably so even for the handful of governors who, like Yegor Stroyev in Orlov oblast, had been elected to office in April 1993.

49 This quote comes from a useful discussion of this process in Vladimir Lysenko, "A 'Little Constitution' Can't be At Odds With The Big One," *Rossiikie vesti*, 18 April 1995, p. 2. (Translated in *CDPSP* 47, no. 16 (1995), 8–9).

50 Tsvetkov's description, which appeared in *Kommersant-Daily* on 30 May 1995, was also translated in *CDPSP* 47, no. 22 (1995), 16.

51 Born in 1947, Lisitsyn was elected as chair of the ispolkom in the city Rybinsk in May 1990. He was supported by the democratic movement. He was appointed governor by Yeltsin on 3 December 1991 in place of V.A. Kovalev,who had been elected ispolkom chair over Lisitsyn by the more conservative oblast soviet in May 1990. Kovalev was the standard-bearer of the old nomenklatura and sided with the putchists in August 1991. As a result, he was removed from office by Yeltsin. Lisitsyn had been a member of the Russian Supreme Soviet and on December 12, 1993 was elected to the Federation Council as a candidate of Russia's Choice.

52 This view was given in an interview with the author in Yaroslavl on 17 June 1995. His view was echoed by other journalists interviewed by the author who suggested that the lack of free media is true elsewhere in Russia's regions.

53 The use of this term to describe the obkom first secretary's position in the old Soviet system can be found in the now classic work by Jerry Hough, *The Soviet Prefects* (Cambridge, MA: Harvard University Press, 1969).

54 See Clark, "Central Authority and Local Governance in Post-Communist Russia," p. 23. Clark also sees some differences from obkom secretaries of the past: governors are characteristically more likely to be indigenous and technically proficient (pp. 11–13).

55 Yeltsin has been reluctant to use the power he has claimed for himself; until January 1996, no governors had been appointed, punished or removed following the decree of October 1994. Moreover, there had been elections of governors not supported by him, including Eduard Rossel in Sverdlosk oblast. However, on 22 January 1996, Yeltsin dismissed the governors of Chita, Ivanovo, and Kaluga oblasts, according to *OMRI Daily Digest,* 24 January 1996. As the report notes, this leaves the regions affected with one representative instead of two in the Federation Council because elections for governors will not take place until December 1996. Earlier in January, Yeltsin had also dismissed six presidential representatives (Kursk, Smolensk, Novosibirsk, Bryansk oblasts; Krasnodar Krai; Agino-Buryat okrug). See ibid., 15 January and 24 January 1996.

56 Led by the deputies of the CPRF faction, the State Duma decided on 8 October 1995 to appeal the decree to the Constitutional Court. Among other reasons, the Communist deputies had won twenty-two out of twenty-four seats in an election to the city duma in Volgograd on 1 October and had every reason to believe they would do well elsewhere in municipal elections. The results of elections in Volgograd were reported in *OMRI Daily Digest,* 2 October 1995; the Duma's appeal to the Constitutional Court was reported in ibid., 9 October 1995.

57 The decree is translated in the Foreign Broadcast Information Service, *Daily Report: Central Eurasia* (hereafter *FBIS-SOV*), 19 September 1995, pp. 1–3.

58 Data reported by Jerry Hough from a nationwide survey conducted in 1993 found that 73 percent wanted direct elections for governors with only 5 percent supporting presidential appointment. Hough, "The Russian Election of 1993," p. 13. See also Wishnevsky, "Russia's Policy Towards the Regions," p. 6.

59 Public pressure would appear to support the decentralization of authority to the regions. In research reported by Jerry Hough, when respondents were asked whether the "center" or the regions could better act to improve the economy, 19 percent opted for the center, 37 percent favored joint control with the regions,

and 31 percent advocated strong regional administrations (13 percent were not responsive). Hough, "The Russian Election of 1993," p. 12.

60 In addition to those in Moscow, Nizhny Novgorod and Omsk oblasts, elections were authorized for 17 December 1995 by way of exception in Belgorod, Novgorod, Novosibirsk, Orenburg, Primorsky Krai, Tambov, Tomsk, Tver and Yaroslavl (for a total of thirteen gubernatorial elections in 1995 including Sverdlovsk.) Of the twelve elections held on 17 December, ten were won by incumbents. In only two of them were candidates elected who were supported by the Communist Party (all from the south): Mukha in Novosibirsk and Ryabov in Tambov. The rest could be regarded as reformists and had been appointed by Yeltsin or ran as candidates of the party of power, "Our Home is Russia." For a useful summary of these elections see Marc Zlotnik, "Russia's Governors: All the President's Men?" paper prepared for the Conference on Hyper Federalism: Russian Decentralization in Comparative Perspective, Princeton University, 9–10 February 1996.

61 Walter Lacqueur, *The Long Road to Freedom* (NY: Scribners, 1989), p. 8. For a more extensive review of the cultural continuity thesis, see Jeffrey W. Hahn, "Continuity and Change in Russian Political Culture," *British Journal of Political Science* 21 (1991), pp. 393–421.

62 Robert V. Daniels, *Is Russia Reformable?* (Boulder, CO: Westview Press, 1988), p. 39.

63 For an interesting (and critical) analysis of this argument by a Russian specialist, see Grigorii Vainshtein, "The Authoritarian Idea in the Public Consciousness and Political Life of Contemporary Russia," *The Journal of Communist Studies and Transition Politics* 11, no. 3 (September 1995).

64 S. Frederick Starr, "A Usable Past," *The New Republic*, 15 May 1989. For a more extended treatment, see *The Legacy of History in Russia and the New States of Eurasia*, ed. S. Frederick Starr (Armonk, NY: M. E. Sharpe, 1994).

65 These strands include the idea of a "constrained" autocracy, a Russian Orthodox Church independent in its own sphere from the Russian state, and an "enlightened" Russian patriotism. See Nicolai Petro, *The Rebirth of Russian Democracy: An Interpretation of Political Culture* (Cambridge, MA: Harvard University Press, 1995).

66 There has been a good deal of criticism directed at the use of survey research in Russia based on methodological grounds, including some cautionary remarks by the author. Some of the criticism was justified in the early stages of doing field research in Russia by the lack of qualified specialists and of quality control. Much of this criticism is no longer valid. For a discussion of the validity of using survey research in Russia and a review of the literature see Wyman, "Public Opinion, Parties and Voters," pp. 591–94.

67 These generalizations represent the author's best effort to summarize a substantial number of studies that have appeared on the topic of political culture in the former communist countries since 1990. The degree to which any of the following authors would accept any or all of these generalizations would certainly vary and they should not be held responsible for this author's interpretation of their findings. The author's own research may be found in Hahn, "Continuity and Change in Russian Political Culture" and Jeffrey W. Hahn, "Changes in Contemporary Russian Political Culture," in *Political Culture and Civil Society*

in Russia and the New States of Eurasia, ed. Vladimir Tismaneanu (Armonk, NY: M. E. Sharpe, 1995). The work of the team from the University of Houston includes: James L. Gibson, Raymond M. Duch, and Kent L. Tedin, "Democratic Values and the Transformation of the Soviet Union," *Journal of Politics* 54, no. 2 (May 1992); Raymond M. Duch, "Tolerating Economic Reform: Popular Support for Transition to a Free Market in the Former Soviet Union," *American Political Science Review* (hereafter, *APSR*) 87, no. 3 (September 1993); James L. Gibson and Raymond M. Duch, "Political Intolerance in the USSR," *Comparative Political Studies* 26, no. 3 (October 1993); James L Gibson, "The Resilience of Mass Support for Democratic Institutions and Processes in the Nascent Russian and Ukrainian Democracies," in Tismaneanu, *Political Culture and Civil Society*. Research reported by a team of scholars from the University of Iowa includes: William Reissinger et al., "Political Values in Russia, Lithuania and Ukraine: Sources and Implications for Democracy," *British Journal of Political Science* 24 (April 1994); Arthur Miller et al., "Reassessing Mass Support for Political and Economic Changes in the Former USSR," *APSR* 88, no. 2 (June 1994); and William Reissinger, Arthur H. Miller, and Vicki L. Hesli, "Political Behavior Among the Post-Soviet Republics," paper presented at the 27th Annual Meeting of the AAASS in Washington, DC, October 26–29, 1995. Research conducted by specialists at the United States Information Agency includes: Richard B. Dobson, "Whither Russia: Trends in Russian Opinion Since 1991," paper prepared for the 1994 Meeting of the World Association for Public Opinion, Danvers, Massachusetts, 12 May 1994; Mary E. McIntosh et al., "Politics Meets Market Democracy in Central and Eastern Europe 1991–1993," *Slavic Review* 53, no. 2 (Summer 1994). Related findings are also to be found in William T. E. Mishler and Richard Rose, "Legislatures and New Democracies: Public Support for Parliaments and Regimes in Eastern Europe," Glasgow, University of Strathclyde Studies in Public Policy, no. 217 (1993) and David S. Mason, "Attitudes Toward the Market and Political Participation in the Post-Communist States," *Slavic Review* 54, no. 2 (Summer 1995), among others.

68 Setting aside the federal cities of Moscow and St. Petersburg, of these eighty-nine federal units the most important are the republics and oblasts because they are where the overwhelming majority of Russian citizens live. (The six krai or territories have essentially the administrative status of an oblast but contain one or more ethnic minority groups.) The analysis presented here is limited to a comparison of how democratization has proceeded in the republics and oblasts. Moscow and St. Petersburg, although clearly important, are politically idiosyncratic and do not lend themselves easily to a comparative analysis of Russian regional government. A more detailed look at Moscow is provided in Timothy J. Colton, *Moscow: Governing the Socialist Metropolis* (Cambridge, MA: Harvard University Press, 1996) and Robert W. Orttung, *From Leningrad to St. Petersburg: Democratization in a Russian City* (NY: St. Martin's Press, 1995).

69 For an assessment of the provisions of the 1993 Russian Constitution as they relate to federalism, see Edward W. Walker, "Federalism-Russia Style," *Problems of Post-Communism* 44, no. 3 (July–August 1995). Walker considers most of the criticisms regarding inequality unfounded (p. 11).

70 Wishnevsky, "Problems of Russian Regional Leadership," p. 9.

71 Although the treaty was favorable to Russia's claim that Tatarstan is a member of the Federation and as such subject to its laws, a number of provisions, especially concerning taxes and the use of local resources were favorable to Kazan. See Elizabeth Teague, "Russia and Tatarstan Sign a Power Sharing Treaty," *RFE/RL Research Report*, 8 April 1994.

72 On the treaty with Yakutia, see *Moskovskie novosti*, 25 June–2 July 1995 and on the treaty with Buryatia, see Yelena Tregubova's article in *Segodnia*, 7 July 1995. The other republics with bilateral treaties are North Ossetia, Bashkiria, and Kabardino-Balkaria. Tuva was also expected to conclude a treaty before the end of the year. *OMRI Daily Digest*, 12 January 1996 indicated that there are nine such treaties in existence.

73 The four oblasts that had signed such agreements with the center include Sverdlovsk, Kalinigrad, Orenburg, and Krasnodar Krai. Others are likely to follow. See *OMRI Daily Digest* for 12 and 31 January 1996. The quotation is by Zlotnik, "Russia's Governors," p. 30.

74 This section draws heavily on the information provided in Glubotsky et al, *Organy vlasti sub"ektov Rossiiskoi Federatsii.*

75 Yelena Tregubova in *Segodnia*, 18 August 1995.

76 One bright note for the democratic parties came when the candidate for chief administrator of the Siberian Republic of Khakasia supported by Russia's Choice won by getting 70 percent of the vote compared to 22 percent for the Communist and Agrarian parties. They also elected nine of fifteen members of the city council, but generally lost in rural areas. See the article by Vasily Ustyuzhanin in *Rossiia*, no. 14 (May 1995), translated in *CDPSP* 47, no. 22 (1995), 16.

77 These data are reported in Tables 2, 3, and 4 of Darrell Slider, Vladimir Gimpelson, and Sergei Chugorov, "Political Tendencies in Russia's Regions," *Slavic Review* 53, no. 3 (Fall 1994).

78 Reformist parties identified by the authors included Russia's Choice, Yabloko, the Party of Russian Unity and Accord or PRUA, and the Russian Movement for Democratic Reform or RDDR. See Slider et al., "Political Tendencies in Russia's Regions," pp. 715–16.

79 The odd exception was Mordovia in what Slider et al. suggest was "perhaps the only case of open collaboration between local communists and the LDPR." Mordovia does have a majority Russian population (61 percent). Slider et al., "Political Tendencies in Russia's Regions," p. 723.

80 *Vesna 89: Geografia i anatomniia parlementskikh vyborov*, ed. V.A. Kolosov, N.V. Petrov, and L.V. Smirniagin (Moscow: Progress Publishers, 1990) pp. 69ff.

81 The data from the 1991 election and the 1993 referendum are reported in Aleksandr Sobyanin, Eduard Gelman, and Oleg Kayunov, "Politicheskii klimat v Rossii v 1991–1993," *Mirovaia ekonomika i mezhdunarodnye otnosheniia*, no. 9 (1993), 20–32. For further details regarding which oblasts and republics are included in each of these macro-regions, see Teague, "North-South Divide," pp. 7–23 and Slider, "Political Tendencies in Russia's Regions," p. 718.

82 Nikolai Petrov, "Elektoral'nyi landshaft Rossii i ego evolutsiia," an unpublished manuscript made available to the author in June 1995. Petrov's observations are similar to those of Donna Bahry and Lucan Way cited earlier.

83 What the authors label quadrant III is characterized by support for a strong center *and* state control over the economy. Slider et al., "Political Tendencies in Russia's Regions," p. 729.

84 *Ibid.*, p. 732. It is not clear to the author of this chapter whether deputies who once held "nomenklatura" status under the old regime are necessarily opposed to reform *per se*, or whether they are primarily opposed to reforms proposed by Yeltsin. It seems likely that there are some real divisions along these lines among deputies affiliated with Ziuganov's CPRF.

85 From the "Revised Research Guidelines for Country Study Writers."

86 Some of these findings, including the author's, may be found in Tismaneanu, *Political Culture and Civil Society*. For dissenting views, see Stephen Whitefield and Geoffrey Evans, "The Russian Election of 1993: Public Opinion and the Transition Experience," *Post-Soviet Affairs* 10, no. 1 (1994) and Matthew Wyman, "Russian Political Culture: Evidence from Public Opinion Surveys," *Journal of Communist Studies and Transition Politics*, March 1994.

87 Parrott, "Parties, Political Participation, and Post-Communist Democratization," p. 6.

88 See, for example, Robert Sharlet, "Russian Politics on the Eve of the Parliamentary Campaign," *CSIS Post-Soviet Prospects* 3, no. 9 (September 1995).

5   The development of political parties in Russia

Michael Urban and Vladimir Gel'man

Introduction

This chapter concerns the formation and development of political parties in Russia over the course of four distinct periods, dubbed here: (1) late-Soviet (1988–91), and characterized by the struggle of Russian political society against the Communist party-state, a struggle in which political parties first appeared; (2) postcommunist (1991–93), a period marked by the ascendance of the executive, its duel with the legislature for authority, and the consequent reconfiguration – and degeneration – of the party system; (3) Fifth Duma (1993–95), defined by the constitutional order imposed by the president following the elimination of his antagonists in the Supreme Soviet, one in which new legislative elections stimulated party development even while the negligible authority exercised by the legislature inhibited the influence of parties and thus restricted their development; and (4) elections to the Sixth Duma (1995–), which includes a survey of the election campaign and the balloting of December 17.[1] The central problem that we address involves the relative weakness and incoherence of Russian parties and, attendantly, the rather marginal role that they have played (in most respects) in the country's government and political life. We use two related sets of categories to frame this problem, examining the way in which it has appeared concretely in the respective periods and outlining changes in its manifestation over time.

The first set of categories – "identity" and "interest" – refers to that which political parties express. If politics represents a society's dialogue with itself – one in which problems are thematized, solutions debated and, eventually, decisions adopted – then political parties might be regarded as major partners in this ongoing conversation. The political identities that they project serve to distinguish themselves from one another and, in so doing, to create out of their discursive interaction a party system. Interaction produces identities in a "negative" way, as a given party can only be distinguished from others by purporting to be something that they are not. However, it is the "positive" claims by political parties to be organized embodiments of one or another political identity – in the Russian case, democrats, communists, patriots or various permutations and/or combinations of these – through which identities are themselves manifest. And each manifestation is an appeal for public support on the basis of those elements that are valorized within the respective identity construct. So, whereas, say, Russia's patriots accent the language of "nation" and "state," democrats speak the dialect of "individuals," their "rights" and so forth. Any of these identities, mediated by language and symbols, is thus both an invitation to the public to define the world of politics in a particular way – to understand their problems and the sources of, and solutions to, them from the standpoint of that definition – and a set of invidious distinctions drawn by its purveyors between themselves and their opponents.

The second term in this pair – "interest" – is, in principle, readily conjoined to the first one. Knowing the identity assumed by a given party should indicate which social and economic interests that party seeks to represent. However, the short history of Russia's political system would not vouch for the truth of that proposition. On one hand, organized political forces have exhibited a capacity to advance certain interests and to sanction certain practices obviously at odds with their self-concepts (communists, for instance, calling down God's blessings on the Motherland, or democrats consecrating the shelling of the country's parliament); on the other, social and economic interests have devoted relatively little attention to political parties as vehicles for achieving their ends. The second pair of categories provides an explanation for this apparent anomaly in the first.

The second pair of categories includes "state" and "political society." The former refers to hierarchically organized bodies that deliver authoritative injunctions backed by coercive force; the latter, to that sphere of life in which questions, issues or concerns relevant to the public are voiced for the purpose of influencing the course of state activity. Parties and parliaments would count as political society's premier institutions. That unique product of their particular practices – acts of parliament (laws) – generally represents the principal influence on state activity, either authorizing or prohibiting action on the part of its hierarchically organized bodies.

The decoupling of identity and interest can be traced to the particular relationships that have prevailed in Russia between state and political society across the periods surveyed here. Despite the sweeping changes that have characterized Russian politics over these four periods, the relationship between state and political society has been in one respect remarkably constant: namely, the state has vastly overshadowed the institutions of political society and drastically inhibited their influence on its actions. Among the reasons that might be adduced to account for that condition, none in our view would hold greater import than the role played by elections. In this respect, we need recall that never in Russia's history have those in possession of state power submitted the issue of their continuing tenure to the verdict of the voters. While elections may have been called for purposes such as conferring the mantle of popular approval on those holding state power, demonstrating to others outside the country that Russia (or, earlier, the USSR) should be regarded as a democratic country, or conducting a purge of officialdom (turnover in high office has been at least a side effect of all the elections discussed here), no election to date has actually been inscribed with the question, who shall govern us? As a result, elections have featured a surfeit of affective behavior (the signification of identities) and a corresponding dearth of the instrumental considerations (attending the claims of various interests). Since those occupying state offices with the capacity for issuing authoritative injunctions have been remarkably unconstrained by authorization and/or prohibitions emanating from political society, social and economic interests have tended to take their "business" directly to those offices themselves, while actors in political society have maintained a corresponding preoccupation with identity politics, distinguishing themselves from one another less on the basis of those interests that they claim to represent than by means of strong significations advertising who they claim "to be."

Party formation in the late-Soviet period

The appearance of political parties in Soviet Russia constituted a counter-movement to the disintegration of the Communist party-state. The temporal dimension of that disintegration – from the reforms associated with perestroika to the anti-communist revolution accomplished by a mass political mobilization that was itself both cause and consequence of party formation in the late-Soviet period – involved more or less discrete stages, each of which conditioned the opportunities for political organizing in ways different from the others. Responding to the opportunities confronting them at one time or another, individuals and groups engaging in political organization arrived at a common destination – the inauguration of political parties – but did so along separate routes whose signposts were imprinted on the characters and identities of the parties that had followed them. Our discussion here concerns those conditions contingent on party formation that were associated with communism's declining hegemony. Its aim is to outline the broad contours of Russian political society as it emerged out of – and, to one degree or another, in opposition to – the communist order. This section is subdivided according to various routes to party formation and the corresponding party types that travelled them.

Route 1: from the informal movement

Following the 1986 revision of regulations governing amateur societies that permitted groups to organize independently of the institutions maintained by the Soviet party-state, millions of individuals availed themselves of the opportunity to found or to join so-called "informal" associations springing up around members' interest in music, art, literature, education, sports, historical preservation, ecology and so on. By 1987, these informals had developed into a nationwide movement, more and more politicized by conflicts with local authorities attempting to limit their spheres of activity and by the appearance of political-oriented individuals within their ranks who typically assumed leadership roles very quickly.[2] Many clubs devoted to social questions soon turned to political ones, just as the urge to discuss was rapidly replaced by the call to act, whether in the form of petition drives, staging pickets and rallies, or publishing semi-legal newspapers. By 1988, a number of groups had crystallized around distinct political identities ranging from anarchists, at one end of the political spectrum, to monarchists at the other. Indeed, in May of that year, one of these groups (Democratic Union) had proclaimed itself a political party. Although that effort proved premature, openly breaking the Soviet taboo against party formation stimulated other groups to begin thinking along those same lines. The experience of the USSR's competitive elections in 1989 – in which scores of informal groups conducted successful campaigns for candidates running against party-state officials, as well as the chance to repeat and to expand upon that effort as the 1990 elections in Russia approached – added powerful incentives to form parties.

These incentives, of course, were conditioned by the rules of the political game, rules made by those in possession of state office for the obvious purpose of legitimating their authority via the mechanism of public elections.[3] Nowhere would this be more evident than in the decision of the Communist Party's leadership to delay the removal of constitutional strictures against organizing political parties until 13 March 1990; that is, until *after* elections in the USSR (1989) and Russia (1990) had been staged. Consequently, when parties began to appear in the aftermath of those elections, they were deprived of that singular circumstance defining the nature of their counterparts in conventional party systems: competing for seats in a legislature, organizing the electorate and sculpting themselves in the process. Party formation in Russia thus banked steeply *away* from a politics of interest in which social groups – themselves in an incipient stage of development – might be represented by various parties appealing for their support in an election and toward a politics of identity in which organizational coherence would be sustained by the collective adoption of particular political discourses developed by various circles within the informal movement that distinguished one party from another. In short, party development was "ingrown."

The three major parties that grew out of the informal movement were the Social Democratic Party of Russia (SDPR), the Russian Christian Democratic Movement (RCDM) and the Constitutional Democratic Party (CDP). Given both their lineage and the fact that they never competed in elections as distinct organizations, these were identity-based parties *par excellence*. The SDPR, which was founded in May 1990, drew its membership from informal groups such as the Social-Democratic Union, the social-democratic faction of Democratic Union, Moscow's Democratic Perestroika and Perestroika of Leningrad, as well as similar social-democratic clubs in dozens of Russia's large cities.[4] Its identity was pitched against all things Soviet with images of Western social democracy supplying the requisite positive markers. Proclaiming themselves bearers of all putative social interests and opposed on that basis to the rule of the Communist nomenklatura,[5] the SDPR eschewed the "tradition of social-democracy in Russia" and opted for a "contemporary . . . social-liberal orientation in the European sense."[6] Although such a "Western" party would seem strangely out of place in Russia, the men and women of the SDPR constructed one all the same. Its members who had been elected as individuals to legislatures at various levels generally comprised their most disciplined and effective factions; party leaders penned landmark pieces of legislation such as Russia's Declaration of Sovereignty and the Supreme Soviet's draft of a new constitution;[7] the SDPR created its own trade union affiliate (Sotsprof), its own publishing house (Sotsium); and, with a remarkably well-developed arrangement for internal financing,[8] put out the widest array of national and regional newspapers of any political party in Russia.[9]

In sharp contrast to the secular "Western" identity constructed by the SDPR, the RCDM's leadership relied on heavily mythologized moments gathered from Russia's past to distinguish their organization. Confronted with rivals who had already organized a proto- party, the Christian Democratic Union of Russia, in August 1989, those from a number of Russian Orthodox circles who initiated the RCDM defined their project from the first as a restoration of a Russian state based on tradition and, above all, on the Russian Orthodox Church.[10] Paradoxically, whereas the SDPR rejected the extant tradition of Russian social democracy, the "traditionalist" RCDM embraced a "Christian-democratic" identity in full recognition of the fact that there had never been a Christian democratic tradition in Russia. Moreover, the RCDM's self-concept – especially in the hands of party leader, Viktor

Aksyuchits – reduced Christianity to Russian Orthodoxy, thereby further confusing its identity construct, warping its communicative capacities and driving its discourse steadily in the direction of fundamentalism and its internal structure toward authoritarianism. Once the Communist Party – whose odious presence in Russia had sustained the RCDM's Christian *democratic* identity of opposition to communism – had been overthrown, the party rapidly repaired to the ranks of a resurgent fundamentalist movement, affiliating itself with ultra-nationalist and fascist forces.[11]

The third of the parties surveyed here began in October 1989 as a proto-party – the Union of Constitutional Democrats – that amalgamated certain liberal-democratic groups active in the informal movement around an explicit project to revive Russia's "constitutional- democratic" tradition.[12] However, at the May 1990 congress at which this "Union" would give birth to a Party of Constitutional Democrats (PCD), the issue of identity – the correct interpretation of the principles of constitutional democracy – became so vexed that it split the new party in two.[13] Thus Russia acquired both a PCD and a CDP, the latter of which outstripped its competitor with respect to membership (about 2,000 as compared to the PCD's 600–800) and high profile leaders (Mikhail Astaf'ev and Dmitrii Rogozin). Ironically, like the RCDM, the CDP refitted its profile once its Communist nemesis had been dispatched and incongruously bore the standard of Russian constitutional democracy within the communist-nationalist camp.[14]

Route 2: from the interior of the CPSU

This route toward party formation followed the signposts of factional activity inside the Communist Party, despite the persistence of its formal rules to the contrary. Identity for the groups considered here was also a central issue, but since they first appeared *within* the CPSU, it did not amount to drawing distinctions between themselves and the Soviet order entirely. Instead, the distinctions were introduced between themselves and that brand of communism represented by the Gorbachev leadership, valorizing certain themes drawn from socialist/communist thought and weaving them into alternative communist discourses. Initially, the programs advanced by these factions represented efforts to persuade others in the CPSU to adopt the discourse – and the identity – embedded in each.

Four parties eventually crystallized out of these factions within the Communist Party, their paths entangled with one another. (One of these, the Russian Communist Party, is considered, below). Two of these factions traced their roots to the Moscow inter-club party group, an association of CPSU members active in the informal movement that was set up in spring 1988 to influence debates at the Communist Party's Nineteenth Conference.

The group continued to function thereafter and became an "informal" presence within the CPSU.[15] By 1990, in anticipation of the Communist Party's Twenty-Eighth Congress, the group divided into the Marxist and Democratic platforms: the former (and smaller) emphasizing a renewal of socialism along the lines of direct democracy and worker's control; the latter drawing its inspiration from Eurocommunist theories underscored the virtues of parliamentary democracy.[16] To make matters more confusing, a section of the Democratic Platform formed a tactical alliance with the Marxist Platform at the Twenty-Eighth Congress and refused to follow their nominal leaders out of the CPSU after the Congress.

The Marxist and Democratic platforms sired three political parties. The first was the Republican Party of Russia (RPR), formed in October 1990 by that section of the Democratic Platform that had dissolved its ties with the CPSU.[17] The second was the People's Party of Free Russia (PPFR), formed initially in August 1991 as the Democratic Party of Communists of Russia on the basis of a union between that section of the Democratic Platform that had remained in the CPSU (led by Vasilii Lipitskii) and the Communists for Democracy faction in the Russian legislature whose leader, Aleksandr Rutskoi, had been elected vice president of Russia in June. The specific impetus for the inauguration of the PPFR was the expulsion of Lipitskii and Rutskoi from the Communist Party itself.[18] The third, after many "initiative committees" had collapsed under the weight of sectarian squabbles, grew out of the remnants of the Marxist Platform in 1992 as the Labor Party – which contained few, if any, actual laborers.[19] Like the parties originating in the informal movement, none of these three managed to contest an election under its own name.[20]

Route 3: against the CPSU

In May 1990, two distinct political currents converged to found the Democratic Party of Russia (DPR), the premier anti-communist party of the time. One came from the loose assembly of voters' associations that had campaigned for their respective candidates in the 1990 elections under the nationwide umbrella of Democratic Russia. Following those elections, the largest of these associations (led by Lev Ponomarev in Moscow and Marina Sal'e in Leningrad) began an organizational effort to found a political party.[21] The second current consisted of a number of individuals associated with Democratic Russia whose activities in the Inter-Regional Deputies' Group – a faction in the USSR's legislature – had won them national reputations: Gennadii Burbulis, Arkadii Murashev and, especially, Nikolai Travkin.

The DPR was initially conceived as a mass party uniting all democratic forces for the purpose of toppling the CPSU. The issue of who would lead that effort, however, provoked a bitter dispute between Travkin's supporters, who wanted a disciplined party with Travkin at the helm, and those from the voters' associations who favored the organizational arrangement to which they had become accustomed during election campaigns – maximum inclusion, minimal program and collection leadership. Relying on quite ruthless tactics, Travkin's group prevailed, essentially commandeering the organization launched by Ponomarev and Sal'e who therefore walked out with their supporters and founded another (much smaller) party – the Free Democratic Party of Russia (FDPR) – on the spot. Consequently, the DPR became a disciplined anti-communist party and the largest non-communist party in Russia at the time (with a peak membership approaching 50,000), but never the mass party envisaged by its founders.[22]

In contrast to the parties surveyed, thus far, the DPR expended very little energy on cultivating a distinct political identity, working out a consistent program or debating political principles. Instead, its character was action-oriented, focusing on overthrowing the Communist system and building a well-oiled party machine poised to capture office in the elections expected to ensue thereafter. A sociological study has disclosed a profile of this party's elite fully congruent with those objectives: upwardly mobile individuals, many with aspirations to succeed in private business, who had no record of political activity prior to entering the DPR.[23] Alone among the parties formed during the late Soviet period, the DPR managed to stage its own elections campaign in 1993 and gained representation of its party list in the State Duma. However, the party did not survive the 1995 elections as its leaders affiliated with competing blocs and the DPR effectively collapsed as an organization.

Route 4: revolutionary movement

Once Travkin had stolen "their" party out from under them, the leaders of Russia's voters' associations immediately restarted their project to create a political organization capable of bringing all of Russia's "democratic forces" under one roof.[24] A flurry of organizational conferences during summer and autumn of 1990 led to a national congress in late October that launched the movement, Democratic Russia. The leadership and cadres included in these efforts consisted of "outsiders," either individuals who had not affiliated with any of the new political parties or those whose current party ties were of marginal consequence (such as Ponomarev and four other members of his FDPR who were elected to Democratic Russia's twenty-seven-member organizing committee; or Murashev, the organizing committee's chairperson who broke with the DPR a few months later).[25]

This moment in October 1990 was the realization of efforts begun as early as 1987 to unite the country's "democratic forces" into a single organization. Whereas earlier projects to create a national center for informal groups, an all-union anti-communist party (Democratic Union), a unionwide (or Russian) popular front, a national voters' association and, most recently, the divisive inauguration of the DPR had all gone wide of the mark, the recipe perfected by Democratic Russia's organizers succeeded brilliantly. Its ingredients included: (1) no specific program beyond a commitment to overthrow communism by peaceful and democratic means; (2) provision for all affiliates – parties, trade unions and public associations – to retain their separate identities and pursue their own strategies and tactics; (3) organization of the movement's own local and regional bodies which both elected officials and individuals unaffiliated with any of its member groups could join; (4) establishment of the movement's own financial basis and newspaper.[26] Within months, Democratic Russia's membership climbed into the hundreds of thousands.[27] In spring 1991 it waged a successful presidential campaign for Boris Yeltsin that broke the back of the Communist system.[28] In August, it rallied millions of people across the country in a massive display of civil resistance that defeated the Communist *coup d'etat*. Within months of its victory over communism, however, Democratic Russia splintered and then withered as an organization, as the parties within it bolted, its leadership split and members left in droves.[29] The remainder of the organization joined Egor Gaidar's Russia's Choice as a junior partner in the 1993 elections; thereafter, it reconstituted itself as a separate political party[30] but withdrew from the 1995 contests, throwing its support to the strongest of the democratic contenders, Yabloko.[31] How might we account for its spectacular rise and fall?

The opportunity structure to which Democratic Russia's organizers responded in 1990 was shaped by the parliamentary elections that year. Candidates affiliated with the Democratic Russia bloc captured some 40 percent of the seats in the Russian Congress of People's Deputies – that large and infrequently convening legislature that delegated most legislative activity to a smaller, full-time organ (the Supreme Soviet) yet retained constitutional entitlement to be the locus of all legitimate authority – and majorities in the city councils of Moscow, Leningrad and a few other large cities. The acknowledged leader of the democratic movement, Boris Yeltsin, was elected Chairperson of the Russian Supreme Soviet and the enactment of his program for creating a sovereign Russian state represented the end of Communist rule in Russia. Thus, a palpable political alternative to communism had appeared for the first time, encouraging support for Yeltsin, the Russian state and an unspecified "reform."[32] Simultaneously, these same developments signalled the fact that the Soviet party-state was entering its final phase of disintegration, unable to check a mass revolutionary movement pitted against it. Democratic Russia stimulated, organized and harnessed that movement, requiring no particular program beyond anti-communism and support for Yeltsin. Its loose organizational structure represented an open invitation for all to join.

These factors contributing to its success as a revolutionary movement also accounted for its downfall as a political organization. For its Herculean efforts on behalf of Yeltsin and his government, it received effectively nothing beyond the satisfaction of victory over communism. No government posts, no influence in policy circles, no consideration for its demand for immediate national elections following the defeat of the August 1991 putsch – the singular organization-building issue confronting it at that critical juncture. Fractured and diminished, it retained some internal coherence and organizational capacity by means of personal ties established between its officers and functionaries and certain individuals in government that supplied the organization with discrete material incentives such as salaried jobs or access to state property, then being "privatized." All of this transpired between individuals; none of it between Democratic Russia and the government.[33] Eventually, what had been a mass democratic organization found itself shilling for an increasingly authoritarian regime pursuing an economic reform impoverishing most Russians while creating a new class of wealthy individuals consisting primarily of old communist officials, organized criminals and bunko artists.

Route 5: opportunism

The difference between responding to opportunity and "opportunism" can be measured with venality's yardstick. For those parties discussed to this point, the disintegration of the Communist system represented an opportunity to establish independent political organizations. For those surveyed here, it was the chance to pose as independent political organizations in order to enter into a cooperative relationship with the Communist Party from which they would derive material resources and grants of authority. The first "opportunist" party to appear in the late-Soviet period was the Democratic Party of the Soviet Union, founded in August 1989 by Lev Ubozhko, Vladimir Bogachev and R. Semenov – all recently expelled from Democratic Union for harshly criticizing one of its leaders in the official press.[34] However, owing to Semenov's election as party leader, Ubozhko and Bogachev immediately left to found their own Democratic Party which split again in a few weeks time when Bogachev joined another refugee from Democratic Union, Vladimir

Zhirinovskii, to establish the Liberal Democratic Party of the Soviet Union (LDPSU). By October of 1990 Ubozhko was expelled from "his" Democratic Party for making unauthorized proclamations on prime-time Soviet television and for suppressing debate at a party congress with para-military forces.[35] He and his followers then declared themselves the Conservative Party.

The LDPSU was apparently sponsored by the CPSU and the KGB, which funneled cash directly to Zhirinovskii, who used the money to "recruit" delegates to its March 1990 founding.[36] Zhirinovskii straddled both sides of the political fence from the start, intoning the standard slogans of the democratic movement – such as "We want to be a European industrial society"[37] – and delivering Russian chauvinist harangues at nationalist/fascist rallies.[38] In October 1990, he had been expelled from "his" LDPSU, but immediately formed with his followers another organization of the same name. Together with other small opportunist parties and groups, Zhirinovskii's LDPSU formed a "Centrist Bloc," the Communist Party's idea of an alternative to the democratic movement which entered into "negotiations" with the Soviet Prime Minister, Nikolai Ryzhkov and the Chairperson of the USSR's Supreme Soviet, Anatolii Luk'yanov, toward the (preposterous) purpose of forming with the CPSU "a coalition government of national accord."[39] This stratagem came to nothing and the Centrist Bloc quickly collapsed along with effectively all of its constituent units,[40] save Zhirinovskii's LDPSU which – thanks to a nomination secured by a Communist vote in the Russian legislature and the material assistance contributed by the CPSU – sustained his bid for the Russian presidency in June 1991 which netted him 7.8 percent of the vote and a place in the limelight of national politics.[41]

Route 6: restoration

The principal party of restoration, the Russian Communist Party (RCP), was formed in June 1990. Its constituent currents consisted of a number of organizations fielded by, or composed of, party-state officials reacting to the disintegration of the Communist system – first as a form of pressure on Mikhail Gorbachev to rein in his reforms, later as an attempt to staunch the democratic revolution by advocating, and participating in, the August 1991 *coup d'etat*. These currents included: the bogus "workers' organization," the United Front of Working People, fielded by sections of the Communist Party apparatus in industrial centers;[42] the Peasant Union, its rural counterpart organized by party-state officials in the agricultural sector;[43] and the Soyuz ("Union") deputies' groups in the USSR's Congress of People's Deputies.[44]

These forces formed an electoral association – the Bloc of Public and Patriotic Movements of Russia – that contested the 1990 elections and failed to win a single seat in the national legislature. Accordingly, their political strategy focused thereafter on capturing control of the CPSU, which they would use to restore the Soviet order by turning back the political clock to pre-perestroika time. In some respects, they succeeded. The Communist Party's leadership steadily capitulated to their demand to create a Russian party within the CPSU,[45] and in June 1990 that party came into existence with Ivan Polozkov – the CPSU's Krasnodar boss whose anti-reform actions had earned him the reputation of perhaps the country's premier restorationist[46] – at its head. The RCP can be credited with influencing the rightward direction of Gorbachev's government from autumn 1990 till spring of 1991 and with preparing the way for and supporting the coup that briefly unseated him in August. Two days after the coup's defeat, Yeltsin banned the party by decree. With some new faces and a modified political posture, it reappeared in February 1993 as the Communist Party of the Russian Federation (CPRF).

Party deformation and reformation in the postcommunist period

The failed *coup d'etat* of 1991, the banning of the CPSU and the subsequent collapse of the USSR fundamentally changed Russia's political landscape. But contrary to the apparently salubrious implications of these events for democratization and, thus, for party development, they in fact led to the opposite result. Here, it would be important to recall that the status of new parties in the previous period was conditioned by their opposition to the CPSU. The disappearance of that nefarious "other" stabilizing the identities of the various parties coincided with an all-around regrouping of organized political forces that occurred against the backdrop of fading public interest now that the heroic period of anti-communist revolution had passed. However, the marginalization experienced by parties in this period, the erosion of their memberships and the relentless efforts of their leaders to staunch their growing insignificance by forming new coalitions and undertaking various public campaigns can be traced primarily to Yeltsin's strategy of reform. His approach concentrated power in the executive branch which ruled around or – when necessary – against the national legislature, installing his appointees as a governing class of officials in the regions and localities. Moreover, since new parliamentary elections were not called while those to the post of regional governor were "postponed," party development marked time. Parties in this period were sustained as small (and usually fluid) factions in the national legislature, but its size and design ensured that they would play a relatively insignificant role in its internal organization and operations. Thus, party activity was in fact deprived of substance. The transition to the system of personal appointments (that is, regional heads of the administration and representatives of the president) gave birth to the phenomena of quasi-party clientelism whereby jobs in one or another region were filled on the basis of recommendations advanced by various political parties. Rather than a form of patronage that obligated appointees to their respective party patrons, this process – because it stipulated that appointees suspend their party membership – tended to sever relations between the new officials and the parties from which they had come. As a result, party nominations produced personalized, rather than organizational, forms of clientelism. Yesterday's party activists were now embarked on government careers in which ties to very different sets of patrons – officials in the Administration of the President or those in the government apparatus – mattered more. Politicians thereby utilized party organizations to recruit new cadres and to whip up public support for themselves when circumstances so required. At the same time, however, they were running party organizations into the ground.

By the beginning of 1992, parties (irrespective of their political orientation) consisted only of weak factions in a weak parliament and slender networks of supporters and activists in the country's regions. There was little or no occasion for mobilizing their cadres, financial or informational resources for real political struggle. Therefore, after the onset of the 1992 economic reform when key political actors conducted an open struggle for the redistribution of power and authority, political parties were converted into appendages of the protagonists. With respect to classifying parties in this period, we would emphasize that that which had existed previously in the form of the triad – "communists," "democrats," "national-patriots" – did not fundamentally change but began to be increasingly saturated by more complicated tones and shades as certain compound identities were forged from these basic elements.

National-Patriots

As Vladimir Prybilovskii has noted, the historically determined division into "red" and "white" national-patriots was preserved up to the end of 1991.[47] The collapse of the USSR only deepened the divide between these groups both on the ideational-theoretical level and on the personal one. Moreover, the first wave of "white" patriots – which had been eclipsed as a political force by the democratic movement in its struggle with the Soviet regime – gave way after communism's collapse to a second wave recruited primarily from among those erstwhile democratic politicians who were denied the spoils of office and influence in the postcommunist regime. At the end of 1991 and the beginning of 1992, a few large "white" national-patriotic associations were formed, among them the Russian Social Union headed by

Sergei Baburin (a former democrat), the Russian National Union led by Aleksandr Sterligov (a former KGB officer), and the Russian Popular Assembly (led by former democrats such as Viktor Aksyuchits and Il'ya Konstantinov of the RCDM and Mikhail Astaf'ev of the CDP). At the same time, a number of smaller groups were formed and reformed out of the various wings of nationalist society: Pamyat, the National Republican Party of Russia (NRPR) headed by Nikolai Lysenko and Zhirinovskii's Liberal Democratic Party of Russia (LDPR). Owing in part to their mutually-exclusive claims to represent the nation – as well as to the bombast typically marshalled to authenticate those claims – the national-patriotic opposition remained throughout the period surveyed, here, the most marginalized and fragmented segment of the Russian political spectrum.

The core of the national-patriots' appeal concerned the loss of empire, the loss of Russia's "greatness." For this "crime" they accused the Yeltsin government, which they portrayed as a collection of traitors doing the bidding of the Western powers intent on forcing Russia to its knees, if not wiping the Russian state and civilization off the map entirely.[48] The shrill pitch of their rhetoric was reinforced by the conditions of competition for leadership of the anti-Yeltsin opposition – competition among the various national-patriotic groups themselves and between them and a resurgent communist movement, most of whose organizations inscribed their own bizarre brands of patriotism into new versions of communist ideology. In autumn of 1992, effectively all of the national-patriotic organizations combined with their communist counterparts to launch the "left–right" opposition to Yeltsin's "occupation regime," christening themselves the Front of National Salvation (FNS). This coalition immediately became the dominant bloc in the Russian legislature, thereby fusing to the institutional interests of the parliament – championed by its "Speaker," Ruslan Khasbulatov – a radical majority bent on bringing down the president and his government. But this unity of purpose was offset by colliding ambitions within the FNS, especially by the resurrection of a large communist party under the leadership of Gennadii Zyuganov, who sought to capture the entire left-right constituency for his new Communist Party of Russian Federation (CPRF).

Communists

The banning of the CPSU and the confiscation of its property severely limited the organizational resources of all those in the left and communist movement intent on maintaining, or founding new, political parties. At the same time, however, it stimulated that differentiation already apparent within the communist camp itself by drastically reducing the supply of material and organizational resources at the disposal of leaders and functionaries who would otherwise deploy them to staunch centripetal tendencies, as we observed above, with respect to the Democratic Platform. The formation of various parties on the basis of the territorial organizations of the CPSU – from the moderate PPFR and Socialist Party of Working People to the orthodox Russian Communist Workers' Party (RCWP) and All-Union Communist Party of Bolsheviks (A-UCPB) – only reflected the process of diversification of the left movement already under way in 1990 and 1991.[49] Although during the 1992 struggle in the Constitutional Court to remove Yeltsin's ban on the old communist party – the so-called "affair of the CPSU" – that wing of the party led by Zyuganov was able to become the center of consolidation for communist organizations, the fragmentation of the left movement has not been surmounted up to the present day.[50]

In contrast to the national patriotic movement, whose ideological differentiation has been driven by disputes over the interpretation of a heavily-mythologized past, for the communists the key thing has been their relation to the Russian present: from the complete unacceptability of each and every change in the direction of the market and democracy that is characteristic of Viktor Anpilov's RCWP and the (smaller) A-UCPB to the partial acceptance of the market and parliamentarianism that marks the orientation of the CPRF. The issue of whether to participate in the elections called by Yeltsin for December 1993 reprised the early-century controversy on the Russian left between the "recall group" (who insisted on abandoning work in the parliament in order to concentrate on underground methods of political struggle) and the "liquidators" (who favored parliamentary work and advocated disbanding all underground organizations). In this instance, the RCWP refused to participate in the 1993 elections while the CPRF waged an impressive grassroots campaign.

Democrats

Russia's democratic parties were among the principal casualties of the postcommunist transition. Between the 1991 putsch and that of autumn 1993, the democratic camp suffered a serious attrition of leaders, activists and rank-and-file members, as well as the defection of entire parties to one or another of the opposition coalitions arrayed against Yeltsin's reforms. In this respect, the arrested development of parties on the (initially) democratic wing of the political spectrum represented a singular case of those factors conditioning the overall weakness of the party system in the 1991–1993 period, especially the conversion of the governmental institutions of Russia (president and parliament) into the primary actors of political struggle. In conditions in which both opposing sides relied upon their institutional clients – whether soviets in the case of parliament or the administrative apparatus in the case of the presidency – these institutions were transformed into their own kinds of "parties," while parties *per se* were condemned to the role of political "cannon fodder," as was clearly demonstrated by the violent termination of the constitutional order in October 1993. Political parties still were unable to influence the direction of policy or the institutions of power via elections or to participate in the formation of a government. Nonetheless, power holders required a basis of support beyond the institutions that they controlled: hence, the formation in 1991 and 1992 of "committees of reform," "forums of the democratic forces" at one pole and, at the other, the FNS. Both sides – president and parliament – utilized the rally, the demonstration and other shows of public enthusiasm merely as devices to mobilize larger publics for their own narrow interests. The illusion of unity within this framework of counter-poised camps – the "left–right opposition" and "the Union of Democratic Forces" – depended in both cases on the framework of the struggle against the common enemy. And not unsurprisingly, after the obliteration of the bipolar system by armed force in October 1993, these coalitions simultaneously collapsed themselves.

Centrist parties

The final development of note during this period would be the failed attempt by certain parties to form a "political center," putatively between the democrats and the left–right opposition, mediating the conflict between president and parliament. The first efforts along these lines actually began at the twilight of the Soviet order with the creation of the Movement for Democratic Reforms (MDR), a coterie of perestroika-era luminaries such as Aleksandr Yakovlev and Eduard Shevardnadze who joined forces with certain individuals carving out careers within or near the democratic movement (Gavriil Popov, Moscow's mayor, vice president Rutskoi, and Arkadii Vol'skii, the chief spokesperson for the "industrial lobby" among them). In the face of its failure to annex Democratic Russia as a mass base and with the collapse of its putative constituency, the USSR, the MDR quickly faded. Many of those active in its leading circles undertook subsequent attempts to form "centrist" organizations which ultimately resulted in the appearance of two competitors for that niche.

The first was the Russian Movement for Democratic Reforms (RMDR), led by Popov and Anatolii Sobchak (mayor of St. Petersburg), which formed in early 1992; the second – and, for a time, more consequential "centrist" bloc – was also initiated at this time with the announcement of a coalition between Travkin's DPR and Rutskoi's PPFR.[51] These parties had shied away from allying with the national-patriots and, although Rutskoi was the country's vice president, neither had any influence in Yeltsin's government.

In June 1992, the DPR and PPFR were joined by another "centrist" group, the newly-proclaimed party "Renewal" that arose out of Vol'skii's Russian Union of Industrialists and Entrepreneurs, an association composed of factory directors and local officials smarting under the hardships induced by Yeltsin's reforms. The product of their three-way alliance, Civic Union, appeared under the conditions attending Russia's postcommunist transition to be a potent political force. Included were arguably the country's most formidable party machine (the DPR), another sizeable party disposing of a significant bloc of voters in the parliament (the PPFR) and most of the captains of Russian industry represented by Renewal which immediately assumed the leadership of another large parliamentary faction. However, Civic Union's influence – which for a while was considerable and led to a reshuffling of Yeltsin's cabinet in summer 1992 and to major alterations in his economic reform – only bloomed in the hothouse conditions produced by the executive-legislative conflict and the consequent grouping of most of political society around one or the other of those poles. In that context, the strategic advantage was thought to accrue to those in the center.[52] When bipolarity replaced any pretense of accommodation after the Seventh Congress of People's Deputies in December 1992, this would-be center collapsed. Anticipating new elections, the DPR left the coalition in summer 1993; the PPFR was banned after the bloody events of September–October 1993; and Vol'skii led the rump of Civic Union into the December 1993 elections in which it failed to capture two percent of the national vote.

The Fifth State Duma and realignments in the party system

The spiral of executive/legislative conflict in 1993 appeared to make early parliamentary elections all but inevitable. That prospect – reinforced by the April referendum's majority vote for early elections to the legislature and Yeltsin's summoning of a Constitutional Convention in June whose ostensible purpose (a new constitution) coincided conveniently with its strategic one (decommissioning the Congress of People's Deputies) – triggered a new round of differentiation in political society. Old alliances were sundered, new ones engendered and government officials, party leaders and activists scrambled to patch together organizations to wage the coming campaigns. The democratic quarter of Russia's political field arguably featured the most thoroughgoing realignment in that respect. The appearance of Russia's Choice was indisputably the main event.

Russia's Choice represented the first successful attempt by those controlling a significant segment of state offices to field a political organization. In this instance, the principal characters included Yeltsin's close associates Gennadii Burbulis and Mikhail Poltoranin, his chief of staff, Sergei

Filatov, and the two leading "technocrats" from his reform cabinet, former acting prime minister Egor Gaidar and (then) first deputy prime minister, Anatolii Chubais. According to patterns not unfamiliar in postcommunist states,[53] the Gaidar-Chubais team had parlayed its links to international capital into a power base in domestic Russia politics. The backing of the World Bank, International Monetary Fund and similar institutions determining the terms of credit critical to Russia's economic transformation constituted their base within the government; that base and those credits were then used to erect their political organization. Under Chubais, the State Property Committee instructed its regional organs in March 1993 to create "private" associations that soon amalgamated as the Association of Privatized and Privatizing Enterprises (APPE) headed by Gaidar. This arrangement brought together three powerful sets of actors: state officials in possession of property; those to whom it would be passed; and international capital. In consideration for the property acquired from the state, the APPE tithed its members to finance Russia's Choice; in return for their political largess, members would be eligible for the $1.5 billion in assistance then made available by international financial institutions to the Russian economy, monies that were channelled by the Gaidar-Chubais team almost exclusively to those in the APPE.[54] By the time of its official founding in October 1993, Russia's Choice had added to its base of state offices, property and finance, the bulk of the mass media[55] and Democratic Russia's constituency organizations. Despite its overwhelming advantages, however, Russia's Choice polled poorly in the December balloting. The regulations installed by presidential decree had specified two methods for staffing the new State Duma: 225 seats to be filled by proportional representation by any party receiving a five-per-cent minimum of the national vote; and an equal number filled by first-past-the-post elections in territorial districts. In the national voting, Russia's Choice garnered only 15.5 percent.[56] Many of its candidates were elected in the district races, making it initially the largest faction in the Fifth Duma, but most of these deputies would defect before the Duma's two-year term had expired (see table 5.1).

Three other electoral organizations were cobbled together by democratic groups to contest the 1993 elections: the RMDR, replete with a renewed leadership composed of celebrities and other notables; the Party of Russian Unity and Accord (PRES), another network of state officials centered around the State Committee for the Affairs of the Federation and organized as a would-be "party of the regions";[57] and Yabloko ("Apple"), whose name derived from the surname initials of the bloc's three leading figures – Grigorii Yavlinskii (economist and former deputy prime minister), Yurii Boldyrev (former head of the President's Control Administration) and Vladimir Lukin (then Ambassador to the United States) – which included the

Table 5.1 *Representation of Russian parties, blocs, and factions in the Fifth State Duma*

Faction/group	Seats won in December 1993			Realignment by factions	
	National	Districts	Total	Spring '94	Fall '95
Russia's Choice	40 (15.5%)	56	96	76	53
Yabloko	20 (7.9%)	8	28	28	27
PRES	18 (6.7%)	12	30	30	19
DPR	14 (5.5%)	7	21	15	8
Women of Russia	21 (8.1%)	2	23	23	23
CPRF	32 (12.4%)	15	47	47	46
APR	21 (8.0%)	34	55	55	53
LDPR	59 (22.9%)	5	64	64	59
New Regional Policy	–	–	–	–	65	35
Union of 12 December	–	–	–	37	11
Stability	–	–	–	–	37
Russia	–	–	–	–	35

Source: G. Belonuchkin, information-research group, Panorama, Moscow, 1995.

RPR and the SDPR and presented itself as the democratic alternative to Gaidar's shock therapy, Yeltsin's authoritarian practices and his foreign minister's unduly pro-Western foreign policy. While both PRES and Yabloko received enough votes to surmount the 5 percent threshold for representation in the Duma, the RMDR failed to do so and soon exited the Russian political stage.

As a consequence of the two-week civil war that gripped Moscow in the advent of these elections, both the communist and national-patriotic camps were thrown into disarray and hasty realignment. The only group among the latter that managed to appear on the ballot was the LDPR. As the sole contender from this constituency, Zhirinovskii's party staged a brilliant campaign and won a plurality (22.9 percent) in the national balloting. Yeltsin's initial ban on all communist organizations induced those in that quarter with ties to the rural sector to launch the Agrarian Party of Russia (APR) as a way around his restrictions. Once the ban was lifted, the CPRF joined the race as the "other" communist party on the ballot. Although the CPRF and APR entered the Fifth Duma as city and country "cousins," respectively, parliamentary politics would introduce considerable divisions between them, just as the rough and tumble of work in Russia's new legislature would rewrite the map of political parties generally.

From the first it was clear that the bi-polar structure of Russian politics that had left its imprint on party development from 1989 to 1993[58] had given way in the Fifth Duma to a (shifting) multi-polar configuration. Indeed, change in this respect was already apparent during the election campaign, as parties within both the democratic and opposition camps assumed contrary positions on Yeltsin's draft constitution whose ratification via referendum was concomitant with the parliamentary elections. Whereas Russia's Choice endorsed the draft wholeheartedly, Yabloko opposed it as an instrument of authoritarian rule; for that same reason, the LDPR supported it, while the DPR and CPRF condemned it for reasons not unlike those advanced by Yabloko. Once this constitution came into effect, its provisions assigning a lopsided measure of authority to the president nudged political parties toward further differentiation. On one hand, the Duma could influence neither the composition nor the policies of the government; on the other, its legislative capacities – to say nothing about the actual implementation of the laws that it might pass – have been severely restricted by the upper chamber (elected in 1993, but nonetheless composed mainly of regional-level politicians whose careers depend on the president),[59] by Yeltsin's veto power and by the Constitutional Court whose majority has listed strongly toward presidential preferences.[60] In short, conditions militated against stable coalition politics, a fact evinced by the absence of anything resembling firm party coalitions in the legislature. Moreover, the surfeit of powers awarded to the president has fractured the party system in another respect as parties maintained an eye on the forthcoming presidential elections and attempted to position themselves propitiuously for them.

This consideration would be most apparent in the cases of the LDPR, the DPR and Yabloko, each of which has been a "leader-oriented" organization intent on capturing the presidency. But whereas the LDPR and Yabloko, their respective presidential hopefuls heading the factions in the Fifth Duma, suffered relatively little attrition, the DPR unravelled in rivalries, especially after Travkin resigned the party leadership in order to assume a position in the government (see table 5.1). Their competitors for the oppositionist, centrist and democratic niches – the CPRF, PRES and Russia's Choice, respectively – did not sport presidential timber during the Fifth Duma and, accordingly, displayed more "programmatically-oriented" profiles. Indeed, the dissipation experienced by both PRES and Russia's Choice over the duration of the Duma's two-year term – culminating in the 1995 failure of each to achieve representation in its successor – might be attributed in part to the fact that, although both began as "pro-presidential" parties, neither included a credible contender for the presidency, thus cautioning would-be backers to look elsewhere for returns on their political investments. The remaining two parties entering the Fifth Duma, the APR and Women of Russia (an electoral organization based on the Soviet-era's female nomen-klatura), were "corporatist-oriented," purporting to represent discrete constituencies: the rural-agricultural sector in the first instance; women's issues (home and hearth), in the second. Here, too, both parties were disadvantaged by the absence of a presidential candidate and neither would subsequently garner the necessary 5 percent vote to return its national list to parliament.

The watershed separating Russia's 1989–93 bi-polar political structure from the multi-polarity that developed during the Fifth Duma appeared in the voting of February 23, 1994 on a resolution to grant amnesty to those charged with high crimes for their participation in the events of October 3–4, 1993 and the attempted *coup d'etat* of 1991.[61] Unsurprisingly, the resolution drew the support of the government's principal opponents: the LDPR, CPRF and APR. But it was also backed by the centrist DPR and Women of Russia, as well as by the pro-government party, PRES. As the legislative process proceeded, the line distinguishing pro-government factions from oppositionist ones was blurred even more. According to Aleksandr Sobyanin's data, Yeltsin's government could usually count on the backing of about 180 deputies, but the actual composition of that group was subject to continual change.[62]

In considerable measure, the shifting sands underlying the government's base of support in the Duma were occasioned by Russia's Choice's claim during the elections to being simultaneously "the party of all democratic forces" and "the governing party." Hardly had the Duma begun its work before Boris Fedorov – former minister of finance and a prominent leader of Russia's Choice – had gathered around himself a complement of defectors from the faction to form another parliamentary group, the Union of 12 December, which by spring had supplemented its ranks with 5 refugees from the LDPR and a number of previously unaffiliated deputies.[63] The attempt to build a liberally-oriented cadres party on the basis of Russia's Choice and its extra-parliamentary network of activists across the country only accelerated the decline of what had seemed such a formidable political organization a year earlier. By the time of its founding (June 12–13, 1994) the new party – Democratic Choice of Russia (DCR) – had been deserted by the remains of Democratic Russia as well as by a host of the faction's well-known members, among them individuals previously prominent in government: Burbulis, Poltoranin and Ella Pamfilova.[64] To some degree, defections were due to the longstanding short-shrift that the Gaidar-Chubais team had given to their base of activists in Democratic Russia. But what seemed to bring that matter to a head this time was the fact that DCR leaders openly disavowed any intention of becoming a mass democratic party,[65] setting their sights instead – in the words of DCR ideologue and Duma member Grigorii Tomshin – on representing the interests of "big capital."[66] Underscoring that fact was the unanimous election of Oleg Boiko (Chairperson of National Credit Bank and President of the Olbi conglomerate) as Chair of

DCR's Executive Committee,[67] and the arrival of new figures from the business sector, some with apparent connections to the criminal underworld.[68]

Although DCR registered support for the government and its putative course of reform, DCR influence on actual policy was effectively nil. To be sure, its members occupied important governmental positions – Chubais as first deputy prime minister and Andrei Kozyrev as minister of foreign affairs – but neither displayed any loyalty toward the parliamentary faction or the party to which they nominally belonged. The onset of the Chechen War in December 1994 spelled the end of the DCR's attempt to marry liberal political principles to power. Its parliamentary faction, with former-dissident Sergei Kovalev in the lead, forthrightly condemned the government's aggression; for his part, Foreign Minister Kozyrev condemned the disloyalty of his erstwhile colleagues and resigned from the party. Boiko resigned, too, taking with him a number of the DCR major financial supporters. With the scandal that erupted in the following year over party member Vladimir Bauer's (allegedly corrupt) disposition of the perquisites attached to the Duma's Committee for Organizational Work that he chaired, another milestone was passed in the disintegration of what once had been the major democratic bloc.

To distinguish themselves from their former comrades, Fedorov's Union of 12 December had confected an identity that combined liberal *economic* principles with a *political* posture braced around statist and national-patriotic slogans. Consistent with that posture, Fedorov supported the launching of Russia's Chechen military campaign in no uncertain terms, thus discrediting himself in the eyes of most of Russia's liberals and provoking defections among his remaining supporters (among them, Irina Khakamada who attracted many of the disaffected to her new bloc, Common Cause). By February 1995, Fedorov's quest for a liberal-patriotic synthesis had led to the creation of a new party, dubbed – in obvious mimicry of Silvio Berlusconi's Forza Italia! – Forward Russia!

PRES's parliamentary experience was hardly any happier. During spring and summer of 1994, the faction had attempted to assemble a centrist bloc by forging an alliance with Women of Russia, New Regional Politics (formed by deputies elected in districts and theretofore unaffiliated with any parties) and a number of independents in the Duma. But this project came to nothing. Equally, the party's efforts to assume the mantle of spokesperson for regional interests – or, more accurately, those of the regional elites – were doomed once its leader, Sergei Shakhrai, was removed as Minister for the Affairs of Nationalities and Regional Policy in May 1994. Inasmuch as regional interests have been serviced via direct bargaining among executive structures, Shakhrai's departure from his ministerial post eclipsed any prospects for attracting or sustaining the support of regional officials. PRES, therefore, sought to create a base on lower rungs of the federal ladder, courting organizations such as the Union of Russian Cities, the Russian Union of Self-Administration, the Union of Small Towns of Russia and the Russian Zemskoe Movement. This strategy also proved disappointing. The top-down statist form of federal relations prevailing in Russia meant that these grassroots organizations of officials had little, if any, influence on real decision making.[69] Thus deprived of a base among regional elites, PRES – contrary to its proclaimed identity as the "party of the regions" – reconfigured itself as a party of local self-administration (a sub-regional party) seeking to redraw the lines of federal authority in favor of its new-found constituency. But these efforts, too, ended in failure. Instead of passing PRES's bills on local self-administration, the Duma opted for competitive drafts submitted by a group of left-wing factions. Whatever hopes PRES may have had for becoming the voice of Russia's regions vanished with Shakhrai's endorsement of the government's war on Chechnya.

Contrary to the zig-zag trajectories of the factions discussed thus far, Yabloko in the Fifth Duma pursued a course consonant with its 1993 electoral posture as the "democratic opposition." Not coincidentally, the faction's membership remained almost completely intact (see table 5.1), while its voting record indicated that it did not support a single significant initiative of either the president or the government (see table 5.2). Since the organization of the Duma awards to factions the paramount role in composing committees and setting the legislative agenda,[70] their influence in the Duma far outweighs their numbers alone. As a coherent faction in parliament, Yabloko was able to avail itself of that advantage. Yet, since the constitutional order within which parliament functions contains no effective provisions for controlling the government, conditions were ideal for radicalizing this leader-oriented "democratic opposition." As the country's economic and political crises deepened during the Duma's term, Yabloko was caught in a squeeze whereby the increasing need to oppose what they regarded as a disastrous course of government policy coincided with the futility of parliamentary methods for doing so. By fall 1994, the pinch was already apparent. Yabloko abstained from taking a position on a vote of confidence that came before the Duma on October 27, arguing that the measure was not radical enough inasmuch as it would not lead to dissolving the government but – more likely if passed – to dissolving the Duma. Instead, Yabloko continued, the constitution should be amended "to put the authorities under the control of society and to conduct presidential elections [a year ahead of schedule] in 1995."[71] Since none of this was within the authority of the Duma itself, Yabloko's rhetoric amounted to no more than a civics lesson.

Table 5.2 *Positions taken by Russian factions on key votes in the Fifth Duma*

Issues	Positions of factions							
	RC	CPRF	LDPR	WR	APR	DPR	PRES	YaBL
Amnesty	−	+	+	+	+	+	+	−
Agreement on social consensus	+	−	+	+	−	+	+	−
Budget for 1994	−	−	+	+	+	+	+	−
No confidence in government (Oct. 27, 1994)	−	+	+	+	+	+	−	0
Support for war in Chechnya	−	−	+	−	+	=	+	−
Budgets for 1995 and 1996	+	−	+	+	+	−	+	−
Amendments to Constitution	+	+	−	+	+	+	−	+
No confidence in government (June 21, 1995)	−	+	+	+	+	+	−	+
Support for initiative to impeach the president	−	+	=	−	+	+	−	0

Notes: Plus signs indicate "yes" votes; minus signs, "no" votes; equals signs indicate either no position taken or position changed; zeroes indicate abstention. The capital letters identifying factions are the same as those used in the text. Here, "RC" stands for Russia's Choice; "WR" for Women of Russia; and "YaBL" for Yabloko.

Source: G. Belonuchkin, information-research group, Panorama, Moscow, 1995.

But the anti-Yeltsin tone of that statement would be amplified in a few weeks time when Yabloko would condemn both president and government for launching "war in the Caucasus" and would add its weight to resolutions on that score put before the Duma by the CPRF.[72] Comparable transformations occurred among those parties entering the Duma under the banners of communist or national-patriot opposition. Although the LDPR, especially in the persona of its bad-boy leader, continued to pose as an irreconcilable opponent of the government, it backed the government on all but one of the critical votes in the Duma (see table 5.2). While perhaps disappointing Yeltsin by supporting the 1994 amnesty, it refused to endorse the CPRF's initiative to impeach him. The LDPR's peculiar political posture (shrill opposition to the government combined with a near-spotless track record of support for it) along with the equally peculiar approach taken by its leader to parliamentary work (semi-hysterical outbursts, fisticuffs, hair-pulling and so forth) insured the faction against cooperative arrangements with other groups and thus deprived it of any significant posts or serious influence in the legislative process.

Although the APR entered the Duma as the rural counterpart of the CPRF, legislative work – and the readiness of the government to accommo-date its demands – quickly transformed it into a "lobby" securing state subsidies for its agricultural clients and resisting any measures that might undercut their effective monopoly in that sector.[73] The APR thus acquired a new partner, the government, toward which it tendered crucial support in budget votes and muffled its criticisms of government decisions, particularly the military actions in Chechnya. In so doing, it came into increasing conflict ideologically with its erstwhile ally, the CPRF.

For its part, the CPRF was the only opposition faction able significantly to improve its political position over the course of the Fifth Duma. It effectively used the parliamentary rostrum to disseminate the party message and efficiently deployed its legislative resources – paid staff, instruments of communication – to that end as well. With its large competitor, the RCWP, on the parliamentary sidelines, it assumed the visible leadership of the communist camp. Moreover, since the CPRF adhered steadfastly to the positions that they took on one or another issue, they became a dependable partner for other factions and groups, thus forging a number of successful coalitions around various bills that they either authored or supported. These two years of parliamentary work would thus raise an important question about the CPRF: should it be numbered among Russia's democratic institutions?

This question is more easily asked than answered. The CPRF, particularly its territorial organizations, still contains a heavy complement of so-called orthodox Marxist-Leninists. Under pressure from that quarter, its Duma faction, headed by party leader Gennadii Zyuganov, refused to sign the president's "Agreement on Public Consensus" in spring 1994 and, in the following year, launched a campaign to impeach Yeltsin, despite the insurmountable legal and political obstacles to such an undertaking. With respect to the war against Chechnya, the CPRF has sponsored and supported anti-government resolutions and spoken out forcefully against the actions of the federal forces. But it has never publicly disclaimed the use of force *per se* as a means for ending the conflict. In terms of its internal organization and affairs, the CPRF may be the most addicted to democratic procedures and parliamentary discipline of any of the Duma's factions. The singular attempt by the government to coopt it – the January 1995 appointment of faction member Valentin Kovalev as Minister of Justice – resulted in an immediate vote that expelled Kovalev from the faction. Yet, paradoxically, it is this very penchant for democracy *inside* the CPRF that gives many observers pause when the question turns to the commitment of this party to democratic principles in the larger polity. Their concern consists in the fact that some CPRF leaders make no secret about their intentions to change radically the country's politico-economic course should their leader, Zyuganov, win the 1996 presidential election. They are prepared to disregard law and the courts in order to do so and to silence criticism by nationalizing anti-communist newspapers.[74] Should Zyuganov succeed in his bid for the presidency, the question remains open as to whether an anti-democratic majority can be marshalled within the CPRF and whether it would be sufficient to overcome the commitment to democracy displayed by most of the party's parliamentary faction over more than two years of legislative work.

Elections to the Sixth State Duma, December 1995

At the approach of the 1995 elections, Russia's political field included some 261 political parties, public movements and associations officially registered as potential participants. Since proportional representation would be maintained for half of the Duma's seats – along with the rule specifying that parties must receive a minimum of 5 percent of the vote to send the candidates on their lists to the legislature – the great majority of these parties and associations would be expected to form larger election blocs in order to have some chance of passing that five-per-cent threshold. And, for a time, that indeed occurred. Throughout 1994 and into 1995, Russian political society was convulsed by a seemingly endless series of initiatives, conferences and organizing efforts promising to consolidate the fractured forces in the respective political camps and thus present to the electorate a relatively clear choice among competing political identities:[75] democrats, communists, national-patriots and centrists (freely translatable as either "none of the above" or "all of the above"). However, by summer of 1995 when rhetoric about "unity" would necessarily give way to hammering out real coalitions and deciding whose candidates would appear on election lists, the entire edifice of would-be united blocs crumbled and a new scramble of last-minute negotiations ensued that would determine the actual contestants. As summer wore on, some eighty-one political organizations canvassed the country to secure the minimum 200,000 signatures on petitions to appear on the ballot.[76] By the end of the registration period in October, 67 of them had submitted such petitions to the Central Electoral Commission (CEC)[77] which, in turn, determined – sometimes on orders from the Supreme Court in the wake of the CEC's initial rejection of applications – that 43 of them had satisfied its requirements for ballot registration.[78]

How might this surfeit of contenders be explained in the face of both election rules that would "punish" small groups that failed to consolidate into larger blocs and the marathon of ostensible efforts to achieve that consolidation that antedated the campaign itself? Leaving aside the not unimportant influence of "subjective" factors – that is, the vaulting ambitions, personal animosities and longstanding rivalries that characterize Russia's political class generally – we would draw attention to three conditions that promoted fragmentation, all of which stem from the enormous concentration of power in the presidency. First would be the presidency itself and the manner in which it dominates the horizon for the country's politicians. Indeed, the issue of who would eventually stand for that office as the candidate of one or another of the heralded "unified" blocs had been the missing brick in the facades of unity erected by communists and national-patriots in the run-up to these elections.[79] Parliamentary elections thus appeared for many would-be nominees for the presidency as "primaries" in which their names would be promoted and their organizations tested in political battle. Concomitantly, the impetus to combine forces in order to win a larger share of seats in a rather powerless parliament was understandably weak. Second, Yeltsin initially vetoed the Duma's law on elections because it retained the provision of proportional representation for one-half of the seats in parliament. He preferred reducing that percentage to one-third, thus (assumedly) advantaging pro-presidential candidates elected in districts where the political weight of his governors would affect the balance. Negotiations ultimately led to a horse trade: Yeltsin relented on his demand, but the Duma was required to limit the number of candidates on party national lists to twelve, with the provision that all other seats that might be awarded to a party would go to candidates on its regional lists in correspondence with its vote shares in the regions.[80] Since there was no way of predicting the rank order of regional returns for one or another electoral amalgamation, there was no way of determining which regional lists would be named to the Duma and which not. Ergo, the distribution of slots on regional lists did not figure into negotiations among would-be partners. And with only twelve places on national lists to share, coalition formation was severely impeded.[81] Finally, the CEC's provision of 115 million rubles of public monies to finance the campaign of any party securing registration served to broaden the field by: (1) bankrolling weak contenders, and (2) offering, in the face of effectively non-existent financial monitoring,[82] tidy sums of money that could easily be diverted from actual campaigning and into private pockets.

Rather than containing the political differentiation that had accompanied the Fifth Duma, these conditions further encouraged it. Faced with the common task of distinguishing themselves from competitors, parties and blocs within each of the country's four political camps exfoliated. Reviewing the identities projected by the major contenders in each quarter, we get a glimpse of how that process unfolded.

Democrats

Yabloko and DCR entered the race as the principal contenders in the democratic camp, with the former counting on a minimum of 10 percent of the national vote. Yet each party enjoyed a somewhat different base of support among those of Russia's voters generally inclined toward the democratic column. Yabloko voters were more often found in an older age cohort, were less frequently self-employed and evinced little support for the radical economic reform and pro-Western foreign posture associated with Gaidar. As such, there was little in the arithmetic of this election that would conduce to an alliance between them and – since each was shadowed by competitors poised to poach on its vote share – much to caution against it. A Yabloko-DCR alliance would dilute the identity of each partner and thus trigger the defection of erstwhile supporters: potential Yabloko voters might be attracted to the social-market program put forward by its newly-formed competitor, the Party of Self-Management of Working People (PST); their DCR counterparts may prefer the unvarnished economic-liberalism espoused by Forward Russia! or Common Cause.[83] Indeed, a would-be Yabloko-DCR partnership was vicariously incarnate in the Pamfilova-Gurov-(Vladimir) Lysenko bloc, whose figures on left and right of the hyphenated troika had run on Gaidar's and Yavlinskii's tickets, respectively, two years earlier. As indicated in table 5.3, competitors subtracted a considerable share of votes from both of the principal democratic contenders. DCR thus failed to surmount the five-per-cent hurdle and was actually outpolled by the PST whose relatively strong showing seemed to have come at Yabloko's expense.

National-Patriots

Whereas the LDPR had had the national-patriotic field to themselves in 1993, four other major competitors appeared in 1995 to slice into its share of the national vote: the Congress of Russian Communities (KRO), featuring both a more reserved brand of national-patriotism and – according to pre-election opinion polls – the country's leading contender for the presidency, recently-retired general Aleksandr Lebed; the movement Derzhava (Great Power), led by former vice-president Rutskoi who also made no attempt to conceal his presidential ambitions; the Stanislav Govorukhin Bloc, christened for its leader, the film director and leader of the DPR's parliamentary faction whose presidential possibilities were widely mooted; and Nikolai Lysenko's NRPR, a fascist organization in all but name. To make things even more crowded in

Table 5.3 *National vote for parties and blocs in Russia: 1995 with comparisons to 1993 (in percentages)*

Parties and blocs	1995	1993
Democrats		
DCR	3.9	15.5
Yabloko	6.9	7.9
PST	4.0	–
Forward Russia	1.9	–
Common Cause	0.7	–
Pamfilova–Gurov–(V.)Lysenko	1.6	–
National-Patriots		
LDPR	11.2	22.9
KRO	4.3	–
Derzhava	2.6	–
Govorukhin Bloc	1.0	–
National Republicans	0.5	–
Communists		
CPRF	22.3	12.4
APR	3.8	8.0
Communists-Laboring Russia	4.5	–
Power to the People	1.6	–
Centrists		
NDR	10.1	–
Rybkin Bloc	1.1	–
PRES	0.4	6.7
Women of Russia	4.6	8.1
Union of Labor	1.6	1.9[a]

Note: [a]Then known as Civic Union.

Source: *Byulleten' Tsentral'noi izbiratel'noi komissii Rossiiskoi Federatsii*, no. 1 (1994), pp. 52–67; preliminary results for 1995 elections provided by the Central Election Commission of the Russian Federation.

this field, the size of the vote share on which national-patriots could firmly rely was in steep decline, from as much as 20 percent to as little as 10 percent, apparently as a result of Yeltsin's cooptation of their preferred solution to the Chechen crisis (armed force) that, when actually implemented, had yielded results sufficiently disastrous to disabuse many millions of their erstwhile political sympathies.[84]

Nonetheless, the LDPR emerged from the national-patriotic pack as the only party to surmount the five-percent barrier for representation in the Duma (see table 5.3). In the face of the LDPR's modest showing in most pre-election polls (whose figures reflected only about half of the vote total that the party actually won) and the challenges mounted against it – particularly by KRO (which counted, in addition to Lebed's popularity, much of the now-split DPR led by Sergei Glaz'ev, the Socialist Party of Working People, and KRO leader Yurii Skokov's Federation of Commodity Manufacturers)[85] – this result represented perhaps the election's main surprise. In our view, it derived in large part from the outrageous persona so assiduously cultivated by Zhirinovskii and from the extensive (and singularly entertaining) television campaign mounted by the LDPR that played upon that outrageousness.[86] For those fed up with government, politics and politicians, and incensed by the steep and steady socio-economic deterioration of the country surrounding them, no other party rivaled the LDPR as a voter's vehicle to convey his own outrage, symbolically thumbing his nose and shaking his fist at them all.

Communists

From its inception, the CPRF had fashioned itself as a patriotic party, jettisoning notions of class struggle and internationalism while underscoring its devotion to Russian national interests and traditions, including a call to declare Russian Orthodoxy as the state religion.[87] Its patriotic orientation thus served as reason (or excuse) to eschew alliance with other communist organizations in 1995, rejecting in particular the proposal put forward by the RCWP and a few other orthodox Marxist–Leninist parties to stand with them in the elections as a Union of Communists.[88] While it thus distinguished itself from its competitors on the left – principally the Communists-Laboring Russia coalition – it drew a slightly different demarcation between itself and its rivals in the national-patriotic camp. Whereas patriotism for, say, the LDPR or KRO exclusively concerned the Great Russian identity, the CPRF's was a more nuanced approach. Zyuganov, in particular, made room in his broader church for those national minorities and religious denominations deemed loyal to the Great Russian people.[89] Although the CPRF lost some of the communist vote to its more orthodox competitor, Communists-Laboring Russia, and, to a lesser extent, to Power to the People led by Baburin and former Soviet Premier Nikolai Ryzhkov[90] (see table 5.3) – it retained the great bulk of that constituency while stealing votes from the national-patriots as well.[91] Indeed, its momentum going into the campaign

Table 5.4 *Leading Russian parties in the 1995 elections: distribution of seats in the Duma by district and national races*

Parties & blocs	Candidates nominated in districts	Winners in districts	Seats allotted by proportional representation	Total seats won
CPRF	131	58	99	157
LDPR	187	1	50	51
NDR	108	10	45	55
Yabloko	71	14	31	45
APR	90	20	–	20
DCR	75	9	–	9
KRO	90	5	–	5

Sources: Central Election Commission of the Russian Federation.

was sufficient to attract a number of the APR's regional organizations to its side, a development that would account for that party's failure to cross the five-per-cent threshold.[92] Organizationally, the key elements in the CPRF's victory were its old-fashioned, grass-roots campaign, testifying both to the limited effectiveness of money and television in this election and to the CPRF's peerless status as a political machine. The data assembled in table 5.4 indicate the decisive effect of its machinery, both in the national voting and in the country's 225 electoral districts. As had been the case two years earlier, parties proved unable to coordinate their efforts at district level. Despite pre-electoral talk about withdrawing their respective candidates in certain districts in order to support one another's nominees in reciprocal fashion, effectively nothing of the sort occurred once the races were underway.[93] Consequently, with a surfeit of contenders – some 2,700 in all, averaging about twelve candidates per seat[94] – a well-organized party could capitalize on that situation by mobilizing sizeable minorities in districts across the country. Among those seven parties sponsoring a sizeable complement of candidates in the districts (see table 5.4), the number of victors running on the CPRF ticket nearly matched that of all others combined. Unsolicited assistance was also rendered to the CPRF by Yeltsin and those in the state propaganda apparatus who throughout the campaign portrayed the communists as the principal opponent of the president and his government, thus indicating to the disaffected how they might vote most effectively against the president and his government.

Centrists

In addition to three holdovers from the 1993 races – PRES, Women of Russia and the Union of Labor (based on Vol'skii's old Civic Union, now reincarnate as the Russian United Industrial Party, plus the Federation of Independent Trade Unions) – the 1995 centrist contingent included two new parties, both conceived in the Administration of the President.[95] In April 1995, Yeltsin had unveiled the new arrangement at a meeting with the Duma's recently-formed Stability faction – itself the creation of big banks, the gas industry and certain key officials in the presidency and government[96] – proclaiming the formation of a "right-center" bloc (to be headed by Prime Minister Viktor Chernomyrdin) and a "left-center" one (to be led by Duma Chairperson Ivan Rybkin) in order "to oust [from, presumably, the Duma] the extremist wings both left and right."[97] Since none of the established centrist parties passed the five-per-cent threshold, and since Rybkin's bloc, finding itself bereft of expected allies,[98] stumbled to disaster at the polls, we conclude this section with a few remarks on Chernomyrdin's Our Home Is Russia (Nash dom – Rossiya, or NDR).

NDR was Russia's premier power bloc, comprising a complex web of government offices, private capital and state-private conglomerates (chief among which would be the energy sector's Gazprom, the world's largest profit-making organization)[99] decked out as a political party. Revolving around its state-capitalist center were satellite elite configurations in the regions, involving many thousands of government officials[100] (including those superintending privatization)[101] and tied directly to the Administration of the President by their respective heads of administration, some forty-six of whom sat on NDR's central council.[102] Its national staff was headquartered in the apparatus of the government and consisted of the government's past and present senior personnel officers.[103] Indeed, NDR was indistinguishable from the state itself, including those state organizations such as the CEC, its regional counterparts and state television that in Russia have been as much participants in the election process as referees or observers. These associations and its composition framed NDR as an iconic organization, unable to signify anything beyond itself. Its campaign watchword was "stability," a message best decoded as "things could be worse."[104] Its political objectives were perhaps most frankly summarized by the head of its Voronezh chapter, the regional head of administration there who proclaimed that NDR's goal was "to stop those who today are striving for power"[105] – or, in other words, "we who are in power are striving to keep it."

NDR thus marshalled effectively all the resources of the state behind its campaign efforts. Billboards (provided free of charge) throughout Russia's

Table 5.5 *Paid political television advertising by selected Russian parties and blocs, November 1–December 15, 1995*

Parties/blocs	Overall expenditures (in US dollars)	Air time (in seconds)	Number of spots
NDR	1,942,203	40,483	768
Rybkin Bloc	909,392	17,459	387
LDPR	884,944	16,328	519
KRO	597,102	9,710	549
DCR	595,319	6,908	309
Yabloko	354,171	3,651	161
Forward Russia	262,754	3,325	167
Women of Russia	204,167	2,187	130
PRES	172,501	2,392	83
CPRF	3,208	55	1

Source: Analitik Ltd., Moscow (December 18, 1995).

urban landscapes sported its imposing – if self-satirizing – campaign image of Chernomyrdin's sober face against the background of Russia's national colors, the party's name and logo (a pyramid in tricolor), with the prime minister's hands joined at finger tip in the shape of a roof, intended to symbolize "Our Home" but readily suggesting another meaning inasmuch as "roof" in contemporary Russian slang refers to an official body playing host to organized crime. Naturally, party leaders (especially Chernomyrdin) appeared nightly on national news broadcasts making campaign statements in their "official capacity," just as one or another news spot featuring an interview with an official or military officer always seemed to film its subjects in front of an NDR poster or seated next to a framed portrait of the prime minister. In addition to the governmental resources that it poured into its campaign, NDR raised the largest war chest from private contributions of any party in the race. No precise sums would be available in this respect, due to the absence of anything resembling accounting and auditing procedures. But NDR's outspending of competitors would be clearly indicated by its purchase of televised advertising, considering that TV ads represented some 85 percent of all campaign expenditures for advertising in these races.[106] The data presented in table 5.5 show that NDR led the field in this respect, its total greater than that of its two nearest competitors combined. These data also underscore our earlier point about the effectiveness of the CPRF's campaign which made almost no use of television. Outspent by NDR by a factor of 605:1, it outpolled Chernomyrdin's party by more than 2:1 even accepting the official vote totals for the NDR, which appear to have been fraudulently inflated.[107]

Conclusion

If public elections represent modern democracy's *conditio sine qua non*, then its quintessential institution is perforce that agency which structures national voting in coherent and meaningful ways: the party system. Conversely, as our survey of Russia's political parties would indicate, public elections have a critical impact on the structure of the party system itself. Until the issue of who should govern has been submitted to the country's voters for a definitive answer – and, at this writing, it appears to be scheduled for the presidential elections in summer 1996 – the gap between state and political society cannot be expected to be adequately bridged. And without this bridge that an authentic election would supply, we would expect the continuation of the division between the politics of interest – whose principal locus is the state itself – and the politics of identity transpiring in political society.

Our survey of the development of Russia's party system would find support for that proposition in each of the four periods that we have examined. Party formation in Russia's late-Soviet period was arrested until after the 1990 elections had been held. Moreover, those mounting the effort to organize parties had already imbibed the bitter experience of those elections (as well as those for the USSR's new legislature in 1989) conducted under the tutelage of the Soviet party-state in which formal rights, rules and procedures had a habit of disappearing in practice. The multitude of more or less isolated struggles against the party-state in those elections formed the backdrop for party formation thereafter. In all cases – excepting opportunists and restorationists – it focused political energies on one overriding desideratum: to remove the CPSU from power, a result regarded as indispensable to the project of inaugurating democracy and, with it, a real party system. In their formative stage, then, parties appeared as collections of political activists grouped together under various identity constructs, all of which spoke various dialects – "Christian-," "constitutional-," "social-democratic" and so forth – of the same anti-communist language.

When Russia's anti-communist revolution succeeded, the bi-polarity evident during the late-Soviet period carried over into the postcommunist years. Once again, elections – in this case, their absence – would appear to be the primary factor shaping the party system. Since elections were not called immediately after communism's collapse, party development was set back enormously. Here, it is enough to recall the fact that those parties formed in the preceding period – and, therefore, the organized political forces that would have campaigned in the elections that they demanded for early 1992 – had all effectively exited Russia's political stage by 1995. Their undoing was in almost all cases coextensive with the history of the postcommunist period when, instead of engaging in electoral struggle, political society regrouped as footsoldiers for the battles waged between president and parliament.

The elections of 1993 revived party development, but in ways peculiar to those elections themselves. The authorities' ban on a number of parties and political associations was significant in that respect, as was the apparently extensive degree of ballot fraud that they practiced.[108] However, the constitution imposed by Yeltsin was of even greater import in reconfiguring the party system.[109] The combination of an authoritarian presidency with an ineffectual parliament reinforced the division between state and political society, thus impeding a fusion of interests and identities in the latter and structuring political forces in a new multi-polar pattern wherein political differentiation was incommensurate with political coherence. As we observed in that respect, the cleavage between supporters and opponents of the government's substantive policies was crosscut by another one involving support or opposition to the authoritarian presidency from which those policies ultimately derived.

These constitutional considerations – not least of which was the prospect of elections in June 1996 to the presidency itself – exerted a powerful influence on the field of contenders in the 1995 elections to the Sixth Duma. Relatively undeterred by the confusing spectacle of 43 different parties and blocs appealing for their support, 64.5 percent of Russia's voters were reported to have turned out, a figure which – even if inflated by ballot fraud[110] – represented a significant increase over the 54.8 percent turnout officially reported two years earlier. However, despite the appeals of propagandists on state television urging the voters not to "waste" their ballots by voting for any of the smaller parties unlikely to cross the five-per-cent threshold for representation,[111] nearly half of the electorate (49.5 percent) did just that. Since only four parties managed to cross that barrier, the surfeit of political representation in the election has resulted in a corresponding dearth of representation in the Duma. That problem evident in the national voting has been compounded by the results of the races in territorial districts. Since no provision for run-offs was included in the election law, relatively small pluralities usually proved sufficient to send candidates to the Duma. Overall, some 70.8 percent of the votes cast in district races went to the losers.[112] With so many parties shut out of office and so many voters denied representation, the prevailing arrangements do not bode well for the stability of Russia's party system and, by that measure, for Russian democracy generally.

In conclusion, we would be remiss to neglect mention of the influence that Western governments and institutions have had on Russia's party system and the country's overall experience with democracy. Whereas Russia's postcommunist history began with large percentages of the public supporting the idea of democracy – and, correspondingly expressing favorable attitudes toward the (democratic) West – by 1995 some two-thirds of the population regarded the policy of Western governments as a hostile force "directed toward the weakening of Russia."[113] Despite professed good wishes and even the best intentions regarding "democracy" and "reform" in Russia, Western actions have had profoundly deleterious effects on both. Economically, Western assistance has not arrived in quantities that would begin to match expectations. Indeed, almost all direct US aid between 1991 and 1995 (totaling some $3.5 billion) paid salaries for, and remodeled the offices of, US consulting firms contributing a very questionable "expertise" to the cause of democracy in Russia.[114] Yet, since the West continues publicly to support "reform," it is identified in the minds of many as complicit with that savage form of state-capitalism that has taken shape in Russia. Politically, a similar story can be told. Regardless of public endorsements for the cause of democracy in Russia, Western governments supported the authoritarian presidency that emerged during the postcommunist period, including Yeltsin's abrogation of the constitution in September 1993 and his subsequent shelling of the parliament. His codification of the authoritarian presidency into the country's new constitution as well as his reneging on his promise to hold presidential elections in June 1994 drew no criticism from Western governments. Even the unspeakable carnage that his generals have wrought in Chechnya has elicited no more than a few hesitations. Our point, of course, is not that the West inherently bears some responsibility for promoting democracy in Russia. Rather, it is that Western governments and institutions both have claimed that responsibility for themselves and have discharged it in ways counter-productive to their professed intent. The ensuing disillusion in Russian society with both the West and democracy itself can be measured in part by the results of the recent elections. The governing party captured a humiliating 10 percent of the national vote; subsequently, it has formed a *de facto* coalition in the Duma with the party of Zhirinovskii;[115] and some four years after communism's collapse, that same spectre has again appeared in Russia.

Acronyms

APPE	Association of Privatized and Privatizing Enterprises
APR	Agrarian Party of Russia
A-UCPB	All-Union Communist Party of Bolsheviks

CEC	Central Electoral Commission
CDP	Constitutional Democratic Party
CPRF	Communist Party of the Russian Federation
CPSU	Communist Party of the Soviet Union
DCR	Democratic Choice of Russia
DPR	Democratic Party of Russia
FDPR	Free Democratic Party of Russia
FNS	Front of National Salvation
KRO	Congress of Russian Communities
LDPR	Liberal Democratic Party of Russia
LDPSU	Liberal Democratic Party of the Soviet Union
MDR	Movement for Democratic Reforms
NRPR	National Republican Party of Russia
NDR	Our Home is Russia
PCD	Party of Constitutional Democrats
PPFR	People's Party of Free Russia
PRES	Party of Russian Unity and Accord
PST	Party of Self-Management of Working People
RC	Russia's Choice
RCDM	Russian Christian Democratic Movement
RCP	Russian Communist Party
RCWP	Russian Communist Workers' Party
RMDR	Russian Movement for Democratic Reforms
RPR	Republican Party of Russia
SDPR	Social Democratic Party of Russia

NOTES

1 We are using for the last two categories the official terminology employed in Russia, according to which the new legislature elected in 1993 is regarded as a successor to the Fifth Russian Duma dissolved by the Emperor in 1917.
2 Michael Urban, *The Rebirth of Politics in Russia* (Cambridge: Cambridge University Press, 1997), ch. 5.
3 Discussion of this point for the 1989 and 1990 elections can be found in ibid., chs. 6 and 8. For the 1993 elections, see idem, "December 1993 as a Replication of Late-Soviet Electoral Practices," *Post-Soviet Affairs* 10 (April–June 1994), 127–58.
4 On the SDPR's founding congress, see: *Alternativa*, no. 1 (30 May–12 June 1990); Dmitrii Khrapovintskii, "Partiya sotsial-demokratov," *Soyuz*, no. 19 (May 1990), p. 10; N. Solyanik, "Pomen'she by ambitsii," *Narodnyi deputat*, no. 12 (1990), pp. 75–77. SDPR membership stood at 4,000 at the party's inception, grew to some 7,000 by the end of 1990 and declined thereafter. Mikhail Malyutin, "Sushchestvuet li v SSSR mnogopartiinost'?" (Moscow: mimeo, May 1991). On the SDPR's pre-history, see: Vladimir Pribylovskii, *Slovar' oppozitsii: novye politicheskie partii i organizatsii Rossii* (Moscow: Postfactum, 1991), p. 40; "Esdeki," *Panorama*, no. 8 (September 1989), 1–2; D.A. Pankin, *Sotsial-demokraticheskaya partiya Rossiiskoi Federatsii: kratkii spravochnik* (Moscow and Petrozavodsk: Inform-Sluzhby, Board of SDPR, 1991), pp. 28–30.

5 *Al'ternativa*, no. 1 (30 May–12 June 1990), 2; V.E. Lyzlov in Dmitrii Khrapovit-skii's "Partii nachinayut i . . ." *Soyuz*, no. 17 (April 1990), 19.

6 Oleg Rumyantsev, "Nash put' k sotsial'noi demokratii," *Narodnyi deputat*, no. 2 (1991), 86. A left-wing current in the SDPR that would not concur with this definition of social-democracy was formed around Galina Rakitskaya. Its position paper, "Levaya fraktsiya v SDPR" (19 April 1991), set out a counter-identity for the party, harkening back to when the unionized working class in the West formed the backbone of social-democratic and labor parties. This faction left the SDPR in 1993.

7 "Sotsial-demokraty v Rossiiskom parlamente," *Novosti sotsial-demokratii*, no. 2 (1990), 2–6; interview given by Denis Pankin (SDPR Executive Secretary) to M. Urban (23 April 1991).

8 "Ob utverzhdenii Polozheniya o tsentral'noi finansovo-kommercheskoi komissii pri Pravlenii SDPR," Reshenie 2-go plenuma Pravleniya SDPR (Moscow: mimeo, 5 August 1990).

9 Pankin, *Sotsial-demokraticheskaya partiya Rossiiskoi federatsii*, pp. 35–6.

10 For example, "Dvizhenie Khristianskoi Demokratii v Rossii," in *Rossiiskoe Khristianskoe Demokraticheskoe Dvizhenie: Sbornik materialov* (Moscow: Duma Khristianskogo Demokraticheskogo Dvizheniya, 1990), p. 3.

11 V. Aksyuchits, "Vystuplenie na Sobore RKhDD," *Put'*, no. 7 (1992), 3. His speech to the Congress of Civic and Patriotic Forces in February 1992 appears in ibid., no. 2 (1992), 3.

12 "Soyuz Konstitutsionnykh Demokratov: paket programmnykh dokumentov" (Moscow: mimeo, 1989).

13 Ol'ga Golenkina, "Zapiski na mandatakh," *Grazhdanskoe dostoinstvo*, no. 21 (June 1990), 3; V. F. Levicheva and A. A. Nelyubin, "Novye obshchest-venno-politicheskie organizatsii, partii i dvizheniya," *Izvestiya TsK KPSS*, no. 8 (1990), 149–50. For details, see "O pretenziyakh na kadetskoe nasledstvo," *Grazhdanskoe dostoinstvo*, no. 3 (23–30 May 1991), 8.

14 In 1992, the PCD joined the Russian National Assembly and Front for National Salvation. Its leader, Mikhail Astaf'ev, was co-chairperson of the former and sat on the latter's executive bodies.

15 Yu. Gladysh, "Ot partiinogo kluba k 'Demokraticheskoi platforme,'" *Narodnyi deputat*, no. 6 (1990), 59–62; M. Malyutin, "Za kem poidut massy," ibid., no. 5 (1990), 45–6. In June 1989 this group, renamed the Moscow party club, began meeting at the premises that the Sevastopol district CPSU committee had previously afforded to the informals. "Zayavlenie o sozdani Moskovskaya partiinaya kluba (kommunisty za perestroiku)" (mimeo, no date [Moscow Bureau of Information Exchange (hereafter, M-BIO) archives, fond DP 079–052]); "K kommunistam v pervichnykh partiinykh organizatsii raikomakh [sic] MGK KPSS" (mimeo, no date [M-BIO archives, fond DP 079–052]).

16 Synopses of their programmes appeared in "Est' mnenie," *Izvestiya* (10 June 1990).

17 M. Steven Fish, *Democracy From Scratch: Opposition and Regime in the New Russian Revolution* (Princeton: Princeton University Press, 1994), pp. 86–88.

18 Urban, *The Rebirth of Politics in Russia*, ch. 10.

19 O. Grigor'ev, V. Lepekhin and M. Malyutin, *Partiya truda v sovremennoi Rossii: neobkodimost' i vozmozhnost'* (Moscow: Institute for the Study of Extraordinary [ekstremal'nykh] Processes, 1991); B. I. Koval' and V. B. Pavlenko, *Partii i politicheskie bloki v Rossii* (Moscow: Narodnaya Neftyanaya Investitsionno-promyshlennaya evroaziatskaya korporatsiya, 1993), pp. 103–8.

20 The Republican Party of Russia entered the Yabloko coalition for the 1993 elections, and splintered thereafter, retaining a separate identity but not as an electoral organization. The People's Party of Free Russia was forbidden to participate in the 1993 elections, and metamorphosed thereafter into two competing organizations: the Social Democratic Union (Lipitskii) and Derzhava (Rutskoi). The Labor Party joined other democratic-socialist groups in an electoral bloc in 1993, but was denied a place on the ballot, allegedly for irregularities in its signatures list.

21 V. Kriger, "Pochemu ya ne mogu vstupit' v partiyu kotoruyu sama sozdavala," *Golos izbiratelya*, no. 12 (1990), 4; Konstantin Zavoiskii and Vladimir Krylovskii, *S chego nachinaetsya partiya* (Moscow: Ekspress-Khronika, 1990).

22 Urban, *The Rebirth of Politics in Russia*, ch. 9.

23 Sergei Mitrokhin and Michael Urban, "Social Groups, Party Elites and Russia's New Democrats," in *Russia in Flux: The Political and Social Consequences of Reform*, ed. D. Lane (Aldershot, UK: Edward Elgar, 1992), pp. 62–81.

24 "Obrashchenie orgkomiteta po sozdaniyu dvizheniya 'Demokraticheskaya Rossiya'" (Moscow: photo copy, no date [M-BIO archives, DR, fond no. 1, doc. 17]).

25 "Spisok chlenov orgkomiteta po sozaniyu dvizheniya 'Demokraticheskaya Rossiya'" (Moscow: photo copy, no date).

26 Political parties and other affiliated organizations were represented on DemRossiya's Council of Representatives, whose membership, numbering at various times between 200 and 300, also included delegates from DemRossiya's regional units who were not party members. Parties were also represented on the more important Coordinating Council, but there they were a distinct minority (eleven representatives on a body of forty-eight members in spring 1991). The Coordinating Council, which elected the co-chairpersons, was thus the real stronghold of those in DemRossiya making political careers outside of its affiliated parties, as indicated by the roster of the first six co-chairpersons elected in December 1990: Afanas'ev, Popov, Ponomarev, Murashev, Yakunin and Viktor Dmitriev. "Demokraticheskaya Rossiya" (M-BIO archives, DR, fond no. 1, document 167.) "Soobshchenie N 2 Orgkomiteta po sozdaniyu dvizheniya 'Demokraticheskaya Rossiya'" (Moscow: photo copy, no date).

27 Membership estimates vary from the 200,000–300,000 cited by Pribylovskii (*Slovar' oppozitsii*, p. 8) to a figure of 1.3 million that appeared in *Nezavisimaya gazeta*, 25 April 1991, p. 1.

28 Michael Urban, "Boris El'tsin, Democratic Russia and the Campaign for the Russian Presidency," *Soviet Studies* 44, no. 2 (1992), 187–207.

29 Urban, *The Rebirth of Politics in Russia*, ch. 10.

30 *Segodnya*, 24 May 1994, p. 2; ibid., 7 September 1995, p. 2.

31 *OMRI Daily Digest*, 1 November 1995.

32 The fact the presidency had not been established yet in Russia did not dissuade
    DemRossiya's organizers from this view. See Arkadii Murashev's remarks quoted
    in Aleksandr Davydov's "Otkrylsya s"ezd 'Demokraticheskoi Rossii,'" *Izvestiya*,
    20 October 1990 and Andrei Vasilevskii, "Demokraty: ob"edinenie i razmezhe-
    vaniya," *Panorama*, no. 13 (December 1990), p. 3.

33 Urban, *The Rebirth of Politics in Russia*, ch. 11.

34 This paragraph is based on Pribylovskii, *Slovar' oppozitsii*, pp. 7, 13, 17.

35 N. V. Proselkov and A. V. Cherepanov, "Informatsionnoe soobshchenie ob
    itogakh II S"ezda Demokraticheskoi partii," *Zona: gazeta neravnodushnykh*,
    November 1990, p. 4.

36 "Coup or Operetta?" *Moscow News*, 18–25 November 1990, p. 6; "Raskoly,
    raskoly, raskoly . . .," *Soyuz*, no. 13 (27 March–3 April 1991), p. 10.

37 Quoted in Natalya Izyumova, "LDP Set to Hold Congress in Kremlin," *Moscow
    News*, 6–13 May 1990, p. 7. Zhirinovskii himself said that the LDPSU's
    orientation was indistinguishable from that of the other democratic parties:
    Izvestiya, 1 April 1990.

38 Stepan Orlov and Vadim Prokhorov, "PervoAprel'skaya partiya," *Panorama*, no.
    7 (July 1990), p. 5.

39 "Coup or Operetta?"; G. Alimov, "A. Luk'yanov: 'My otkryty dlya dialoga,'"
    Izvestiya, 2 November 1990. DemRossiya regarded the Centrist Bloc as either the
    creatures or the tools of the KGB. "Demokraticheskie sily o perspektivakh
    demokraticheskogo razvitiya," *Demokraticheskaya Rossiya*, no. 3 (September
    1990), p. 4.

40 "A est' li trentristskii blok?" *Izvestiya*, 29 March 1991.

41 Urban, "Boris El'tsin, Democratic Russia."

42 Urban, *The Rebirth of Politics in Russia*, ch. 7.

43 A. Aidak, "S"ezd krest'yam gotovitsya . . . apparatom," *Izvestiya*, 25 April
    1990. Don Van Atta, "Political Mobilization in the Russian Countryside: Creating
    Social Movements from Above," in *Perestroika from Below: Social Movements
    in the Soviet Union*, ed. J. Sedaitis and J. Butterfield (Boulder, CO: Westview,
    1991), pp. 57–62.

44 Aleksei Kiva, "'Soyuz' oderzhimykh," *Izvestiya*, 11 May 1991; Joel C. Moses,
    "The Challenge to Soviet Democracy from the Political Right," in *Pere-
    stroika-Era Politics: The New Soviet Legislature and Gorbachev's Political
    Reforms*, ed. R. Huber and D. Kelley (Armonk, NY: M. E. Sharpe, 1991), esp.,
    pp. 109–110.

45 Robert Orttung, "The Russian Right and the Dilemmas of Party Organization,"
    Soviet Studies 44, no. 3 (1992), 463.

46 For a political portrait of Polozkov, see Lyudmila Telen', "Zapovednaya zona?"
    Narodnyi deputat, no. 10 (1990), 52–61.

47 Vladimir Pribylovskii, *Natsional'no-patriotickeskie ob"edineniya "Pamyat"*
    (Moscow: Institut gumanitarno-politicheskikh issledovanii, 1991), pp. 1–10.

48 For a representative sample of national-patriotic discourse at this juncture, see
    Michael Urban, "Contending Conceptions of Nation and State in Russian
    Politics," *Demokratizatsiya*, no. 4 (1993), esp., pp. 9–11.

49 Ya. Ermakov, T. Shavshukova and V. Yakunichkin, "Kommunisticheskoe
    dvizhenie v period zapreta: ot KPSS k KPRF," *Kentavr*, no. 3 (1993), 65–80.

50 Tat'yana Shavshukova, "Kommunisty i sotsialisty v yanvare 1993 goda," *Politicheskii monitoring*, no. 1 (1993), 167–79.
51 Michael Urban, "State, Property and Political Society in Postcommunist Russia: In Search of a Political Center," in *In Search of Pluralism in Soviet and Post-Soviet Politics*, ed. C. Saivets and A. Jones (Boulder, CO: Westview, 1994), pp. 132–9.
52 Michael McFaul, "Russian Centrism and Revolutionary Transitions," *Post-Soviet Affairs* 9 (July–September 1993), pp. 196–222.
53 Joanna J. Mizgala, "The Ecology of Transformation: The Impact of the Corporatist State on the Formation and Development of the Party System in Poland, 1989–93," *East European Politics and Societies* 8 (Spring 1994), 358–68.

54 Evgenii Krasnikov, "Politicheskoe predstavitel'stvo biznesa," *Predely vlasti*, no. 4 (1994), 138–9; Vladimir Gel'man and Ol'ga Senatova, "Politicheskie partii v regionakh Rossii," *Politicheskii monitoring*, no. 8 (1993), 22–37.
55 Vyacheslav Bragin, director of State Television, and Mikahil Poltoranin, head of the Federal Information Center, were leading members of Russia's Choice. On their use of the public airwaves for campaign purposes in 1993, see Michael Urban, "December 1993 as a Replication of Late-Soviet Electoral Practices," *passim*; James Hughes, "The 'Americanization' of Russian Politics: Russia's First Television Election, December 1993," *Journal of Communist Studies and Transition Politics* 10 (June 1994), 125–50.
56 All data reported for the 1993 elections have been taken from *Byulleten' Tsentral'noi izbiratel'noi komissii Rossiiskoi Federatsii*, no. 1 (1994), 52–67. On the 1993 elections generally, see *Vybory v Gosudarstvennuyu Dumu: 7 oktyabr'–14 dekabrya*, ed. V. Dorofeev, Yu. Solodukhin and E. Topoleva (Moscow: Postfactum, 1993); Richard Sakwa, "The Russian Elections of December 1993," *Europe-Asia Studies* 47 (March 1995), 195–227; Matthew Wyman, Stephen White, Bill Miller and Paul Heywood, "Public Opinion, Parties and Voters in the December 1993 Russian Elections," ibid. 47 (June 1995), 591–614; Stephen Whitefield and Geoffrey Evans, "The Russian Elections of 1993: Public Opinion and the Transition Experience," *Post-Soviet Affairs* 10, no. 1 (January–March 1994), 38–60.
57 Petr Sidorov, "Tendentsii rossiiskoi politiki v avguste 1993 goda," *Politicheskii monitoring*, no. 8 (1993), 17–18.
58 A. Salmin, *Rossiiskaya partiinaya sistema v 1989–1993 gg: opyt stanovleniya* (Moscow: Nachala-press, 1994).
59 Oleg Ochin, "Predupredit fal'start," *Segodnya*, 26 April 1994, p. 10; Dmitrii Volkov and Rustam Narzikulov, "Senatory namereny funktsionirovat' ne po-parlamentski," ibid., 28 April 1994, p. 2.
60 A clear indication of the Constitutional Court's role in this respect would be its April 1995 ruling that a majority vote in the Duma consists of one-half plus one of that body's membership as it appears in the constitution (450 members), irrespective of how many seats might be vacant at a given time or how many of its members may not have turned up to cast votes. This decision obviously has retarded the legislative process by raising the threshold for an actual majority.

61 Donald Barry, "Amnesty Under the Russian Constitution: Evolution of the Provision and Its Use in February 1994," *Parker School Journal of East European Law* 1, no. 4 (1994), pp. 437–61.

62 A. Sobyanin and V. Sukhovol'skii, *Demokratiya, ogranichennaya fal'sifikatsiyami* (Moscow: Proektnaya gruppa po pravam cheloveka, 1995), pp. 73–109.

63 *Segodnya*, 26 May 1994, p. 2.

64 Ibid., 31 May 1994, p. 1, and 15 June 1994, p. 2.

65 See Egor Gaidar's report to the DCR's founding congress, *Otkrytaya politika*, no. 2 (1994), 49–54.

66 *Nevskoe vremya*, 3 June 1994, p. 1.

67 Viktor Alekseyenko, "Gaidar Gets Support from Financial Circles," *Moscow News*, 17–23 June 1994, p. 2.

68 *Nezavisimaya gazeta*, 25 February 1994, p. 2.

69 See Jeffrey Hahn's chapter in this volume.

70 Moshe Haspel, "Internal Organization in a Developing Legislature: Committees in the Russian Duma" (paper presented to the Annual Meeting of the Midwest Political Science Association, Chicago, 6–8 April 1995).

71 *Reformy dlya bol'shinstva: Ob"edinenie "Yabloko"* (Moscow: EPItsentr, 1995), pp. 256–57.

72 Ibid., pp. 258–60.

73 Of particular import in that respect was the Land Code composed by the APR that preserved corporatist interests in the agricultural sector by effectively prohibiting the buying and selling of land. The Duma's favorable vote on the Land Code in the first reading (July 1995) thus blocked the path for land reform in the legislature. *Segodnya*, 23 November 1995, p. 2.

74 See, for instance, the interview given to Yu. Feofanov by CPRF leader Yurii Ivanov, *Izvestiya*, 22 February 1996.

75 Gleb Cherkasov, "Khronika neudavshegosya splocheniya," *Segodnya*, 14 November 1995, p. 3.

76 On the mechanics of the election process and the composition of the contending partners and blocs, see: *Previewing Russia's 1995 Parliamentary Elections*, ed. Michael McFaul and Nikolai Petrov (Washington, D.C.: Carnegie Endowment for International Peace, 1995); *Pre-Election Report: The December 1995 Parliamentary Elections in the Russia Federation* (Washington, DC: National Democratic Institute for International Affairs, 1995).

77 For names, leaders and an analysis of the profiles of these 67 groups, see Dmitrii Yur'ev, "Peizazh pered bitvoi," *Segodnya*, 21 October 1995, p. 3.

78 For analyses of these forty-three contenders, see the sources cited in note 76 (above) and *Argumenty i fakty*, no. 49 (December 1995), pp. 8–9.

79 Gleb Cherkasov, "Tret'ya popytka sozdaniyu 'bolshoi antiel'tsinskoi koalitsii,'" *Segodnya*, 14 May 1994, p. 3; Viktor Khamraev, "Lidery oppozitsii eshche raz potreboval edinstva," ibid.; "The Opposition Gets Organized," *Moscow News*, 3–9 June 1994, p. 1.

80 On the history of the adoption of the Law on Elections, see V. Razmustov, "Istoriya prinyatiya zakona o vyborakh deputatov Gosdarstvennoi Dumy," *Nezavisimaya gazeta*, 29 November 1995, pp. 1, 5.

81 For specific examples, see *Segodnya*, 9 September 1995, p. 2.

82 The CEC had a staff of (at most) fourteen individuals charged with monitoring the campaign spending of the forty-three national parties and blocs as well as that of some 2,700 candidates running in electoral districts. See Rustam Narzikulov, "Na deputatskii rynok vybroshen tovar stoimost'yu 370 mln dollarov," *Segodnya*, 28 November 1995, pp. 7–8.

83 Igor' Klyamkin, "Elektorat demokraticheskikh sil," in *Analiz elektorata politicheskikh sil Rossii*, ed. A.I. Ioffe (Moscow: Komtekh, 1995), pp. 13–18.

84 Leontii Byzov, "Rossiiskie natsional-patrioty i ikh elektorat," in Ioffe, ed., *Analiz elektorata*, pp. 53–4.

85 The internal make-up of KPO was quite eclectic. It began initially in January 1993 as the Union for the Rebirth of Russia, a cultural-political organization headed by former CDP leader Dmitrii Rogozin (*Nezavisimaya gazeta*, 16 January 1993, p. 2). A few months later, many of these same individuals created the Congress of Russian Communities (KRO), signifying their interest in securing the rights of Russians still living in the "near abroad." In 1993, both groups joined the (unsuccessful) Fatherland bloc to contest the December elections. By early 1995, KRO had graduated into a political party in its own right, electing the influential Skokov as its leader (*Segodnya*, 25 February 1995, p. 2). In preparation for elections that year it attracted one of its old partners from the Fatherland bloc, the Socialist Party of Working People (*Segodnya*, 1 September 1995, p. 2), and a wing of the DPR keen to back it because of Lebed's then bright prospects for the presidency (*Segodnya*, 8 August 1995, p. 2).

86 The sources of the LDPR's ample financing remain a mystery. Assumedly, the party no longer benefitted, as it appeared to in 1993, from old communist money held in foreign bank accounts. The LDPR may have received support in 1995 from certain right-wing organizations in Europe, but the major suspicions circulating in Moscow in December 1995 were that much of its financing had come from Yeltsin's inner circle (for whom Zhirinovskii represents a convenient "scarecrow") and/or from arms manufacturers in the United States and France (for whom a perceived foreign threat is essential to a good business climate).

87 Vladimir Sirotin, "National Communism," *Moscow News*, 2–8 September 1994, p. 6.

88 *Segodnya*, 29 August 1995, p. 2.

89 Maryanne Ozernoy, "Neo-Communist Ethnic Politics: Multi-Ethnic Fundamentalism," *Prism* (The Jamestown Foundation) 2, Part 1, no. 1 (12 January 1996).

90 Although Power to the People – composed of Baburin's Russian All-People's Union, Mothers for Social Justice, the Union of Officers and the movements Soyuz and Fatherland – projected a national-patriotic identity, we have numbered it among the communist organizations because of the close ties between most of those groups and the Soviet order, personified by Ryzhkov, who topped its national list.

91 Aleksandr Segal, "Elektorat levykh sil," in Ioffe, ed., *Analiz elektorata*, p. 42.

92 *Segodnya*, 22 December 1995, p. 2.

93 *Nezavisimaya gazeta*, 24 November 1995, p. 1; ibid., 29 November 1995, p. 2.

94 Data provided by CEC at press conference, Moscow, 29 November 1995.

95   The strategy to install "from above" a two-party system in Russia was apparently authored by Shakhrai. It called for the formation of a "right-center" and a "left-center" party, each of which would divide governmental and legislative posts between themselves in staggered fashion – a ministerial appointment for one, for instance, implied a deputy minister's job for the other – thus assembling a two-party government prior to the elections themselves. Apparently, this arrangement broke down during the plan's implementation phase. On the plan itself, see: Egor Bykovsky, "Two 'Superparties' Bent on Sharing Power," *Moscow News*, 28 April–4 May 1995, pp. 1–2; Gleb Cherkasov, "Generaly gotovyatsya k proshloi voine," *Segodnya*, 19 May 1995, p. 3; Vera Selivanova, "Partiya vlasti: depolitizatsiya politiki," ibid., 31 May 1995, p. 3. On its implementation, see: Sergei Parkhomenko, "'Sluga dvukh gospod.' Versiya 1995 goda," ibid., 3 October 1995, p. 2; interview given by Sergei Shakhrai to A. Smirnov, *Izvestiya*, 14 December 1995.

96   Lyudmila Telen, "Money Increasingly Controls Politics," *Moscow News*, 24–30 March 1995, p. 3.

97   Quoted in Gleb Cherksov, "Prezident rasporyadilsya obespechit' uspekh na vyborakh," *Segodnya*, 26 April 1995, p. 1.

98   It appears that Rybkin attempted to enlist those who eventually formed the Union of Labor, as well as the APR (on whose list he had appeared in 1993) and Women of Russia, all without success. See: *Segodnya*, 12 May 1995, p. 2; ibid., 22 August 1995, p. 2; *OMRI Daily Digest*, 13 September 1995.

99   Vladimir Lepekhin, "Problemy izucheniya sovremennoi elity Rossii," *Predely vlasti*, no. 4 (1994), 90–101.

100 *Segodnya*, 31 October 1995, p. 2.

101 Ibid., 31 August 1995, p. 1.

102 Ibid., 13 May 1995, p. 1.

103 Ibid., 28 April 1995, p. 1.

104 Klyamkin, "Elektorat demokraticheskikh sil," pp. 11–12.

105 Quoted in *Segodnya*, 5 July 1995, p. 3.

106 Ibid., 23 January 1996, p. 10.

107 Given NDR's direct associations with government and the role played by most heads of administration – whose personnel networks include district- and regional-level electoral commissions – it appears likely that some falsification of results in favor of NDR occurred. More directly evident would be falsification of the vote in the military, whose officers were ordered by the Russian Ministry of Defense to support NDR's efforts (US Government Diplomatic Cable, Moscow, 21 September 1995). Thus, whereas the Ministry of Defense reported a vote in the armed services of over 60 percent for NDR (*Nezavisimaya gazeta*, 22 December 1995, p. 2), exit polling in military units indicated that only 30–40 percent of service personnel cast their ballots in that way (*OMRI Special Report: Russian Election Survey*, 18 December 1995).

108 Kronid Lyubarskii and Aleksandr Sobyanin, "Fal'sifikatsiya 3," *Novoe vremya*, no. 15 (April 1995), pp. 6–12; Tatyana Skorobogatko, "Were the Election Returns Rigged?" *Moscow News*, 22–28 July 1994, p. 1.

109 We regard this constitution as "imposed" inasmuch as public debate on it was effectively disallowed, while the low condition set for its adoption by public

referendum (a majority vote with 50 percent turnout) apparently was not, in fact, met. *Izvestiya*, 4 May 1994.

110 *Moskovskii komsomolets*, 29 December 1995, pp. 1-2.

111 The spots (beginning in early December) performed by Boris Grushin, head of the polling firm, Vox Populi, that offered nightly voter "education" on the evening news program, Vremya, would be the outstanding example of this practice.

112 Dmitrii Babovskii et al., "Parlamentskie vybory 17 dekabrya 1995 goda kak prezidentskie 'praimeriz,'" *Segodnya*, 5 April 1996, p. 3.

113 Klyamkin, "Elektorat demokraticheskikh sil," p. 16.

114 Aleksei Gorshkov, "Teknicheskaya pomoshch' SShA Rossii popadaet k amerikanskim konsaltingovym kompaniyam," *Segodnya*, 5 April 1996, p. 2.

115 Ibid., 17 January 1995, p. 2.

Belarus, Moldova, and Ukraine

6 Belarus: retreat to authoritarianism

Kathleen J. Mihalisko

Fully a decade has passed since Mikhail Gorbachev initiated the liberalizing policies that dramatically altered the fate of Soviet communism and led to the demise of the world's last great empire. The implementation of perestroika and glasnost unintentionally catalyzed forces that overwhelmed and destroyed the very system Gorbachev sought to repair, in what came to resemble a historically irresistible chain reaction. What propelled these events faster and farther than any Western policy-planning scenarios had ever conjured were the aspirations of subjugated nations – Balts, Ukrainians, and others – toward national self-determination and independence from Moscow. Speaking of another time and place, R. F. Foster, the eminent historian of modern Ireland, once observed that "belief in deliverance" remained distinct in the Irish mind through "the different layers of the palimpsest of historical experience," a belief described by a fellow Irishman as the idea of "freedom as an end in itself and of independent government . . . as the solution of all ills."[1] Much the same spirit took hold throughout the USSR.

The initial reluctance of some US and European policy-makers to come to grips with the breakup of the Soviet Union (recall President George Bush's trip to Kiev on the eve of the August 1991 putsch, when he urged Ukrainians to avoid nationalist excesses and sign Gorbachev's proposed Union treaty) eventually ceded to the realization that national aspirations, far from threatening regional stability, strongly favored the democratic transformation of the communist bloc and were a logical extension of the nation-building processes that have characterized twentieth-century Europe. The imperatives of nationhood provided the crucial context for the transition to democracy and free markets.

Belarus, the focus of this paper, provides a singular exception to the trend. With catastrophic irony, Belarus's initial opening to Western reforms has been cancelled indefinitely by its first democratically elected president in history, Alyaksandr Lukashenka, who since coming to power in 1994 has suspended the post-Soviet constitution in practice to establish a lawless regime of personal dictatorship. The Belarusian leader summarized his leadership approach in a November 1995 interview with the German newspaper *Handelsblatt*, wherein he praised Adolf Hitler's "good deeds" in prewar Germany and suggested that a similar kind of iron-willed regime was needed in Belarus.[2] Even more revealing of his character, it was clear in context that Lukashenka thought such comments would be received as flattery, not offense, by *Handelsblatt*'s readers. The president has been true to his word: surrounded by armed thugs instead of statesmen, Lukashenka currently prosecutes a campaign to drive parliament out of business and crush his critics. Two of these recently became the first politicians from the former Soviet bloc to receive political asylum in the United States.

These sad developments actually owe less to fascism, with its current of extremist nationalism, than to the basic traditions of Soviet totalitarianism. It is the absence of nationalism – in its primary definition of devotion to the interests of a nation – that makes Lukashenka possible. With the express endorsement of the population, the Belarusian president restored the Soviet republican flag and emblem in place of the historical symbols of independence and is pursuing a course of full reintegration with Russia in the expectation that the USSR, or something akin to it, will be reconstituted after Boris Yeltsin leaves the scene. In the process, Lukashenka has evolved into a staunch opponent of NATO expansion, which would bring the Western alliance to Belarus's border with Poland. Although to considerable degree a pawn of Russian hegemonists, the Belarusian president's ongoing assault on democratic and market reforms bears only his imprimatur. Unlike Russia itself and every country in the Central–East European region, Belarus has not been accepted into the Council of Europe – a dubious distinction for a country located square in the geographic heart of the European continent.

It is not that Belarusians have no viable claim to nationhood, as some observers maintain; nations arise, thrive or perish in accordance with many conditions, and in Belarus's particular case, historical and geopolitical circumstances left its people with a weak national consciousness at the moment the Soviet Union ceased to exist. It would be disingenuous to say that Belarusians sought "deliverance" from the USSR. Many did, to be sure, but a majority were comfortable with the higher standards of living they enjoyed *vis-à-vis* other Soviet republics and in relation to their own background as a quintessentially downtrodden Slavic peasantry. As nowhere else in the postcommunist region, Western concepts of modern democracy confronted a void.

Precisely how that void stymied progress and gave rise to a dictatorship will be detailed below, beginning with an examination of nationality issues in history and how they shaped Belarusian social and political life before the advent of Gorbachev. That will serve as a backdrop to an expanded discussion of the essence of the ruling Communist Party until 1991, institutional responses to reform in the first years of independence, and the friction between prodemocracy parties and the gamut of factors resistant to change. It is proposed to demonstrate how Lukashenka, a ruthlessly ambitious product of the countryside, managed to "connect" with the public in a way that democrats could not, and to develop a case study of populism-turned-despotism. Of especial concern is how the new president exploited the weak foundations of representative government, democratic processes, and legal norms into a general indictment of the parliamentary system. Not to be overlooked in our survey is the all-important role of Russia in alternately helping and hindering the prospects for democracy in Belarus.

Historical roots and dilemmas of Belarus

Earlier we took note of the centrality of Belarus's geographic position in Europe. As a location it has contributed immeasurably to the country's misfortunes over time. It is the historian's task to calculate the number of foreign armies that have passed through or occupied this sizeable piece (207,600 square kilometers, as presently constituted) of landlocked, unobstructed territory along the Berlin–Moscow axis. World War II was the deadliest of many major conflicts, claiming the lives of 20 percent of the Belarusian population as well as destroying the city of Minsk and some 90 percent of the country's infrastructure. Belarus's significance as a military corridor did not diminish in the postwar period. The Belarusian SSR[3] acquired the world's highest ratio of soldiers to civilians (1:43) as well as the sixth largest arsenal of nuclear missiles. It remains an area of vital geo-strategic importance to the framers of Russian national security interests.

Belarus (Belaia Rus, or "White Rus," in antiquity)[4] perhaps qualifies as the innocent bystander of East European history. Tatars, Teutonic Knights, Poland versus Muscovy, Napoleon, two World Wars and a Cold War: all this traffic notwithstanding, its own record of offensive military action and belligerence is practically nonexistent. Belarusian martial activities have been overwhelmingly defensive, with notable premodern examples being the halt of the Tatar advance into "White Rusian" regions and the defeat of the Teutonic Knights in joint effort with Lithuania and Poland (1410 Battle of Grunwald). In 1514, near today's city of Orsha, White Rusian, Lithuanian, and Polish forces crushed a large Muscovy offensive in a battle that patriotic Belarusian groups still commemorate.

Official Soviet historiography, which served Moscow's policies of Russification, devoted volumes to demonstrating that the entire thrust of Belarusian and Ukrainian history had aimed at "reunification with Russia" and reconstitution of the single Rusian state lost in Kievan times. Accordingly, Belarusians and Ukrainians did not and could not aspire to separate paths of development from Russia any more than parts of one body yearn to detach themselves. The dogma required much distortion of facts to prove that Polish and Lithuanian "oppression" prevented Belarusians from achieving their cherished goal until, in the late eighteenth century, the tsarist empire reunited them with their Russian brethren. But realities were altogether different.

White Rus's path of development following the dispersion of the Kievan state led it to forge close ties with Lithuania. (The process may have been facilitated, according to some ethnologists, by the preexistence of mixed Baltic–Slavic bloodlines in the region since the Dark Ages.)[5] The two peoples, Lithuanian and White Rusians, coexisted on peaceable terms in a single state that is most commonly known by its shorter name, the Grand Duchy of Lithuania (GDL), but whose full name was Grand Duchy of Lithuania, Rus, and Samogitia. At its height in the fourteenth to sixteenth centuries, the GDL was an influential power on the crossroads of the Catholic and Orthodox worlds. Debate rages endlessly in efforts to prove or disprove that the duchy was as much a Belarusian as a Lithuanian state. Nationally-minded Belarusians – whom we will call the Belarusianist school – establish and legitimate their claim to statehood largely with reference to the GDL.

Belarusian-American historian Jan Zaprudnik has called the GDL a "polyethnic dynastic empire where local customs and the Christian Church were respected and where new Lithuanian rulers, still pagan, underwent acculturation by the ruled."[6] Originating in the thirteenth century, the duchy was stitched together by Lithuania's heathen princes to defend against the crusading Teutonic and Livonian Knights. By the end of the following century it stretched from the Baltic coast to the Black Sea, encompassing Lithuania, all of Belarus, and western Ukraine. In 1323, its capital was transferred from Navahradak in present-day Belarus to Vilnius, thus fixing that city's place as the center of Lithuanian and White Rusian life for centuries to come.

The duchy's pagan rulers were heavily influenced by the culturally advanced White Rusians in the areas of government, administration, legal structures, finances and letters. As Lithuania did not have a written alphabet until its belated conversion to Christianity (late fourteenth to early fifteenth centuries), old Belarusian was adopted as the official language of the ducal chancellery and courts. In that role Belarusian gave birth to the exceedingly rich treasure of legal documents, 600 volumes in all, called the Litouskaia Metryka (Lithuanian Archive). Similarly, the Statutes, or codes of law, of the GDL were composed in Belarusian; promulgated in three stages in the 1500s, they formally remained in effect until the nineteenth century. The overwhelming role of their language[7] and civilization, according to Belarusianists, justifies regarding the GDL as the formative vehicle of White Rusian/Belarusian statehood. The golden age of Belarusian culture reached its zenith during the European Renaissance and was epitomized by the publisher-scholar Francisak Skaryna (d. 1552?), who produced many of the Slavic world's first printed texts in the Cyrillic alphabet, including the Bible.

As for sheer political influence, however, the case becomes more problematic after the year 1385, when Grand Duke Jogailo (in Polish, Jagiello – whence Krakow's Jagiellonian University takes its name) was crowned King Wladyslaw II of Poland on condition of accepting the Catholic Christian faith in Lithuania. Before long, the influence of the Orthodox White Russians *vis-à-vis* the unified Catholic dynasty began to wane. Finally, two events in the sixteenth century assured Poland's direct authority. In 1569 the GDL, severely weakened by the Muscovy advance, was forced to consolidate with the Kingdom of Poland into a Commonwealth, the Rzeszpospolita polska; and while retaining its separate status, institutions, and privileges as part of the bargain, the duchy lost its Ukrainian territories to the Polish Crown. That was followed in short order by the 1596 Union of Brest establishing the Uniate (Eastern-rite) Catholic Church in place of Orthodoxy in the Common-wealth's eastern territories. Latin displaced Belarusian as the language of record, and the subsequent Polonization of the gentry drastically undercut the GDL's remaining distinctions.

As a prototype Belarusian state, therefore, the GDL satisfied many conditions in the earliest centuries of its existence but in time became an instrument of Poland's eastward expansion. Several points emerge from the foregoing outline that, despite the distance in time, are pertinent to our comprehension of Belarus:

Importantly, the White Rusians did not form a guiding, powerful elite – dynastic or military – of their own. Authority, instead, was diffuse, with most White Rusian cities enjoying the Magdeburg right of self-government and elections. It is a point of pride for many Belarusians that their ancestors appeared remarkably egalitarian by the standards of their time as well as tolerant of other peoples, religions, and languages, as evidenced by the fact that the GDL was a haven for Tatars, European Jews, and others fleeing their homes for one or another reason.[8] The White Rusians, in addition, did not institutionalize war and competition in the manner of their medieval contemporaries elsewhere (a process, by the way, that spurred on the development of European nation states).

Many Belarusianists have lauded the qualities of egalitarianism, tolerance, and peaceableness as immutable characteristics of their people. But if we accept these assertions as justified, it is necessary to ask whether the same traits combined to deprive the national consciousness of the chance to define itself against outsiders. The Belarusian historical record is bereft of galvanizing moments or legends of the sort that normally stir ethnic/patriotic loyalties and serve as the basis for populistic edification. The emergence of Ukrainian identity, to use a contrasting example, owes much to the exploits of the Cossacks, who became the repository and symbol of the national spirit, and who, furthermore, permitted future generations of Ukrainians to regard themselves in heroic terms against defined adversaries. White Rus's past glory resided in the higher realms of culture, yet the coalescence of Belarusian national aspirations in centuries to come was severely hindered by a dearth of larger-than-life figures and causes for the *Volk* to rally around.

The White Rusians' seeming capacity for peaceful coexistence was not shared by the more ambitious states in the region, Poland and Russia, and the vaunted principle of toleration may have opened wide the door to assimilation. The Polonization of culture, religion, family ties, language, and institutions in the Commonwealth lands starting in the sixteenth century posed a serious risk to the continuity of Belarusian ethnicity. Nevertheless, most Belarusianist historians contend that life under the Poles was preferable to existence in the tsarist "prison of nations."

Belarus under the Tsars

The Commonwealth of Poland was dismembered and partitioned among Russia, Austria, and Prussia in 1772–95. The GDL, with borders roughly corresponding to present-day Belarus and Lithuania, was annexed by Russia under the reign of Catherine II and officially ceased to exist with the abrogation of its Statutes in 1840. The names "Belaia Rus" and "Lietuva" (Lithuania) were officially banned and replaced by designations such as "Northwest province"; the Uniate Church, then the majority religion of Belarusians, was outlawed; and draconian restrictions on use of the Belarusian and, later, Polish languages went into effect. The GDL's academic institutions, in Polacak and the more important University of Vilnius, were closed. Signs of rebellion and ethnic unrest in the former Commonwealth met with swift, often murderous, reprisals, as happened, for example, in the aftermath of the 1830 Polish uprising.

Belarusians and Ukrainians had the added burden of being the object of the "reunification" thesis to justify the tsars' harshest measures of Russification. Of no small consequence to Ukraine, however, was that the Uniate lands of Galicia and Transcarpathia were shielded by having passed to the Catholic Austro-Hungarian empire, where conditions were distinctly less repressive. In time, Uniate West Ukraine became the fountainhead of nationalist resistance to Russia, a role it preserved throughout the Soviet period and until the present day. The Belarusian cause was not so fortunate, although scholars continue to debate the contentious issue of Uniatism in Belarus. Allegiance to Rome, after all, had been forcibly imposed on Orthodox believers by Polish rulers in league with the Vatican. This furnished a compelling reason to return Belarusians to the "true faith." Yet the Orthodoxy of nineteenth-century tsars was a Russian institution to the core and an especially effective instrument of assimilation owing to the Church's close proximity to ordinary, illiterate peasants for whom matters spiritual counted more than matters literary.

Tsarist severity also was prompted by the spread of "subversive" ideas on the heels of Napoleon's drive across Europe, with the tragedy of the Decembrists and Tsar Nicholas I's reactionary reign being the best known examples. The yawning gap between imperial despotism and the revolutionary foment gripping Europe brought new nationalisms to the fore. Modern Belarusian nationalism and vernacular literature originated with a small circle in multiethnic Vilnius, where anti-tsarist fever ran high. Publicists and writers, that is, the most literate people of their day, were the dominant force in the new movement, which sought to arouse the dormant "White Rusian" consciousness via and for the sake of the oppressed native language. The most celebrated names of the period were Francishak Bahusevich (1840–1900), the father of Belarusian literature, and Kastus Kalinouski (1838–1864), publisher of an underground newspaper called *Peasant Truth.*

Kalinouski was a true firebrand. The anti-tsarist insurrection in Poland in 1863 inspired him to organize an uprising in the "Northwest province," where destitution was reaching new heights as a result of Aleksandr II's emancipation of the serfs without ceding them land. As in Poland, the effort was brutally suppressed and its perpetrators put to death or exiled. Kalinouski, sentenced to hang in 1864, penned a *Letter from the Gallows* beseeching his people to resist the "Muscovite slavery" or face perdition.[9] Like the majority of his insurgents, Kalinouski came from the gentry, not the peasantry, but his last words reportedly were "we have no noblemen, we are all equal."[10]

The sad "peasant truth" was that Kalinouski's martyrdom was in vain. The peasantry, then constituting 90 percent of the Belarusian population, could not read newspapers and manifestos, were suspicious or resentful of gentry, and had interests turning on basic survival and the occasional act of expropriation. But the most complex problem of all was that "Belarusianness" itself, as manifested in the speech and customs of the villages, had come to be inextricably associated in the peasant mind with the lowest possible status in the feudal order of things. It was tantamount to inferiority inasmuch as the ruling classes had a different speech (Russian or Polish). The Belarusian peasant, furthermore, had no more conceptual tools to bring to the question of linguistic and ethnic differences than the medieval French or German knave: heightened consciousness required the dissemination of vernacular literature and values from elite groups to the broader layers of society, and that process had scarcely begun in late nineteenth-century Belarus. That their native tongue was a ticket to liberation, as the ultraconscious intellectuals claimed, was innately impossible to grasp.

For all the injustice to what is a richly expressive Slavic language, the stigma of inferiority proved so resilient that it finds reflection today in President Lukashenka's utterances, as in a recent pronouncement that, "you can't express anything great in Belarusian, it is a poor language. There are only two great languages in the world, Russian and English."[11] A century ago, Lukashenka might have said "Polish" in place of "English."

To Yazep Lyosik (1884–1940), a prominent writer and activist, we owe a telling commentary on the futility of rallying the countryside around nation-minded goals. Although it dates to shortly after the October Revolution of 1917, readers would do well to bear in mind that the comment could well describe the mood in Belarusian villages as late as 1996:

At our meetings our peasants declare that they don't need autonomy and don't need their language. No one on earth renounces their own language, save for our peasants . . . They do so out of ignorance. Knowing that our peasantry is downtrodden and dark, the enemies of Belarus use this and say, "Ask the people!" And did you [Bolsheviks], we [Social Democrats] reply, ask the people before starting the revolution?[12]

The complete alienation of Belarusians in their rural masses from urban life and urban dynamics merits attention in this context. In Lyosik's day, fully 98 percent of towns and cities like Minsk consisted of non-Belarusians, primarily Russians, Poles, and Jews. These, Jan Zaprudnik has noted, had their own political parties and goals "not necessarily coinciding with – and in some cases antagonistic to – the Belarusian revival."[13]

It is doubtful that many of these groups were aware of or paid the slightest heed to a handful of Belarusian-speaking intellectuals, and the towns offered practically no scope to agitators for Belarusian self-determination. The urban proletarian class that was the *raison d'être* of the Marxist parties was virtually synonymous in Belarus with Jewish workers. Accordingly, the broadest, most active, and most visible party in the "Northwest province" was the famous Jewish Social-Democratic Bund, based in Minsk and Vilnius.[14]

The nationalists, therefore, were forced to concentrate on penetrating the mass consciousness of a peasantry barely aroused from its feudal torpor, and did not meet with great success. Their counterparts in Ukraine, facing similar social conditions, fared considerably better owing, among other factors, to the stronger impulses of the historical memory and the existence of a prosperous bloc of peasants who consciously opposed the tsarist system.[15]

Still, in terms of assuring that Belarusian identity had a viable future despite the odds, the nationalists accomplished much. The first Belarusian political party, the Socialist Hramada (Union) was formed in 1902 and began publishing its own organ, *Nasha Niva* (Our Field) with the introduction of some political and minority freedoms in the empire following the 1905 revolution. *Nasha Niva* brought together the best and brightest of the Belarusian cultural revival and had a profound impact on intellectual life.

In the path of revolution, war, and genocide

The opportunity for nationalists to influence political events had to await the October Revolution and the end of World War I. With the empire of the Romanovs in full collapse, the Hramada-Nasha Niva group poised to form a government and declare an independent Belarusian National Republic. That milestone occurred in Minsk on March 25, 1918, a few short weeks after Bolshevik Russia signed its armistice with Germany at Brest-Litovsk. What marred the debut of the BNR and national government was that it came about under German sponsorship and over the objections of some nationalists who opposed collaboration with the Kaiser's occupation forces.[16] The BNR's government later proved its ineffectiveness when faced by the rampaging brutality of the Germans in retreat, and many of its members fled either to Germany or crossed over to the Russian communists. Lenin's Red Army, thwarted in an earlier attempt to declare Soviet power in Belarus, occupied the country in December 1918 without much ado.

Even with a different outcome, the BNR would have faced an insurmountable threat from the side of newly freed Poland, which had already revived its claims to the Polish Commonwealth lands of the Grand Duchy. The Bolsheviks responded in February 1919 by merging Belarus and Lithuanian territory in a single Soviet Republic with the inelegantly abbreviated name of Litbel. The outbreak of the Russo-Polish War meant the Belarusian populace had no respite from hostilities, occupation, and reoccupation for another two years. The peace of the 1921 Treaty of Riga came at a terrible price, however: Belarus was bisected into West (including the city and region of Vilnius), which was incorporated into Poland, and East, which reverted to Russia and became the Belarusian Soviet Socialist Republic (BSSR). Remnants of the national government of 1918 had no say in these matters.

With the end of "war communism," the Bolshevik regime was forced into tactical retreats on the economic, social, and cultural fronts in order to keep itself in power. The quasi-capitalist New Economic Policy was accompanied, at Lenin's insistence, by favorable policies toward the Soviet republics and regions. *Korenizatsia*, or "nativization," brought indigenous cadres into administrative positions once monopolized by Russians. Crucial strides were made in education, led by the opening of the Belarusian State University and the Institute of Culture in 1921–22. The latter, which changed its name in 1928 to the Academy of Sciences, fast become a haven for nationalist scholars and ground-breaking studies of such long-forbidden topics as the Grand Duchy. Outstanding writers and poets – Janka Kupala, Jakub Kolas – and Belarusian-language publicists thrived at a time when the Belarusification, linguistic and otherwise, of public life had the highest-level sanction. This was a period of significant ethnic maturation and went a long way toward restoring layers of the "palimpsest of historical experience."

The BSSR increased from a mere 1.5 million inhabitants in 1921 to 5 million in 1926 when Moscow transferred nearly 30,000 square miles of ethnically Belarusian territory from the Russian SFSR. Slightly more than 80 percent of the population after this territorial extension consisted of Belarusians, with Jews the second largest group (8.2 percent) and Russians the third largest (7.7 percent). Jews, concentrated in the cities, effectively managed the BSSR economy and held nearly 50 percent of all economic-related government positions in the NEP era due to an absolute lack of experienced cadres among the titular nationality.[17] Ethnic Belarusian gains through *korenizatsia* centered, instead, on state agricultural and administrative posts.

Belarusians did not outnumber Russians and Jews in the local Communist Party ranks until the late 1920s, and under conditions where national communism (alternatively, "communist nationalism" or "national democracy") was the prevalent line. Where Ukraine had its famous commissar Mykola Skrypnyk to infuse communism with nationalism, Belarus had historian Usevalad Ihnatouski, the first president of the Academy of Sciences. Ihnatouski promoted the view that the abolition of classes in Soviet society, as applied to the peasant Belarusian masses, was equivalent to national liberation.[18]

National communism held sway until the rise of Josef Stalin. All its proponents, together with the cream of Belarusian culture, were swept away in Stalin's repressions of the *natsdemy* and native intelligentsias beginning in 1929. Ihnatouski committed suicide in 1931, standing no chance of escaping eventual "liquidation." An estimated 2 million Belarusians lost their lives to the purges, forced collectivization, starvation and deportation. The figure includes some of the 4.5 million West Belarusians in Poland who were reunited with the BSSR under the terms of the Molotov-Ribbentrop Pact of 1939 (Vilnius, it should be noted, reverted to the newly created Lithuanian Soviet Republic that same year). The most notorious NKVD killing field, active from 1937–41, was the Kurapaty forest outside Minsk, where tens of thousands were shot and buried in mass graves.[19]

Belarus's tragedies culminated not in Kurapaty but in Adolf Hitler's invasion of the Soviet Union in 1941. In terms of percentage, Belarus's population loss (25 percent) in World War II was the largest of any other region of the USSR; the pre-war level of 9.1 million would not be regained until the early 1970s. Altogether, the Belarusian population declined by 12.7 percent between 1939 and 1951 versus 4.7 percent for the USSR as a whole.[20]

It is important to note the impact of that conflict specifically on the national psyche. The present paper has argued that the course of Belarusian history lacked a defining, galvanizing moment of the kind that among other peoples caused national-patriotic affinities to crystallize. The Great Fatherland War, as it came to be known, provided that defining moment for many Belarusians, to the exclusive benefit of Soviet patriotism. In their authoritative study *Utopia in Power*, Mikhail Heller and Alexander Nekrich pointed out that the anti-German resistance in Belarus, counting as many as 100,000 partisans, had the vast support of the population. Collaborationists, mainly nationalists (who saw in Germany a savior from Stalinist atrocities), were few in number and generally despised as the Nazis' own murderous penchant, inflicted first on Belarus's Jews, was evident to all.[21] Resistance fighters and Red Army liberators filled the role of the missing popular heroes of Belarusian history, and that, in turn, abetted the process of forging a strong Soviet identity at the mass level.

Forming a Soviet society

The "palimpsest of historical experience" was extirpated in its near entirety in the postwar BSSR, and the engineering of a Russian-speaking *homo sovieticus* met with greater success in Belarus than in any other Soviet republic. The process unfolded along the parallel lines of urbanization/modernization and linguistic and cultural Russification. The inherited weaknesses of Belarusian society (undeveloped ethnic consciousness, rural unsophistication), together with the massive scale of human and material destruction in preceding years, fundamentally contributed to the progress of "Sovietization."

At the time of the first postwar census of 1959, the BSSR had the Soviet Union's third largest proportion of collective farmers in its population (53 percent), exceeded only by Moldova (71 percent) and Tajikistan (57 percent). Conversely, its percentage of workers (33 percent) was among the lowest of the fifteen Union republics,[22] and at the time included a large number of Russian workers who had migrated to Belarus to rebuild infrastructures and replace the skilled labor, mainly Jewish, annihilated in the war.

234   *Kathleen J. Mihalisko*

Table 6.1 *Demographic trends in Belarus since the 1950s*

	1950s	1970s	1980s
Percentage of population	(1959)	(1979)	(1989)
Rural	77.8	45.1	34.6
Urban	22.2	54.9	65.4
Average annual rates	(1951-61)	(1971-79)	(1990-99)[a]
of population growth (%)	0.5	0.6	0.3
Age distribution (%)	(1959)	(1979)	(1989)
15-24	17.4	18.0	13.9
25-49	32.4	33.7	34.3
50-59	9.2	11.2	12.6
Over 60	10.6	14.0	16.1
Levels of education[b] (%)			
Primary	58.8	50.1	40.4
Secondary	38.2	43.4	49.6
Post-secondary	3.0	6.5	10.0

Notes: [a]Estimate. [b]Indicates attainment of completed or partial education at each level among persons over fifteen years of age.

Sources: US Department of Commerce, *Statistical Abstracts of the United States*; Paul S. Shoup, *The East European and Soviet Data Handbook*; UNESCO, *Statistical Yearbooks*; United Nations, *Demographic Yearbooks*.

With the BSSR earmarked in Moscow's planning for rapid industrialization, the socio-demographic and economic landscape of Belarus was set to change dramatically. By 1990 only one-fifth of the population remained engaged in agricultural work as collective/state farmers or foresters, as against 42 percent employed in industry and construction and 38 percent in the service or professional occupations.[23] The urban share of the population more than doubled from 31 percent in 1959 to 66 percent in 1989–90,[24] and, in fact, the rate of urbanization beginning in the late 1950s exceeded the all-Union average for the duration of the USSR's existence.

Reconstructed after the war with every dreary aesthetic in the book of Soviet urban planning, Belarus's cities inspired neither imagination nor a historical outlook. But their inhabitants attained unprecedented levels of prosperity, modernity, and security under communism, a fact that for many apparently overrode the system's defects. At the time Mikhail Gorbachev assumed the position of CPSU General Secretary, Belarus was outpacing other Soviet republics in economic growth and industrial output, and annual increases to labor productivity in industry and agriculture were the highest in the USSR.[25] An American specialist attributed Belarus's economic boom (and might the BSSR have been the Soviet Union's answer to Germany's economic recovery miracle?) to large amounts of capital investment; a specific industrial mix – machinery, electronics, chemicals, textiles " that favored a "technologically modernizing economy"; and the republic's location in the developed Baltic–East European region.[26] Similarly, key indicators of social well-being were among the highest in the Soviet Union and in some cases, such as infant and maternal mortality rates, they compared very favorably on a European-wide level.[27]

Educational gains were also impressive. Although the 1989 census showed nearly one-quarter of the Belarusian population aged 25 and over having only primary or no formal schooling, these can be considered the last vestiges of the prewar peasant society. Postwar generations benefited from substantial spending on education (typically 5-6 percent of GDP) such that, today, fully 77 percent of the national workforce has at least completed secondary education and illiteracy is unknown. The quality of secondary schools was on par with all-Union standards, but was mixed when it came to institutions of higher learning. These ranged from excellent in the technical fields to mediocre in the social sciences and economics; many of the most talented minds and artists quit Belarus for Moscow where opportunities and facilities were superior.

The price the Soviet system exacted for educational achievement was the Belarusian language. Linguistic Russification went hand in hand with the modernization of Belarus starting in the 1950s. As thousands of schools opened to accommodate the growing urban population and influx from the countryside, they offered instruction in Russian only or in mixed language arrangements preparing students for an eventual transition to Russian. Consequently, on the eve of the Soviet Union's demise, there were no Belarusian-language schools or classes in any urban area of the BSSR. In rural areas, schools with Belarusian as the language of instruction were closed by the hundreds as young people deserted the villages. There was no better way to undermine the very crux of Belarusian ethnicity than to raise up-and-coming generations in Russian.

At the same time, Russification proceeded in relentless fashion in the realms of book and newspaper publishing, culture, public life, the work-place – in short, every corner of modern existence. Even though the same processes applied to the other Soviet nationalities, they had deeper and more far-reaching effect in the BSSR as much because of the similarity of the two languages, Russian and Belarusian, as because of the popular predisposition to regard attachment to the native tongue as an impediment to social mobility and cultural maturity. A majority of ethnic Belarusians (80 percent) in the 1989 Soviet census declared Belarusian as their native language, but later sociological studies established that it was, and is, rarely spoken at home, much less outside the home.

Official language data were intended anyway as window-dressing. Soviet nationality policy based itself on a purposeful contradiction: outwardly the peoples of the USSR were "flowering," inwardly they were "merging." Russification never was a *proclaimed* policy of the CPSU or Soviet government despite its ubiquitous enforcement. This duplicity added a confused and paradoxical dimension to existing Belarusian problems with self-identity:

> The turn-of-the-century Belarusian peasant had a distinct folk culture and spoke a tongue that differed substantially from the Russian literary language, but he was not aware his language was the equivalent of Russian or Polish. The Soviet Belarusian was practically no different from the Russian in culture, spoke (and continues to speak) Russian, and didn't know Belarusian or knew it poorly. At the same time, he knew for certain he was Belarusian, a citizen of the BSSR – an equal Soviet republic and even a member of the United Nations – and that his native language was Belarusian.[28]

It is not surprising that many Western observers have fallen prey to the misconception that Belarusians consider themselves Russian. They do not; but neither do many know what "Belarusian" is outside a Soviet context.

Cultural elites and the Communist Party

Similar to the role they had played before the Bolshevik Revolution, Belarusian cultural elites took it upon themselves to defy – and decry – the trend they dubbed "national nihilism," particularly with respect to the language question. The republican Writers' Union and its organ, *Litaratura i mastatstva* (Literature and Art), took the lead. It was only with the advent of glasnost that details emerged of the writers' sharp clashes with the party leadership over language and cultural policies as far back as the 1960s and continuing through the era of Leonid Brezhnev. Voices of opposition in the BSSR were not as overt as in other republics, but behind the scenes they worked in interesting ways. Several writers, including Ales' Adamovich and the world-renowned Vasil Bykau (Bykov), avoided joining the Communist Party at a time when said membership was a virtual prerequisite for Soviet writers. Bykau courageously resisted years of KGB harassment for his moral views, but, rather like Boris Pasternak in the 1930s, escaped a worse fate because the consequences of putting him away were greater than the price of keeping him around.

Nevertheless, Belarus's cultural dissenters stopped short of creating a full-fledged human and national rights movement; for instance, there was no Helsinki rights committee in the BSSR.[29] The republic produced only one anti-

Soviet dissident, Mikhael Kukabaka, who spent many years in the gulag. By and large, nationally-minded intellectuals poured energy into activity for which there was already historical precedent, namely, defending linguistic-cultural survival, but shrank at setting any new Belarusian precedents of challenging authority.

The Belarusian Communist Party's (CPB) perpetual attacks on "nationalism" were a good indication that the cultural intellectuals were a bothersome force. This was a party organization whose core leadership bore no relation to Ihnatouski's "national communists" and which rigorously fulfilled the Kremlin's expectations to "merge" Belarusians with Great Russians. Deviations like the Petro Shelest' affair, in which Ukraine's first secretary was removed for his pro-Ukrainian orientation, were out of the question. During the Brezhnev era, the CPB was guided by an uncompromising reactionary line fixed by its long-time ideological secretary, the neo-Stalinist Savelii Paulau (who, strange to say, currently heads up a state-funded institute in Minsk). Paulau and his followers made Belarusophobia, anti-intellectualism, and "anti-Zionism" the steady fare of party discourse.

It was, however, their capacity for toadying to Moscow that made the reputation of Belarusian Party leaders in other corners of the Soviet Union. The BSSR strove in every way to be a showcase republic. The title was deserved, given its good economy, comparatively high living standards, "denationalized" population, and muted internal dissent.

The overseer of Belarus's transformation into a Soviet showcase was Piotr Masherau (Masherov), CPB first secretary from 1965 until his death in 1980. Even if his is not a popular name with nationally-minded intellectuals, who recall him as the engine that drove Russification, Masherau was genuinely popular with the public at large because he radiated concern about ordinary citizens. In 1988, demonstrators at the first mass anti-Soviet protest in Minsk laid flowers at his grave (at which time, no doubt, the loyal Party leader turned over). His death in circumstances unheard-of for a Politburo member – killed in an accident while being chauffeured in the highway lane reserved for high-ranking officials – gave rise to conspiracy theories involving his alleged disapproval of corruption in Brezhnev's Kremlin. It is somewhat unfortunate that the Masherau phenomenon has not received adequate attention from specialists, inasmuch as he seems to have personified "socialism with a human face" for many Belarusians.

Perestroika and independence

Belarus abruptly ceased being a showcase on a precise date, April 26, 1986, the day of the explosion at the Chernobyl nuclear power station a few kilometers south of the border with Ukraine. An estimated 70 percent of the radioactive fallout from the accident was deposited on the BSSR, in particular the oblasts of Homel' (Gomel') and Mahileu (Mogilev). The Chernobyl incident and its aftermath is too complex to cover here other than to note that the evacuation of populated areas was limited and delayed for political reasons, resulting in the needless exposure of thousands of children and adults to contamination. It took another two years for the Kremlin's policy of glasnost to mature enough for information on the scale of the disaster to reach the Belarusian public through newspapers. It is useful to recall, in that connection, that the international embarrassment of the official cover-up of the catastrophe helped kick-start glasnost in the first place. Chernobyl, therefore, had historic political fallout as well, which for Belarus's self-satisfied Party leaders had worse implications than invisible doses of radiation.

Anti-Soviet opposition in Belarus came together and gathered momentum due to several coinciding events: the belated release of information about Chernobyl; the unofficial archeological excavation, in 1988, of the NKVD's massacre site in Kurapaty, which provided the first forensic evidence of Stalinist genocide ever publicized in the Soviet Union; and increasing freedom to air nationality grievances. As might be expected, the cultural intelligentsia was most active in the latter arena, but so, too, were a growing number of radically-minded student groups that had come into being with the liberalization of Soviet laws pertaining to organizations. Finally, the formation of Popular Fronts in the neighboring Baltic republics took Belarusian intellectuals and activists by storm. Close ties were established in the summer of 1988 with Lithuania's *Sajudis*, and October of that year witnessed the launching of the Belarusian Popular Front for perestroika (BPF) – the first such movement to establish itself outside the Baltic states.

The original roster of BPF founders read like the membership list of the Writers' Union. Within a few months, however, most of that literary elite with the exception of Bykau were gone, having capitulated to communist pressure either to quit the BPF or lose their Party membership and material privileges. That left the BPF leadership in the hands of Zyanon Paznyak, the archeologist responsible for the Kurapaty discovery, as well as youth group leaders and others without communist ties. Paznyak formulated a platform the pillars of which were national revival and sovereignty (later, independence), democratic reforms, human rights, and restitution for the crime of Chernobyl. The goals, in short, were every bit as revolutionary as those of the Balts and Ukrainians. In retrospect, though, the abandonment of the BPF organization by the *crème de la crème* of the intelligentsia served to lower the Front's authority in the eyes of the public and marginalized its members.

It is difficult to imagine a sharper dichotomy of ideologies than existed between the CPB and the national-democrats in the BPF. Ironically, the first secretary at that time, Yafrem Sakalau, had been one of Gorbachev's first republican-level appointees, hand-picked to implement modest experiments in economic reform when perestroika was a new idea. Sakalau and the upper echelons of the CPB soon lined up behind Yegor Ligachev, the Soviet leader's formidable conservative foe on the Politburo. At home they made no concessions to reformist forces. The aforementioned demonstration that stopped by Masherau's grave was violently dispersed by police; and in 1989 the BPF was forced to hold its first constituent congress in "exile" in Vilnius. These and other incidents earned the BSSR the unfortunate epithet "Vendeé of perestroika" (after the region in France that took up arms against the Revolution), coined by the writer Adamovich and widely repeated in the liberal Soviet press.

The Party leadership employed more subtle means as well to limit the impact of Moscow's liberal reform course on Belarusian institutions, the media, and political life. An important and enduring case in point was the USSR's first multicandidate elections to the republican Supreme Soviets (hereafter: Councils) in March 1990. Belarus, as distinct from the other Union republics, chose to reserve a designated number of seats (50 out of a total 360) in the legislature for the archconservative war veterans' and handicapped associations. The ruse, which blatantly violated the "one person, one vote" principle of the Soviet Constitution, was copied from the newly-created USSR Council of People's Deputies. Other means were found to prevent BPF candidates from reaching the ballot; as it happened, the Front won only 7.5 percent of the mandates, that is, 26 of 360 seats, versus 86 percent for the CPB.[30] Many Party officials obtained deputy mandates by running unopposed in rural districts.

What the BPF opposition faction lacked in numbers it made up for in determination. The most significant item on their agenda was to ensure that Belarus followed in the footsteps of the RSFSR and Ukraine by passing a Declaration of State Sovereignty, by no means a foregone conclusion given the overwhelming antireformist profile of the deputy corps. According to one account, newly-elected Supreme Council chairman Mikalai Dzemyantsei – a proverbial colorless apparatchik – initially rejected the BPF's proposal to bring the matter to the vote, then changed his mind after consulting with Moscow and discovering that the Soviet leader did not object to the "parade of sovereignties," in Gorbachev's oft-repeated phrase, as long as the republics enshrined their intentions to sign his proposed Union Treaty.[31] That gave the Communist parliament in Minsk reason to hope that other provisions of the sovereignty Declaration would be nullified in practice, and accordingly it was approved on July 27, 1990, with barely a quorum present owing to a principled boycott by many hardliners.

Those were the somewhat tenuous circumstances under which Belarus became a sovereign republic with the right to pursue its own domestic and foreign policies and, crucially, to become a nuclear-free, nonaligned state eschewing participation in military blocs. Dzemyantsei and the head of the Belarusian government, Vyacheslau Kebich, indeed devoted most of their energies to the proposed Union Treaty to the exclusion of filling sovereignty with real content. Meanwhile, the Central Committee of the CPB continued on a course of barely concealed opposition to Gorbachev, with some members, notably, Vitsebsk oblast' Party secretary Uladzimir Hryhoreu, gaining Union-wide notoriety for their public condemnations of perestroika's architects.[32] As it was obvious there were no prospects for creating a pro-reform faction within the CPB, moderate to liberal rank-and-file members quit the Party by the tens of thousands, especially in the wake of Boris Yeltsin's spectacular defection from the CPSU.[33]

Space does not permit discussion of all the reactionary causes (Nina Andreeva's Bolshevik bloc, Russian interfronts, and so on) that CPB officials courted to one or another degree. The main point, and one that severely injured the prospects for democracy, was that Belarus's Party elite did not find it expedient or necessary to coopt the national-democratic agenda of their opponents, in contrast to their counterparts in other regions of the Soviet Union. Minsk did not give birth to a Brazauskas, a Kravchuk, or – heaven forbid – a Yeltsin. In reference to an organization having some 650,000 members, this fact speaks volumes about the dearth of nationally-minded individuals in the ruling party.

Equally revealing was the want of a critical mass of pressure at the "grassroots" level to force the leadership into accepting reform, sovereignty, and change. The Popular Front in 1991 had seen very disappointing results in its effort to become a broad-based organization and faced much public indifference both in Minsk and especially in the "provinces." As for Paznyak, the same moral force that made him the bravest of regime opponents (and probably the most courageous Belarusian of his day) also made him too strident and extreme for Belarusian tastes. What could mobilize the masses if not democracy, independence, and freedom from "Muscovite tyranny," as Kalinouski had put it?

It was, literally, the high price of a cafeteria sandwich that sparked the worst unrest in Belarus in the final days of Soviet power. In April 1991, when the all-Union government ordered sweeping price increases to take effect in the USSR, workers at a Minsk factory walked off the job at lunchtime and were joined by tens of thousands of others in spontaneous nationwide strikes and protests that lasted two weeks. Over 100,000 workers participated at the height of the strikes, raising demands that were economic and political in nature.[34] Although the situation defused when the Kebich government agreed to raise salaries, the strikes were a milestone in several respects: not only did they give rise to an independent trade union movement and a general sense of workers' empowerment, they also solidified the concept of sovereignty in demonstrating that Moscow was no longer capable of addressing the needs of Belarusian citizens.

The specter of a *Solidarność* scenario raised alarm in Communist Party circles to new heights. How the CPB proposed to keep itself in power and rescue the socialist order is extremely significant. Their most desired outcome was evident as early as the March 1991 plenum of the CPSU Central Committee, on which occasion Anatolii Malafeyeu (Malofeev), Sakalau's recent replacement as CPB first secretary, proclaimed that, "the country can be saved from collapse only by declaring a state of emergency on the territory of the USSR."[35] The statement and other suspicious activity in Belarus[36] in the summer of 1991 suggested that a few Minsk comrades had foreknowledge of a *putsch* attempt, but more importantly, it was certain that said eventuality had their full support.

A contingency plan also emerged in the event that Gorbachev (and newly-elected President Yeltsin) survived, consisting of preparations to establish an independent Belarusian communist regime. In the months preceding the ill-fated August coup d'état, Party leaders became sudden converts to national communism and spoke of making overtures to the cultural intelligentsia. Malafeyeu was quoted in print speaking Belarusian – a definite sign that something queer was afoot.[37] The revered name of Piotr Masherau reappeared in print, presumably to evoke fond thoughts of the Party's closeness to the people. The thrust of it all was to legitimize Communist authority in national context, and it was in this regressive manner that patriotism came into vogue.

The CPB quickly returned to its natural state of being when the *putsch* unfolded. The Central Committee on August 21 adopted a resolution in support of the State of Emergency Committee (GKChP) and awaited its triumph. The posture said less about the Party, insofar as its loyalties were well known, than it did about the Belarusian government, whose highest levels beginning with Kebich were staffed exclusively by Central Committee members. Indeed, military and security organs on government instruction worked behind the scenes in anticipation of orders from the GKChP,[38] while in public the entire government and state apparatus maintained a conspicuous silence about events in Moscow. Belarusian TV was prohibited from showing Yeltsin leading the resistance and print media faced a prompt revival of heavy censorship.

When the coup attempt collapsed and with the Communist Party on the verge of being suspended over Soviet territory, the Belarusian Party formally broke off from the CPSU in an effort to avoid the ban and, reverting to its contingency plan, supported the initiative of the Popular Front parliamentary opposition to declare Belarus's independence from the USSR. That declaration, on August 25, was the result of a compromise whereby the BPF agreed to the caveated form of "political and economic" (as opposed to national) independence at the insistence of parliament's Communist majority, in exchange for an indefinite ban on CPB activity.

It is a sobering thought, in previewing the chances for Belarusian democracy, that the newly independent country would be led for the next four years by the same officials who had stood prepared to accept the GKChP and the restoration of the pre-Gorbachev order. The government remained intact until 1994 with Kebich at its head; the Supreme Council was replaced only at the end of 1995. A report by a temporary state commission detailing widespread official complicity in the abortive coup was quashed in December 1991 and never seen again.[39]

The sole sacrifice, however important, was parliamentary chairman Dzemyantsei, who had handled himself maladroitly during the August events. In September he was forced to cede the chair to his deputy, Stanislau Shushkevich, one of very few political centrists in the Supreme Council and one who took national independence in stride. If Dzemyantsei, like all the others, had kept his position, it is unlikely that the December 8 founding agreement of the Commonwealth of Independent States (CIS) would have taken place when or as it did, in that Dzemyantsei was not a man to do business with Yeltsin or Ukrainian president Kravchuk. Belarus's participation in the original CIS accord was essential in order to null and void the original 1924 Union Treaty between the three Slavic republics (BSSR, UkrSSR, and RSFSR) that created the USSR. It was indicative of Shushkevich's realism and national-mindedness that he backed the secret Yeltsin-Kravchuk plan and offered a place, Belavezha, for the historic talks to underscore that Belarus was to be an equal partner.

Shushkevich's involvement in the dissolution of the Soviet Union came as an unpleasant shock to much of the population. (The BPF had legitimate reasons for not wanting to bring the declaration of independence to a popular referendum, as Ukraine did.) When last consulted, 83 percent of Belarusians had voted in favor of upholding the USSR in the all-Union plebiscite of March 1991, and until the present day, reliable opinion polls show majorities believing that the breakup of the USSR was a bad thing for Belarus.[40] The solitary vote cast against the Belavezha accord in any of the three parliaments concerned belonged to a Belarusian – people's deputy Alyaksandr Lukashenka.

The spectrum of political parties

Preceding sections have dealt extensively with the numerous factors that worked against Belarus's democratic development, above all the ramifications of weak national consciousness and the absence of conditions for mobilization around acutely felt national goals. Consideration should be given at the same time to factors that inherently favored (and favor) democratic progress.

The absence of ethnic strife in Belarus is one such advantage. Its present population of 10.2 million consists of Belarusians (78 percent), Russians (13 percent), Poles (4.1 percent), Ukrainians (2.9 percent), Jews (1.1 percent) and others. Relations among these ethnic groups are harmonious, in keeping with the ancient Grand Duchy tradition. Overt anti-Semitism in this century has been limited to the excesses of a few Brezhnev-era hacks, and there is no basis for conflict between the ethnic majority and minorities. Moreover, as much as Belarus's geographic location condemned it to constant invasion, what's past is past and the overall region is striving to integrate with Western democracies. Belarus is well positioned in principle to anchor the stability of Eastern Europe.

Another advantage concerns the orientation of its noncommunist political parties toward self-same ideals of integration with the West and Belarus's transformation into a modern European state with a market-based economy. A majority of new parties and political organizations came into being during perestroika and all advocate change by peaceful democratic means. For that matter, the low propensity for convulsive social or political violence can be seen as an another plus favoring democratization in principle. The spectrum of national-democratic organizations and parties is as follows:

The Popular Front, headed by Zyanon Paznyak, has been the leading opposition force since its founding in 1988. As a matter of law, the BPF contests elections as a party but otherwise functions as a movement with a nonfixed membership. The Front is also actively involved in the Independent Trade Unions of Belarus (led by, *inter alia*, Syarhei Antonchyk) which obtained a lease on life during the workers's unrest in April 1991 but whose primary means of assistance at this time is foreign sources (AFL-CIO, Solidarity). The Washington-based Freedom House has reported significant growth in their membership, from 7,000–8,000 in 1993 to 24,000 the following year.[41]

The Front had a caucus of 26 opposition deputies (50 percent of whom represented Minsk districts) in the Supreme Council whose term expired in 1995 and some of its members have been elected to city councils. In addition to Paznyak, other well-known BPF people's deputies in the previous parliament were Uladzimir Zablotskii, Syarhei Navumchyk, and the aforementioned Antonchyk. Although it held few commission chairs – and no ministerial posts at any time – the BPF deserves the credit for opening the legislative venues to democratization.

The BPF's fortunes have taken a dramatic turn for the worse under President Lukashenka, and it has no members in the Supreme Council elected in December 1995 to a five-year term. In the summer of 1996, Paznyak and Navumchyk became the first politicians from the postcommunist region to request and receive political asylum in the United States. More will be said on the subject below.

Not represented in the Supreme Council but espousing objectives broadly consistent with those of the Popular Front are the National Democratic Party (founded 1990; several co-chairmen; membership 300) and the Christian-Democratic Association (founded 1991; Piotr Silka, coordinator; membership 100). The latter traces its origins to the Belarusian Christian-Democratic Party in Polish-held West Belarus.[42]

The Social-Democratic Union (Hramada) identifies with the European social-democratic school and favors a strong state presence in a market economy. Founded in 1991, the untimely death the following year of its chairman, Mikhas Tkachou, a leading intellectual, was a serious blow. Since then its chairman has been Aleh Trusau, lately joined by Stanislau Shushkevich as co-chair. It has approximately 1,000 members. Until 1995 the Hramada had twelve deputies in the Supreme Council and was closely aligned with the BPF; today it has just two representatives in parliament.

The United Democratic Party, founded in 1990, counts 1,500 members drawn from the liberal (and Russian-speaking) technical/professional intelligentsia. It emphasizes political and economic freedoms in the context of national independence, but does not regard Belarusian linguistic revival as a paramount concern. The UDP is engaged in opposition initiatives and has its own institute in Minsk for the study of sociopolitical and socioeconomic trends. Co-chaired by incumbent people's deputy Alyaksandr Dabravolskii, the UDP appears to have folded recently into the United Civic Party (below).

The Peasant Party (founded 1991; Yeuhen Luhin, chairman) claims hundreds of rural members and has a small number of deputies in local councils in addition to one member in parliament. Its platform stresses the privatization of land as well as basic human and national rights. In addition, a Peasant Union (founded 1989; Kastus Yarmalenka, president) represents the interests of several hundred private farmers and is devoted to the expansion of private farming.

The Green Party, with one Supreme Council seat, and the related Belarusian Ecological Union (founded 1989; Boris Savitskii, chairman) have been relatively well represented in local councils in Chernobyl-affected areas and elsewhere.

Attempts to stake out a political middle between the national-democratic camp here described and the Communist/communist-leaning bloc have not been successful owing to the extremely polarized nature of Belarusian politics. The absence of a reformist pro-Belarusian wing in the former CPB has had all-round negative repercussions in the search for consensus.

At present, what might be termed the "center" is occupied by economic leaders and the fledgling entrepreneurial class. The Party of National Accord (founded 1992; Leonid Syachka, chairman) long had a one-person agenda, set by the well-known industrialist Henadz' Karpenka, one of four vice-chairman of the Supreme Council. It has eight representatives in the Supreme Council and as such is the largest noncommunist-allied bloc, with social-democratic allegiances. A similar United Civic Party (founded 1995), with seven incumbent deputies, has been built around Stanislau Bahdankevich, ousted by Lukashenka last year as chairman of the National Bank and a fierce critic of the president's economic policies. Additionally, a Union of Belarusian Entrepreneurs, headed by people's deputy Viktar Karyahin, is active politically in trying to improve economic and business opportunities.

Turning to "the left," the Party of Communists of Belarus (PCB; Vasil Navikau, chairman) established itself in 1992 as the successor party to the banned CPB and legitimate heir to the latter's confiscated financial assets. Bitter feuds broke out between the old guard around former first secretary Malafeyeu and upstarts who wanted the legacy for themselves. When, in early 1993, the communist-dominated Supreme Council voted to relegalize the CPB (it will be recalled that 86 percent of deputies once belonged to it), the upstarts moved to squelch the Malafeyeu group.

The majority of legislators elected in 1990 (including Lukashenka) did not renew their memberships in the rechristened Party of Communists.

The PCB is the largest party of any type in Belarus, with approximately 40,000 members from reregistration. Significantly, it is mainly entrenched in rural areas and has considerably less clout with the "vanguard proletarian class" in urban industrialized centers. It is primarily on account of the rural vote that the PCB also boasts the largest number of deputies – forty-two – in the parliament elected in 1995. The weighty Communist bloc is led by Syarhei Kalyakin; Navikau serves as first deputy chairman of the Supreme Council. A Socialist Party is represented by one deputy, Vyacheslau Kuznetsau, who is also the chairman and, possibly, the only member of that party.

The Agrarian Party is of growing interest because a leading member, Semyon Sharetskii, currently occupies the position of Supreme Council chairman. It is represented in the sitting parliament by 33 members, making it the second largest bloc after the PCB. The four-year-old party, composed of collective and state farm officials, recently has distanced itself from the

PCB on the question of Belarusian sovereignty, which the Agrarians support. Sharetskii is currently locked in conflict with his fellow agricultural professional, Lukashenka, over the president's course of personal dictatorship.

Several groups exist on the extremist fringe. The Movement for Social Progress and Justice (MSPS, formerly, Movement for Social Progress, Democracy and Justice) was created in 1991 by self-styled Bolshevik Viktor Chikin. Chikin held aloft the torch of hardline communism during the CPB ban. Judging by the quantity and print quality of publications, all reactionary, that his group produced, it is likely he benefited from hidden government funding. One of Chikin's closest lieutenants, Syarhei Haidukevich, held a visible position under Kebich. The MSPJ prides itself on being visible to the public eye, as per a recent spate of anti-NATO rallies. A newly emerged Republican Party for Labor and Justice which contested and won one seat in the 1995 national election may be an arm of the MSPJ.

Vladimir Zhirinovskii's Liberal-Democratic Party has a branch in Minsk and to all appearances has Lukashenka's ear. It was the Liberal-Democrats, for instance, who urged the president in August 1995 to order the withdrawal of school history textbooks written after independence on grounds of "nationalistic excesses." Zhirinovskii himself supported Lukashenka in the 1994 presidential elections.

Finally, the Slavic Assembly (Slavyanskii sobor) and White Rus' (Belaia Rus') promulgate the union of the Russian, Belarusian, and Ukrainian peoples in a Slavic superstate and are virulently anti-Western. Membership is secretive. Both have operated in Belarus since perestroika, at which time they were linked to the Russian "interfront" movements in the Baltic states. Popular Front chairman Paznyak has dubbed the pan-Slavs a Russian fifth column.[43] Perhaps more important than the groups themselves is that Lukashenka in 1995 heralded pan-Slavism as "the state ideology of Belarus."[44]

Only a small fraction – less than 5 percent – of the Belarusian population belongs to political parties,[45] with the Party of Communists accounting for a major share of that proportion.

Belarus is a long way from the concept of broad-based constituencies and so far only the Communists, self-evidently, possess the experience and resources to achieve something like it with their firm hold on the rural vote. Democratic parties for their part are overly compacted into Minsk and exceedingly weak in regional centers.

Reform and independence under seige

Belarus was the last country in Eastern Europe and the NIS to replace its Soviet-era parliament (May and December 1995) and the last to create the post of president and hold a presidential election (June-July 1994). The former point owed much to the self-preservation interests of the Supreme Council's communist majority and the public's numbed reaction to the collapse of the Soviet Union. The latter point was due to personalized politics, on the one hand, and reformers' concerns, on the other, that the position might be abused to accumulate powers in the wrong pair of hands. This vacuum of leadership was as hazardous to Westernization as it was beneficial to Russian designs to reintegrate its empire.

Opposition deputies accorded high priority at the outset of national independence to introducing democratic electoral laws and holding preterm elections, a path that had the unquestioned support of all democratic parties and forces on the landscape who faced exclusion from the political process for the next few years. A draft BPF law provided for elections by party lists and single-member constituencies to guarantee fair representation. So armed, a total of eighteen organizations in early 1992 formed a "New Belarus" coalition to begin a petition drive for a nationwide referendum on preterm elections (in other words, a petition in favor of holding a referendum on whether early elections should take place). The somewhat torturous route – asking the people if they wanted to be asked something again – was dictated in part by legalities. Despite the daunting task of having to collect some 400,000 signatures to meet constitutional requirements for consideration by the Supreme Council, the petition drive exceeded that goal, in what was the opposition's greatest success to date in the area of mass political activism.

The Supreme Council invalidated the entire initiative on false pretext and instead "recommended that elections be held in March 1994, one year ahead of time – a concession that was quickly forgotten. It was not to chairman Shushkevich's credit that he took part in this exercise in pure cynicism, and in ensuing months he had cause to regret his role in depriving the nation of a chance to render its verdict on a parliament that, as Shushkevich himself often admitted, was beyond repair and incapable of implementing reforms.

Shushkevich was a meandering moderate at a time when bold steps were needed to steer Belarus into the future. Having burned many bridges to the Popular Front camp where vision abounded, Shushkevich chose for his corps of advisors an indifferent group of acquaintances who, in some cases, had never been outside the Soviet Union. Shushkkevich was, without question, committed to sovereignty and independence but failed during his tenure to put forth any kind of blueprint for democratic statehood. Whether that had more to do with temperament (a physicist by training, he boasted of his affinity for the little elements of politics) or with his highly tenuous position in the communist-dominated Supreme Council, is a matter for debate. What is certain is that he built up no base of support for himself or reformist coalition of any kind, preferring to be a lone ranger.

The question of "national communism" never did arise again as an alternative to democratization. Moscow spared reform opponents in Belarus the indignity of having to speak Belarusian by moving to reassert its domination over the "near abroad" mid-way through the Commonwealth's first year, in what became a process of steep erosion of sovereignty. The trend can be traced to the CIS summit in Tashkent in May 1992, when both Shushkevich and Ukrainian president Kravchuk refused to sign a collective security agreement with Moscow on grounds that it violated their countries' principles of neutrality and military nonalignment. The implications for Moscow can be readily surmised against a background where at the given moment Polish president Lech Walesa was proposing a NATO-bis security alliance of Central-Eastern Europe, the Baltic states, Belarus, and Ukraine.[46] If anything, the imperative of maintaining Belarus as Russia's corridor to Europe intensified as Ukrainian defiance of Moscow increased.

Shushkevich's stand on neutrality, which, in his credit column, he never abandoned, set off a rapid chain of events establishing once and for all Russian intentions toward Belarus in particular and the CIS in general. A mere two months after Tashkent, Prime Minister Yegor Gaidar called his Belarusian counterpart, Kebich, to Moscow and ordered him to sign a sweeping bilateral agreement creating a "common" economic, political, and social "space" (*prostranstvo*) between the two countries and recognizing Russian command over the 30,000 Belarus-based strategic troops and relevant technical and production facilities. Its practical effect was to give the Russian government free reign to subvert its neighbor's independence, not at all difficult considering that fealty to the Center was in the genes of Minsk officials.

The main points of pressure were military and economic. If Belarus's stated goal of nuclear disarmament was set in motion with the withdrawal or elimination of the tactical and strategic arsenal (START and NPT were ratified in 1992), the twin goal of neutrality, intended as the principle basis of its international conduct, came under assault inside the country from the predominately Russian officer corps and Ministry of Defense staff[47] as well as directors of military-industrial enterprises that relied on Russian orders.[48] On the economic front, Russian oil prices and supplies, on which Belarus is totally dependent, became a sword of Damocles in bilateral relations. In early 1993 Kebich put before the Supreme Council a proposal to sign the collective security pact and to enter an "economic and defense union" with Russia. The initiative was overwhelmingly approved in spite of Shushkevich's expressions of outrage.

As for a "common political and social space," such a proposition had much less appeal as long as Yeltsin, the loathed nemesis of Minsk communists, was at the helm of the Russian Federation. It is all but certain that leading Belarusian politicians colluded in some way with ringleaders of the anti-Yeltsin insurgency that was destined to end in the dramatic October standoff at the Russian White House. One of these was Lukashenka, then a leader of the Supreme Council's "red" majority bloc, who met with soon-to-be disgraced Russian speaker Ruslan Khasbulatov to show Belarusian support for a "political union," presumably with a Russia stripped of its democrats. Belarusian as well as Russian parliamentarians went on record as favoring the renunciation of the Belavezha accord. No less a personage than Kebich, whose complicity during events two years earlier has been noted, told a gathering in Homel' in September that he was directing his efforts "not toward the resurrection of the Soviet Union – which is practically impossible – but toward its creation in a renewed form,"[49] echoing precisely the aim of forces behind Khasbulatov and Vice President Aleksandr Rutskoi.

The rout of those forces in October was a victory for Russia's new democracy but did not alleviate pressures on the newly independent states to align themselves behind Moscow. To the contrary, the hardliners' challenge forced a shift to the right in policies toward the CIS, as seen, *inter alia*, in the fact that foreign intelligence chief Yevgenii Primakov (currently Russian foreign minister) soon was tasked with drawing up a plan to reintegrate the Commonwealth states in the fullest possible sense.[50]

In Belarus, the ignoble episode was followed by less, not more, democracy. Following the arrest of the White House insurgents, BPF parliamentary faction leader Zyanon Paznyak called for Lukashenka and three of his allies to be stripped of their deputy's status for activities against the Belarusian state. Not only did that not occur, but Lukashenka at the given moment was conniving with Kebich (the Kremlin does not have a monopoly on Byzantine plots) to topple Shushkevich. Appointed earlier in the year to an extraordinary commission to investigate state corruption – which amounted to a mandate from the prime minister to dig up dirt on Shushkevich – Lukashenka publicly denounced the Supreme Council chairman with unsubstantiated petty allegations in December. At the start of 1994 Shushkevich was replaced by the straight-laced Myacheslau Hryb, regarded as a pliant tool of the communist majority.

Institutions and power struggles

Shushkevich's removal cleared the way to the adoption, in March 1994, of a new constitution providing for a presidency and a new delimitation of executive and state powers. The timing was not accidental and had everything to do with the fierce rivalry between Shushkevich and Kebich for the position of first Belarusian president. Kebich did not want his chief potential contender to enter a presidential race from the strong position of parliamentary speaker; while Shushkevich's personal standing in opinion polls (a 59 percent confidence rating in mid-1993)[51] provided yet more reason for Kebich and his supporters in the Supreme Council to stall the electorate's verdict for head of state. It is not, after all, the practice of Belarusian leaders to "ask the people" when the outcome is unpredictable. Hence, the backroom manoeuvering to bring down Shushkevich, already in the cards as he continued to oppose the collective security pact, was Minsk's answer to an election primary.

At the same time, Popular Front leaders had serious – and prescient – misgivings of their own about the potential abuse of presidential powers and remained open to the option of establishing a parliamentary republic. Most of their fears, though, revolved around Kebich's intentions for elected office. Until the eve of the presidential election in June 1994, no one, least of all the prime minister, took seriously the chances of any candidate other than Kebich.

As noted earlier, the Soviet-era Council of Ministers and government apparatus were still in place in 1994. What changes occurred were due to expansion, with positions materializing to accommodate unemployed CPB nomenklatura (Malafeyeu, for instance, went to the forestry ministry) or to compensate for the collapse of all-Union ministries. Arguably, the only institution to undergo significant change and restructuring was the military as a result of the formation of a national armed forces in the context of reduced troop levels (from over 400,000 Soviet personnel in 1991 to 90,000 Belarusian troops in 1996) and the implementation of CFE and nuclear disarmament obligations. Elsewhere, institutional sclerosis was the absolute norm. A most instructive example can be seen in the paleolithic Soviet trade union structures, still every bit intact today and chaired by the equally dinosaurian Viktar Hancharou, who has been railing against Solidarity for the past fifteen years.

Kebich's policies oriented themselves toward the rebuilding of ruptured economic ties with Russia and the thorough-going reintegration of the former Soviet republics;   the creation of a more efficient "social economy," in Kebich's phrase, via the gradual introduction of market mechanisms; and the preservation of social and socioeconomic stability through centralized control

Table 6.2 *Indicators of economic trends in Belarus since 1989*

	1989	1990	1991	1992	1993	1994	1995[a]
GDP	8.0	-3.0	-1.2	-9.6	-11.6	-21.5	-10.0
Industrial output	n.a.	n.a.	-0.2	-6.0	-11.0	-19.3	-13.0
Rate of inflation	1.7	4.5	84	969	1,188	2,220	700
Rate of unemployment	n.a.	n.a.	n.a.	0.5	1.5	2.5	3.7
GNP per capita	n.a.	n.a.	n.a.	n.a.	6,360	n.a.	n.a.
% Workforce in non-state sector[b]	19.7	26.1	29.1	35.0	36.9	40.2	n.a.
% GDP from private sector[b]	n.a.	n.a.	n.a.	n.a.	n.a.	6.1	n.a.

Notes: GDP – % change over previous year; industrial output – % change over previous year; rate of inflation – % change in end-year retail/consumer prices; rate of unemployment as of end of year; GNP per capita – in US dollars at PPP exchange rates. [a]Estimate. [b]Non-state includes collective farms, cooperatives, limited and leased companies, economic and social organizations, and mixed enterprises.

Sources: European Bank for Reconstruction and Development, *Transition Report 1995: Economic Transition in Eastern Europe and the Former Soviet Union* (London: EBRD, 1995); European Bank for Reconstruction and Development, *Transition Report Update, April 1996: Assessing Progress in Economies in Transition* (London: EBRD, 1996).

for an indefinite transition period. The third strategy succeeded best in the first two years of the Commonwealth's existence, when Belarus posted comparatively low rates of inflation and output decline,[52] but the inevitable freefall commenced even as more reform-minded countries, Russia included, were recovering from the worst of the economic crisis. In the five years since the Soviet Union's collapse, Belarus has lagged behind every country in the region in key aspects of economic reform: by 1995, less than 10 percent of GDP derived from private activity and no measures had been taken yet to privatize agriculture or large state-owned enterprises.

The pursuit of various economic, monetary, and even budgetary unions with Russia that was a hallmark of the Kebich government, went beyond the objective realities of Belarus's historically tight integration with the USSR and lack of natural resources. Reintegration was intended as a substitute for Western-backed economic reforms. This was evident from the constant connections the prime minister drew between economic salvation and integration with Russia, whereas one searches in vain for any statement of his linking recovery to the development of a free market economy.

A government critic suggested that the drive to reintegrate had a baser component as well: "Now that privatization in Russia is in full throttle, it is becoming very attractive to the Belarusian nomenklatura who see chances to enrich themselves that do not exist in Belarus with its socialist mentality."[53] The explanation was quite realistic, although Belarusian citizens saw plenty of examples of "enrichening" activity closer to home and came to view their government as steeped in corruption. It is well known that Kebich became a wealthy man as head of the independent Belarusian government and was involved, among other things, in selling millions of dollars in promissory notes abroad. Several attempts to investigate charges of corruption against Kebich were resolutely quashed during and after his tenure, most recently at the end of 1995.

One of the most disturbing and portentous trends under Kebich was the executive's usurpation of powers at the expense of the legislature. Although the prime minister and his twenty-member Council of Ministers were in principle appointed individually by the Supreme Council, in practice they functioned in conditions of unaccountability. Kebich's one notable failure was his attempt in 1992–93 to remake the Belarusian KGB into a ministry, a move resisted by the never-renamed intelligence agency so that it might continue operating as a state within a state, likewise accountable, in practice, to no one in particular within the Republic of Belarus. The prime minister's authority was further augmented by the lack of a head of state. The Supreme Council chairman, or speaker, had no power outside parliament's chambers, and as Shushkevich's case demonstrated, not a great deal within. Absent, too, a commander in chief, the armed forces of Belarus were subordinate to a minister of defense chosen by Kebich; strategic forces answered to Moscow.

The accumulation of executive powers was abetted in addition by critical defects of the Soviet state system that remained in place in the first years of independence. The Supreme Council was a part-time body only, with just 70 out of 345 deputies working in the legislature on a full-time, professional basis. Furthermore, because the Soviet-era Constitution did not respect the principle of separation of powers, a great number of elected representatives worked simultaneously in executive organs,[54] a situation that gave rise to a slew of dubious group interests having nothing to do with voter constituencies. And in view of parliament's all too evident paralysis and endless squabbling in the face of mounting economic despair, it is easy to understand why the parliamentary system itself stood on the verge of popular indictment.

The rise of Lukashenka

The forty-one year-old Lukashenka, a poorly educated former state farm director, spent his life and career in the countryside before coming to Minsk in 1990 as a newly elected deputy to the Supreme Council. It is no trivial point that his wife and son never joined him in the capital and still milk cows in a village in Mahileu oblast'. Time and again Lukashenka has demonstrated in masterful fashion how well he grasps the mentality and priorities of the simple *narod* [people]. He understands, for instance, that blunt talk, an aura of honesty, and "closeness to the people" are what they yearn for in a leader. He also knows that many approve of a strong fist: in a 1992 poll asking Belarusians how best to overcome the economic crisis, 56 percent of respondents (with multiple choices possible) cited "order and discipline" and 41 percent said "strengthening the fight against corruption and embezzlement," as compared to 25 percent who mentioned "speeding up privatization" or "creating conditions for entrepreneurship."[55] Shortly after his election as president, Lukashenka summarized his personality traits as "on the one hand, severity, on the other, softness to the point of tears."[56]

Lukashenka's talent for striking all the right populist chords and drawing attention to himself became evident when he turned his position as state corruption "watchdog" against the Kebich government. In March 1994, directly after the first presidential election was set, Lukashenka announced his entry into the race with a spectacular televised denunciation of corruption at the highest levels of defense, foreign affairs and other ministries, citing specific names. In spite of it all, it was a testament to arrogance that presidential candidate Kebich paid little heed to Lukashenka during the campaign, being confident that the support of the *nomenklatura* both at home and in Moscow would carry him to an easy victory. On one of his numerous campaign-related trips to the Russian capital, the Belarusian prime minister asked journalists from *Izvestiia* to support him not against Lukashenka but against Paznyak, the Popular Front's presidential candidate who had no realistic chances of being elected.[57]

Official Moscow, it appears, took Lukashenka more seriously. In what is a revealing passage in every way – begging the question whether Kebich was running for president of independent Belarus or Party *obkom* secretary[58] – the prime minister told agrarian officials during a campaign stop in Polacak:

Russia gave us, [Prime Minister] Chernomyrdin personally gave me two million tons of oil at $20 a ton for the election. And we want to give this oil to the villages, understand? . . . It's worth $85 but we get it for $20! . . . I'll tell you a secret, yesterday his first deputy – Chernomyrdin's on vacation – gave me a call. It seems I'll be flying back to Russia this week. They asked me directly, how can we help, Slava, how can we help? There's a lot of alarm in Russia about the situation here, they're especially concerned in Russia about Lukashenka . . . The man is finished.[59]

Moscow had reason to be wary of Lukashenka, given his ties to the anti-Yeltsin camp. More than that, Russian if not Belarusian officials knew that "red crusaders" posed a threat to the lucrative interests of the nomenklatura. Kebich's conclusion that Kremlin disapproval would eliminate his opponent needs no elaboration.

If the prime minister turned more frequently to Moscow than to Belarusian voters for electoral support, Lukashenka relied on his ability to fan the flames of popular vengeance at those deemed responsible for collapsing living standards. He continued to denounce corruption, called for the reimposition of fixed prices, and vowed to merge the Belarusian economy with Russia's. In the first round of balloting in June he received 45 percent of the vote; Kebich, 17 percent; Paznyak, 13 percent; and Shushkevich, 10 percent. During debates going into the July 10 runoff, Lukashenka levelled his charges of corruption directly at Kebich, waving documented "proof" in front of cameras. He won by a lopsided 80 percent of the vote, all the more startling considering that he had no organization behind him, had been a complete unknown to the general public before the month of March, and, like other candidates with the exception of Paznyak, had run as an independent (under the Constitution, the president of Belarus may not have a party affiliation).

It should not be assumed that Lukashenka intended to carry out his populist mandate to expose corruption. The accusations against Kebich and his ministers were not pursued; ironically, the same functionaries, who never hesitated to bring libel suits against investigative journalists, did not seek restitution from Lukashenka for defaming them before a national audience.

Presidential powers in theory and in action

The Constitution of 1994[60] declared Belarus a presidential republic with three branches of executive, legislative, and judicial power. Among the privileges the new president obtained as head of state and executive in chief was the right to appoint a Cabinet (formerly, Council) of Ministers consisting of: the prime minister and his deputies; the minister for foreign affairs; the ministers for finance, defense, and internal affairs; and the chairman of the KGB, all subject to Supreme Council approval. Hence, the first shakeup of the Belarusian government since Soviet times was carried out by Lukashenka, and some of his choices immediately revealed that he intended to keep his hands firmly on the controls. Kebich's replacement as prime minister was a minor figure, Mikhail Chihir. In addition, soon after his election Lukashenka sought and obtained from the Supreme Council the right to appoint "governors" to the six oblasts of Belarus.

The new Constitution provided for a leaner, 260-member unicameral parliament but, critically, it failed to introduce a strict separation of functions or a full-time legislature. The relevant article states that a deputy "shall exercise his powers in the Supreme Council on a professional basis or, if he so desires, without suspending his activity in industry or administration" – an invitation to conflict of interest, insofar as the majority of these jobs would be related to the monopolistic government. And although members of the Cabinet, other executive appointees, presidential advisors, and judges are expressly barred from seeking elected office, the prohibition has been flagrantly violated in practice (see table 6.5).

Balance otherwise was observed between the executive and legislative branches. The president enjoys the right to veto laws but may be overruled by a two-thirds majority of parliament, and he does not have the authority to disband the Supreme Council. The calling of national elections, referendums, and the passage of laws and constitutional amendments are exclusive to the legislature. The president can issue decrees provided they do not violate the Constitution, as determined by a Constitutional Court whose members are appointed by parliament. Appointments to the Supreme Court and Office of the General Procurator are likewise within parliament's sole competence.

It is important to realize that the 1994 Constitution recognized the supremacy of law in the Republic of Belarus; guaranteed equal protection under the law; and enshrined the highest international norms with respect to the range and inviolability of fundamental human rights, including but not limited to freedoms of speech, assembly, access to information, and association. Nevertheless, it was precisely in the arena of rights and rule of law where Lukashenka wasted no time in demonstrating his "severe" side, starting with the media.

The government of independent Belarus had restricted the development of an independent media by retaining a tight monopoly over printing and broadcasting facilities and distribution outlets. Most television and radio stations continued to be state-owned and under the purview of Alyaksandr Stalyarou, the chief Soviet-era censor; in several instances, private cable stations were closed when their content displeased officials. A modest amount of independently-produced or Western-made programming of nonpolitical content was permitted.

Greater scope for editorial and financial independence existed in the print media, where privatization had made inroads among smaller publications devoted to business, culture and politics. Two private news-gathering services functioned alongside the official Belinfarm news agency. Even so, all major newspapers, accounting for 90 percent of national circulation, belonged – and still do – to the government or Supreme Council,[61] and many had become less interesting and probing than they were in 1988–91. The largest Russian-language daily never took the trouble to change its name, Soviet Belorussia (*Sovetskaia Belorussiia*) and was a dependable government mouthpiece. A bright spot was the parliamentary organ *People's Newspaper* (*Narodnaia gazeta*), a product of the glasnost era, which had survived conservative attempts to sanitize its editorial line and remained one of the most critical papers in the Republic of Belarus. Essential sources of news and information, and beyond the capacity of domestic authorities to control, were the universally available and considerably freer airwaves and press of the Russian Federation.

Constitutional provisions and new legislation, guaranteeing freedom of the press and prohibiting monopolies, were enacted in 1994 under the Popular Front's influence but came into immediate conflict with Lukashenka's intolerance of opposition, criticism, and the mere potential for same to occur. Eight independent newspapers had to suspend publication when the government cancelled their printing facility contracts in the latter part of the year. On December 20, just one year after the dissemination of Lukashenka's trumped-up charges against Shushkevich, the text of a BPF report to parliament on corruption in the president's own administration was excised from newspapers moments before they went to print, forcing them to come out with blank spaces.

The situation immediately aroused concern in the international community – Freedom House, for one, dropped Belarus from the "partly free" press category in 1993 to "not free" in 1994 – and alerted forces within the country to the pending expiration of democratic hopes. It is no exaggeration to say that since then the Belarusian media have come to enjoy less freedom of expression than they had under glasnost and are used to foster a cult of personality around Lukashenka, his every waking hour and every word of his typically long-winded speeches relayed faithfully to audiences in place of real news. The president's increasingly numerous opponents, no matter the position they occupy or where they stand on the political spectrum, are systematically denied access to the print and electronic media.

Emergence of a "rogue regime"

The foregoing may have left open the question for some readers of Lukashenka's relationship to the communists. Essentially, after 1991 Lukashenka was one of many "red" politicians who did not find it personally or politically expedient to associate with the Party after its relegalization. The Party was irredeemably discredited in urban Belarus. More to the point, it had ceased being the source of power. After the collapse of the Soviet Union, that source had shifted rapidly to the executive organs of government, and only tangentially or secondarily to elected office.

Belarusian communists, like the comrades in Russia, broke down into two broad groups after the CPSU was banned: the pragmatists who underwent "capitalization" by learning to profit financially from their positions; and the ideologists or true believers who strove to restore the Party's authority. But Lukashenka's limitless personal ambitions led him into a third direction of his own, namely, gathering power unto himself. As the only parliamentarian to vote against ratifying the Belavezha accord, he quickly established his impeccable credentials with leading revanchists in Moscow and won their enduring support, probably less to advance his cause in Belarus than to put himself in line for an important Kremlin title in a reconstituted Soviet Union or Slavic superstate. That goal indeed appears to be the driving force of his life, and it is most likely that Lukashenka decided to settle for second best – becoming leader of Belarus – soon after the arrest of his Russian parliament friends in the October 1993 debacle.

In Minsk, though, Lukashenka had no real use for the revived Communist Party and even less desire to compete with rivals for preeminence (say, with Navikau, who briefly ran as PCB candidate for Belarusian president). Many of the comrades looked askance at him anyway because his youth had precluded his rising through the normal ranks. Being outside the nomenklatura, too, Lukashenka had none of the usual power structures or bases behind him at the time of his election. To buttress his authority he homed his authoritarian instincts and megalomania on the security organs and the creation of executive "vertical structures."

Less than a year into his presidency, in April 1995, riot police acting on Lukashenka's orders beat up Popular Front deputies on the steps of the Supreme Council, in what was a first manifestation of regime violence. Ever since, the special interior ministry troops (OMON) have become a most visible reminder of how Lukashenka prefers to deal with critics, being used against peaceful demonstrators with escalating brutality and frequency. In two years, the number of security forces is estimated to have risen to about 180,000, or double the size of the armed forces.[62]

Also expanding is the number of administrative posts reporting directly to Lukashenka throughout the country which effectively override other authority. It is known, in fact, that the president has fired a number of local elected officials and at one time sought, without success, the Supreme Council's approval to abolish the local soviets. In what is but the latest example, the president recently instituted what he described as "an informational-political vertical" consisting of raion- and oblast-level administrators who are responsible for "informing the population" about the president and maintaining his ties with the public and youth. These officials were described in the Russian press as tantamount to *stukachi*, or informants, one of the most dreaded words in the Soviet-era lexicon.[63] As author Vasil' Bykau described matters just one year into Lukashenka's tenure: "It is not the law or the Constitution that reign supreme in the country but the unpredictable will of the president, with his 'vertical structures' and bulletproof-vested, black-masked bodyguards.[64]

Their new-found prominence notwithstanding, the loyalty of the power organs to the Belarusian president cannot be taken for granted, and Lukashenka is demonstrably anxious to ensure that his security people do not follow the Russian example of becoming influential players in their own right. Lukashenka, by the way, has avoided involving the military in his domestic agenda, so of central concern is the Ministry of the Interior and the KGB. Coordination is exercised through the Council of Security, headed by the president with KGB chief Viktar Sheiman as State Secretary. Here it is noteworthy that the Council's apparatus is famously prone to purging, demotions, and presidential cronyism, notably on the interior ministry side which has jurisdiction over the "black-masked" forces but also in the KGB's higher levels.[65] Such instability leaves the impression that not everyone relishes the direction Lukashenka is taking and the chance to bloody up the citizens of Belarus: if the aim is to create a police state, what the president has wrought thus far is best described as a rogue regime.

Consider, for example, the figure of Major-General Valentin Agolets, a former commander of USSR internal forces from Tashkent who rose to the position of Belarusian interior minister in late 1995. "Rose" may be an understatement, because at the time of his appointment Agolets was in career disgrace as an exposed crook.[66] His reversal of fortune came in the wake of a major shakeup at Interior in October of that year, when Lukashenka fired minister Yurii Zakharenka and his deputies on grounds of – no surprise – corruption, but in reality because the ministry had balked at the use of its police to crack down on striking transportation workers the previous August.

The selection of Sheiman, too, was highly irregular and hinted of problematic relations between the president and career KGB officers. The latter have been quoted off the record with sardonic comments such as, "Today you criticize Lukashenka, tomorrow you sell out the country," and reserve officers have aired complaints about being squeezed out of medical and other perks by the presidential Council of Security staff.[67] Sheiman's biography is that of a low-level crony, having served as chief of Lukashenka's bodyguard during the presidential campaign and, prior to that, chief of staff of an airborne assault unit in Brest.[68] Since his promotion in 1995–96 to the top post in the KGB, journalists have dubbed him the "Great Mute" for his refusal to speak in public.

It is unlikely in any case that a more talkative personage would shed light on the crucial subject of whose national security interests the Belarusian KGB really serves. The organization was unique on post-Soviet territory not only for retaining its name but also for the fact that its republican structures underwent no changes after 1991. There was no "repatriation" of cadres in the service of a newly sovereign country. It is difficult therefore to fit the KGB into a particular national context. Interestingly, General Valerii Kez, the former Deputy State Secretary of the Council of Security, now occupies "an important position" in Moscow after being punished for producing compromising material on Sheiman's own cronies.[69]

What is certain, however, is that the KGB of Lukashenka's administration has exuded a Stalinesque obsession with spies and saboteurs. Predictably, the economy's continued dismal performance and the possibility of social unrest have nothing to do with The Leader's policies but are the work of external and internal enemies. The aforementioned transportation strikes in August 1995 were blamed on "foreign emissaries" from the AFL-CIO and Solidarity.[70] Large demonstrations in Minsk in spring 1996 resulted in dozens of arrests, hospitalizations, and injuries courtesy of Agulets's troops and were followed up in short order with a rare pronouncement by Sheiman that the KGB would reorient its investigative priorities from organized crime to antistate activities. Lukashenka did not distance himself from a bizarre and much-publicized outburst in July 1996 by Russian Duma deputy Viktor Iliukhin, with backing from Vladimir Zhirinovskii, about a CIA plot, allegedly involving $254,000 and eighteen to twenty operatives in Warsaw, to foment unrest in Belarus and overthrow its president.[71]

The state of the electorate

As catastrophic and lawless as Lukashenka's regime has become, one should not lose sight of the fact that he came to power in a reasonably democratic election and has never been guilty of misreading the pulse of the population. This is not to imply that Belarusians condone violence – these incidents occur only in Minsk and are not covered by official media – but Lukashenka's rule is a logical outcome of the population's entrenched Soviet mentality and widespread nostalgia for the relative prosperity and stability of the old system. Whereas a US-governed sponsored opinion poll in 1995 found broad support in the abstract for democratic principles such as freedom of speech, it also discovered that two-thirds of Belarusians would be willing to forego such freedoms for a strong leader who could solve the country's economic problems.[72] Lukashenka is aware that promises to put the economic house in order can be used like a narcotic to justify anti-Westernization policies. The question is, when does the public begin making the connection between those policies and the economy's failure to improve?

Of course, the desirable way for citizens to answer that and related questions is through the democratic election process. Yet one of the most egregious effects (or causes?) of Belarus's political culture in the first half-decade of independence was that the population did not come to associate the parliamentary system in fact or *in principle* with changes for the better. Table 6.3, based on a representative sample of voting-age adults surveyed in 1993,

Table 6.3 *Interest in politics and voting intentions in Belarus, 1993*

	Rural	Urban	Secondary education or less	Higher education	Men	Women
% replying "yes":						
Are you very/somewhat interested in politics?	54	58	49	67	66	49
Would you vote this week if.... ?	50	46	41	51	51	44
Differential	-4	-12	-8	-16	-15	-5

Notes: Sample size = 1,990.
Sources: RFE/RL and Novak Laboratory of Axiometric Research, Minsk, 1993.

compares positive responses to the question, "Are you very/somewhat interested in politics?" to the hypothetical query, "Would you vote this week if parliamentary elections were held?" with the following results:[73]

The findings reflected a high degree of skepticism with respect to voting, with just 51 percent of highly educated voters willing to go to the polls; and a discrepancy between interest in politics and interest in voting that was most pronounced among men (-16 point differential), urban residents (-12) and the highly educated (-16) – in other words, the very groups that tend in general to be most politically active. Note, in addition, that the rural voters polled in 1993 were more inclined to vote (50 percent) than their urban counterparts (46 percent). The same survey revealed that urban women were among the least likely group in society to want to vote: only 42 percent replied they would participate in a parliamentary election as against 48 percent of rural women.

Table 6.4, based on the same respondent sample, compares satisfaction with the political situation and confidence in parliament to affirmative voting intentions. Against the background of 1993, when parliament was irreconcilably gridlocked and unwilling to implement reforms, the results in table 6.4 brought the extent of skepticism into even sharper focus: the more dissatisfied the respondent with the political situation or parliament, the smaller the chance that he or she would appear at the polls. Conversely, high levels of satisfaction with the prevailing situation correlated with stronger voting intentions. If just 42 percent of Belarusians with "no confidence at all" in the Supreme Council said they would vote in a hypothetical election that

Table 6.4 *Political satisfaction and voting intentions in Belarus, 1993*[a]

	Are you satisfied with political situation? %	Would you vote this week if...? % replying "yes"	Do you have confidence in parliament? %	Would you vote this week if...? % replying "yes"
Great deal	2	→ 59	5	→ 74
Some	15	→ 60	29	→ 58
Not much	51	→ 48	35	→ 44
Not at all	17	→ 44	15	→ 42

Note: [a]Degree of satisfaction with political situation/Degree of confidence in parliament among overall Belarusian population, cross-tabulated by percentage in each of four row categories who expressed a positive intention to vote; n=1,990.

Sources: RFE/RL and Novak Laboratory of Axiometric Research, Minsk, 1993.

week, the corresponding figure among people with "a great deal of confidence" was 74 percent.

The inverse relationship between motivation for change and motivation to vote was also mirrored in economic attitudes. Although not shown here for reasons of space, proponents of a market economy were least likely to say they would vote in a hypothetical parliamentary election despite the glaring fact that the Supreme Council as constituted in 1993 was opposed to market reforms. There was, overall, no discernable correspondence between liberalism/reform-minded views and faith in the parliamentary process. Rather, it was the most conservative and "preservationist" elements who exhibited the greatest interest in going to the polls.

The reason derived not so much from a conscious desire to deliver a vote of confidence in the given Supreme Council as from the residual dictates of Soviet civic duty, according to which citizens were required to turn out at the polls and "approve" the Communist slate by a 98 percent margin. In rural areas especially, such reflexive obedience was to prove an immensely useful tool for the revived Party of Communists, determined to stage its electoral resurgence from the countryside in time for the 1995 parliamentary elections.

As for the more critically minded urban electorate, the opposite pattern of disorientation and apathy was conditioned by the absence of a clear alternative to the status quo in the form of developed parties and magnetic ideas. The age-old Belarusian problem of galvanization had reasserted itself. According to the same 1993 survey, the Popular Front in 1993 could count on the support of no more than 16 percent of potential voters, while among nonpotential voters it had the sympathy of just 11 percent. The predicament of the BPF, unable to convert most Belarusians to its agenda of national rebirth, bore much in common with the situation of nationalists in 1917–18.

The failed elections to parliament

Spring 1995 marked the end of the five-year term of the Supreme Council and local soviets and signalled the inevitability of general multiparty elections. Unlike the Russian Federation, Belarus's new electoral legislation did not incorporate a party list system, as the political opposition had wanted, but instead provided for candidates in each of 260 electoral districts to be nominated by legally qualifying parties or to run as independents, provided they met certain requirements. By law, all registered candidates were guaranteed equality of access to media and to state-sponsored campaign financing but were barred from raising or accepting funds from sources independent of the public treasury. Behind its egalitarian appearances, the election law assumed a level of impartial democratic behavior on the part of controlling government and state organs that did not exist either before or especially with Lukashenka as president.

Another serious flaw was a provision invalidating election results in districts where voter turnout was below 50 percent of eligible voters (defined as citizens of Belarus aged eighteen and over). This threshold, originating with the "red" majority, was intentionally calculated to maximize the number of invalid results in urban voting districts, where democratic parties were the stronger force, thereby overvaluing the rural, that is, guaranteed nondemocratic, weight in parliament. It could not have occurred to the communists at the time they devised their neat trick that it risked keeping them out of power, too. It did, on the other hand, occur to Lukashenka. From the outset of the election season it was evident he intended to exploit the law's deficiencies and his own strategic talents to force a popular verdict against parliamentarianism and in favor of his absolutist authority.

With the election date set for May 14, the president proposed to the outgoing assembly that it schedule a simultaneous national referendum consisting of the following propositions: granting Russian parity with Belarusian as the official language of Belarus, a status that the indigenous tongue alone had enjoyed since 1990; exchanging the Belarusian flag and emblem, inherited from the Grand Duchy and adopted as the national symbols in 1991, for their slightly modified Soviet versions; achieving economic integration with Russia; and finally, according the president the right to dissolve parliament in event of a crisis. On the eve of the Supreme Council's vote in April to accept or reject the president's initiative, outraged Popular Front deputies staged a hunger strike in protest that ended in the aforementioned beating incident. The rest of the deputy corps got the message and speedily approved the first three questions as binding plebiscites and the fourth, on dissolving parliament, as a consultative referendum.

While devoting all the state's efforts toward propagandizing his four-point referendum, Lukashenka actively strove to sabotage the parliamentary elections. Among the measures he imposed were:

– a media blackout on information and reports pertaining to candidates, platforms, and parties, accompanied by the preventive dismissal of Mikhail Katyushenka, liberal chief editor of the youth newspaper *Znamia iunosti*. Official refusals to air debates and interviews further ensured that candidates remained invisible to the electorate;

– the publication of newspaper editorials disparaging both Western parliamentarianism and the incumbent Supreme Council, and suggesting that presidential rule was the only way out of the current crisis;

– a delay in the release of election-related government funds until the month of May and a limit for each candidate of $50 for campaign expenditures, barely sufficient to print 20,000 leaflets. A total of 20 billion Belarusian rubles were allocated to the elections, in contrast to the 100 billion rubles reportedly spent that month on the annual World War II Victory Day celebration;[74]

– the airing of programs on state television linking the Popular Front and Belarusian national symbols to Nazi collaborationists.

In a more graphic display of contempt, on May 14 the Belarusian leader cheerfully spoiled his ballot slip in front of television cameras with the explanation that no one on it was worth voting for. Lukashenka's example and tactics had their desired effect. A respectable 65 percent of the electorate turned out at the polls to overwhelmingly endorse all four referendum propositions but most ignored their election ballots. A mere eighteen candidates out of a total pool of 2,348 office-seekers won mandates in the first round due to a mass of invalidations.

A chorus of Western condemnation elicited somewhat more statesmanlike behavior during the runoff two weeks later in the remaining 242 electoral districts. Too late to rescue a disastrous situation, only 101 additional seats were filled on May 28, leaving Belarus, with 119 newly elected legislators, far short of the two-thirds quorum (or 174 deputies) required to form a constitutionally viable parliament. Statistics showed that turnout was twice as high in the villages as in the cities,[75] adhering, as it happened, to the pattern of voter motivation discussed in the previous section. The absolute majority of valid election results came from rural areas.

The urban electoral districts were a different story. In the regional capitals of Brest, Homel', Hrodna, Mahilou and Vitsebsk, many individual seats were contested by ten or more candidates, all virtual unknowns owing to the un-democratic conduct of the elections. The result was another plague of low turnouts and invalidations. Nowhere was the competition among candidates – and disorientation of voters – more intense than in Minsk, which failed to elect a single representative to the Supreme Council after two rounds of voting.

Not only had Belarusians failed to elect a working parliament in their first post-Soviet national election, but the outcome, such as it was, also spelled a near-complete rout of the urban-based democratic parties. The Popular Front, which had fielded the largest proportion of candidates, did not capture a single seat in the wake of state television's malicious slander. What is more, candidates who did not obtain a majority of votes in their districts, irrespec-tive of whether results were validated or invalidated, were disqualified by law from participating in further election rounds. That eliminated Paznyak (in whose case questions arose about ballot-box tampering) as well as hundreds of other democratic activists from the field in future runoffs. Another group that was trounced consisted of incumbent legislators of all persuasions who stood for reelection: only a handful of leading names such as speaker Myacheslau Hryb came out of the calamity of invalidations with their mandates intact.

In terms of parties, the resounding victors were, naturally, the Commu-nists sweeping in on the reliable rural turnout. The results in table 6.5, showing the party affiliations and professional backgrounds of winning candidates in the May elections, speak eloquently for themselves.[76]

Of further interest is that many of the communist election victories in rural districts went to the most familiar leaders of the *ancien régime*, such as former BCP first secretary Malafeyeu and the irrepressible Uladzimir Hryhoreu of Vitsebsk, mentioned earlier as a singularly notorious opponent of Gorbachev's policies. Procommunist groups with less name recognition, such as the Party of Labor of Justice, fared no better nationwide than the national-democratic parties. Briefly put, villagers remained true to Soviet "election" traditions. Similarly, it was by presenting themselves to the most politically backward constituencies that candidates who had no business seeking elected office, such as presidential appointees and staff, flaunted the Constitution to obtain seats in parliament.

Local soviet elections took place on June 11 and 25, but benefited, perversely, from the growing insignificance of local authority. An average of less than two candidates vied for each of 28,244 constituencies. Despite low turnouts, the relatively empty field abetted the attainment of valid results, and 86 percent of seats were filled.[77]

Citing the numerous irregularities, international election monitors judged Belarus's parliamentary election "neither free nor fair," placing the centrally

Table 6.5 *Newly elected deputies in Belarus, 1995*

	No.	% of total (119)
Most common party affiliations:		
Agrarian Party		
(communist-allied)	30	25
Party of Communists	27	23
Party of National Accord (centrist)	2	2
All others	5	4
Unaffiliated	55	46
Most common professional backgrounds:		
Kolkhoz/sovkhoz directors	33	28
Raion executive officials	17	14
Factory directors	12	10
Presidential staff employees	10	8
Police	5	4
Other national officials	5	4
Local soviet chairmen	4	3
Military	2	2
All others	21	18

Source: Belarusian Radio, May 29, 1995.

located European country in the same category of political offenders with the Central Asian states. Immediately after the May 28 round, the Council of Europe suspended Minsk's application for membership. None of this had much impact on Lukashenka's popularity ratings. In an independent survey of public opinion conducted in June 1995, 36 percent of Belarusians thought their president was doing a "good" to "excellent" job, up from 24 percent in December 1994, with an additional 34 percent describing his performance as "satisfactory."[78] His triumph on the referendum questions, which passed by margins of 70 to 80 percent, confirmed that his retrograde agenda had widespread appeal. At great expense to the state, down came the flag and emblem of independent Belarus, up went their Soviet look-alike replacements.

The parliamentary system in crisis

The failed election opened the door to a presidential putsch. Consistent with his drive toward unfettered personal rule, Lukashenka refused to recognize the Supreme Council as a legitimate body because its term had expired but opposed the scheduling of more elections to fill out the parliament-in-waiting with sufficient numbers for a quorum. Meanwhile, he began to govern by decree, issuing one after the other in excess of his powers and without regard for constitutional norms. Two of the earliest were issued in August 1995 in response to the outbreak of strikes by Minsk subway and bus workers whose grievances included serious wage arrears and threats to public safety posed by drivers in hunger-induced weak condition. After police crushed the strike action and arrested its organizers, one of whom was people's deputy Syarhei Antonchyk, Lukashenka outlawed independent trade unions by decree and unilaterally abolished deputies' immunity from prosecution in order to take revenge on Antonchyk, author of the report on corruption in the president's administration.

Characteristically, the Supreme Council majority did not overly concern itself with the assault on workers' rights and freedom of association; but it was outraged by the attempt to strip its members of their immunity and at other examples of Lukashenka's concerted usurpation of its powers. Running on a self-extended mandate, the lame duck parliament was not entirely incapable of fighting back. The Constitutional Court under its authority overturned five decrees on grounds of violating the Constitution and in the process become the chief institutional buttress against presidential dictatorship in the second half of 1995.

The crisis transformed the most unlikely individuals into defenders of parliamentary values and constitutionalism. Speaker Myacheslau Hryb, for one, broke with his record of tame complacency to become an outspoken Lukashenka critic. Rather more unexpected was the hero status attained by Constitutional Court chairman Valerii Tsikhinya, a product of the Soviet-era justice ministry who had no democratic credentials whatsoever. Since the end of last year, the crucial role of his Court in opposing the president's voracious power-grabbing has been recognized in several independently conducted ratings of Belarus's leading politicians. These have shown that political experts in Minsk invariably rank Tsikhinya as the second most influential person in the country, behind only Lukashenka and well above the ninth- or tenth-ranking Prime Minister Chihir.[79]

Even more urgently, of course, Lukashenka had to be prevented from instituting what he termed "direct presidential rule" in place of a parliament. It was manifestly clear from his sabotaging of the elections that the president did not discriminate between national-democrats, moderates, and communists when it came to excluding his former fellow parliamentarians from the corridors of power: when one has the unquestionable support of The People, why bother indeed with their other elected representatives? Groups that had the most to lose if a new assembly did not convene protested the loudest, above all, the Party of Communists, which not only decried Lukashenka's "dirty fighting methods" but formally adopted the position that the office of president should be abolished.[80]

The Supreme Council confronted Lukashenka with its intention to seek a reduction of the validation threshold to 25 percent of voters retroactive to May (in effect to reverse the invalidation of many deputies' reelection bids) and to press ahead with third and fourth election rounds on November 26 and December 10. Forced to accept the runoffs, Lukashenka warned that parliament would cease to operate if these failed again and did everything in his power to ensure such an outcome. On the eve of the third round, demonstrating his mastery of Bolshevik techniques, he sent his personal aides to physically intimidate members of the Constitutional Court into ruling against the proposal to lower the 50-percent turnout minimum. Hryb, by now thoroughly blacklisted along with Tsikhinya, was prevented from broadcasting an appeal to citizens to go to the polls.

The fate of Belarusian parliamentarianism was truly a cliffhanger that was decided the evening of December 10 with just an hour or two to go before voting stations closed. Until that point, the Central Electoral Commission, still short several dozen validations, was pessimistic about the success of the elections. A last-minute spurt of voters, however, sufficed to validate returns from 16 districts in Minsk alone and nudge overall nationwide turnout to above 50 percent. Anecdotes had it that the eleventh-hour "miracle" was due to people chancing to stop by the polls while out walking their dogs.[81] It would be more satisfying to attribute things to a sudden collective recollection of Lukashenka's broadcast remarks on November 23 in praise of Hitler's leadership style, but evidence for that explanation is lacking. Whatever the cause, the total number of elected candidates rose to 198, more than enough to form a constitutionally viable if understaffed parliament.

In the final round, a few gains were posted by middle-of-the-road parties and the PCB augmented its strength by a dozen seats. None of the second-tier Popular Front candidates were elected, which altogether eliminated the national-democratic faction from the Supreme Council. Further details on party representation in the new assembly, which first convened in January 1996, were presented above (see "The Spectrum of Political Parties"), but here it would be helpful to describe the political-ideological blocs in broad strokes.

The PCB, with forty-two deputies in all, became the largest bloc; it espouses "a Belarusian-Russian confederation and eventual restoration of the USSR," in the words of Party leader Vasil' Navikau.[82] Sympathetic to the Communists' economic and social agenda, but in favor of preserving Belarusian sovereignty, are the Agrarians with thirty-three representatives including new Supreme Council chairman Semyon Sharetskii. Close to one-half of the deputy corps – 96 out of 198 present members – are independents, but within this group is a "presidential bloc" consisting of approximately forty deputies who are employed in Lukashenka's administration. The president's chief aide, Uladzimir Kanouleu, heads this faction, which calls itself "Accord," and is a member of the Presidium of the Supreme Council at Lukashenka's insistence. At the risk of belaboring a point, "Accord's" existence is a mockery of the Constitution.

Fewer than thirty deputies belong to the centrist-liberal camp, which is still in the process of defining itself and susceptible to the competing personal ambitions of well-known individuals like Shushkevich, industrialist Henadz' Karpenka, and former National Bank chairman Stanislau Bahdankevich. As one who had a public falling out with Lukashenka over economic policies, Bahdankevich arguably is the most prestigious liberal reformer in parliament. Like Tsikhinya, his rating as one of the most influential players in Belarusian politics – in fifth place – has been consistent.

The march to dictatorship continues

The "neo-Soviet" constellation of forces in parliament would appear to be wholly compatible with Lukashenka's world view. Regardless of the long-standing acrimony between the president and the PCB, the Communists are indebted to Lukashenka for dismantling "nationalist" symbols, guaranteeing the continued supremacy of the Russian language, and rolling back the few tentative steps Belarus had made toward integration with Western Europe. In short, the executive and legislature should be marching in step to the radiant past. Paradoxically, the political crisis in Belarus has grown to such immense proportions that matters are now virtually out of control.

To begin with, Lukashenka has continued on the path toward one-man rule in spite of the convocation of a new parliament. Presidential chain-of-command structures controlling the economy and state finances have mushroomed along with the vertical political-social structures touched on in a preceding section. The course of privatization and market reforms have been set back accordingly and with deliberate intent. Irrespective of their opposing views on the desirability of a market economy, liberals and communists alike agree that the accumulation of economic and financial powers in one set of hands has teetered between the destructive and the despotic.

One trend set in motion by Lukashenka and Chihir is the renationalization of financial institutions, beginning, in late 1995, with the forced merger of the Belarusbank stock company and the state Savings Bank as an initial step toward creating a "Superbank" for the largest in-country accounts (primarily, oil refineries and the chemical industry). The state came away owning a 99-percent share of Belarusbank but complications with plans for the "Superbank" subsequently clouded the question of just compensation for the original shareholders.

More drastically, in April 1996 Lukashenka signed a decree nationalizing the Interbank Currency Exchange (ICE) and imposing a ceiling on the quantity of Russian rubles and hard currency that banks are permitted to buy. One immediate effect was to consign nonstate firms employing tens of thousands of workers to a low-priority category of access to foreign currency. Many consequently faced bankruptcy.[83] Additionally, nine solid investment projects had to be cancelled; the nationalized entity, according to ICE's ex-chairman who was sacked by separate presidential decree, operates at a loss of 4 billion rubles per month and endures indirect losses of tens of millions of dollars.[84]

Another tendency, referred to in the literature as "administrative-disciplinary" measures, involves the assignment of government and executive officials to take responsibility for factory or farm operations. For example, the "Horizont" television manufacturer, a crown jewel of the Belarusian Soviet economy that did not privatize or adapt to market conditions, is under "direct presidential rule"; the shop is run by a so-called "presidential council of the labor collective" reporting to a deputy prime minister. Other well-known enterprises already under or slated for this regimen are the Minsk Watch Factory and the "Integral" electronics plant.

Domestic critics fear that ultimately, plants which do not submit to "direct presidential rule" will be subject to the highest taxation rate, a ruinous 70 percent, on the value of their goods, while "presidential" firms receive favorable rates.[85] For that there is a sordid precedent: Lukashenka's office owns and manages two commercial firms – "Torgekspo" and the "Mahmoud Esembaev" concern – that are specifically exempt from any taxation, at a cost to the treasury, say parliamentary sources, of hundreds of millions of dollars.[86]

It is difficult to overstate the lawlessness of these measures in terms of protection for investors, the rights of shareholders, state finances, and the overall functioning of market mechanisms. To take another instance, Lukashenka recently granted himself the added privilege of "liquidating" any enterprise that did not undergo "republic-wide registration," the hitch being that procedures for said registration do not exist in the books. The steps will no doubt further discourage much-needed foreign investment in Belarus, already the lowest per capita in the entire postcommunist expanse (in 1993, foreign investment stood at $1 per capita in Belarus, as against an average $50 in the NIS and $250 in Eastern Europe).[87]

Inevitably, too, Minsk has badly undermined its standing with world lending institutions. Last April officials of the International Monetary Fund singled out Belarus as the region's only backpedaler on market reforms and the sole exception to their optimistic prognoses for the foreseeable future of the NIS economies.[88] In order to refute that picture and claim the economy is stabilizing, Chihir's government has resorted to artificially boosting output with mass subsidies and a form of quotas for inefficient, outmoded enterprises. The approach might be likened to the "acceleration" program launched in the USSR in 1985 to produce as many (unwanted) goods as quickly as possible.[89] In that connection, the Belarusian prime minister himself conceded that unsold inventory rose 30 percent in the first quarter of 1996.[90]

However, the chief executive's ongoing takeover of the economy is a rear guard action as compared to the intensification of his front-line battle against the Supreme Council. Small matter that parliament no longer has a Popular Front faction to demonize; the hunt for "enemies of the people" and "trash" – two of Lukashenka's own choice epithets – has grown to encompass the entire national legislature as well as most oppositionist institutions. Writes one observer, "Among those inscribed on Lukashenka's enemy list are Supreme Council deputies, practically all political parties and movements, the Constitutional Court, [free] trade unions and the independent media."[91] (On the latter point, it bears mentioning that persecution of what is left of the independent press recently forced two newspapers to move their facilities to Vilnius.)

The descent into absolutist dementia is best seen in chronological form:

– on March 24, 1996 40,000 demonstrators rally in Minsk to mark the anniversary of the founding of the independent Belarusian Republic in 1918 and to protest the imminent signing of a Lukashenka-Yeltsin accord establishing a "Belarusian-Russian confederation";

– the accord is signed April 2 in Moscow, prompting another large demonstration organized by the Popular Front. Arrest warrants are issued for BPF leaders Paznyak and Navumchyk, who escape police by fleeing to Ukraine and eventually to Warsaw;

– Paznyak returns to Minsk to take part April 26 in a march commemorating the tenth anniversary of the Chernobyl disaster, which again draws 40,000+ people and takes on anti-Lukashenka tones. OMON forces attack with clubs and send dozens of injured to hospital. Close to 200 people are arrested, including seventeen citizens of Ukraine representing Rukh, the Ukrainian parliament, and the militant Ukrainian National Assembly-Ukrainian National Self-Defense Organization (UNA-UNSO). Foreign journalists and a few diplomats are among those abused by riot police.

– Yurii Khadyka and other arrested BPF members go on hunger strike in prison; Paznyak again flees to Poland; and on May Day, another demonstration is violently dispersed, with police seizing the audio-visual equipment of Russian journalists;

– Agulets uses the internationally embarrassing incidents to carry out another purge of the interior ministry, bringing in several "heavies" of Lukashenka's acquaintance from Mahileu oblast'; Sheiman reorients the KGB's energies to combatting subversion and steps up harassment of journalists and members of parliament. For instance, in June, three thugs break into the home of political commentator Yurii Drakohrust and severely beat his wife, forcing the pair to leave Belarus.

– in June-July, Paznyak and Navumchyk leave Warsaw for the United States, becoming the first Belarusian dissidents in history and the only politicians from the post-Soviet region to request political asylum;

– in mid-July, Lukashenka declares he will seek to extend his term from five to seven years and amend the constitution to increase his powers. This leads to a development without precedent and hitherto unthinkable in the eight-year history of the Belarusian opposition: the leadership of the Party of Communists sits down with the Popular Front and five other parties to form a round table alliance.

– comprised of parliamentary speaker Sharetskii for the Agrarians, the PCB's Navikau, Khadyka of the BPF, Bahdankevich for the United Civic Party, Shushkevich and a Social Democrat, the group of seven releases a public declaration on the general crisis in Belarus. In it the president is accused of gross management of the economy and financial system, disgracing Belarus on the European and world arena, and wasting time fighting enemies in the Supreme Council, Constitutional Court, and media. The declaration calls on Lukashenka to join the political parties at the negotiating table;

– the president calls a joint meeting of the Council of Security and Cabinet of Ministers, telling them "there will be no dialogue with politicians who are discussing plans to estrange me from power;" and tells the nation in a two-hour broadcast address that "those who are thinking to oust me will be ousted first."[92] He also bans demonstrations for the duration of the harvest season.

– on July 25, Viktor Iliukhin, who chairs the Russian Duma's national security committee, exposes the CIA plot to topple the Belarusian president, adding for extra color a UNA-UNSO twist to the story and the revelation that Langley planned to assassinate Popular Front leaders and pin the blame on Lukashenka. Within a few days the United States grants Paznyak's and Navumchyk's request for asylum.

– Iliukhin and Zhirinovskii also send cables to Minsk warning of Belarus's infiltration by hostile Polish Jews. Belarusian state TV picks up these themes in nightly programs that manage to tie all the president's opponents to foreign conspiracies.

It was against this alarming background and proliferating calls for his impeachment that Lukashenka in early August unveiled his plan to submit a new version of the constitution and other questions to a popular referendum on the November 7 anniversary of the Bolshevik Revolution. If Yazep Lyosik were alive he would recognize this as the very same "Ask the people" retort he heard from the Bolsheviks in 1917.

The key changes Lukashenka had in mind were to make the Supreme Council a bicameral assembly, with members of the upper house to be appointed by the president; extending the president's term to seven years; and granting the executive the privilege to appoint 50 percent of members of the Constitutional Court. Impeachment provisions would also be struck from the constitution such that the president could be removed from his post only if he changed citizenship. The plebiscite would also include questions on outlawing private land ownership and changing the national holiday from July 27, anniversary of the Declaration of Sovereignty, to the day Belarus was liberated from Nazi occupation.

Later Lukashenka proposed to tack on a referendum item about preserving capital punishment – a guaranteed winner in the court of public opinion – in a move almost certainly aimed at justifying Belarus's exclusion from the Council of Europe. The president is nothing if not clever, and the idea probably derived from a dispute in Ukraine over compliance with the ironclad CE requirement that member states abolish the death penalty. It would then be possible for Lukashenka to claim before his own people and to the Europeans that Belarus cannot join the CE, not because it ignores human and democratic rights but because the citizens demand the highest sentence for criminals.

The round table alliance struck back August 28 with an ultimatum to the president to rescind sixteen unconstitutional decrees or face impeachment. Sharetskii dubbed the referendum a constitutional coup but the parties were disadvantaged in formulating a response because Lukashenka's constitution was not circulated to members of parliament until the month of September. The president had left it in Moscow to be vetted first by Russian foreign affairs minister Yevgenii Primakov.

The Russian factor

Primakov, as previously noted, had been charged with the task as then chief of Russian foreign intelligence to codify Moscow's policies toward the newly independent states. That effort bore fruit on September 14, 1995, when

President Yeltsin issued a decree titled "On the Establishment of the Strategic Course of the Russian Federation with Member-States of the CIS incorporating the recommendations of Primakov and leading policy organs.

The eight-page decree specified concrete measures to reassert Russian hegemony over the former Soviet republics in the spheres of politics, defense and security, economics, culture, science, communications and international relations, among others.[93] In accordance with the Strategic Course, policies toward the CIS states must be based on firm intolerance of conduct which runs counter to Russian "vital interests." It called for a range of "financial, economic, military-political and other measures to protect the rights and interests of Russian minorities in the "near abroad," in what sounds like a recipe for destabilization. Of no less importance were Yeltsin's instructions to work toward the deployment of Russian Federation border troops along the outer periphery of each of the Commonwealth states as well as the merger of Russian and CIS positions in relations with the United Nations, OSCE, NATO, the European Union, and the Council of Europe.

Months before the Strategic Course was promulgated, Belarusian-Russian relations began corresponding remarkably to these prescriptions in the large and small details, and most transparently in the defense and security realm. The very first action Lukashenka took after his referendum triumph in 1995 was to enter in a Customs Union with Moscow providing for joint border patrols. Since then he has referred to the extension of *Russia's* border to Poland and offered to forge a corridor between the Russian mainland and Kaliningrad oblast', all the more provocative in terms of Poland's territorial integrity. Belarusian air defense remains fully integrated and under the command of Moscow; one can be confident that the orders to shoot down two American balloonists in the tragic incident of September 1995 did not originate in Minsk.

Areas of coordination are many, and need not distract attention from the overriding issue of Belarus's strategically critical place in military alliance with Russia from the time it renounced neutrality in 1993. That role was further underscored when, only days before Yeltsin signed his decree, Lukashenka suddenly stood up as a front-line spokesman for opposition to NATO expansion, a position he zealously promotes to the consternation of leaders elsewhere in Central and Eastern Europe.

What pertains to Russia's vital security interests is no less relevant to the pipelines transporting Russian oil to Europe. Traversing both Belarus and Ukraine, recurring disputes between the latter and Moscow over right-of-use fees have compelled Russia's mighty Gazprom to concentrate new projects in Belarus. For all the bluster from Belarusian leaders about obtaining "cheap" Russian fuel, the fact is, the discount on average has amounted to no more than 10 percent of world prices;[94] Minsk, meanwhile, retains its friendly policy of levying transport charges on Moscow at the circa 1968 level.[95] More than that – and a trend that promises to be of enormous import in the years to come – are ongoing efforts by Ukraine and the Baltics to reduce if not eliminate their dependency on Russian oil. Currently under construction are the Baltic transportation project with a terminal in Buting, Lithuania, and a terminal in the Odessa area that would carry Iranian oil via Turkey to Ukraine and thence to other points in Europe. The Balts and Ukrainians likewise envision hooking up these lines on the north-south axis, inevitably drawing Belarus into the picture.[96] This is a scenario capable of inducing paroxysms at Gazprom, and one would expect the Belarusian regime as presently constituted to block it on Moscow's behalf.

If these constitute weighty considerations in determining Belarus's significance to the Kremlin, the question remains to what extent Russia is willing to honor the tradeoff: propping up Belarus's reform-resistant economy.

Lukashenka has been frustrated more than once in his overtures to Yeltsin and Chernomyrdin. Just two weeks after his inauguration as president, he hastened to Moscow promising to negotiate full economic and monetary union as "the only way to overcome the crisis" in Belarus. The two Russian leaders, stung by "Slava" Kebich's downfall, sent Lukashenka home empty-handed. In the end their rebuke ushered in a brief period of economic liberalization and sovereignty-minded policies on the part of Lukashenka's administration. Prices on basic foodstuffs and consumer goods were freed in August 1994 and Bahdankevich, then in the post of National Bank chairman, made progress toward introducing a Belarusian currency. Even the spineless Chihir came into the Cabinet as a market advocate.

When Lukashenka took his case for economic reintegration with Russia to The People by means of the referendum, the results of which – 80 percent in favor – were entirely predictable, he did so with the intention of having a populist weapon against Western reform proponents at home and, secondly, to convey a message to Moscow that it was time to get serious about upholding its end of the bargain with its Belarusian client state. The issuance of the Strategic Course, signed by Yeltsin in his accelerating alignment with the political right, found Lukashenka effectively cancelling the sovereignty drive and dropping many pretenses at reform. Bahdankevich clashed with the president over the change in course and was dismissed.

The creation in April 1996 of a Belarusian-Russian confederation was the latest development in the four-year-long game of economic unions, monetary unions, defense pacts, integration, restoration, "common social spaces" and so on *ad infinitum*. It is strange, to say the least, that the new entity is formally called the Union of Sovereign Republics – SSR in Russian – when one of its two members is a Federation. How this politically-motivated

Anschluss will change relations in a substantive sense remains to be seen. At the end of the day, Russia derives immeasurably greater benefit from Belarus's vassalage than what it gives in return. Lukashenka isn't close to getting what he urgently needs, namely, that Russians subsidize his unprivatized economy and buy up overstocks of black-and-white "Horizont" Tvs instead of Sonys. Unfortunately, he is not inclined to accept that things no longer work that way.

Another dimension is being added with respect to Russian toleration of Lukashenka's increasingly crazed conduct. Despite having vetted both his latest referendum questions and constitution with Primakov before showing them to the Belarusian legislature, parliamentary sources assert that his plan to hold the plebiscite and the president's excesses in general have no support in the Kremlin.[97] As a champion of Moscow's interests in the region and the near abroad, Lukashenka is at once a public relations disaster and, of greatest concern, a factor of destabilization in Russia's only remaining "window to the West." More harm than purpose is served by encouraging a paranoid red dictatorship in the midst of would-be NATO allies.

It is not surprising, therefore, that on a trip to Moscow September 7 seeking help against a parliament he said was stockpiling weapons and preparing to take up arms against him, the Belarusian leader encountered a few doors slamming in his face. His claim to Interfax news agency to have met with Yeltsin was firmly denied by the Kremlin press service. In the tradition of the beleaguered Belarusian communists in 1991, however, there is always sovereignty to fall back on. According to a Belarusian journalist, Lukashenka "dramatically changed the tone of his statements about Russia after his return from Moscow. He began to persistently underscore the importance of Belarus's sovereignty (which he used to call 'junk') and complained that certain opponents of the president are looking for support in the West as well as the East."[98]

Conclusion

So it remains to "ask the people" for their support in crushing democracy. Naturally, the stakes of the November 7 referendum are not presented to the population in those terms, but so complete is the information blackout in Belarus about events and realities that the view is easily distorted. To the public Lukashenka shows only his "soft to the point of tears" side, like Uncle Stalin, crying for a child dying of a Chernobyl-related illness or leading workers on an old-fashioned Soviet *subbotnik* (a free day's labor for the state).

Again, one is struck by his deft exploitation of every defect in the national, political, and social psyche, and how masterfully he frames his case for a new constitution that would give him unlimited totalitarian powers. Blaming incompetence in parliament and certain "ambitious politicians . . . destroying the state" for the failure of his own policies to alleviate their misery, Lukashenka has told Belarusians that his constitution is "based on the example of countries such as Russia, France, and Italy, which give the president legislative powers, the right to dissolve parliament, to decide on the resignation of the government, and to announce republic-wide referendums and parliamentary and local elections."[99] Who in Belarus would not want to be in the same advanced constitutional company as Russia and Western Europe? To close the deal, Lukashenka has also incorporated into his draft those paragraphs of the USSR Constitution pertaining to social guarantees like full employment.

Much less impressive is how the Supreme Council is reacting to the crisis. After all, it is within its powers to stop the referendum, impeach Lukashenka, and get on with it, yet somehow it doesn't happen in conditions where democratic values, respect for the supremacy of law, and accountability to the nation have not penetrated parliament itself. Among the ideas under discussion in the round table alliance is to move up the schedule for another election runoff to November 7 and/or hold a parallel referendum on whether to abolish the post of president, as the communists are urging. But given all precedents, these options seem torn from life and are likely to backfire spectacularly. The urban working class, for instance, may not perceive Lukashenka's real motives but it does know a thing or two about the Communist Party and will interpret its proposition, All Power to the Soviet, for what it is and vote against it. Which leads to the issue, too, of what Belarus is left with if Lukashenka is ousted – a solid bloc of reactionaries like Syarhei Kalyakin forming the largest faction in parliament.

Incredibly, Lukashenka is the only strong Belarusian leader in history and the first to find the means to galvanize the masses. However despised by intellectuals, business people, journalists, most of the Minsk political establishment, democrats, communists, some part of the KGB and even by the Kremlin, the most recent poll figure shows he has the full support of 42 percent of the population.[100] It is up to the remainder to decide how long he stays. Significantly, blue-collar unrest appears to be building. If Lukashenka makes good on his intention to disband parliament and rule without it, at some point he will run out of scapegoats and have to be held personally accountable for drastic unemployment (unofficially estimated at 600,000 to 700,000 workers), continued impoverishment (incomes for 90 percent of the population are below the Minimum Consumer Basket level) and, in line with a recent World Bank recommendation, the halt of further loans to Belarus. Lukashenka's proposition to build communism without so much as a Communist Party, his sworn enemy of the moment, or anything resembling a national or political ideology is without historical precedent and ultimately doomed to fail.

One fervently hopes that when the time comes, an individual of *national and moral consciousness* will emerge who is capable of mobilizing the population around better, democratic ideals; and who will exploit not its weaknesses but the peaceable and tolerant character of the Belarusian people, so paradoxically at odds with the current regime.

NOTES

1 R. F. Foster, *Modern Ireland, 1600–1972* (London: Penguin, 1988), p. 569.
2 *Handelsblatt*, 23 November 1995. Again according to Lukashenka, Hitler "ruined all the good he achieved by launching the war." The interview was broadcast in its entirety on Belarusian radio, but on November 27, in attempted damage control, Lukashenka's press office claimed the comments had been deliberately distorted by the president's political enemies. Only six weeks earlier, on October 13, Lukashenka had delivered an emotional four-hour address to World War II veterans in homage to their sacrifices for the Soviet motherland.
3 The term Belarusian SSR is equivalent to Belorussian SSR. The "Beloruss-" spelling, derived from Russian, fell out of use after 1991 and will not appear in the body of this chapter for consistency's sake.
4 Precisely why the northwestern Rusian (adjectival form of Rus) lands acquired the appellation Belaia, i.e., White, is not known for certain, but recent scholarship suggests an original religious connotation (white, or true, Orthodox faith) that later came to encompass Rusian lands which successfully resisted Tatar domination. See Jan Zaprudnik, *Belarus: At a Crossroads in History* (Boulder, CO: Westview Press, 1993), pp. 2–3, who also provides most of the historical background on which this discussion is based. Dr. Zaprudnik also points out that Belaia and Rus were not combined to form the name Belarus until the late nineteenth century, but for our purposes we will make retrospective use of "Belarus."
5 Ibid., pp. 8–9.
6 Ibid., p. 3.
7 The Belarusianist school tends to minimize the objective impossibility of composing texts in the Lithuanian vernacular; even the acquisition of a writing system upon Christianization required a long period of adaptation. The first document in Lithuanian appeared only in 1525, consisting of a translation of prayers.
8 Yauhen Reshatau, *Notes From the History of Belarus* (http://www. freedom.ncsa.uiuc.edu/ ~ zelenko/history.html) (1994). Reshatau writes that conditions in the GDL "attracted oppressed people from other countries . . . The liberal policy of [Grand Duke Vitaut IX] toward them meant they were free to use their language, religion and traditions."
9 Zaprudnik, *Belarus: At a Crossroads*, p. 58.
10 Reshatau, *Notes*.
11 *Narodnaia gazeta*, 1 February 1995.

12 Yazep Lyosik, *Tvory* (Minsk: Belarus, 1994), p. 255.

13 Zaprudnik, *Belarus: At a Crossroads*, p. 67.

14 Leonard Shapiro, *The Communist Party of the Soviet Union*, 2d ed. (New York: Vintage Books, 1971), p. 22. Shapiro writes of the Bund in former GDL territory that "apart from the Georgian party, it was the only broadly based workers' party with anything like a democratic organization in Russia." The First Congress of the All-Russian Social Democratic Labor Party, organized by the *Bund* at the urging of Lenin, then in exile, was held in Minsk in 1898.

15 Richard Pipes, *The Formation of the Soviet Union* (New York: Atheneum, 1974), p. 149.

16 Ibid., p. 151.

17 Ivan S. Lubachko, *Belorussia Under Soviet Rule, 1917-1957* (Lexington: University of Kentucky Press, 1972), p. 69.

18 Zaprudnik, *Belarus: At a Crossroads*, p. 77.

19 After the Kurapaty site was excavated in 1988, an official investigation into the massacres was obstructed for years by hardliners insisting that the killings had been carried out by Nazi extermination squads. The Belarusian Office of the General Procurator concluded only in 1996 that the Belarusian NKVD was responsible and that "at least 30,000 people were buried" in Kurapaty, although unofficial estimates have put the figure at closer to 250,000. Press Release, "Belarus Authorities Confirm Stalin NKVD Blame for Atrocities Site," Embassy of the Republic of Belarus, Washington, DC, 5 July 1996.

20 Ralph S. Clem, "Belorussians," in *The Nationalities Question in the Soviet Union*, ed. Graham Smith (London: Longman, 1990), p. 113.

21 Mikhail Heller and Aleksandr Nekrich, *Utopia in Power: the History of the Soviet Union from 1917 to the Present*, trans. from the Russian by Phyllis B. Carlos (New York: Summit Books, 1986), pp. 397-98.

22 *Naselenie SSSR za 70 let*, ed. L.L. Rybakovskii, USSR Academy of Sciences, Institute of Sociology (Moscow: Nauka, 1988), pp. 163-64.

23 BSSR State Committee on Statistics, *Narodnoe khoziaistvo Belorusskoi SSR v 1989 g.* (Minsk: Belarus, 1990), p. 24.

24 Ibid., p. 14.

25 Clem, *The Nationalities Question*, p. 116.

26 Ibid., p. 116.

27 *Republic of Belarus: Country Economic Memorandum*, World Bank Report No. 11349-BY, May 12, 1993, Annex G, p. 15.

28 Dmitrii Furman and Oleg Bukhovets, "Belorusskoe samosoznanie i belorusskaia politika," *Svobodnaia mysl'*, no. 1, 1996, pp. 57-75.

29 Zaprudnik, *Belarus: At a Crossroads*, p. 111.

30 Only 345 of 360 seats were filled in 1990 after three rounds of voting.

31 Kathleen Mihalisko, "Belorussia as a Sovereign State: An Interview with Henadz' Hrushavy," *Report on the USSR*, no. 35, 1990, pp. 21-23.

32 Kathleen Mihalisko, "Prospects for 'The Last Bulwark of Bolshevism in Eastern Europe'," ibid., 9 August 1991, pp. 15-19.

33 *Zviazda*, 29 November 1990.

34 Kathleen Mihalisko, "The Workers' Rebellion in Belorussia," *Report on the USSR*, 26 April 1991, pp. 21-22; and "Workers and Soviet Power: Notes from Minsk," ibid., 5 July 1991, pp. 15-21.

35 Quoted in *Znamia iunosti*, 2 May 1991.
36 For instance, in July Malafeyeu hosted an unusual set of meetings with leaders (soon to be jailed) of the pro-Soviet Communist factions from all three Baltic republics.
37 Mihalisko, "Prospects for 'The Last Bulwark . . ." pp. 15–19.
38 *Report of the Temporary Commission of the Supreme Council of the Republic of Belarus in Evaluation of Actions by the State of Emergency Committee and its Supporters* (abbreviated title), Minsk, December 1991, p. 59.
39 *Femida*, 15 December 1991.
40 Nationwide public opinion survey for 1994, Radio Free Europe/Radio Liberty and Novak Laboratory of Axiometric Research, Minsk.
41 *Nations in Transit: Civil Society, Democracy and Markets in East Central Europe and the Newly Independent States* (Washington: Freedom House, 1995), p. 33.
42 Zaprudnik, *Belarus: At a Crossroads*, p. 157.
43 Zyanon Paznyak, "Nash narod – hliboko ta seryoz'no khvoryi," *Ukraina*, no. 13 (1995), 3–4.
44 Belarusian Radio, 19 August 1995.
45 *Nations in Transit*, p. 33.
46 This is discussed in more detail in Kathleen Mihalisko, "The Belarusian National Dilemma and its Implications for US Policy-Makers," *Demokratizatsiya*, no. 1 (1993/94), 108–19.
47 According to *Vo slavu rodiny*, 17 September 1992, no more than 30 percent of Belarus-based officers were Belarusian; the Ministry of Defense staff was 20 percent Belarusian.
48 Kathleen Mihalisko, "Belarus: Neutrality Gives Way to Collective Security," *RFE/RL Research Report*, 23 April 1993, pp. 24–31.
49 *Narodnaia gazeta*, 18-20 September 1993.
50 *Moskovskie novosti*, 17–24 September 1995.
51 Kathleen Mihalisko, "Politics and Public Opinion in Belarus," *RFE/RL Research Report*, 15 October 1993, p. 50.
52 *Republic of Belarus: Country Economic Memorandum*, p. 12.
53 *Narodnaia gazeta*, 10 March 1994, as quoted in Furman and Bukhovets, "Belorusskoe samosoznanie i belorusskaia politika."
54 See "State System" by Vladimir Novik, Supreme Council of Belarus (http://www.lang.uiuc.edu/HUM382/stateSys.html) (1994).
55 *Sovetskaia Belorussiia*, 25 March 1992.
56 Ibid., 1 September 1994.
57 *Izvestiia*, 26 August 1995.
58 The author owes this observation to Furman and Bukhovets, "Belorusskoe samosoznanie."
59 The transcript of Kebich's talk in Polacak appeared in *Narodnaia gazeta*, 17 June 1994, and in Furman and Bukhovets, "Belorusskoe samosoznanie."
60 The Belarusian Constitution may be viewed on the Internet (http://www.uni-wuerzburg.de/law/index.html [note that the hyphen is part of the address]). This useful site, maintained by the Department of Law at the University of Hamburg, contains the English-language version of every post-Soviet constitution.
61 *Nations in Transit*, p. 34.

62 Ustina Markus, "Lukashenka's Proposed Referendum," *OMRI Analytical Brief*, no. 255, 2 August 1996 (http://www.omri.cz).

63 *Kommersant-Daily*, 22 August 1996.

64 Quoted in *Moskovskie novosti*, 10-17 August 1995.

65 *Segodnia*, 22 August 1996.

66 *Izvestiia*, 19 January 1996, reported on the basis of documents that in 1994, Agolets had been relieved of duties as first deputy commander of Belarusian internal forces for gross irregularities involving his living quarters and possessing a suspiciously large amount of cash and valuables.

67 *Segodnia*, 26 June 1996.

68 NTV Moscow, 13 September 1996.

69 *Segodnia*, 22 August 1996.

70 Belarusian Radio, 21 August 1995.

71 *Novaia gazeta*, 5–11 August 1996; and *Moskovskie novosti*, 4 August 1996.

72 "Belarusians Remain Committed to Most Democratic Principles," *USIA Opinion Analysis*, M–117-95, 11 August 1995.

73 See Mihalisko, "Politics and Public Opinion in Belarus," as a source for the tabular data and analysis in this section.

74 *Segodnia*, 28 April 1995.

75 Belarusian Radio, 29 May 1995.

76 Belarusian Radio, 29 May 1995. Other sources may show slight differences in party affiliation figures.

77 *Nations in Transit*, p. 36.

78 *Analiticheskii biulleten' agenstva RIO*, no. 51, 25 June-2 July 1995.

79 In monthly surveys of 60 political experts jointly sponsored by *Nezavisimaia gazeta*, Vox Populi Service, and Skaryna, Ltd., 1996; see, for example, *Nezavisimaia gazeta*, 9 February 1996.

80 *Nezavisimaia gazeta*, 5 January 1996.

81 *Obshchaia gazeta*, 14–20 December 1995.

82 Quoted in *Nezavisimaia gazeta*, 5 January 1996.

83 *Delovoi mir*, 7 August 1996.

84 See the comments by former ICE chairman Uladzimir Biryuk in *Segodnia*, 27 August 1996.

85 *Delovoi mir*, 7 August 1996.

86 *Segodnia*, 30 August 1996; Minsk correspondent Syarhei Anis'ka also writes that Lukashenka has repelled attempts by the Control Chamber of the Supreme Council to investigate the commercial activities of the Directorate of Presidential Affairs.

87 *Delovoi mir,* 7 August 1996.

88 Robert Lyle, "Former Soviet States Generally Doing Well," *RFE-RL Special*, 24 April 1996 (http://www.rferl.com).

89 *Novaia gazeta*, no. 28, 5–11 August 1996.

90 *Delovoi mir*, 7 August 1996.

91 *Segodnia*, 30 August 1996. The Constitutional Court of Belarus overruled Lukashenka's ban on independent trade unions in November 1995.

92 *Segodnia*, 9 August 1996 and *Moskovskie novosti*, no. 31, 4–11 August 1996.

93 Presidential Decree No. 940, 14 September 1995.

94 U.S. Department of Commerce sources.

95   Based on 1995 calculations provided by Ukrainian energy ministry sources.
96   *Novaia gazeta*, no. 28, 5–11 August 1996.
97   *Svaboda*, 13 September 1996.
98   Ibid.
99   Radio Minsk, 6 September 1996.
100 Provided in September 1996 by the press secretary of the Belarusian Popular Front.

7   The politics of democratization in postcommunist Moldova

William Crowther

Introduction

This chapter examines the political transition in post-Soviet Moldova. While it is clearly too early in the process to provide a comprehensive review of democratization in the republic, an effort is made to identify those factors that have been most influential in determining the course of events thus far. The argument will be advanced that Moldovan democratization to date has been affected most powerfully by (1) the character of the immediate transition from communism, (2) the international environment, (3) the course of intra-elite politics in the early transition, (4) the interest cleavage structure in Moldovan society, and finally (5) the process of political party formation.[1]

The first section of the following discussion reviews the historical context in which the Moldovan transition began. As the eastern-most region inhabited by a Romanian-speaking population, Moldova's position has long been ambiguous. Moldovan culture has clearly been influenced by its interaction with the Slavic population of the region, as well as by the Romanian tradition. Furthermore, Moldova, as a border region, has been politically insecure for centuries.

The analysis of the historical context assesses the impact of both the pre-Soviet and Soviet periods. Particular attention is addressed to the character of interethnic relations, which was critical to the direction of the mobilization process in Moldova. Historically, relations between the diverse peoples that inhabit Moldova have been mixed, but on the whole positive. In many rural areas, Moldovan and non-Moldovan inhabitants coexisted in relative harmony for centuries and for the most part have continued to do so up to the present. But conditions in the cities, where the effect of immigration was greatest during the Soviet period, were less positive at the time of the postcommunist transition.

A second legacy of the past that has clearly affected current democratization efforts is an ambiguous national identity. Moldova's historic development is closely related to that of neighboring Romania by bonds of language and culture. Yet the influence of the present republic's Slavic neighbors has also been considerable, producing in Moldova a unique culture that is recognizably distinct from that of the western Romanian region. On the breakdown of the USSR, a committed minority among ethnic Moldovans opted for "Romanian" national identity and worked for unification with the Romanian state. The majority of the population, however, gravitated toward Moldovan identification and political independence. The dialogue between these two forces has been crucial to the democratization process.

For purposes of brevity, examination of Moldova's international relations will be limited to those factors that have interacted decisively with domestic politics. Firstly, Russian support for efforts by separatists to make Moldova's Transdniestrian region an independent state will be assessed. Even before Moldova's final break with the USSR in August 1991, separatist forces declared sovereignty in the heavily Gagauz-populated southern districts and in the Transdniestrian region on the eastern bank of the Dniester river. In addition to the obvious foreign policy challenges presented by this situation, the external environment also shaped Moldovan domestic politics, limiting the options available to the Moldovan government in addressing the minority issues facing the new republic (and the course of economic reform as well). This fact has affected both intra-elite politics and the mass mobilization process. Secondly, Romania, because of its proximity and interest, has equally affected Moldovan domestic politics, most directly by conditioning the sovereignty and national identity debates since 1989. Its role will also be addressed.

Analysis then turns to the politics of the transition period itself. On independence Moldova was faced with the dual tasks of developing democratic institutions and managing the transition to a post-Soviet economy. These tasks were undertaken in an environment of intense political competition and popular mobilization. The argument is advanced that the course of intra-elite politics in the republic during the 1989–91 period was crucial in ultimately channeling mass mobilization conducive to democratization. The structure of social cleavages in the republic and their impact on democratization are also explored. Mass attitudes, it will be shown, played a crucial role in the Moldovan transition, both during the period of anti-Soviet mobilization and later, during the political consolidation of an "ethnically moderate" successor regime.

Finally, the process of party formation is examined. Party formation is a key factor, if clearly not the sole factor, in the democratization process. Data will be presented to suggest that party formation is underway in Moldova, and that the outcome produced by the first wholly democratic legislative elections, held in October 1994, was consistent with mass-level opinion on key issues in the republic.

Moldova before Communism

The origin of the Moldovan population dates back to the period from A.D. 105 to approximately A.D. 270, when Roman colonists intermingled with the local population of the region. An independent principality including the territory of the present Moldovan republic was established in the mid-fourteenth century, but was short-lived. During the second half of the fifteenth century, it came under increasing pressure from the Ottoman empire and was finally reduced to the status of a tributary state. Moldova reemerged as an independent political actor only in the twentieth century. In the intervening years, Moldova's identity was closely tied to that of the Romanian speakers to its west. Cultural differentiation between eastern and western populations is apparent, however. The distinction between Moldovan and Romanian identity was engendered in part by externally determined political divisions. Territory on the west bank of the Dniester river now included in Moldova was ceded by the Ottoman Empire to Russia in 1792.[2] The remainder of current Moldova, Bessarabia, was annexed by Russia following the Russo–Turkish war of 1806–12. Western Moldova was united with Walachia in 1859 through the joint election of Alexandru Ion Cuza as prince of both principalities in January 1859, forming the basis of modern Romania.[3] During the period of Russian control, Tsarist authorities encouraged a substantial migration into Moldova. The population influx included Russians and Ukrainians, and Bulgarians and Gagauz colonists from the Balkan peninsula. Cities in the region became very diverse ethnically, as did rural society in the southern zone. The most concentrated ethnic Moldovan population was found in the central region. In the north and on the east bank of the Dniester, Romanian villages coexist with those of Russians and Ukrainians, and in the south with Gagauz and Bulgarians.

Historically, the economy of Moldova was weakly developed. Growth lagged prior to the mid-eighteenth century for a variety of reasons, including principally recurrent periods of the political instability. Traditionally the main economic activity of the region was agriculture. Most of the population was engaged in peasant agricultural production, and rural poverty was endemic. The small urban economy was based almost entirely on commerce, with the late addition of food processing and limited consumer goods production.

Bessarabia changed hands once again in the early twentieth century as a consequence of the Russian revolution. When Imperial power disintegrated, leaders in Bessarabia formed a National Council (the *Sfatul Ţarii*) and voted to unite with Romania in March 1918. But rule from Bucharest proved less than entirely felicitous. Administrators from the capital did little to improve local economic conditions and engendered substantial hostility through their use of tax and police authority. The Romanian efforts to impose cultural assimilation on the minority population of the region left in its wake a legacy of hostility toward Romanians that continues to play a role in Moldovan politics half a century later. Meanwhile, in October 1924, Russia's new communist authorities formed a competing political unit, the Moldovan Autonomous Soviet Socialist Republic (MASSR). The MASSR, whose capital was Tiraspol, encompassed fourteen districts (raions) on the east bank of the Dniester and was administered as part of the Ukrainian Soviet Socialist Republic.

Soviet Moldova and the legacy of communism

Along with Latvia, Lithuania, and Estonia, Bessarabia was among those territories annexed by the USSR as a consequence of the Ribbentrop–Molotov agreement. In June 1940, Bessarabia was occupied by Soviet troops. The Soviet Socialist Republic of Moldavia was formed on August 2, 1940, through its merger with the already established MASSR.[4] Postwar incorporation into the USSR was traumatic, as it was elsewhere. The calamities that befell the rural population of other regions at an earlier stage in Soviet history were now visited upon Moldova. During 1946–47 the region experienced a serious drought and famine. Party leaders failed to reduce compulsory grain collections in response, with the result that a great many people died of hunger and malnutrition related diseases.[5] Immediately on the heels of this disaster, Moldova's peasantry was subjected to forced collectivization, which saw some 10,000 or more families deported as kulaks.[6] The suppression of class enemies, mass famine and starvation, and then the collectivization campaign, appear to have been no greater in scope or more brutal in Moldova than in other areas of the Soviet Union. But the historical proximity of these events is in comparison quite near. Lingering anger concerning the events of this period and demands for public disclosure concerning them were evident during the anti-Soviet mobilization of the late 1980s.

As a consequence of the annexation, many members of the Romanian-speaking intelligentsia migrated west into Romania, while others were purged by the new Soviet authorities. This, along with the influx of Slavic populations from other parts of the USSR, substantially altered the character of the republic's population. The impact of early Soviet development policy acted to intensify hostility toward Russia that had already been engendered by annexation. Industrialization in Moldova transformed the distribution of occupations among ethnic groups. Non-Moldovans' presence in the urban economy was reinforced, leaving Moldovans in less skilled and less highly paid urban occupations and in the agricultural sector. This effect was most marked in the early postwar period. As of 1970, Moldovans made up only 35 percent of the republic's urban total population, while 28.8 percent was comprised of Russians, and another 19.6 percent was Ukrainian.[7] By the latter part of the Soviet period, this demographic trend had in fact reversed itself. In 1989 Moldova's total population of approximately 4,348,000 was comprised of Moldovans 63.9 percent, Ukrainians 14.2 percent, Russians 12.8 percent, Gagauz 3.5 percent, and Bulgarians 2.0 percent.[8] The 1989 census indicated that the ethnic Moldovan proportion of the urban population had increased to 46 percent, while Russians declined to 23.4 percent.[9] Yet the perception of discrimination remained strong among many Moldovans.

Animosity was also generated by Soviet cultural policy. Moldova presented special problems in this realm because of the artificial nature of its boundaries with Romania. Moscow undertook a determined effort to separate Moldovans from Romanians. Clearly, some basis exists to support the view that a separate "Moldovan" identity is historically founded. But Soviet authorities' efforts to differentiate the two populations from each other (often quite artificially) became the basis of substantial popular resentment.

Although political conditions were harsh in Moldova, the region did experience substantial economic development under Soviet rule. During the interwar years, Tiraspol and the neighboring areas in Transdniestria were the site of substantial industrial activity. Following World War Two, the new republican capital, Chişinău, joined Transdniestria as the focus for development activity. By the end of the Soviet period, industry accounted for more than one-third of Gross National Product. But while Moldova made substantial strides in relation to its own previously underdeveloped condition, it remained backward in comparison with other regions of the USSR. Capital investment and industrial employment rates were below national averages. In the early 1980s, Moldova produced lower national income per capita than any other non-Central Asian republic. Access to higher education also lagged. With 620 per 1000 population with higher education, Moldova found itself last in the USSR in 1984.[10] At the close of the Soviet period, Moldovan rural population density was the highest in the USSR. In 1987 Moldavia was the fourth least urbanized of the Soviet republics, at 47 percent urban population, followed only by Uzbekistan, Kirgizia, and Tajikstan (see table 7.1).[11] Adding to its woes, Moldova suffered from extreme corruption, even by prevailing Soviet standards. This was in part the result of close ties between the Moldovan leadership and the Brezhnev patronage network (Leonid Brezhnev having been the Republican Communist Party leader for a time). During the era of Brezhnev's tenure as General Secretary of the CPSU,

Table 7.1 *Indicators of demographic trends in Moldova*

	1950s	1970s	1980s
Percentage of population	(1951)	(1979)	(1989)
Rural	82.5	61.2	53.4
Urban	17.5	38.8	46.6
Average annual rates	(1951-61)	(1971-79)	(1990-99)[a]
of population growth (%)	2.5	1.0	0.4
Age distribution (%)		(1979)	(1989)
15–24	n.a.	18.7	14.4
25–49	n.a.	33.0	34.7
50–59	n.a.	10.5	10.3
Over 60	n.a.	10.8	12.6

Note: [a]Estimate.
Sources: US Department of Commerce, *Statistical Abstracts of the United States*; Paul S. Shoup, *The East European and Soviet Data Handbook*; UNESCO, *Statistical Yearbooks*; United Nations, *Demographic Yearbooks*.

Moldova became the site of continual official abuse. Ivan Ivanovich Bodyul, who presided over the Communist Party of Moldova as First Secretary from 1961 until beginning of the 1980s, was a trusted supporter of Brezhnev. Under his administration corrupt members of the republican Party apparatus are said to have siphoned off millions of rubles and to have used their connections with higher level leaders to shield themselves from prosecution.

Although Brezhnev's demise may have opened the door to change elsewhere, the end of the "era of stagnation" had little immediate impact on Moldova. In addition to his obvious skill in clinging to office, Bodyul's successor as leader of the CPM, Simion K. Grossu (the last of the pre-Gorbachev republican First Secretaries to be removed, finally, in November 1989), proved to be a tenacious opponent of reform. Although Grossu assumed the rhetoric of perestroika and glasnost in official communications, little or no effort was made to implement changes mandated from above or to reach an accord with reformist leaders inside Moldova. Perestroika's early achievements were therefore limited at best. Political conditions improved marginally, if at all. While higher consumer goods production quotas were said to have been met and surpassed in response to calls from above for economic reform, actual supply improved only minimally or worsened.

These are the general conditions that pertained as Moldova entered the process of transition from communism in the latter part of the 1980s. First, although substantial economic development occurred during the Soviet period, the republic remained largely agricultural and weakly developed within the context of the USSR economy. Second, substantial division existed between ethnic communities, but the extent of hostility varied between the rural (largely Moldovan) and urban (heavily russophone) populations. In many rural areas, Moldovan and non-Moldovan populations had coexisted in substantial harmony for well over a century. But within the urban population, where the proportion of immigrants to the republic was high and resource competition (for employment and housing) was intense, interethnic tension was significantly greater. Third, Moldova had no pre-Soviet model of indigenous national-level democratic institutions to fall back on once the constraints of the Soviet system were removed. Although it had participated in Romanian political life during the interwar period, national level politics were almost exclusively "Bucharest" politics, and far removed from affairs in Moldova. Furthermore, democratic tendencies in Moldova itself were vigorously suppressed up to the very end of the Soviet period. Finally, the "national" identity of the indigenous population was in question. Strong strains within Moldova's historical development tied the region to "greater Romania." As events have since shown, however, an equally compelling attachment to "Moldovan" national consciousness was also present.

Anti-Soviet mobilization

Reform currents emerged openly in Moldova only in 1987, when members of the creative intelligentsia mobilized around the issue of selecting a replacement for the head of the republican writers' union.[12] This controversy escalated into a contest for control over the cultural establishment, during the course of which reformers gained control of several mass circulation news organs and began to espouse publicly the cause of restructuring. From this base, a campaign for fundamental change was launched by those in favor of furthering democratization. By early 1988, at least two popular organizations had formed to press for reform. The first of these, the Democratic Movement in Support of Restructuring, appears to have been primarily an organization of the intelligentsia, committed to general economic and political reform.[13] A second, significantly more nationalist-oriented group, the Aleksey Mateevich Literary–Musical Circle, became active in May 1988.[14]

It was within this context of increasing public opposition that preparations began for election to the All Union Congress of People's Deputies. Both the electoral process itself, which unfolded from January through March 1989, and the outcome of the elections reflected the relatively low level of organization that the opposition had achieved at the point when elections occurred. Despite the formally democratic nature of elections to the Congress of People's Deputies, the Communist Party establishment, still under the leadership of First Secretary Grossu and clearly not committed to pluralism and openness, was easily able to dominate most of Moldova's forty-three electoral districts. Most nominating meetings appear to have been well orchestrated by local Party authorities. This conclusion is supported both by the nature of the nominees put forward and by the tenor of debate in nominating sessions. Generally speaking, even those selected who were not obviously associated with the Party apparat were supported by local authorities. Of 125 persons nominated, only nine were clearly identifiable as either representatives of the reform movement or were persons who ran as non-Party candidates. Party and state personnel, on the other hand, comprised thirty-seven candidates.

Despite a formal commitment to multi-candidate competition, in over one-third of Moldova's electoral districts (fifteen out of forty-three) only one contestant appeared on the March 1989 ballot. The overwhelming majority of these non-competitive districts were allocated to members of the political establishment: six members of the CPM apparatus, three military officers, and three high level state personnel. The remaining three unopposed candidates were intellectuals. Two of the latter (including author Nikolai Dabija), though members of the Communist Party, were clearly identifiable as leaders of the reform movement. The extent to which the republican political establishment was able to influence the elections in those cases where its vital interests were at stake (for example, in cases considered important enough to warrant providing individuals with uncontested elections) is suggested by figures on voter turnout (see table 7.2). In essence, these data indicate the strongest turnout in districts where a single person was nominated and advanced as a candidate, while least support is evidenced in multi-nominee two-candidate elections. The primarily rural "safe districts" were allocated, among others, to S. K. Grossu, first secretary of the CPM, the president of the Council of Ministers, the president of the republican Supreme Soviet, and the head of the republican komsomol organization. Although the elections of March 1989 indicated the Communist Party's continued dominance and ability to stage elections in the traditional manner in most areas, the data provide another striking message as well. That is, when faced with open competition with representatives of other social groupings, the Party's representatives did exceedingly poorly. If one examines the vote per candidate for all districts, including single candidate districts, members of the apparatus place third behind military personnel and intellectuals in per candidate vote. But if single candidate districts are removed from the count, and if voters were given a choice of selecting some one other than an apparatchik, the Party officials' share of the vote drops to last place among all social categories (see table 7.3). Even more strikingly,

Table 7.2 *Elections to the Congress of People's Deputies in Moldova, 1989:*
average turnout by type of district

Type of district	Number of districts	% turnout
One nominee, one candidate	7	94.2
All one-candidate	15	92.8
All two-candidate	28	89.8
All districts	43	90.8

Table 7.3 *Elections to the Congress of People's Deputies in Moldova, 1989: average share of*
vote by type of candidate (in percent)

Candidate	All districts	Two-candidate	One-candidate
Military	79.71	n.a.	79.71
Opposition	68.56	61.71	91.00
Intellectuals	60.44	53.18	82.23
CPM apparatchiks	54.91	33.05	84.31
State personnel	51.72	45.84	57.61
Managers	51.25	51.25	n.a.
Peasants	45.35	45.35	n.a.
Professionals	44.54	44.54	n.a.
Workers	42.96	42.96	n.a.

in these competitive races, members of the apparatus were able to win in
only one out of eight contests, in comparison, for example, to five out of
eight wins for enterprise managers. The population was, in fact, less willing
to vote for party apparatus members than for any other group represented in
the elections (see table 7.4). Among those who failed to win election were
the first secretary of the Chişinău City Committee and the first secretaries of
three of the Communist Party's Raion Committees. It appears from these
results that by 1989 the party apparatus was still able to dominate the
elections, but at the same time that conservative members were under
significant pressure from opposition forces. The electoral process itself was
extremely useful to the reformers, who employed the publicity generated by
the campaign and the relative security conferred by the status of official
candidates to advance their cause. Furthermore, the electoral success of
several opposition leaders, despite the conservative effort to hinder their

Table 7.4 *Elections to Congress of People's Deputies in Moldova, 1989: competitive races*[a]

Candidate	Number	Wins	Wins (%)
Opposition	6	4	66
State personnel	3	2	66
Managers	8	5	62
Kolkhoz/Sovkhoz directors	5	3	60
Peasants	2	1	50
Intellectuals	9	4	44
Professionals	6	2	33
Workers	7	1	14
CPM apparatchiks	8	1	12

Note: [a]Two-candidate elections in which the candidate's opponent was not a member of the same social category.

campaigns, proved critical in succeeding months by legitimating their movement and providing a crucial link with moderate elements within the Communist Party.[15]

The reformers' new status as elected officials thus constituted a significant step in altering the political ambience in Moldova. Signalling the change in circumstances, in early June the Party leadership extended official recognition to the Popular Front of Moldova, the leadership of which was drawn primarily from the Democratic Movement. On June 11, 1989, the Popular Front held its first public meeting, attended by high level Party and state representatives, to discuss methods of promoting language reform and related issues.[16]

The efforts of reformers focused initially on revision of Moldova's language laws, especially provisions mandating Russian as the language of public communication and Cyrillic versus Latin script for use in written Moldovan. Despite limited concessions on the part of republican authorities on these issues, political unrest escalated through 1988 and 1989. On August 27, 1989, pro-reform activists staged a massive demonstration, the "Grand National Assembly," in central Chişinău. This event was a crucial juncture in the mobilization process. Confronted with mass opposition, party conservatives were unsettled, while reformers were encouraged to press for decisive change. On August 31, 1989, the republic's Supreme Soviet passed a version of the state language law favorable to the Romanian speaking majority, and the recently formed Moldovan Popular Front became increasingly assertive.[17]

Given the heavily nationalist appeal of the anti-Soviet opposition, it should hardly come as any surprise that the early stage of Moldova's transition was accompanied by intense interethnic conflict.[18] The prospect of the Romanian speaking majority gaining political influence touched off a sharp response by Russian speaking inhabitants of the republic. Many Russians gravitated toward Edinstvo, a pro-Russian mass movement whose strongest base of support lay in the heavily industrialized cities on the east bank of the Dniester river. Gagauz-Halk, the main organization representing Moldova's Gagauz minority during the early transition period, aligned itself with the Russian activists and demanded that the southern districts where their population is concentrated should be granted political autonomy.

Just as important as the popular upsurge was the simultaneous breakdown of formerly authoritative institutions. The Communist Party found itself in a state of increasing disarray. During a Central Committee Plenum called in September 1989 to discuss ethnic strife, a number of delegates held Secretary Grossu personally responsible for the republic's woes, and called for his resignation.[19] The heads of the Tiraspol and Bender Party organizations were criticized for promoting (Russian) nationalism within the Party. Reformist Party members, on the other hand, were rebuked for participating in opposition demonstrations.[20] Within weeks after this meeting, Grossu was removed as Party First Secretary and replaced by Petru K. Lucinschi, a staunch reformer and Moscow's choice for the position.

It was within this context of heightened mobilization that campaigning for 1990 legislative elections occurred. The final version of the law governing the election provided for quite open competition, relative to the earlier Soviet system. Opposition candidates were able to campaign actively throughout the republic. Individual candidates were provided with space in the republican Central Committee's newspapers. The journal of the Moldavian Writers' Union, *Literatura și Arta* published the Popular Front's official platform, which called for full sovereignty, a return to the use of traditional national symbols, demilitarization, private property and a free market, and full political pluralism.[21]

In the process of the 1990 campaign, a partial rapprochement was established between the reformist wing of the Communist Party and the Popular Front. Many of the reformers, who were enjoying a surge of renewed popularity under the leadership of Lucinschi, but who found themselves increasingly at odds with party hardliners, were beginning to seek alternatives to their Communist affiliation.[22] The Popular Front, for its part, was open to the overtures of Party moderates. The candidacies of a series of reform-minded Communist leaders, including Mircea Snegur, were endorsed by the Front. Snegur, a Central Committee Secretary since 1985, was appointed president of the Moldavian Supreme Soviet by S. K. Grossu in July

1989. By early 1990, he had clearly associated himself with the Popular Front and its political program. In order to generate mass support, activists from both the Moldovan and minority communities employed ethnic appeals during the campaign. It was the ethnic Moldovan opposition, though, that benefited most from the process of ethnic mobilization.

By the February 25th election date, Popular Front-approved candidates were on the ballot in 219 out of Moldova's 380 electoral districts (see tables 7.5 and 7.6 for the political affiliation and ethnicity of nominees and deputies). The results of the first round of elections confirmed the main trends that appeared during the nominating process. Competitive races were held in 373 districts, and turnout was 83.4 percent of the electorate.[23] Approximately one third of deputies elected to the republican Supreme Soviet were Moldovan Popular Front adherents.[24] With the support of centrist deputies the Popular Front was able to command a majority of the votes in the new legislature.

This initial transition election thus produced a fundamental change in the leadership of the republic. With the Popular Front's support, Mircea Snegur, was named president of the Supreme Soviet, despite his status as a leading member of the Communist Party. Ion Hadarca, president of the Popular Front Executive Council, and other Front members also took up leadership positions in the legislature. Mircea Druc, an avidly pro-Romanian member of the Popular Front hierarchy, was appointed prime minister.

The shift in political control to the ethnic Moldovan opposition was accompanied by increasingly serious interethnic confrontation. A series of provocative actions by Popular Front legislators (under the influence of pan-Romanian extremists who achieved a position of dominance within the Front) fueled minority concerns with regard to their future in a republic controlled by the titular nationality. Such changes as reinstating the pre-revolutionary flag as the emblem of the republic and an extremely divisive measure introduced by Moldovan nationalists (but narrowly defeated) that would have changed the name of the legislature from Supreme Soviet to *Svatul Ţurii* were of little practical consequence, but proved tremendously divisive.[25] Furthermore, while ethnic Moldovans accounted for 69 percent of the deputies, they dominated the institution, accounting for over 83 percent of the legislative leadership positions.[26]

The minorities' initial experience with the emerging democratic legislature thus did little to encourage any conviction that post-Soviet institutions could restrain the behavior of the majority population. In May 1990, following a succession of street confrontations in the capital that were orchestrated by radical Popular Front leaders in order to intimidate their opponents, 100 russophone deputies withdrew from the republican Supreme Soviet. At the same time, in areas in which non-Moldovans formed a local majority, city

Table 7.5 *Social background of nominees and legislative deputies in Moldova, 1990*[a]

Status	Nominees		Deputies	
	N	%	N	%
Party members	1,382	86	305	81
Popular Front	219	13	101	27

Note: [a]Both tables 7.5 and 7.6 were formulated on the basis of returns after the second, March 10, 1990 runoff.

Sources: Information used in the tables was extracted from *Moldova Socialistă*, January 27, 1990, p. 1; *Literatura şi Arta* no. 8, February 22, 1990, p. 3; *Literatura şi Arta* no. 11, March 15, 1990, p. 1; *Moldova Socialistă*, March 17, 1990, p. 1. Nine more repeat contests were held on April 22, 1990. This round decided only two more contests. Elections were invalidated in four district elections because less than 50 percent of the electorate participated, and in three others because neither candidate obtained the necessary number of votes to be elected. A fourth round of elections was accordingly scheduled for June 17. *Moldova Socialistă*, April 28, 1990, p. 2.

Table 7.6 *Ethnicity of nominees and legislative deputies in Moldova, 1990*

Ethnicity	Nominees		Deputies		Population
	N	%	N	%	%
Moldovan	1,170	72	254	69.2	63.9
Russian	137	9	57	15.5	12.8
Ukrainian	170	11	35	9.6	14.2
Gagauz	45	3	12	3.3	3.5
Bulgarian	45	3	8	2.2	2.0

and district authorities began to develop alternative representative institutions. Local governments in the cities of Tiraspol, Bender, and Ribniţa enacted measures suspending application of central government edicts.[27] In late August 1990, representatives of the Gagauz minority announced the formation of their own republic in the southern region, while the hard-line Communist leadership in Transdniestria declared the formation of the Transdniestrian Moldovan Soviet Socialist Republic. Little interethnic conflict developed within the bulk of Moldova (Bessarabia), but increasingly serious fighting occurred between the separatist regions and Moldova's central government. This reached a peak in the open battles of mid-1992.

Consolidation of the initial stage of Moldova's transition came in August 1991 as a consequence of the anti-reform coup in Moscow. Chişinău's response to the coup was immediate and unequivocal; it denounced the coup as illegal and anti-democratic and declared independence, founding the new Republic of Moldova on August 27, 1991. In stark contrast, the leaders of the separatist regions declared for the coup plotters. When their hopes were dashed by events in Moscow, they asserted their independence from Moldova and vowed to uphold the values of the Soviet Union. The new Republic of Moldova thus entered into its existence as a postcommunist state with its sovereignty already challenged and its government controlled in part by pan-Romanian nationalists whose long-term commitment to the new state was limited at best.

Post-Soviet Moldova

Democratization and the international environment

Democratization efforts in Moldova have been complicated by foreign policy issues since the beginning of the independence movement. The new republic has been threatened by separatist movements which enjoyed the support of external sponsors, as well as by domestic and foreign "pan-Romanian" activists. The conflict over Transdniestria, in particular, became the focus of intricately intertwined domestic and international problems confronting the Moldovan government. Moldova's sovereignty and territorial integrity cannot be isolated from the status of its non-Moldovan minorities. Extending concessions to the minorities is crucial to allaying minority fears of majority domination and ending separatist efforts. Yet, the perception of excessive concessions both inflames extremists among the republic's Romanian-speakers and raises concerns in Bucharest.

The strongly nationalist strain that emerged in the course of anti-Soviet mobilization in Moldova during the late 1980s was highly disconcerting to the republic's ethnic minorities. Anti-Moldovan feelings ran particularly strong in the heavily Russian urban areas on the eastern bank of the Dniester. Perceiving efforts of the majority ethnic group to destabilize the status quo as threatening to their interests, in 1989 ethnic-Russian elites undertook independent political action themselves in order to bloc concessions to the Moldovans. They also appealed to leaders in Moscow to either defend the status quo or, alternatively, to permit the minorities areas to detach themselves from Moldova and form independent political entities of their own.

Limited confrontations began to occur even before independence, between August and late November 1989.[28] On August 16th, Russian-speaking workers initiated strikes that quickly spread through enterprises in Tiraspol, Bender, and Chişinău. Strike leaders, many of whom were enterprise managers from large enterprises in the east bank cities, announced the formation of an independent Union, the "Union of Moldovan Working People," to press for what they considered a more just nationality policy.[29] Passage of the law on state law on August 31, 1989, despite the strikers' efforts to the contrary, encouraged further escalation. Minority activists became convinced that Party and state authorities had succumbed to ethnic Moldovan pressure and could no longer be depended upon to defend their interests. Dissatisfaction with the outcome of the legislative process quickly spread to the general population of Russian speakers, reinforcing the strike movement. The strikes spread to over 150 factories, shut down much of the republic's rail system, and lasted for more than a month. Strike committees consolidated their control over enterprises and gained increasing public support. In several predominantly Russian-speaking localities, Communist Party and government bodies took positions favorable to the strikers, contrary to the direction of republican officials.[30] During the following months, agitation for secession gained strength throughout the minority regions of the republic. This separatist activity was encouraged by Soviet military commanders, who supported the formation of the Transdniestrian Moldovan Soviet Socialist Republic in mid–1990, and abetted the transfer of arms from 14th Army stock piles to the separatist militia.[31]

Throughout 1990 and 1991, relations between Chişinău and Tiraspol, the capital of the breakaway Transdniester republic, were characterized by mutual denunciations and sporadic violence. But in early 1992, conditions took a sharp turn for the worse as a consequence of the Transdniestrians' attempt to consolidate control over the west bank city of Bender (Tighina) with the support of the 14th Army. With nationalists in the parliament demanding action, President Snegur undertook to disarm units of the separatist militia by force. This attempt met with armed resistance, and by May 1992, the conflict had escalated into full-scale civil war.

Resolving the separatist crisis has been profoundly complicated by the involvement of the Russian Republic. The fate of the ethnic-Russian population has been a source of concern for political leaders in Moscow, and this consideration necessarily effects Moldova's relationship with Russia and the CIS. Despite some indications of support for conciliation, the record of Moscow's involvement in Transdniestria has been ambiguous at best. The July 1992 cease-fire agreement which brought an end to the worst of the fighting in Moldova was reached with the support of President Yeltsin. But no final resolution of the conflict was achieved. Russian negotiators publicly supported a political settlement of the crisis based on substantial Transdniestrian autonomy within Moldova, but have not been willing to impose this outcome on the Transdniestrian separatists.[32] The continued presence of Russian forces made the military suppression of the Tiraspol government impossible and encouraged the Transdniestrians not to compromise.

The 14th Army thus played a central role in efforts to resolve the Transdniestrian conflict, yet arrangements for removal of Russian forces from Moldova have been markedly slow. The force, which was estimated at several thousand in 1995, is deeply imbedded in the local population. Many of its officers have settled their families in the region. Enlisted personnel have been locally conscripted. Hence "withdrawing" the force in large part amounted to an agreement to dismantle the command structure, demobilize forces, and withdraw weapons stock piles rather than to withdraw troops. A key issue for Moldovan leaders faced with this situation has thus been the fate of these soldiers (they should not be transferred to the authority of the Tiraspol government) and the final disposition of their weaponry.

On August 10, 1994, Russia and Moldova initialed an agreement, over the objections of Tiraspol, calling for the withdrawal of the 14th Army within three years. In a major concession, Moldova accepted that the troop withdrawal should be synchronized with a political solution to the separatist conflict. This agreement, which was immediately denounced by leaders in Tiraspol, was followed by months of controversy. In Moscow, nationalists declared that the document must be ratified by the legislature. After one false start in late 1994 due to nationalist resistance, Russian Ministry of Defense officials announced that the 14th Army was to be reorganized and downgraded and did not mention its provocative commander, General Lebed, as the new officer in charge. In order to facilitate withdrawal of the force, the 14th Army was reorganized into a group of operating forces in 1995. General Lebed announced his return to civilian life, in order to pursue a political career as a leading nationalist politician.

A second complicating factor has been the significance of Transdniestria in the domestic politics of the Russian Federation. While still at his post in Tiraspol, General Lebed made numerous public statements of his nationalist views, despite repeated warnings from his superiors to restrain himself. He stated flatly that he would not "abandon" Transdniestria's Russians. Lebed become a positive symbol for Russian conservatives, who likewise view the abandonment of Russian minorities as anathema. Tiraspol's civil leaders, for their part, actively engaged in a series of reactionary causes inside Russia, including the dispatch of volunteers to the Russian White House to participate in the attempted overthrow of Yeltsin in September 1993.[33] Given these links and the strength of the nationalists in Russia, moderates in Moscow have necessarily been cautious about taking measures to end the Transdniestrian conflict in any way that might leave them open to political attack by conservative forces.

The controversy over Transdniestria obviously complicated other aspects of the relationship between Moldova and Russia, particularly in the period before the 1994 Agrarian electoral victory. Although President Snegur signed the Alma-Alta declaration creating the Commonwealth of Independent States on December 31, 1991, Moldova's parliament, at the time strongly influenced by Popular Front delegates, refused to ratify the agreement. Along with Ukraine and Turkmenistan, Moldova refused to sign a January 1993 agreement that would have strengthened ties between Commonwealth members.

Relations between Romania and Moldova have also become increasingly complicated over the course of the past three years, in part as a consequence of the Transdniestrian conflict. Romania was the first state to extend recognition to Moldova and initially provided it with substantial material support. Close cooperation was fostered by the Moldovans' early enthusiasm for "Romanianism" in response to years of denial of this heritage during the Soviet period. Furthermore, the initial support for reunification expressed by Popular Front leaders, such as Mircea Druc, created a common purpose with nationalist politicians in Bucharest.[34]

All too soon, however, the relationship between the two Romanian-speaking states began to deteriorate. Despite commonalities, Moldovans and Romanians remain culturally distinct. The general response among Romanian nationalists on becoming conscious of differences was that Moldovans had been "denationalized" or "Russified" by the Soviet experience. While this attitude conformed with the view of pan-Romanian intellectuals in Moldova, it has been the source of growing resentment on the part of the majority of Moldovans.

The evolution of the Transdniestrian and Gagauz separatist movements has also been a source in increasing tension between Romania and Moldova. The prospect of unification with Romania is clearly unacceptable to the Russian and Gagauz inhabitants of Moldova. Concern over this issue was central to the outbreak of ethnic conflict. Virtually all aspects of the relationship between Bucharest and Chişinău became politically charged as indicators of movement toward or away from unification. Efforts by Bucharest to provide assistance during the clashes of 1992 were taken as further evidence of near-term unification and acted to increase minority alarm. In essence, it became impossible for ethnic moderate Moldovan leaders to defuse the separatist crisis without assuring minorities that reunification was not in the offing.

Across the border in Romania, however, nationalist elements view concessions to the separatists as evidence of movement toward Moscow and treason against the Romanian nation. Hence, while rapprochement with Bucharest generated domestic conflict, efforts to resolve the conflict through accommodation with the minorities had clear negative ramifications on relations with Bucharest. The pursuit of a "Moldovan" course following the Agrarian Democrats' 1994 electoral victory engendered further hostile discourse. Official assertion of a Moldovan national identity in the 1994 constitution, including labeling the official language of the state "Moldovan" rather than "Romanian," was clearly taken as a cultural affront.

The Moldovan–Romanian relationship presents complications for Bucharest as well. Since assuming office in 1990, Romanian President Ion Iliescu has sought to maintain a positive relationship with Moscow. Actions by Bucharest that could be seen as destabilizing Moldova and that might tip it into civil war would be disastrous, not only demolishing Russian–Romanian relations but, potentially even more serious, drawing Russia into a regional conflict. While Romania's foreign policy interests thus seem quite clear, the highly nationalist tenor of Romanian political discourse makes it is difficult for political leaders of any stripe to take public positions against reunification. Nationalists forces, in particular the Greater Romania Party and the Party of Romanian National Unity, have both played important roles as coalition partners of Iliescu's Party of Social Democracy. Romanian nationalists maintain at least a rhetorical interest in the Moldovan situation, as well as other territorial issues resulting from the Ribbentrop–Molotov pact. They continue to bring pressure to bear on Romania's government from the right and stir in the reunification question.

The collective impact of these pressures has been a sharp decline in relations between Chişinău and Bucharest, especially in the period following the 1994. The cooling of Romanian–Moldovan relations was particularly striking in light of the euphoria of the early transition period. Moldovans' suspicion of and hostility toward Romanian interference in their affairs has increased. Romanian nationalists' distaste for what they perceive as Moldova's continued subservience to Moscow produced a surge of virulent rhetoric in parliament and loss of public support for Chişinău, but little action by the cautious Iliescu government.

Elite politics and the transition process

The transition from Soviet rule touched off a prolonged contest for political power among potential leaders in Moldova. Faced with increasing threats to their interests and having few institutional or normative constraints to limit their behavior, elites entered into a fierce competition for control over the successor regime. With little in the way of political party formation, a weakly developed civil society, and the effectiveness of Soviet era institutions eroding, Moldovan politics became increasingly chaotic. The intra-elite struggle during this early postcommunist phase was crucial because, given the lack of institutionalization, with victory came the power to shape the basic parameters of the new state.

Competition for power was carried out in an environment of escalating social crisis. As occurred elsewhere in the former Soviet Union, during the first phase of the transition, Moldova's economy experienced a massive decline. In part this was an inevitable result of the generalized failure of the Soviet economy. But Moldova's economic decline was also a consequence of the early transition leaders' failure to provide any clear policy direction and the new government's administrative disorganization.

Meanwhile the impact of the separatist conflict on political competition within the ethnic Moldovan elite was evident. Militarization of the crisis and a growing sense of threat from abroad initially strengthened the hand of ethnic extremists. Radicals within the Popular Front, many of whom favored a "pan-Romanian" solution to the questions of Moldova's statehood and identity, successfully fixed legislative and governmental activity on a narrow "national" agenda. This pan-Romanian faction both encouraged mass mobilization and relied on the leverage provided by their followers' occasionally quite threatening street demonstrations.

Moderates found themselves marginalized and their efforts to defuse the crisis ineffective. But even given the heightened tension between the majority and minority populations, efforts to achieve consensus were ongoing. Moldova was, in fact, notably progressive within the former Soviet region in the areas of citizenship and minority rights. Its June 5, 1991 citizenship law gave citizenship to persons who had lived in Moldova before Soviet occupation in 1940 and to persons who resided in the territory at independence or who had at least one parent who was born there, if the person in question was not a citizen of another state. Those living in Moldova at the time of the declaration of sovereignty were given one year to decide whether to take up citizenship.[35] Yet competitive ethnic mobilization counteracted such initiatives, precluding effective articulation of a political and economic reform agenda that might attract support across ethnic lines during the initial regime transition.

Probably the most remarkable single aspect of Moldova's postcommunist transition is the success of efforts to break the cycle of ethnic mobilization and recast political discourse along cross-communal lines. A first step in this shift was achieved in May 1991 through the dismissal of the intensely pan-Romanian Mircea Druc from the post of prime minister and his replacement by the somewhat less radical Valeriu Muravschi. The task of displacing Druc from power was eased by widespread popular dissatisfaction with his administration. As Moldova's transition economic crisis deepened (GDP declined by approximately 14 percent in 1991), the government vacillated, unable to produce a comprehensive reform policy. Further complicating the situation, Druc himself came under intense scrutiny for questionable financial dealings.

Even at this early stage, President Mircea Snegur found himself increasingly at odds with the extremist leadership of the Popular Front. While unable to displace Popular Front legislators, Snegur took steps to distance himself from the organization, casting himself in the role of a moderate advocate of efficient reform. Snegur wisely moved to consolidate his position as an independent political actor by successfully arguing for direct presidential elections. He was confirmed in the office of president through a December 1991 election in which he ran unopposed.[36] The pan-Romanian faction's initial ability to determine governmental policy was thus limited by loss of control over the executive branch, but Popular Front deputies remained a powerful force within the legislature.

In Tiraspol few signs of such moderating tendencies were evident. On the contrary, under the leadership of Transdniestrian President Igor Smirnov, Tiraspol moved in an increasingly reactionary direction. The Transdniestrians' aggressive rhetoric and efforts to gain control of Bender (Tighina) were responsible in substantial part for the major escalation of the conflict in 1992. This, in turn, triggered a second phase in the elite realignment in Moldova.

The military confrontation with Transdniestria (and to a lesser extent the Gagauz), which quickly deteriorated into stalemate, proved highly unpopular with a large majority of ethnic Moldovans. Moldovans' dissatisfaction with the conflict, combined with already deepening concern over the government's failure to pursue reform or respond to the economic crisis, provided a clear opening for ethnic moderates within the Moldovan elite to seize the political initiative. The return to power of Moldova's penultimate (and decidedly reformist) Communist Party First Secretary, Petru Lucinschi, as Ambassador to Russia, signaled that the balance of political forces had shifted. A second prominent reformer from the former communist leadership, Andrei Sangheli, moved back onto the center of the political stage, assuming the prime ministership in June 1992.[37]

The Sangheli government represented a marked departure from the period of Popular Front dominance. The new leadership significantly improved minority representation and promised a more efficient economic reform program.[38] It distanced itself from the position of the Popular Front and pursued a strategy based on reducing both interethnic confrontation and discord between former communists and anti-communists. By taking a more flexible approach, Sangheli's government, in cooperation with an equally accommodationist President Snegur, was able to reduce significantly the level of ethnic hostility inside the area under its control. But the moderate initiatives provoked a strong backlash from still influential pan-Romanianist delegates in parliament, who characterized their opponents as "nomenkla-turists" and "pro-Moscow." As their public support waned, the Popular Front deputies pursued a strategy of obstructionism in parliament designed to block any policy that might compromise their conception of the republic's Romanian identity. The nationalist deputies' very success in blocking reform precipitated a final blow against their remaining power in the legislature.

As political elites continued their struggles over statehood issues and factional politics, the Moldovan economy continued to lose ground. Following independence, agriculture and food industries, which continued to play a central role in economic activity, suffered a series of serious blows. These included an unfavorable shift in Moldova's terms of trade, severe droughts in 1992 and 1994, and the economic disruption associated with the break-up of the Soviet Union. Agricultural output, crucial to the overall performance of the economy, is estimated to have declined 33 percent between 1989 and 1993. World Bank estimates put Gross Domestic Product loss at 21 percent in 1992.[39]

Reform progress was mixed. The privatization program initiated by the government proceeded only sluggishly. Personnel in the State Department of Privatization complained of managerial obstructionism, and the conversion of property proceeded only slowly. New laws did, however, establish the right to hold private property. Among the most important of the reforms introduced prior to the promulgation of the 1994 constitution was passage of the March 26, 1991 Law on Property. This legislation established the right to hold property by individuals, cooperatives, joint economic associations, social organizations, and the state. This right extended to both private property in land and in productive enterprises.

In December 1992, President Snegur, frustrated with the Popular Front's obstructionist tactics, induced a leadership crisis by delivering a speech to the republican parliament warning against the extremes of either unification with Romania or closer integration into the Commonwealth of Independent States.[40] Snegur's public expression of reservation concerning unification with Romania sharpened divisions between Moldovan moderates and more extreme nationalists. Alexandru Moşanu, the pro-Popular Front president of the Parliament, offered his resignation in protest, decrying the influence of former communists within government. Moşanu's effort to rally popular support was futile. Petru Lucinschi returned from his post as ambassador to Moscow to replace him and assume leadership of the parliament.[41]

The shift in favor of the Agrarians and their Socialist Party allies brought the legislative leadership into much closer alignment with President Snegur and Prime Minister Sangheli's government. Moldova's triumvirate of top leaders took little time to conclude that the sitting legislature was no longer viable given changed conditions in the republic. Despite efforts of pan-

Romanian nationalists to resist, the Agrarian coalition orchestrated a parliamentary vote calling for the dissolution of the legislature. Early elections were called for a new parliament. The date of the contest was set for February 27, 1994.

The restructuring of the republican leadership and the decision to call new elections brought to closure the postcommunist elite realignment. The three top positions in the political hierarchy of the republic: the presidency, the prime ministership, and the presidency of the parliament were all held by reform communists, each a former member of the Moldovan Communist Party politburo.[42] Although the commitment of this group to economic transition was an open question, its positions on ethnic issues and democratic political procedures were both markedly more moderate than those of the initial transition regime. The moderate coalition's ability to regain the political initiative resulted in large part from its more experienced leaders' political acumen. But, as indicated below, it also reflected their ability to turn the pattern of political opinion within the general population to their own advantage.

Social cleavages during the early transition period

The depth of divisions within postcommunist Moldovan society became apparent in the turbulent course of the republic's early transition politics. Competing leadership factions struggled over social and economic reform and over majority/minority relations within the newly sovereign state. A similar cleavage structure was also apparent in public opinion.[43] The interaction between elite and mass level politics was critical in determining the course of Moldovan democratization. Tables 7.7 through 7.10 examine aspects of Moldovan, Ukrainian, and Russian perceptions of the minority issues. Both the overall distribution of attitudes and the divergence between the three communities is clear. While half of Moldovans considered the situation of minorities to be "good," only approximately 17 percent of Russians and Ukrainians concurred. Three times more Russians and Ukrainians than Moldovans believed that minority rights were not protected in practice. Other responses concerning minority/majority relations bear out this picture of sharp differentiation.[44]

Ethnic Moldovan and non-Moldovans were equally divided on fundamental questions of sovereignty and statehood. While 70 percent of ethnic Moldovans wanted national independence in 1992, only 31 percent of Ukrainians and 38 percent of Russians agreed. On the other hand, while more than 55 percent of Ukrainians and 48 percent of Russians wanted to participate in the Commonwealth of Independent States, only about 12 percent of ethnic Moldovans desired this outcome.

Table 7.7 *Attitudes towards demands of minorities in Moldova (percent)*

Response to statement[a]	Moldovan	Ukrainian	Russian
Agree strongly	59.3	21.6	18.5
Agree somewhat	16.5	27.4	31.0
Disagree strongly	10.0	27.9	31.5
Don't know	11.7	17.9	17.3
No response	2.2	5.3	1.8

[a]"Minorities demand too much."

Table 7.8 *Attitudes toward the situation of minorities in Moldova (percent)*

Response to statement[a]	Moldovan	Ukrainian	Russian
Agree strongly	52.0	17.4	16.6
Agree somewhat	25.9	44.2	44.4
Disagree strongly	8.2	22.1	21.9
Don't know	11.1	12.1	16.0
No response	2.4	4.2	1.2

[a]"The situation of minorities is good."

Table 7.9 *Attitudes towards minority rights in Moldova (percent)*

Response to statement[a]	Moldovan	Ukrainian	Russian
Agree strongly	8.4	26.8	21.9
Agree somewhat	20.1	31.6	39.1
Disagree strongly	51.9	25.8	22.5
Don't know	16.3	13.2	14.8
No response	2.8	2.6	1.8

[a]"Minority rights are not protected in practice."

Table 7.10 *Attitudes toward the goals of minorities in Moldova (percent)*

Response to statement[a]	Moldovan	Ukrainian	Russian
Agree strongly	51.2	21.1	24.9
Agree somewhat	24.5	29.5	32.5
Disagree strongly	5.7	17.4	16.6
Don't know	15.5	25.3	20.7
No response	2.6	5.8	4.7

[a]"Minorities are self-interested."

Table 7.11 *Attitudes toward privatization of large industry in Moldova (percent)*

Response to question[a]	Moldovan	Ukrainian	Russian
Entirely private	8.5	5.8	4.7
Mixed	27.0	20.5	34.9
Almost entirely state	46.8	55.3	48.5
Don't know	17.0	15.8	10.7
No response	.6	2.6	1.2

Note: [a]The question on privatization in large industry, small industry, services, commerce, agriculture, tourism, and housing was one of a series of questions on property rights. For each of seven sectors respondents were asked if property should be: 1) entirely private; 2) private and some state; 3) almost entirely in the state sector; 8) don't know; 9) no answer.

Table 7.12 *Attitudes toward the pace of privatization in Moldova (percent)*

Response to question[a]	Moldovan	Ukrainian	Russian
Much too rapid	5.4	3.2	1.2
Too rapid	7.8	2.1	3.6
About the right pace	8.7	8.9	8.9
Somewhat too slow	29.1	26.8	23.7
Much too slow	26.2	20.0	26.6
Don't know	20.5	31.6	31.4
No response	2.3	6.8	4.7

Note: [a]"In your view, is the pace of privatization at present: 1) much too rapid; 2) too rapid; 3) about the right pace; 4) somewhat too slow; 5) much too slow; 8) don't know; 9) no response?"

Table 7.13 *Attitudes toward reform in Moldova (in percent)*

Response to question[a]	Moldovan	Ukrainian	Russian
Not necessary at all	4.2	6.8	4.1
Slightly necessary	7.3	6.8	9.5
Necessary	39.9	46.8	33.1
Very necessary	20.5	15.3	18.3
Absolutely necessary	13.1	13.7	17.8
Don't know	13.8	10.0	14.2
No response	1.3	.5	4.7

Notes: Columns may not equal 100 percent due to rounding. [a]"In your view, is reform at present 1) not necessary at all; 2) slightly necessary; 3) necessary; 4) very necessary; 5) absolutely necessary; 8) don't know; 9) no response?"

On the Transdniestrian question, approximately 80 percent of Moldovans favored the continuation of a unitary state with Moldova, while considerably less than half of Russians and Ukrainians did so. Conversely, approximately 29 percent and 38 percent of Russians and Ukrainians respectively favored a solution that would create a federation between Moldova and Transdniestria. Only about 7 percent of Moldovans were willing to accept this solution to the separatist crisis.

In striking contrast to this picture of majority/minority discord, when examination shifts from interethnic relations to other policy realms, differences between communities tend to decline precipitously. This is clearly the case with respect to issues relating to economic reform. Tables 7.11 through 7.13 indicate the range of attitudes concerning privatization and the course of reform. The limited nature of popular support for privatization is evident from the first of these tables. Less than 10 percent of the population favored complete privatization of industrial property, while   approximately half favored retaining state ownership intact.[45] Greater consensus is apparent both within and across ethnic communities in regard to the pace of privatization and the necessity of reform, with the balance of opinion being favorably inclined to reform and the Russian population expressing a slightly more reformist disposition than Moldovans or Ukrainians.

In general, differences between ethnic communities on these issues, which are at the core of the economic aspect of Moldova's transition debate, are not large, and most disappear when one controls for the overrepresentation of Moldovans within the rural population. Although there are quite strong differences of opinion concerning the range of policies under discussion, these differences were not in general determined by ethnicity. This conclusion is supported by analysis of variance for the relationship between ethnicity and scales summarizing the data on these issue orientations.[46]

Furthermore, not all responses concerning interethnic issues were discouraging. For example, the most politically salient of the nationalist political formations on either side of the conflict, the Popular Front and Edinstvo, failed to inspire broad-based popular support even at a time when interethnic conflict was relatively intense. Only approximately 15 percent of Moldovans would express "much confidence" or "very much confidence" in the Popular Front, while only 12 percent of Russians expressed the same degree of support for Edinstvo. Furthermore, popular opinion was surprisingly united on one of the key issues of statehood, unification with Romania. Very few members of the general population, either the Moldovan (12.2 percent) or minority (3.9 percent), desired this outcome, either immediately or in the longer term. This area of concord was critical in the displacement of the pan-Romanian faction and the construction of a new political consensus as the transition proceeded.

These data suggest both the degree of the differences separating Moldova's ethnic communities and the difficulties confronting moderate leaders as long as political discourse focused on interethnic issues. But the 1992 attitudinal data also provided some basis for optimism. The fact that public opinion on key reform issues crosscut rather than reinforced communal lines clearly provided the basis for a non-ethnic appeal, if the salience of the ethnic cleavage could be reduced. This distribution of popular attitudes was crucial in establishing the parameters within which elite factions contested for political power.

Party formation and regime consolidation

Moldova's relative success in negotiating the postcommunist transition to date clearly stems at least in part from the character of party competition that has developed there. With the initial Popular Front leaders in obvious decline for reasons indicated above, the reform communists who predominated in the Agrarian and Socialist Parties determined that consolidation of their newly won ascendancy could best be achieved through electoral validation. Party competition itself in turn appears to have been strongly affected both by the relatively limited role (at least in comparison with more aggrandizing executives in many of the newly independent states) played by Moldovan President Mircea Snegur, and by the logic of intra-elite competition in the republic.

While the executive plays a strong role in Moldova, as elsewhere in the former Soviet Union, the republic's legislature remained the site of decisive political activity throughout the early transition period.[47] Since independence, legislators have made crucial decisions on such fundamental issues as territorial independence, the separatist crisis, and economic reform. Faced with legislative deadlock, the executive branch, under President Snegur, took the legislators' inability to develop policy as an indication of a genuine lack of political consensus. Yet in contrast to the experience of many former Soviet republics, Moldova's executive generally assumed a passive stance rather than pursuing an aggressive extra-legislative political agenda and sought instead to promote a new and more effective legislative coalition. In part this outcome was determined by President Snegur's relative political isolation. His break with his initial Popular Front allies left Snegur without a secure base of support in the legislature. Nor could the president rely on unchallenged control over the executive branch. The former Communist Party apparat that provided a strong extra-legislative power base to executives in similar circumstances in other republics was, in Moldova, already under the control of well-entrenched reform communist leaders in the Agrarian and Socialist parties.

A second key factor determining this outcome appears to have been the complex issue structure in the republic. As indicated in tables 7.11 through 7.13 above, in Moldova one finds a clear reform/anti-reform political cleavage. There was a separate communist/anti-communist cleavage as well, but this was relatively weak. The mildness of the communist/anti-communist division may be explained in part because most legislators, including strong reformers, were elected as communists (which naturally retarded the impetus from within the elite to employ anti-communism as a mobilization tactic), and because anti-communist sentiments in the general population were not markedly intense. Finally, overlaying the reform/anti-reform, communist/anti-communist structures, one finds a third strong set of divisions based on nationality.

The interplay of these factors was critical in Moldovan democratization in general, and in the demise of the Popular Front in particular. Firstly, majority (Romanian speaking) versus minority (russophone) differences led to a breakdown in initial efforts to establish a broadly representative legislature. Complicating the situation, there were both pro- and anti-reformers and pro- and anti-communists on each side of the linguistic divide. These internal divisions frustrated efforts by the initial successor regime to consolidate its hold on power. Second, as the political transition progressed, a new set of divisions emerged within the majority community, including preeminently its legislative representatives, concerning the nature of their national identity itself. This division pitted those identifying themselves as "Romanian" nationalists and those identifying as "Moldovan" against one another. These conditions led to fragmentation of the ethnic Moldovan majority in the legislature.

The end result of this process was that the Popular Front delegation in the legislature, which was initially able to dictate policy when it worked in conjunction with the executive, collapsed, leaving in its wake a legislative vacuum. Consequently, an initially strong executive branch-ruling legislative party institutional alliance also collapsed. In order to pursue his own agenda, the executive was compelled to seek alternative allies in the legislature. Recognizing the need to move more rapidly on reform as a consequence of the continued deterioration of the economy, President Snegur threw his weight behind the Agrarians as they sought to develop a new and more effective legislative coalition. This necessity ultimately acted to increase the political salience of the legislature, since decisions were actually made inside that body through a process of inter-party bargaining rather than outside the institution by the leadership of a single clearly dominant legislative majority party. The renewed importance the legislature invigorated party activity as well, both because breaking the monopoly of the Popular Front opened the political process and because of the prospect of new elections.

A crucial role in the process of party formation was also played by the positioning of competing party elites during the early transition and the nature of the resources that they could bring to bear in their rivalry. As in other postcommunist countries, party structures are generally weak in Moldova. For many parties little organization exists outside of the legislature and a limited committee structure in the capital. Little effort was invested by deputies elected in 1990 in maintaining contact with constituents or in broadening their electoral appeal. Without recourse to any mechanism through which they could discipline members, parties in parliament were volatile and subject to continuous discord and fragmentation. By mid-1992, less than half (45.7 percent) of Moldovan deputies retained their initial 1990 political affiliations.

The experience of the Agrarian Democratic Party ran counter to this general trend. The Agrarians were able to maintain a remarkable degree of cohesion throughout the disruption that occurred within the parliament from 1990 through 1993. Their success is attributable to a variety of factors. The Agrarian deputies were, for the most, associated with the republican agro-industrial complex, either as village mayors or collective farm managers. Hence they shared substantial common material interests, both with respect to reform issues and with respect to resource allocation questions. Many held a common ideological orientation as reform communists. Furthermore, they maintained a powerful presence in the Ministry of Agriculture. This link with the Ministry provided both a channel of influence within the government and a sizeable reserve of organizational and physical resources that could be employed to mobilize supporters in rural constituencies.

Taken together the combination of common policy orientation, political experience and constituency, and an institutional power base made the Agrarians a potent political force. Had they and their allies begun the transition as the initial successor party, they may well have consolidated their position through non-electoral means and inhibited further democratization. But operating from the position of opposition against the authoritarian nationalist Popular Front, they embraced electoral politics as an effective tool in their struggle to regain power. This decision no doubt reflected the confidence of the Agrarians and their allies in their ability to dominate at the polls. It was nonetheless crucial in both reinforcing acceptance of democratic mechanisms and in reinvigorating mass elite-mass political discourse.

While the Agrarians and their allies thus shaped themselves into an increasingly cohesive force, the pan-Romanian group factionalized. Faced with a series of setbacks and the intransigence of the militant leadership, moderate Popular Front supporters defected from the organization and formed the "Congress of the Intellectuals" in order to promote a more limited nationalist agenda. Similarly, managerial elites, discouraged with the failure of the Front to pursue an effective economic policy, broke off to form parties promoting their own agendas. Entering into the campaign for the second legislative elections, the once dominant Popular Front's parliamentary representation was reduced to a mere twenty-five deputies.

The rules governing the 1994 legislative elections were enacted on October 14, 1993. These called for a new legislature that is smaller than its predecessor, with 104 as opposed to 380 deputies. Elections were based on a proportional representation system with a closed party list. In order to avoid causing an impasse concerning representation from the separatist regions or complicating negotiations concerning future territorial boundaries, Moldovan leaders enacted separate legislation establishing a single national electoral district for purposes of the 1994 election.[48] While not ensuring participation in the separatist region, this mechanism allowed elections to go forward, selecting a body of delegates whose constituency was the entire republic, regardless of their individual places of residence.

The election campaign focused on economic reform, competing strategies for the resolution of the separatist crisis, and Moldova's international orientation. The range of ideological positions represented was quite broad. Reform communists, represented primarily by the Socialist Party and the Agrarian Democrats, called for a slower transition to capitalism. The Agrarian Democrats, the Socialist Party, and Edinstvo argued for full participation in the CIS and taking as conciliatory an approach as possible to the minority issue and the separatist crisis. At the opposite extreme of the political spectrum, the Popular Front and the National Christian Party campaigned for unification with Romania, while the more moderate Congress of Intellectuals campaigned for Moldovan independence in the near term but for eventual unification. In addition to this primary competition, several small parties, mostly supported by urban professionals, campaigned for rapid marketization and privatization.

It is hardly surprising that under the circumstances the campaign was subject to some controversy. Members of the pan-Romanian parties, in particular, protested that they were subjected to harassment. Their complaints focused in particular on the rural constituencies where Agrarian support was strongest. It is undoubtedly true that many Agrarian leaders occupied powerful positions in the local power structure, which put them in a position to influence the rural population. While some irregularities did occur, the poor showing of the parties in question outside of urban areas appears to have been primarily a consequence of their lack of organization and limited rural appeal. In the Gagauz region, where difficulties could have been expected, polling places were open by agreement with the Gagauz leadership, and voting went without disruption. In contrast to the Gagauz, Transdniestrian leaders refused to allow voting in their region, but did agree to permit those who wished to cross over into Moldovan territory in order to participate in the elections. Some six thousand people took advantage of this opportunity to cross the Dniester and vote in specially established west bank polling places. At the conclusion of the process, international observers concluded that the elections were "open and fair," and there appears to be no reason to conclude that fraud or coercion played a decisive role in the result.

The outcome in Moldova's second legislative election marked a sharp reversal from the politics of the early transition period (see table 7.14). Turnout was quite heavy, with 79.31 per cent of Moldova's 2,356,614 registered voters participating.[49] The Popular Front and parties identified with "pan-Romanianism" were overwhelmingly rejected in favor of those favoring Moldovan identity and ethnic accommodation. Legislative control passed to the Agrarian Democrats, who won 43.2 percent of the vote and fifty-six of the 104 seats in the legislature. Another twenty-eight seats were won by the Socialist Bloc (the Socialist Party and Edinstvo) which captured 22 percent of the vote and twenty-eight seats. The geographic distribution of these two elements of the vote says much about the current character of Moldovan politics. The Socialist Bloc dominated the urban vote, taking first place in five out of the republic's seven cities, where workers and Russian-speakers are concentrated. The Agrarian Democrats, on the other hand, took first place (usually quite heavily) in all of the rural raions and in the two cities not won by the Socialists.[50] The more extreme nationalist parties suffered a crushing defeat. The Bloc of Peasants and Intellectuals (the

Table 7.14 *Parliamentary elections in Moldova, 1994*

Party/bloc	Number of votes	% vote	Number of seats	% seats
Christian Democrat–Popular Front Bloc	133,606	7.53	9	8.6
Victims of the Communist Totalitarian Regime of Moldova	16,672	0.94	–	–
National Christian Party	5,878	0.33	–	–
Social Democratic Bloc	65,028	3.66	–	–
Bloc of Peasants and Intellectuals	163,513	9.21	11	10.6
Democratic Party	23,368	1.32	–	–
Socialist Party and Edinstvo Movement Bloc	390,584	22.00	28	27.0
Women's Association of Moldova	50,243	2.83	–	–
Ecologist Party "Green Alliance"	7,025	0.40	–	–
Democratic Agrarian Party	766,589	43.18	56	53.8
Republican Party	16,529	0.93	–	–
Democratic Labor Party	49,210	2.77	–	–
Reform Party	41,980	2.36	–	–
Total			104	100

Source: The data in this table are drawn from *Electorala '94: Documente și Cifre* (Chişinău, 1994).

electoral vehicle of the Congress of Intellectuals) won 9.2 percent of the vote and eleven seats, while the Popular Front Alliance won 7.5 percent of the vote and nine seats.

None of the other nine parties and blocs that fielded candidates topped the 4 percent threshold required to enter the national legislature. The failure of the strongly liberal pro-reform Social Democratic Party to surpass the 4 percent threshold was particularly surprising. The Social Democrats enjoyed a highly favorable relationship with western governments and international agencies and included within their leadership high level advisors to President Snegur. Of equal note, though less unexpected, was the failure of the main parties of the emerging managerial interests, the Democratic Labor Party and the Party of Reform, to gain sufficient votes to enter the new parliament. Clearly, the failure of these parties indicates that liberal oriented and pro-reform elites are unable as yet to either reach out of the cities to the rural population or to attract working class support. The outcome produced by the electoral process in Moldova was thus quite consistent with the elite realignment that preceded the 1994 parliamentary contest. This result, however, should not be taken to indicate that elite competition was detached from mass level politics and predetermined the electoral outcome. On the contrary, a considerable part of the explanation for both the course of elite level competition and the electoral result relates to the positioning of competing parties in relation to potential supporters on salient issue cleavages in the society. This conclusion is sustained by analysis of the issue positions taken by parliamentary representatives of the competing parties in relation to the distribution of attitudes within the general population. Questions from the mass survey administered in Moldova in 1992 exploring the distribution of attitudes on the economic privatization and minority relations cleavages addressed above were included in a legislative survey conducted in May 1993. Responses to individual questions were then transformed into scales in both of these areas.[51] The parliamentary questionnaires were distributed through the cooperation of Moldovan legislative leadership, and 188 responses were obtained. Because of changes in the party membership of the legislators that intervened between the two surveys, analysis was not possible for several political groupings. But even restricting examination to the three parties for which complete data are available, the results show both substantial differentiation between parties, and a strong relationship between issue positioning and electoral outcome. The results of this analysis also provide evidence of party formation in the republic.

Figures 7.1 and 7.2 present mean scores for legislators elected in 1990 belonging to three of the country's most significant parties on scales representing attitudes toward property ownership and attitudes toward ethnic minorities. The attitudes of supporters of the three parties and of non-supporters are indicated as well. The actual mean scores, standard deviations, and numbers of cases on which these and the following figures are based are presented in table 7.15. One should expect to find, if mass political parties are developing, that party elites have established identifiable and distinct positions on relevant issue cleavages. It should also be the case that the supporters of the parties analyzed have opinions on salient issues that differentiate them from the general population and that their views are closer to those of their party representatives than those of non-supporters.

With respect to property holding, significant differences exist between the more collectivist Agrarians and Conciliation (the Socialist Party parliamentary faction), and Popular Front legislators (see figure 7.1). Similarly, on the dimension of attitude toward minorities, clear differences separate legislators of the three parties, with the Popular Front occupying an extreme nationalist position (see figure 7.2). Conciliation delegates, on the other hand, take a much more positive position with respect to minorities, while the Agrarians fall approximately between the extremes.

Figure 7.1   *Attitudes toward property in Moldova: group means*

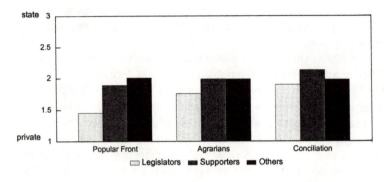

Figure 7.2   *Attitudes toward minorities in Moldova: group means*

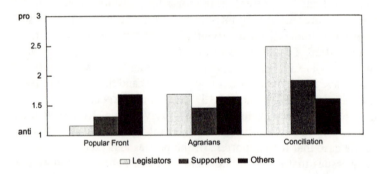

Table 7.15 *Legislators, party supporters, and non-supporters in Moldova: group means, standard deviations, and number of cases*

	Mean	Standard deviation	Cases
Support for private property			
Popular Front legislator	1.4571	.3086	25
supporter	1.8932	.3668	194
non-supporter	2.0110	.4650	926
Agrarians legislator	1.7633	.3376	35
supporter	1.9932	.3993	147
non-supporter	1.9902	.4591	973
Conciliation (Socialist) legislator	1.9018	.3715	16
supporter	2.1359	.4385	62
non-supporter	1.9820	.4511	1,058
Attitude toward minorities			
Popular Front legislator	1.1635	.2115	26
supporter	1.3143	.3886	206
non-supporter	1.6851	.5663	913
Agrarians legislator	1.6875	.4066	32
supporter	1.4565	.4981	138
non-supporter	1.6394	.5611	981
Conciliation (Socialist) legislator	2.4821	.4326	14
supporter	1.9110	.6293	59
non-supporter	1.6005	.5481	1,060

The question of proximity between the issue positions of party legislators, their supporters, and non-supporters is critical. With respect to attitudes toward property holding, only in the case of the Popular Front are party supporters closer to legislators than is the general population. In all three cases, the opinions of party supporters and non-supporters are extremely close, with Conciliation supporters being somewhat more distant from their legislative representatives (more collectivist) than the general population.[52] These results are clearly mixed, indicating that elite opinion is substantially more differentiated than mass opinion on property relations (as is the case with respect to reform issues in general).

On the issue of attitudes toward minorities, clearer mass level differentiation is apparent. In two of the three cases (the Popular Front and Conciliation), party supporters are closer to their legislators than to non-supporters. Polarization is apparent with respect to the positions of these parties, which have strong ethnic agendas. The direction of

Figure 7.3 *Issue positions of legislators and party supporters in Moldova*

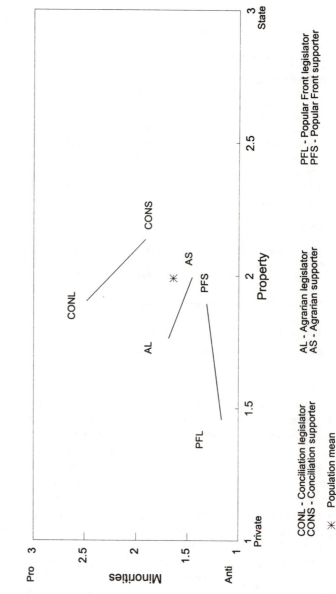

CONL - Conciliation legislator
CONS - Conciliation supporter

AL - Agrarian legislator
AS - Agrarian supporter

PFL - Popular Front legislator
PFS - Popular Front supporter

✳ Population mean

deviation of legislators from supporters reversed in the case of these two parties (for example, Popular Front legislators are more hostile to minorities than their supporters or the population at large, while Conciliation legislators are more favorably inclined to minorities than either their supporters or the population).[53] On the whole, these data reflect distinct party positions on salient policy issue dimensions and the emergence of a structured relationship between the attitudes of party elites and party supporters.

Figure 7.3 seeks to clarify the competitive positions of the Moldovan political parties. Legislative representatives are placed on these two issue dimensions in relation to their supporters (the population mean is also indicated). The Agrarians, occupying a central position between the other competing parties and close to the bulk of the mass population, obviously enjoyed a significant potential advantage which they were able to turn into a massive electoral success in 1994.

The electoral behavior (and to a certain extent the electoral fate of parties in Moldova) is explicable by reference to the parties' proximity to each other and to their potential constituents as indicated in figure 7.3. As one would hope, the party that is closest in position to the bulk of the population, the Agrarian Democrats, emerged as electorally dominant. This party, comprised primarily of ethnic Moldovan reform communists, developed a distinct strategic response to its early exclusion from power by ethnic extremists. Moldova's initial transition party, the Popular Front, was moderately reformist but strongly nationalist. Given the distribution of opinion in the country, the Agrarians were quick to recognize the advantages of assuming a moderate position on the nationalities issue and promoting electoral competition in order to regain the political initiative. They did so by reaching across ethnic boundaries and attacking the Popular Front leaders as authoritarian extremists. But there is no reason that the Agrarians could not have taken up a more nationalist position if they had been confronted with the task of displacing from power opponents who were pro-minority and pro-private property. The ultimate outcome of party competition, which favored an ethnic *inclusionist* outcome, was thus shaped by the short-term politics of the transition and the calculus of elite competition as much as much by structural characteristics of Moldovan society.

From transition to consolidation

The 1994 legislative election and its aftermath brought to a close the turbulent initial phase of the Moldovan democratization process. Top leadership positions, having been realigned prior to the elections, changed little. Andrei Sangheli remained in charge of the government as prime minister, and Petru Lucinschi returned as president of the new parliament. But the legislative elections served to consolidate the moderates' hold on the political system. Outstanding issues were placed on the legislative agenda and acted upon in quick order. Agreement was reached on local autonomy for the Gagauz region, clearing the way for resolution of at least one of the republic's separatist crises.[54]

After a long delay prior to the election, a new constitution was ratified by the parliament on July 29, 1994. This document provided that Moldova should be a democratic republic, established a semi-presidential system, with provisions for separation of powers and judicial review, and guaranteed basic human rights.[55] The new constitution established a strong Constitutional Court, made up of six judges, two selected by the president, two by the Parliament, and two by the Superior Council of the Magistracy. The Court is assigned the power to interpret the constitution and to issue pronouncements on initiatives to revise the constitution. It may make findings concerning the removal of the president, concerning the circumstances in which Parliament could be dissolved, and concerning the constitutionality of political parties. If it functions as it is described, the Constitutional Court will clearly become a very significant institutional actor in the Moldovan political system.

Under the 1994 constitution, the president's role is significantly strengthened. He is conferred with the right to submit issues to the people through referendum and to suspend acts of government which he feels contravene the law until they are decided upon by the Constitutional Court (Article 88). He is also empowered to dissolve Parliament after 45 days if a government is not formed or if passage of a law is blocked for three months.[56]

In keeping with the Agrarians' pre-election commitment to pursue a "Moldovan" course, the constitution called for permanent neutrality and banned the basing of foreign troops in the republic. It reflected the national orientation of the new political majority by removing references to Romanian language and the Romanian people that had appeared prominently in earlier documents. Earlier references to a "national" state were eliminated. In an obvious effort to bring the separatist crisis to a close, the constitution called for special conditions of autonomy to be applied to Transdniestria and the Gagauz region in the south. Revision of this special status requires a three-fifths vote of parliament. Finally, a further crucial change designed to ameliorate fears of linguistic repression by the minority populations was also introduced into Article 13, according to which the state "recognizes and promotes the development and functioning of Russian and other languages spoken on the territory of the country."

On coming to power, the Agrarian government also fulfilled the party's commitment to increasing the pace of economic reform. Prior to the 1994 election the depth of the Agrarians and the Socialist Party allies' commitment in this area was widely questioned, given the close association of both with the former Communist Party.[57] Belying such concerns, the new leadership almost immediately undertook to reorganize Moldova's enterprise privatization efforts. A new Ministry of Privatization was established in April 1994. In June a pilot auction of medium-sized enterprises was held, after which an ongoing privatization program was initiated. According to World Bank reports, more than 800 enterprises were privatized in 1994, and a new privatization program approved in March 1995 called for a further 1,450 firms to be privatized by the end of 1996. In the rural sector, substantial progress was made in converting state enterprises into joint stock companies owned on the basis of shares by their current work force. By the close of 1995, reform progress was evident, and Moldova was widely considered to be among the more progressive post-Soviet states.

The main trends that emerged in the course of Moldova's first five years of independence, relative ethnic moderation and a center-left political consensus, were confirmed in the republic's December 1996 presidential elections. Maneuvering for position in this contest was begun in late 1995 by President Snegur. With the pan-Romanian forces effectively marginalized, President Snegur's remaining rivals were clearly the leaders of the left–wing parties, Petru Lucinschi and Andre Sangheli foremost among them. Despite cooperation with the Agrarians and the Socialist Party in his efforts to defeat the Popular Front, Snegur found himself at a disadvantage compared to his former partners in vying for the support of moderate Moldovans and Russian speakers in presidential elections scheduled for late 1996. Snegur thus took steps to undermine the alliance that had successfully contested the 1994 legislative elections in an effort to pursue more effectively his own political course.

Forming his own political organization, the Party of Revival and Conciliation in Moldova, Snegur campaigned aggressively during late 1995 and early 1996 from his position as the incumbent chief executive. After launching a series of attacks on his opponents for obstructionism and failure to carry out necessary reforms, he argued for the formation of a "Presidential State" in which the directly elected executive would have enhanced power to direct policy. In a sharp reversal of his previous position, President Snegur took up the position that Romanian rather than

Moldovan should be recognized as the state language and attacked his former allies for their "pro-Moscow" orientation.

His obvious efforts to capture the pro-Romanian nationalist support formerly directed to the Popular Front aside, Snegur's appeal to nationalist sentiments for electoral gain failed to attract widespread support. In first round balloting on November 17, President Snegur led the electoral pack with 38.71 percent of the vote, ahead of Parliamentary Speaker Lucinschi with 27.8 percent and Communist leader Vladimir Voronin with 10.26 percent. Prime Minister Andrew Sangheli polled 9.5 percent of the vote, coming in a disappointing fourth place in the election, in which overall turnout was approximately 67 percent.[58]

Despite this first place finish, Mircea Snegur's vulnerability was evident from these results, in which each of the next three finishers shared a common political affinity. Lucinschi campaigned on a program of moderate reform and ethnic accommodation and a moderately pro-Russian stance in foreign policy. He was able to capitalize on a widespread perception that in foreign affairs he would be more able than Snegur to resolve the ongoing Transnistrian dispute, and would be less likely to destabilize the republic by moving to an overtly pro-Romanian policy. At the same time, Lucinschi's reputation as a moderate pro-reformer promised change at a pace that was not threatening to an already economically strapped population, but without giving rise to fears of regression back into Soviet era command policy. It thus came as no surprise that Petru Lucinschi emerged dominant at the conclusion of second round balloting on December 1, 1996, with 53 percent of the vote to President Snegur's 47 percent.

Conclusion

Moldova's political transition began during the Soviet period when, under the prompting of Moscow, reformist elements of the former elite initiated changes designed to open the political process. Since that time, significant progress has been achieved in the direction of democratic consolidation. The political process has become more open to participants from across the ideological spectrum as a consequence of increased freedom of expression and association. Early reforms also provided for increasingly active competition during the first partly democratic election, held in 1990. This election brought into being the transition legislature that governed the country until its dissolution in October 1993. It also played a crucial role in the process of competitive ethnic mobilization that has plagued Moldova throughout its transition.

Three further competitive national elections have been held since independence; for the president of the republic in 1991, for an entirely new post-Soviet parliament in February 1994, and once again for the presidency in 1996. Each of these elections was scrutinized by foreign observers. While the 1991 president election is difficult to assess due to the fact that only a single candidate, Mircea Snegur, campaigned for the post, both contests were found to have been held in compliance with international standards. The 1994 legislative contest was much more crucial in defining the political life of the republic. The year 1994 saw ethnic exclusionists marginalized and control over the new state transferred to forces that are both more moderate with regard to ethnic issues and more committed to the democratic process than their former opponents. The 1996 presidential election saw democratic competition confirmed. Power changed hands as a result of electoral competition, and the troubling movement in the direction of "super-executives" evident in several other post-Soviet republics was rejected along with President Snegur's campaign proposal to form a "presidential republic."

In most domains of public discourse a significant level of consensus has been achieved. A major issue of debate has been the extent of rights to be guaranteed to minorities, particularly the large Russian, Ukrainian, and Gagauz communities. These minority populations were uncertain that they would be able to maintain themselves in Moldova, and their fears were fed by the initially dominant pan-Romanian nationalists. For the most part, such fears have now been allayed. Citizenship, language and human rights legislation, special provision for minority areas, and assurance that Moldova will remain independent have largely resolved minority concerns, with the exception of the intractable Transdniestrian conflict.

Since independence, key Moldovan political institutions have been reformed, and the rules governing their interaction have been updated. The 1994 constitution, introduced in the wake of Moldova's second parliamentary election, both consolidated the early reforms and sym-bolized the culmination of a significant phase in the democratization process. The constitution confirmed and clarified relations that had emerged between the postcommunist executive and legislative branches. It provides for a semi-presidential system in which the executive plays a strong role in directing government, but the legislature remains sovereign, with strong oversight authority.[59]

Moldova has thus made significant progress in instituting democratic politics in the past half-decade. Its successes are even more remarkable given the challenges that it faced from separatists and pan-Romanian extremists in the course of the transition process. Yet further change must clearly occur before Moldova can be considered a "consolidated" democratic regime. Deeper democratization would require the further development of customs and civic beliefs supportive of the democratic process. Although democratic political norms appear to be taking hold, this process of constructing a democratic consensus is clearly still in an early stage. Similarly, little progress is evident as yet in the emergence of independent secondary institutions (interest associations, trade unions, and so forth) that would indicate the growth of autonomous community organizations and independent channels of representation. Moldova's achievement thus far is embodied largely in the fact that an environment has now been established in which progress in these areas may go forward unimpeded by civil conflict.

Appendix

Analysis of variance: hostility to minorities scale by main ethnic groups with education and urban-rural residence

Source of variation	Sum of squares	DF	Mean square	F	Sig of F
Covariates	1.518	2	.759	2.656	.071
Education	.274	1	.274	.958	.328
Urban-rural	.962	1	.962	3.366	.067
Main effects	89.045	2	44.522	155.778	.000
Ethnic groups	89.045	2	44.522	155.778	.000
Explained	90.199	4	22.550	78.899	.000
Residual	374.691	1311	.286		
Total	464.890	1315	.354		

Analysis of variance: minority rights scale by main ethnic groups with education and urban-rural residence

Source of variation	Sum of squares	DF	Mean square	F	Sig of F
Covariates	1.593	2	.797	11.107	.000
Education	.726	1	.726	10.123	.001
Urban-rural	.548	1	.548	7.644	.006
Main effects	10.998	2	5.499	76.678	.000
Ethnic groups	10.998	2	5.499	76.678	.000
Explained	11.640	4	2.910	40.575	.000
Residual	98.039	1367	.072		
Total	109.679	1371	.080		

Analysis of variance: egalitarianism scale by main ethnic groups with education and urban-rural residence

Source of variation	Sum of squares	DF	Mean square	F	Sig of F
Covariates	2.456	2	1.228	1.715	.180
Education	1.520	1	1.520	2.122	.145
Urban-rural	.488	1	.488	.682	.409
Main effects	.163	2	.081	.114	.893
Ethnic groups	.163	2	.081	.114	.893
Explained	2.929	4	.732	1.022	.394
Residual	1009.846	1410	.716		
Total	1012.775	1414	.716		

Analysis of variance: privatization scale by main ethnic groups with education and urban-rural residence

Source of variation	Sum of squares	DF	Mean square	F	Sig of F
Covariates	10.010	2	5.005	23.726	.000
Education	3.333	1	3.333	15.801	.000
Urban-rural	4.523	1	4.523	21.440	.000
Main effects	2.323	2	1.162	5.507	.004
Ethnic groups	2.323	2	1.162	5.507	.004
Explained	11.431	4	2.858	13.547	.000
Residual	282.678	1340	.211		
Total	294.109	1344	.219		

The scale on hostility toward minorities was constructed by calculating the mean response on the following series of four questions after recoding to achieve consistency. Non-answers and non-responses were excluded.

What is your feeling about the following statements? . . .

"Some minorities demand too much."
"The current situation of minorities is good."
"The rights of minorities are not respected in practice."
"Some minorities care more about their own community than they care about the good of the country."

1) agree strongly 2) agree somewhat 3) disagree strongly 8) don't know 9) no response.

The scale on attitudes toward minority rights was constructed by calculating the mean response on the following series of nine questions. Non-answers and non-responses were excluded.

In your opinion which of the following should minorities have at present?

Free general education in one's native language.
Sufficient publications in one's native language.
University in one's native language.
Legal proceedings in one's native language.
Independent television station in one's native language.
Leadership positions at all levels of administration.
Clear anti-discriminatory constitutional provisions.
State support for the promotion of minority cultures.
Local administrative autonomy.

1) yes 2) no 8) don't know 9) no response

The scale on economic equality was constructed by calculating the mean response on the following two questions. Non-answers and non-responses were excluded.

"How large a difference do you think there should be between the wages of the highest paid workers and the lowest paid workers?"

"How large a difference do you think that there should be in the wealth of people with the most money and people with the least money in the country?"

1) a large difference 2) some difference 3) a little difference 4) no difference 8) don't know 9) no answer.

The scale on privatization was constructed by calculating the mean response on the following series of seven questions. Non-answers and non-responses were excluded.

To what extent should economic property be privatized in: 1) large industry 2) small industry 3) services 4) commerce 5) agriculture 6) tourism 7) housing.

1) property should be entirely private 2) property should be some private and some state 3) property should be almost entirely the state sector 8) don't know 9) no answer.

NOTES

The public opinion survey research cited in this chapter was funded by a grant from the National Council for Soviet and East European Research, contract number 806-20. The Moldovan legislative survey was funded in part by a grant from the National Science Foundation.

1 A number of factors generally considered to play a crucial role in democratization are explicitly not addressed in this paper. One category of such factors includes those that are not centrally relevant to the Moldovan transition. Civil-military relations and class politics (mobilized around issues of political access and resource distribution), for example, have played a crucial role in the democratization process elsewhere. In the Moldovan transition, these factors have been most notable by their absence. Likewise, civil associations (professional organizations, trade unions, interest groups, etc.) have played little role in the Moldovan transition. This is not to suggest that any of these factors have been entirely absent, but merely that they have not been crucial in the flow of events thus far. It may (and likely will) turn out that in the longer run they will prove decisive for consolidation of democratic politics, if this in fact occurs.

2 Barbara Jelavich, *History of the Balkans: Eighteenth and Nineteenth Centuries* (New York: Cambridge University Press, 1983), p. 112.

3 Vlad Gheorghescu, *The Romanians* (Columbus, OH: Ohio State University Press, 1991), pp. 146–48.

4 Eight of the fourteen raions that made up the Moldovan ASS were then joined with Bessarabia to form a new Soviet Socialist Republic of Moldova. Districts to the north of the current republic, and the area between the Dniester and Prut rivers to the south were incorporated into Ukraine.

5 "White Spaces in the History of the Republic," *Moldova Socialistă*, 4 August 1988, p. 3.

6 Current accounts of this event suggest that many of those subjected to it were in no way better off economically than their neighbors, and hence that very often there was no actual justification for their exile. A. Tikhorov, "Collectivization: Against White Spaces," ibid., 3 February 1989, p. 3.

7 Viktor Kozlov, *The Peoples of the Soviet Union* (Bloomington, IN: Indiana University Press, 1988), p. 64. On the other side of the coin, in 1970 Moldovans made up 78.2 percent of the rural population. Yu. V. Arutyunyan, *Opyt*

Etnosotsiologicheskogo issledovaniya obraza zhizni: Po materialam Moldavskoy SSR (Moscow: Nauka, 1980), p. 36.

8   "Authority is obtained through Facts," *Moldova Socialistă*, 23 June 1989, p. 2.

9   Vasile Nedelciuc, *Republica Moldova* (Chişinău: Universitas, 1992), p. 16.

10   Michael Ryan and Richard Prentice, *Social Trends in the Soviet Union From 1950* (New York: St. Martin's Press, 1987), p. 74.

11   James H. Bater, *The Soviet Scene: A Geographical Perspective* (New York: Edward Arnold, 1989), p. 84.

12   V. Vizhutovich and E. Kondratov, "Post Script: Concerning the Art of Making Opponents," *Moldova Socialistă*, 23 April 1989, p. 4. This article appeared originally in *Izvestiya*, 21 April 1989.

13   Ibid.

14   G. Doni, "Sensationalism or Publicity," *Moldova Socialistă*, 19 November 1988, p. 4.

15   Among those reformers who became People's Deputies were I. Ciobanu, M. Chimpoi, N. Dabija, and I. Hadarca.

16   *Moldova Socialistă*, 13 June 1989, p. 4.

17   The Moldovan Popular Front was formed out of the mobilization engendered by the efforts of the Democratic Movement in Support of Restructuring and the Mateevich Circle, and it included in its ranks many of the leaders of both those crucial early reform organizations.

18   On the political dynamics of this period see William Crowther, "The Politics of Ethno-national Mobilization: Nationalism and Reform in Soviet Moldavia," *The Russian Review* 50, no. 2 (April 1991), 183–203.

19   *Moldova Socialistă*, 5 October 1989, p. 3.

20   Ibid., 4 October 1989, p. 4.

21   For the full text of the Popular Front's platform see *Literatura si Artă*, no. 6, 8 February 1990, p. 2.

22   Despite its increasing difficulties, the influence of the Moldovan Communist Party remained substantial. According to Petru Lucinschi's report to the Central Committee soon after the first-round election, twenty city and raion Party Committee first secretaries and nine presidents of local soviets won election.

23   *Moldova Socialista*, 1 March 1990, p. 1.

24   Eighty-one percent of deputies were members of the Communist Party. Confusing matters somewhat, some of these, like President Mercea Snegur, were both Communist Party members and supported by the Popular Front. Due to the growing friction between the reform and conservative branches of the Communist Party and the breakdown of the Party's central authority, it is difficult to ascertain in some cases what the affiliation of particular individuals was.

25   For discussion of the confrontation over renaming the republican parliament, see "Strain Without Precedent," *Moldova Socialistă*, 28 April 1990, p. 1. or "Agenda of the Day," *Sovetskaya Moldavia*, 28 April 1990, p. 1.

26   *Moldova Socialistă*, 13 May 1990, p. 1; ibid., 26 June 1990, p. 2–3.

27   For the central government's response to these actions see *Moldova Socialistă*, 13 May 1990, p. 1. On conditions in Bender see S. Ionel, "Meetings during Work Time," ibid., 4 May 1990, p. 3.

28   The first of these centered on the thirteenth session of the Moldavian Supreme Soviet, called primarily to consider the draft language law.

29 See Vasile Trofaila, *Moldova Socialistă*, 29 August 1989, p. 2.
30 In a preview of more serious insubordination yet to come, the Tiraspol city Soviet went so far as to pass a law suspending the implementation of the republican law on state language within its jurisdiction. Under pressure from central authorities this legislation was quickly withdrawn. "The Difficult Path Toward Compromise," *Moldova Socialistă*, November 2, 1989, p. 1.
31 See the account of Charles King, "Eurasia Letter: Moldova with a Russian Face," *Foreign Policy*, no. 97 (Winter 1994–1995), 106–20.
32 Moscow also long held out for an agreement on long-term basing rights for the 14th Army on Moldovan territory, a provision which Moldova flatly rejected.
33 For a full account of links between the Transdniestrian forces and conservatives in Russia see Vladimir Socor, "Dniester Involvement in the Moscow Rebellion," *RFE/RL Research Report*, 19 November 1993, pp. 25–32.
34 Several of the more extreme Popular Front leaders, including Mircea Druc and nationalist poet Larisa Lari, have in fact become prominent in Romanian political circles in the years since pan-Romanian influence declined in Moldova.
35 This period was later extended to 18 months.
36 The results of the election, held on 8 December 1991, were overwhelming. Snegur, who ran unopposed, received 98.2 percent of the votes cast.
37 Sangheli is a former Communist Party raion committee first secretary and later a member of the republican Council of Ministers. He played a prominent role in the removal of the extremely reactionary Simion K. Grossu from the position of party first secretary at the end of the Soviet period.
38 *Moldova Suverana*, 20 August 1992, p. 1.
39 *Moldova: Moving to a Market Economy* (Washington, DC: The World Bank, 1994), p. 5.
40 "Poporul Trebuie Intrebat și Ascultat," *Moldova Suverana*, 26 December 1992, p. 1.
41 *Moldova Suverana*, 6 February 1993, p. 1.
42 The individuals in question were Mircea Snegur, Petru Lucinschi, and Andre Sangheli, respectively.
43 The questionnaire referred to in this paper was administered by personnel of the ethnography and sociology institutes of the Moldovan Academy of Sciences and the National Institute of Sociology of Moldova in June and July of 1992. Approximately 1,600 respondents were selected based upon national probability samples. A stratified sample was drawn based on historical region and type of locality (rural, small towns, and cities). Face-to-face interviews were employed in this project. Members of minority communities were recruited to administer the survey in minority districts, and minority-language versions of the survey instrument were prepared for the use of members of the larger minority groups. Subjects were provided with an opportunity to choose the language in which they wished to respond.
44 When one considers attitudes concerning policy issues related to interethnic relations, a similar image emerges. In the crucial area of language policy, differences are striking. Attitudes concerning language use have been very highly charged due to Moldova's language law, which demanded that employees in positions requiring interaction with the public be able to converse in the state language. In this crucial area, more than 78 percent of Moldovans felt that

Romanian language education should be required for the minority populations, while less than half of Russians and Ukrainians agreed. Conversely, more than one-third of Russians and Ukrainians felt that each ethnic group should learn only its own language, while less than 15 percent of Moldovans agreed.

45 Support for private ownership in other sectors of the economy was greater, but the sharp division concerning property ownership remains obvious. When one considers attitudes concerning policy issues related to interethnic relations, a similar image emerges. For a more detailed discussion of majority and minority attitudes on these issues see William Crowther, "Nationalism and Political Transformation in Moldova," in *Studies in Moldovan: The History, Culture, Language, and Contemporary Politics of the People of Moldova*, ed. Donald Dyer (Boulder, CO: East European Monographs, 1996).

46 See my notes in the Appendix, Analysis of variance: hostility to minorities scale by main ethnic groups with education and urban-rural residence.

47 On the development of the postcommunist Moldovan legislature see William Crowther and Stephen Roper, "A Comparative Analysis of Institutional Development in the Romanian and Moldovan Legislatures," in *The New Parliaments of Central Europe*, ed. Philip Norton and David Olson (London: Frank Cass, 1996).

48 "Resolution on the Procedure for Enacting the Law on Elections to Parliament," 19 October 1993.

49 *Republic of Moldova: Parliamentary Elections, February 1994*, International Foundation for Electoral Systems (Chişinău: TISH Ltd., 1994), pp. 3–5.

50 One of the two cities where the Agrarians took a plurality of the vote was clearly a special case. This was Bender, which was the site of substantial conflict and population movement.

51 For a description of the construction of the scale on hostility to minorities and the scale on attitudes toward privatization, see the Appendix to this chapter.

52 In all of the cases except for that of Agrarian Party supporters and non-supporters, T-tests showed the mean score differences between party legislator/supporter and supporter/non-supporter groups to be significant at the .05 level.

53 In all cases T-tests showed differences between legislator/supporter and supporter/non-supporter groups were significant at the .05 level.

54 For a complete account of the Gagauz agreement see Vladimir Socor, "Gagauz Autonomy in Moldova: A Precedent for Eastern Europe?" *RFE/RL Research Report*, 26 August 1994, 20–8.

55 *Constituţia Republicii Moldova* (Chişinău: Direcţia de Stat pentru Asigurarea Informaţională, MOLDPRES, 1994).

56 This provision seems clearly to be a response to Moldova's difficulty in seeking to promulgate the new constitution and inability to pass legislation relating to the country's international situation under the pre-1994 rules.

57 One can conjecture that opposition to privatization and marketization was eased by the fact that the most dogmatically opposed elements of the former Soviet regime split off in the early transition and became the basis of the Transdniestrian separatist effort. It is also the case that the leadership of the Agrarian Democratic Party is made up primarily of individuals associated with the agricultural sector, who do not have the stake in resisting industrial privatization that their urban

colleagues might. It has been widely speculated that the shift to joint-stock ownership of the former state agricultural enterprises was managed in such a way as to leave the former elite's influence in rural Moldova largely intact.

58 Dan Ionescu, "runoff to Decide Moldovan Presidency," *OMRI Analytic Briefs* 1, no. 478 (19 November 1996).

59 Constitutional progress is also evident in provisions concerning the judicial branch. Lack of judicial autonomy is an obvious consequence of the Soviet system. Courts at all levels were subordinated to political authorities, and defendants' rights were ill-defined and disregarded in practice. These weaknesses are addressed in the constitution through articulation of a strong role for the Constitutional Court, the strengthening of other judicial institutions, and the guarantee of individual rights before the law.

8 Ukraine between proto-democracy and "soft" authoritarianism

Ilya Prizel

What is a democracy?

A democracy must contain the following elements: civil liberties (freedom of speech, freedom of assembly, and so forth); an independent judicial system; public officials held accountable to the law; a vital, free press; and a political system which seeks legitimacy from the public via free, competitive elections. While newly independent Ukraine fully or partially meets some of the above criteria, it fails altogether to pass several key tests of democracy. Whether Ukraine will realize its democratic potential or follow certain disturbing trends towards authoritarianism remains unclear.

On the surface, Ukraine's drive for independence and democratization followed the conditions laid out by Samuel Huntington in *The Third Wave: Democratization in the Late Twentieth Century*. The collapse of the Soviet regime was induced by a decline in the ruling elite's legitimacy. This decline resulted in large measure from higher levels of education, urbanization of the populace, greater awareness of life outside the USSR, efforts of established democracies to stimulate change, and rapid democratization in neighboring countries of Central Europe.[1]

Likewise, the vulnerabilities of a newborn democracy – also enumerated by Huntington – exist in Ukraine as well. Democratic values remain weak among the elite and the population at large. An economic crisis has devastated the country and polarized society. Ukraine also faces pressure from unfriendly external powers. According to Huntington, the success of democracy depends on economic development and growth and a political leadership committed to making democracy a reality.[2] If the success of Ukraine's experiment with democracy depends on these two factors alone, then democracy in Ukraine is in danger of failing.

Historical legacy and political traditions

Of all the polities to emerge from the rubble of the Soviet Union, perhaps none – except for Belarus – was less expected and more meteoric than that of Ukraine. As a result of 337 years of Russian rule, including seven decades of harsh communist administration under the Soviets, Ukraine appeared to be one of the republics least likely to assert its independence and undertake democratization.

Ukraine lacks a political and cultural elite with roots stretching back for a significant period of the nation's history. Historically, such elites have passed on a national idea and notions of self-governance from generation to generation and have provided an archetype from which a contemporary elite feels compelled to derive its legitimacy. Poland, despite forty years of communist rule, retained, along with a national church, its Peasant Party, which since 1919 has remained a powerful player in Polish politics. Hungary's Small Holders Party reformulated itself following the collapse of communism in Budapest. Even Romania, after decades of brutal Stalinist repression culminating in the despotic rule of Nicolae Ceaucşescu, saw the revival of pre-World War II institutions such as the United Peasant Party and national monarchism (centered on the exiled King Michael).

Ukraine, however, has no historical political parties and institutions to draw upon. Decades of foreign rule and the wholesale assimilation and acculturation of various past Ukrainian elites either to Polish or Russian culture produced a nation without a politically usable past. Between 1917 and 1920, the Ukrainian émigré historian Ivan L. Rudnytsky noted, Ukraine, in contrast to Poland, faced a far greater challenge in consolidating an independent state because no Ukrainian counterpart to the Polish *szlachta* existed.[3] Compared with other postcommunist European states, the chronic discontinuity in the national elite has made it far more difficult for present-day Ukraine to develop a coherent sense of purpose – let alone embrace fully the process of democratization – than for its neighbors to the West. The Ukrainian-dominated Cossack Sich of the seventeenth century was neither political nor cultural heir to Kievan Rus. The Ukrainian People's Republic (UPR) was not the heir to the seventeenth century Sich. Contemporary Ukraine is not a continuation of any of its three predecessors.[4] Mykola Rabchuk observed that during the referendum on independence in December 1991, Ukrainians were voting on "a common program for the future, not a common past . . ."[5] This absence of a "common past" retarded Ukrainian democracy from the start and enabled the old elite to survive despite a calamitous economic situation.

Throughout Central and Eastern Europe, diasporas have supplemented and assisted the domestic elites in the reformation of their postcommunist ancestral homelands. Ukraine, unlike most postcommunist states, cannot look to its diaspora as a repository of the nation's precommunist ideal. Although numbering 3 million and well-organized, the Ukrainian diaspora in North America, Western Europe, and Australia are more limited in their ability to influence events in Ukraine than diaspora from the Baltic states or Poland. Polish émigrés, through their publications such as *Kultura* (Paris) and *Aneks* (London), played a crucial role in instilling Western democratic ideals in Poland's intellectual elite.

In the case of Ukraine, most of the diaspora hails from west Ukraine and does not share with the great mass of Ukrainians a common religion, the full Soviet experience, or the identification of World War II with victory. Their influence on events in Ukraine is also divided by waves of emigration and generational lines. Many of the older exiles continue to see Ukraine in terms of its struggle against Poland and, later, the USSR. They are inclined to support, mainly by financial means, nationalist parties ranging from the Republican Party to more extreme groups such as the Ukrainian National Assembly (UNA-UNSO) and others. This financial support has enabled small nationalist groups in Ukraine to publish their newspapers and literature. Nationalist Ukrainian émigrés made themselves felt during the 1992 "Congress of Ukrainians" where, often at their urging, nationalist slogans came to dominate the congress hall. On the other hand, the large influx of younger members of the Ukrainian diaspora from English-speaking countries is providing vital reinforcement to non-government organizations and international organizations, supporting legal reform, women's rights, economic restructuring, party building, and so on. Although the impact of this younger generation is hard to measure, in the long term it may enrich and strengthen democratic institutions and civil society in Ukraine.

The so-called "inner diaspora" (or eastern diaspora) located in Russia and other republics of the former USSR, often overlooked and underestimated, could also have a positive effect on the democratization of Ukraine. The inner diaspora consists of descendants of Ukrainians who voluntarily settled in the Central Asian steppes or were exiled and imprisoned by tsarist or Soviet authorities, people who inhabit ethnically Ukrainian territory which fell outside Ukraine's borders, or those who have simply moved to other cities. Approximately five million Ukrainians live in the Russian Federation, especially in Tiumen, the Pacific Maritime region, and Kuban. They have begun calling for cultural autonomy, dual citizenship, and all that this entails. Fulfillment of their demands hinges on a parallel tolerance of Russian culture in Ukraine. Thus, Russian Ukrainians have become some of the most avid supporters of a culturally and ethnically pluralized Ukraine.[6]

A third group of Ukrainians living outside Ukraine are the approximately one million Ukrainians working temporarily in Poland and Russia. While the impact of this quasi-diaspora on Ukraine's economy and politics has been poorly studied, two general observations can be made. Cross-border trade and repatriated incomes are creating in Ukraine a nascent commercial class whose economic well-being is free from the interests of the ubiquitous nomenklatura. Furthermore, because of the relative economic and political freedom in both Poland and Russia, the economy is stronger and the mass media is largely de-bolshevized. Ukrainian interest in Polish or Russian electronic and print media has grown, ultimately weakening the Ukrainian government's monopoly and manipulation of the media at home. It is interesting to note that one of the oblasts which manifests the greatest degree of privatization is Luhansk, an area where Russian influence is most prominent.

While the collapse of communism in the Baltic states, Poland, Hungary, and Czechoslovakia was generally perceived as the chance to realize their own national aspirations, the collapse of communism also meant a return to the West. This meant aspiring to Western political norms. The unexpected disintegration of the USSR, however, forced Ukraine's political and intellectual elite to focus first on state building and legitimizing, at home and abroad, the existence of an independent Ukrainian state. Reflecting on Ukraine's dilemma, the first Ukrainian President, Leonid Kravchuk, noted that Russia or Poland, both well-established states, are deciding *how* to organize their statehood; Ukraine is still debating *whether* to preserve its statehood. In light of the perceived need to safeguarding independence, Kravchuk and the political elites of all ideologies in Ukraine failed to appreciate Western standards of democracy and relegated the establishment of democracy to lesser importance. In fact, unlike Eastern Europe, where the notion of a return to Europe enjoys broad elite and popular support, Ukraine's place in the world is also far from resolved, and a debate between the "Europeans" and the "Eurasians" continues to dominate the country's intellectual discourse.[7] While this intellectual debate addresses primarily the question of Ukraine's place in the international system, issues of establishing domestic order and a stable democracy are ignored. Just as history affects how Ukraine finds its place in the world at large, historical Ukrainian concepts of democracy complicate its democratization process at home.

Whatever the impact of these diasporas, however, Ukraine still has to overcome other hurdles on the road to democracy. Consisting predominantly of an illiterate peasant population and enduring decades of linguistic and cultural suppression, Ukraine did not experience its intellectual and national awakening until the middle of the nineteenth century. The early shapers of the Ukrainian national identity within the Russian empire came from disparate backgrounds and included towering personalities such as Panteleimon Kulish, Mykola Kostomarov, Mykhailo Drahomanov, Taras Shevchenko, and

Mykhailo Hrushevskyi. All of these thinkers generally agreed that a Ukrainian democracy should consist of a peasant society in loose confederation with communities throughout the orthodox Slavic world.[8] Virtually all nineteenth and early twentieth century Ukrainian thinkers rejected both Russian centralism and Polish aristocratic democracy and linked the idea of democracy with social and economic justice. Even Mykhailo Hrushevskyi, the founder of modern Ukrainian historiography and the man who led Ukraine's attempt to establish statehood after the collapse of the Romanov empire, openly declared that when faced with the choice of socialism or national independence, "the interest of the working people is the highest form of the common good."[9]

The success of the Bolshevik revolution and its proclamation of cultural autonomy (*korenizatsiia*) for Ukraine enticed much of the former leadership of the Ukrainian People's Republic to return to Soviet Ukraine. They believed that the introduction of socialism and cultural autonomy to Ukraine would largely satisfy their notion of democracy. Stalin's forced collectivization, which culminated in an artificial famine killing millions of peasants in Ukraine,[10] thoroughly discredited the belief that the Ukrainian question could be properly addressed so long as the country was in union with Russia. Nevertheless, the commitment to political, social, and economic equality, along with tolerance for minorities, has endured as a key element of Ukrainian concepts of democracy.[11] Within Central and East European history, Ukrainian nationalism has distinguished itself in its identification with social and economic justice.

Another source of weakness in the democratization of Ukraine is the strong psychological association of political pluralism with the demise of the Ukrainian People's Republic (UPR) in 1920. Since the nineteenth century, Ukrainian historiography has perceived a link between the failure of Ukrainian statehood and internal divisions and lack of consensus. Internal discord, it is believed, contributed to uninterrupted domination by foreign countries throughout history, first by the Mongols and Lithuanians, then by the Poles and the Romanovs, and finally by the Soviets. Ukraine's miscarried attempt to secure independence between 1917 and 1920 led to its subsequent partition by Poland and the Bolsheviks and a national disaster. The enormity of the impending disaster, of course, could not have been foreseen, but by the outbreak of World War II, the Bolsheviks had liquidated Ukraine's leading intellectuals, exterminated a large segment of the Ukrainian peasantry, and nearly destroyed Ukrainian culture.

Alexander Motyl has convincingly linked the birth of integral nationalism and authoritarianism in west Ukraine to disappointment in Ukraine's democratic experiment and a feeling of betrayal by the West.[12] Thus, as fascist ideologies spread throughout Europe in the 1920s and 1930s, Galician

Ukrainians, inspired in part by refugees from the short-lived Ukrainian People's Republic, likewise began to associate national identity and statehood with authoritarian leadership and military power, rejecting at the same time foreign ideological and economic influences, whether Marxist or liberal.[13]

After World War II, the nationalist-fascist ideologies prevalent among political groups in western Ukraine were relegated to the fringes. Nevertheless, the notion that some shortcoming of democracy undermined the UPR continues to haunt much of the Ukrainian intellectual elite.[14] It has even led to the disregard of patently undemocratic behavior by contemporary governments, so as not to denigrate Ukrainian statehood. Current Ukrainian legislation permits the Supreme Court, which currently does not exist, to dissolve political parties for anti-Ukrainian activities.[15] While measures for the enforcement of such legislation are nonexistent, its mere presence on the books puts Ukraine at odds with the standards of mature democracies.

These two historical legacies, the concept of the state as guarantor of economic equality and the association of democracy with chaos and the demise of earlier Ukrainian states, remain unquestioned shibboleths of Ukrainian politics. Ukraine's road to independence further reinforced these two legacies.

Ukraine's path to independence and its implications

Throughout Soviet rule, Ukraine maintained a tradition of political dissent. West Ukraine even conducted a guerrilla war against the Stalinist regime until 1955. Numerous studies indicate, however, that the agenda of dissent in Ukraine differed significantly from those of the Russian or Baltic republics. While clearly aspiring to democratize the USSR, the purpose of this democratization was not democracy per se, but the transformation of the highly centralized Soviet Ukraine into a genuinely autonomous republic which would ultimately bring about full independence.[16]

In the post-World War II era, Ukraine did benefit some from Soviet rule and underwent rapid modernization. Between 1959 and 1989, Ukraine shifted from a predominantly agrarian society to an overwhelmingly urban one (see table 8.1). In terms of education, over a similar time period, Ukraine has been catapulted from a backward society to one on par with developed societies. Without these changes, mobilization of the populace would have been impossible. Despite very high levels of education and literacy (see table 8.2), Ukraine's 52 million citizens (73 percent Ukrainian and 22 percent Russian), molded by seven decades of Bolshevism, as well as centuries of tsarist rule, remained highly atomized and politically inert, even as Gorbachev's perestroika and glasnost began to erode Soviet power.[17]

Table 8.1 *Population distribution in Ukraine, 1959-92*

Year	% Employed		
	Rural	Urban	In agriculture
1959	54	46	49.3
1979	45	54	30.8
1989	39	61	n.a.
1992	32	68	21.0

Sources: *Narodnoe khoziaistvo SSSR za 70 let* (Moscow: Gosudarstvennyi komitet SSSR po statistike, 1987); The World Bank, *Ukraine: The Agriculture Sector in Transition* (Washington, DC, 1994).

Table 8.2 *Educational levels of Ukrainian specialists, 1960-90*

Year	% Higher education or specialized secondary education
1960	9.7
1980	22.4
1990	34.0

Source: Stephen Rapawy, "Labor Force and Employment in Ukraine," in *The Ukrainian Economy: Achievements, Problems, and Challenges*, ed. I. S. Koropeckyj (Cambridge: Harvard Ukrainian Institute, 1992).

The repressiveness of the Communist Party of Ukraine (CPU) and the high degree of Russification of Ukraine isolated and alienated Ukrainian dissidents from the Ukrainian population at large. Dissidents in Ukraine devoted a great deal of skill and energy to documenting the policies of "ethnocide" pursued by both the tsarist and Bolshevik regimes and the brutal collectivization and industrialization of Ukraine. Unlike their Polish, Hungarian, Czech, Baltic, or even Russian counterparts, Ukrainian intellectuals gave little thought to the economic future of a postcommunist, postcolonial Ukraine.[18]

During the last twenty years of the Soviet Union's existence, Ukrainian dissent was suspended between two poles. On the left, Ivan Dziuba and his supporters sought to achieve genuine autonomy for Ukraine without dismantling either the Soviet Union or socialism. They drew heavily from the tradition of the "national communists" of the 1920s. On the right, Valentyn Moroz sought to revive the integral nationalist tradition of the Organization of Ukrainian Nationalists (OUN). As an alternative to these two authoritarian ideologies, there emerged in the 1970s the Ukrainian Helsinki Group, led by Danylo Shumuk. The Ukrainian Helsinki Group was truly committed to democracy and rejected racist and authoritarian ideologies, but it also linked human rights with the realization of national independence.[19]

When Mikhail Gorbachev launched perestroika in 1987, the political culture of Ukraine's elite lagged far behind that of either Russia or the Baltic states. Decades of strong-armed rule based on loyalty to Moscow created in Ukraine, as Gray Hodnet argues, one of the most conservative and faithful communist bureaucracies in the USSR. Between 1972 and 1989, Volodymyr Shcherbytskyi, a protégé of Leonid Brezhnev and a quintessential "little Russian," built a powerful political machine noted for its conservatism. With Brezhnev's massive subsidies for heavy industry and Ukraine's status as a major agricultural producer, Shcherbytskyi's power base was not only one of the most conservative in the USSR, it was one of the most corrupt.[20] Under Shcherbytskyi, powerful interlocking political clans *de facto* appropriated vast sectors of the Ukrainian economy as their own private fiefdoms. Motyl has described the political process in Ukraine as a "system of anti-Darwinist self-selection, according to which the worst and the dimmest were most inclined to join the party and the state apparatus."[21]

As glasnost swept the Soviet political scene, the communist parties in the Baltic republics attempted to harness the intellectuals' energy by establishing popular fronts. In Moscow, Gorbachev's central government and Yeltsin's nascent Russian government competed in recruiting liberal intellectuals as a means of attaining legitimacy. In Ukraine, however, the political elite resisted the attempts of Ukrainian intellectuals to catch up with their counterparts in the Soviet Union. Leonid Kravchuk, then the ideological secretary of the CPU, insisted that a popular front was unconstitutional and unnecessary in Ukraine; in his opinion, the CPU fulfilled all political modernizing functions. The stubborn resistance of the CPU ultimately spurred the defection of many communist party intellectuals to more liberal groupings, particularly to the Ukrainian Popular Movement for Perestroika, later to be know as Rukh.

Throughout 1989 the CPU continued to deal with any challenge to its rule in the traditional Soviet manner of harassment and intimidation. Ukrainian dissidents were forced to seek protection from the central authorities in Moscow. Only the direct intervention of Mikhail Gorbachev made possible the publication of Rukh's draft program in *Literaturna Ukraïna*, the organ of the Union of Ukrainian Writers.[22] At the time, Rukh presented itself as "a movement which recognizes the leading role of the Communist Party [and] whose aim is to assist the Communist Party in creating and working out a democratic mechanism."[23] While the Baltic and Soviet communist parties moved increasingly towards accommodation of the democratic forces challenging their power, the well-entrenched Ukrainian elite continued to hold its ground, even resorting to force. In October 1989, one month after the retirement of Shcherbytskyi, the city of Lviv experienced its own Bloody Sunday when OMON troops broke up a procession commemorating the anniversary of the city's founding.[24]

Although the Ukrainian establishment had to confront the notion of mass politics in 1989 and 1990, the growing mass mobilization in Ukraine did not shake the elite's hold on power. Despite public anger over Chernobyl, declining standards of living, revelations of Stalinist atrocities, and the status of the Ukrainian language and culture, the CPU remained in control. The nomenklatura elite could rely on the divided nature of the challenge to its authority. Dissent in Ukraine fell into several distinct groups: disillusioned Marxists, nationalists, western-style democrats, and russophone workers from the east.[25] In the face of such divergent groups, the ruling elite could play the conflicting agendas off one another. The CPU also clung to the hope that the Communist Party of the Soviet Union would at some point reverse Gorbachev's policies. Thus, the CPU took an obstructionist policy in the democratization of Ukrainian political life.

The first challenge to the CPU's monopoly on power occurred in March 1989 when the USSR held quasi-democratic elections to the Congress of Peoples' Deputies. Although communist candidates ran unopposed in most districts, the results were highly embarrassing for the CPU. Irate voters rejected the first secretary of the communist party in Kiev, the chairman of the Kiev city council, and four regional (*obkom*) party leaders. Instead, voters sent to Moscow dissidents such as the journalist Alla Yaroshinska who had exposed corruption in the CPU.

In summer 1989, miners in the Donbas region in eastern Ukraine went on strike. The first phase of these strikes was clearly economic. The miners walked out in July 1989 demanding better wages, safety equipment, pensions, and so on. By 1990 the miners' protests had turned into political demonstrations with calls for an end to the autocratic rule of Moscow's Union Ministries. In the wake of the miners' strikes, Rukh finally managed to build a coalition from nationalists seeking political independence, moderate Ukrainians yearning to end Russia's exploitation of Ukraine, and the miners rebelling against the high-handed administration of the center.

By 1990 opposition groups had begun to coalesce. The convergence of various dissident movements culminated in the formation of a human chain stretching from Lviv to Kiev in January 1990. This demonstration illustrated the phenomenal growth of the Ukrainian national movement, as well as its limits. As impressive as this mobilization was, albeit with some logistical support from the Kiev government, the chain did not go beyond the Dnieper River. It also took place with logistical support from the communist government in Kiev.

Ukraine's first quasi-democratic elections for its republican level parliament took place on March 4, 1990. By this time, the CPSU had given up its monopoly on power, but this was too late to allow the registration of parties for the election in Ukraine. By mobilizing support in the rural areas and engaging in widespread ballot tampering, the CPU won 373 of the 450 seats available, thus easily retaining an absolute majority in the Ukrainian parliament. In the cities, however, the vote was split almost evenly between the CPU, independents, and the Democratic Bloc, a coalition of several groupings. Even though many members of the CPU would go over to the Narodna Rada Bloc (the title of the Democratic Bloc candidates within parliament) or independents, the CPU still enjoyed the support of 239 members of parliament. Within the Narodna Rada, two strains emerged from which parties would begin to coalesce. The first was the Nationalist Bloc. The second was the Moderate Left (see table 8.3).

The Nationalist Bloc

The first genuine opposition groups to emerge adhered to a moderate brand of nationalism. The agenda of these parties was first and foremost political independence for Ukraine. Among these groupings, the largest were the Ukrainian People's Movement for Perestroika (Rukh), the Ukrainian Republican Party, and the Ukrainian Democratic Party.

The Ukrainian Helsinki Union (UHU), later recast as the Ukrainian Republican Party (URP), most likely laid the foundation for this bloc. In 1990, under the leadership of former dissidents such as Levko Lukianenko, Stepan Khmara, and Hryhorii Hrebeniuk, the URP strove for the annulment of the 1922 Union Treaty with Russia, the creation of an independent judiciary, and the enactment of a tough environmental policy. The structure of the URP, with its strong emphasis on its own version of democratic centralism, dismayed many UHU dissidents and sympathizers, who saw in the party structure a retreat from democratic ideals. Despite the prominence of the party's leadership, the party's weak grass roots organization and its emotional commitment to nationalism left it a regional party with most of its 3,000 members coming from Galicia.

The shift from an emphasis on human rights and democracy to an emphasis on nationalism also took place in Rukh. Originally, Rukh's founders conceived of the party as a broad-based democratic coalition in the mode of Poland's Solidarity movement and the popular fronts of the Baltic states. As independence approached, however, Rukh began to suffer from an identity

Table 8.3 *Party representation in the parliament of Ukraine, 1990-91*

Narodna Rada/Democratic Bloc		Uncommitted		Left	
Nationalist Bloc				*Until August 1991*	
Rukh	40	Independents	87	Communist Party of Ukraine (CPU)	239
Ukrainian Republican Party (URP)	12				
Democratic Party of Ukraine (DPU)	23				
Ukrainian Conservative Republican Party (UCRP)	1				
Ukrainian Christian Democratic Party (UCDP)	1			*After August 1991*	
Statehood and Independence for Ukraine (SIU)	1			Socialist Party of Ukraine (SPU)	38
Total	78	Total	87	Peasant Party of Ukraine (PtPU)	c. 44
Moderate Left				Independents	c. 157
Party of Democratic Rebirth of Ukraine (PDRU)	36			Total	239
Social Democratic Party of Ukraine (SDPU)	2				
United Social Democratic Party (USDPU)	1				
People's Party of Ukraine (PPU)	1				
Total	40				

Sources: Derived from Bogdan Szajkowski, *Political Parties of Eastern Europe, Russia and the Successor States* (Essex: Longman Information & Reference, 1994); Dominique Arel, "The Parliamentary Blocs in the Ukrainian Supreme Soviet: Who and What Do They Represent?" *Journal of Soviet Nationalities* 1, no. 4 (Winter 1990-91).

crisis, especially on questions of multi-nationalism and collaboration with reformers within the CPU. One of its initial mottos had run, "Let the Poles of Ukraine live better in Ukraine than in Poland, the Russians better than in Russia, and the Jews better than in Israel." Rukh, however, began to drift toward a more assertive nationalism, and its membership, like that of the URP, soon drew primarily from Galicia. By 1992, when Rukh published "A Concept of State Building in Ukraine," the program envisioned a state constructed on the basis of ethnicity.[26] Although Rukh played a crucial role in mobilizing the Ukrainian public and served as a forum for a wide range of views, it failed to transform itself into a viable political party with nationwide appeal. By the 1994 parliamentary elections, Rukh's role in Ukrainian political life had declined considerably.

Some representatives of the Ukrainian intelligentsia, such as Ivan Drach and Dmytro Pavlychko, attempted to mold out of Rukh the Democratic Party of Ukraine (DPU). The founders of the DPU supported independence but rejected the increasingly authoritarian nature of the URP. Unlike the URP, which considered all members of the CPU traitors, the DPU maintained that enlightened nationalism might convert members of the CPU into "national communists," but that blind nationalism would simply drive wavering CPU members back to Bolshevism.

The moderate nationalist position of the URP, DPU, and Rukh, while objectionable in large areas of eastern and southern Ukraine, came under increasing challenge from ever more nationalist rightwing groupings emerging in western Ukraine, such as the Ukrainian National Party (UNP) led by Hryhorii Prykhodko.

The Moderate Left

The drift toward nationalism occurring among Ukraine's established dissident groups created a backlash among adherents of the moderate left. Disaffected with the political turmoil occurring in the Soviet Union, many nevertheless found the growing nationalism among their erstwhile political allies alarming. One of the first groupings to challenge the political hegemony of the nationalists among the anti-CPU forces was the Ukrainian Social Democratic Party (USDP). Although in favor of market economics, the party remained committed to the welfare system created by the Soviet system and paid scant attention to the national question.

By far the largest of the moderate leftwing groupings in the 1990-94 parliament was the Party of Democratic Rebirth of Ukraine (PDRU). Part of its success stems from its roots in the reform wing of the CPU. The PDRU sought privatization and the creation of a market economy. Uniting several diverse groups, from 1990 until May 1992 the PDRU boasted seven co-chairs. After the collapse of the Soviet Union, this party also promoted closer ties to Russia and the CIS.

Another small yet significant splinter to appear from the left of the Ukrainian spectrum was the Green Party led by Yurii Shcherbak. While the Greens tended to pacifism and indifference to the nationalist question, they increasingly rallied around the idea that Ukraine's ecological problems could not be solved as long as it remained a part of the bureaucratic and authoritarian Soviet monolith.

Despite the proliferation of political parties in Ukraine, the size of their membership remained small, bordering on insignificance. The existence of these parties did alter the political debate in Ukraine, but these parties could neither alone nor collectively challenge the communist elite's monopoly of power. The Communist Party of Ukraine still numbered nearly 3 million members, while the largest opposition party, the URP, claimed 8,879 members. The total membership of the opposition parties did not exceed 40,000.[27] With the opposition split into so many ineffective parties and divided by conflicting interests, the CPU could continue coercing and co-opting the electorate and their representatives. The late demise of bolshevism in Ukraine and the suddenness of independence caught political parties still in the process of formation. None of the parties had gelled into institutions capable of articulating grassroots concerns and formulating effective political agendas. Even after the 1994 elections only 5.1 percent of the population professed any party affiliation, while only 6 percent believed that parties provide support for the people.[28]

Only the weakening grip of the Soviet center forced the CPU to reorient itself and reevaluate its priorities. The red managers and agricultural barons, whose wealth and power were linked to the Brezhnevite system of spoils and the ability of the center to provide economic largess, began to view their economic relationship with Moscow as a liability. As the ability of the central ministries to deliver capital and inputs shrank, the Ukrainian industrial nomenklatura increasingly shifted towards national communism and began to cut their ties to Moscow. By summer 1990, the managers were lobbying the Ukrainian Supreme Rada to nationalize all-Soviet enterprises on Ukrainian soil. This move transformed the Ukrainian industrial nomenklatura from mere administrators into *de facto* proprietors of the second largest industrial concentration in the Soviet Union.

Traditionally, the CPU had looked to Moscow for legitimacy and protection. The failure of the coup in Moscow in August 1991 dealt the final blow to hopes for intervention on behalf of the old order. Paradoxically, however, the attempted coup did more than just free the Ukrainian communist elite from its subservience to Moscow. In the aftermath of the coup, Boris Yeltsin had begun to dismantle the CPSU and undertake the democratization of Russian society. Were this process to expand into Ukraine, it would have threatened the power and privileges of the Ukrainian nomenklatura. Consequently, the nomenklatura embraced independence and the nationalist cause as the main, if not the only, means for survival and a continued hold on power. The Ukrainian Parliament declared Ukrainian independence on August 24, and from then on the ex-CPU elite doggedly resisted a new treaty of union with Russia. The collapse of communism had reversed the Ukrainian Communist Party nomenklatura's relationship with Moscow.

Despite the odious past of Ukraine's communist elite, the process of adaptation proved to be remarkably easy for the old nomenklatura. In fact, as is often the case in post-colonial countries, the old native elite, emboldened by the absence of the powerful mother country, proceeded to assert itself. The recast party nomenklatura, and especially President Kravchuk, quickly built a broad consensus across Ukraine's political spectrum for Ukrainian statehood. The nationalists, sensing the fragile condition of a new Ukrainian state, were willing to overlook the elite's past and endorse the government. They sought to avoid the divisions that had contributed to the collapse of the previous Ukrainian state and so welcomed the communists' conversion to the national cause as the key to maintaining independence. The russophone east Ukraine felt that Kravchuk's past meant his government would avoid reckless Ukrainization and would protect workers from the harsh economic reforms taking place in Poland and Russia. Ukraine's powerful old industrial elite, already national communists, believed Kravchuk would not challenge their political and economic position. All of the nomenklatura mobilized their powers of patronage to guarantee a solid vote for independence and to elect Kravchuk to the presidency in December 1991 (see table 8.4).

Just eight months after the CPU had rallied 70 percent of the country's electorate in favor of maintaining a reformed Soviet Union, the nomenklatura now turned out an overwhelming majority of over 90 percent for independence. This rapid swing in voter preferences reflected the atomized nature of Ukrainian society and the ability of the elite to get out the vote.[29] The swing did not result from genuine political debate and grassroots political mobilization on the part of the opposition groups. Levko Lukianenko said, "The glittering victory of voters was made possible only because both nationalists and communists agitated for independence."[30] The 1991 referendum, as Motyl has noted, was the product of a month-long, Soviet-style campaign of agitation and propaganda.[31] The ex-communist elite presented Ukrainian independence as a way to rectify alleged past exploitation of Ukraine by Russia. No real exchange of views appeared in the newspapers or on television. Analyzing the reaction of the Ukrainian masses to democratization,

Table 8.4 *Presidential elections in Ukraine, 1991*

Candidate	Votes	% of Total
Leonid M. Kravchuk	19,643,481	61.89
Viacheslav M. Chornovil	7,420,727	23.27
Levko M. Lukianenko	1,432,566	4.49
Volodymyr B. Hrynov	1,329,758	4.19
Ihor R. Yukhnovskyi	554,719	1.74
Leopold I. Taburianskyi	182,713	0.57

Source: *Eastern Europe and the Commonwealth of Independent States, 1994*, 2d ed. (London: Europa Publications Limited, 1995).

the Ukrainian philosopher Oleh Bilyi wrote: "Democracy was understood in the mass consciousness as an ordinary resolution of a regular plenary session of the CPSU Central Committee. The only difference was that this 'resolution' was based on real faith in a bright future . . . The main specificity of the induced myth of democracy was the schema of the old catechism. In other words, the affirmation of democracy was implemented in the mass consciousness with the aid of traditional Stalinist ideological methods."[32] The Ukrainian sociologist Viktor Stepanenko described the population's bewilderment during the 1991 referendum: "Everyone is hoping for something better. They will know what they do not want, a fraction of them knows what they want, but no one knows how to achieve it."[33]

Endowed with rich industrial, agricultural, and human resources, Ukraine seemed to possess the greater potential for making the transition from a centrally planned demi-colony to a free-market economy than any other post-Soviet state. Yet, despite its great economic potential, Ukraine lacked both an elite committed to democratic reforms and liberal economics and a fully developed, capable democratic alternative. Because the emergence of free markets often requires decentralization and political freedoms, without genuine converts to liberal democracy, as in the Czech lands, or a rising civil society, as in Poland, newly independent Ukraine failed to transform itself into a thriving economy as well. Ukraine's subsequent development resembled more that of Belarus and Central Asia, rather than that of Central Europe or the Baltic states. The old system neither collapsed as in Czechoslovakia and Russia, nor negotiated a "contractual" retreat as in Poland and Hungary. Ukraine had established a government Ukrainian in form and Brezhnevite in content.

The Kravchuk era

Ukraine emerged as a state with no viable political parties, no modern constitution, no organized political opposition, no national church, and no labor movement with which to challenge the political power of the former CPU elite. As seen above, independence had in fact actually served to reinforce the nomenklatura's hold over the country. Not only had the nomenklatura inherited vast amounts of property and economic resources, it had found itself free of any supervision. Furthermore, the elite could claim legitimacy for having realized the dream of Ukrainian statehood. Independence, validated by popular vote, appealed to the red managers of east Ukraine and the Black Sea coast who benefited from the wholesale redistribution of state assets. According to some estimates, as much as 85 percent of Ukraine's industrial stock belonged to the All-Union Ministries. The continuation of some kind of association with Russia would have meant sharing this social property with Moscow. After the managers had pushed through the nationalization of Soviet property in 1990, political independence assured the undisputed control of the country's wealth. Since Kravchuk's economic team continued to provide huge ruble-denominated credits to the failing industrial and agricultural sectors, it won the support of enterprise managers, blue-collar workers, directors of state farms, and peasants. But independence left the Brezhnevite morass in place.

Given the regime's power base and Kravchuk's own political instincts, the first president of independent Ukraine concentrated on strengthening statehood, his own powers, and the nomenklatura's hold over Ukraine's political and economic institutions. President Kravchuk declared, "The president should be responsible for building the state, while the prime minister should manage the economy."[34] Raising state-building above democratization offered several advantages. On the one hand, Kravchuk's zealous defense of Ukrainian statehood and the promotion of the trappings of independence converted Rukh from the vortex of opposition to a source of support. The leadership of Rukh and the Republican Party, which had initially distrusted and opposed Kravchuk, now sided with him. In turn, Kravchuk rewarded both parties by offering their most influential members ambassadorships, positions as presidential counselors, or high academic posts. As Roman Solchanyk noted "[Kravchuk] succeeded in co-opting both the Rukh program and its top leaders."[35] By meeting the aspirations of the nationalists and pleasing the old economic elite, Kravchuk secured for himself a virtually unassailable position. At the end of 1992, Rukh split, and the faction led by Viacheslav Chornovil engaged in constructive opposition. Lacking an economic power base and unable to dispense patronage, Rukh became increasingly marginalized politically. So long as the Central Bank of

Ukraine could issue virtually unlimited ruble-denominated credits and the government could import energy from Russia well below world market prices, President Kravchuk could meet the contradictory demands of various sectors of the population.

Kravchuk's economic policies avoided the kind of economic liberalization that occurred in Central Europe, the Baltic countries, and, to a lesser extent, Russia. For his prime minister, President Kravchuk turned to Vitold Fokin, the former head of the State Planning Committee and like Kravchuk a product of the CPU's administrative *apparat*. Fokin's policies attempted to replicate Brezhnevite economic policies, albeit on a smaller scale. He issued massive credits to industry and agriculture and held off price liberalization. Privatization, which in addition to bringing about greater economic efficiency, also produces economic and political pluralism, remained confined to the realm of rhetoric.

Brezhnevite economic policies, coupled with accelerating economic decline, ultimately triggered a revolt by the democratic opposition in the parliament. Led by Chornovil, they succeeded in forcing Fokin out on September 30, 1992, but their effort to gather three million signatures and force new parliamentary elections failed. Fokin's political demise did not bring a change of direction. Kravchuk also used the occasion to fire the liberal deputy prime minister for the economy, Volodymyr Lanovyi, a man widely regarded as the Ukrainian Yegor Gaidar, the mastermind behind Russia's reform program. The subsequent appointment of Leonid Kuchma[36] merely signified the replacement of the command administrative faction of the old CPU by a representative of the industrial-managerial faction. The industrial-managerial faction favored some degree of modernization that would enable it to participate in the world economy as its Russian counterparts. The command administrative faction preferred to avoid reforms which might challenge its power and advantages.

Upon taking office, Kuchma promised to trim budget deficits, improve relations with Moscow, and restore economic links with Russia. This raised expectations that Ukraine would finally join the ranks of the reforming countries and curtail the power of the still-dominant nomenklatura. The composition of Kuchma's cabinet demonstrated the degree to which his appointment represented a victory for a rival faction in an intra-elite struggle. Although the new cabinet included among its six vice-prime ministers Ihor Yukhnovsky, an opposition leader, and Viktor Pynzenyk, a liberal deputy from west Ukraine, the rest were drawn from the ranks of managers. Hryhorii Piatachenko and Vadim Hetman, both Fokin appointees, retained their positions as the minister of finance and the chairman of the National Bank, respectively. With a team such as this, the Supreme Rada could, with a clear conscience, confirm Kuchma's cabinet and even grant it emergency powers to bypass the Supreme Rada in making decisions.

Although Prime Minister Kuchma criticized the slow pace of privatization and reforms, he made it clear from the outset that he would avoid shock therapy in reforming the economy. Thus he assured the continuation of the economic distortions that enriched and empowered the old elite. Despite rhetoric about monetary discipline, Piatachenko and Hetman continued to pump extravagant credits into the economy, further fueling Ukraine's hyperinflation and driving the *karbovanets* to ever greater depths. Kuchma's only serious effort to contain the deficit came when he tried to raise the prices of housing, utilities, and other subsidized services to a level closer to market prices. The policy of simply raising prices in the absence of fundamental macroeconomic reform only further impoverished the population. Kuchma blamed his predecessor for tolerating excessive imports of cut-rate Russian energy, which were then re-exported at world prices, enriching corrupt officials, but leaving Ukraine with an enormous debt to Russia.[37] This practice continued, however, during Kuchma's tenure as prime minister.[38] Ultimately, the All-Ukrainian Association of Businessmen accused Kuchma of "curbing market oriented reforms and obstructing the development of private enterprise."[39] Throughout Kuchma's tenure, President Kravchuk remained oblivious to Ukraine's economic problems and regularly attacked Kuchma's policy of easing relations with Russia.[40]

The economic crisis hit Ukraine in 1993, when the Russian government, in rapid succession, freed most prices, expelled Ukraine from the ruble zone, and raised energy prices. No longer able to issue credits in rubles, Kravchuk's government resorted to massive emissions of its own Ukrainian *karbovantsi* in order to prop up industry. This policy resulted in hyper-inflation and a new wave of strikes in the Donbas coal mines, where the deepening economic crisis was most apparent. This region, despite its status as the *creme de la creme* of Soviet industry, depended heavily on massive subsidies as well as Russian inputs and markets. In the Donbas, support for Ukraine's independence and President Kravchuk depended most on restoring the relative well-being and advantages the region enjoyed under Brezhnev. The rapid deterioration of an already bad economic situation in the Donbas resulted in a prolonged period of non-payment of salaries and led to political upheaval, both among the masses and the elite. On the popular level, the economic collapse resulted in the creation of a new Communist Party of Ukraine. The labor unrest of that summer led the Supreme Rada to force parliamentary and presidential elections on President Kravchuk.

Kuchma's tenure as prime minister had turned out a disappointment to all concerned. In the autumn of 1993, faced with the continued free fall of the Ukrainian economy and the growing popular unrest across the country, the

Table 8.5 *Indicators of economic trends in Ukraine since 1989*

	1989	1990	1991	1992	1993	1994	1995[a]
GDP	4	-3	-12	-17	-17	-23	-12
Industrial output	3	0	-5	-7	-8	-28	-14
Rate of inflation	2.2	4.2	91	1,210	4,735	891	375
Rate of unemployment	0	0	0	0.3	0.4	0.4	0.6
GNP per capita	n.a.	n.a.	n.a.	n.a.	n.a.	4,030	n.a.
% Workforce in private activity	n.a.	n.a.	n.a.	17.1	19.6	24.5	n.a.
% GDP from private sector	n.a.	n.a.	n.a.	8.8	46.7	54.2	n.a.

Notes: GDP – % change over previous year; industrial output – % change over previous year; rate of inflation – % change in end-year retail/consumer prices; rate of unemployment as of end of year; GNP per capita – in US dollars at PPP exchange rates. [a]Estimate.

Sources: European Bank for Reconstruction and Development, *Transition Report 1995: Economic Transition in Eastern Europe and the Former Soviet Union* (London: EBRD, 1995); European Bank for Reconstruction and Development, *Transition Report Update, April 1996: Assessing Progress in Economies in Transition* (London: EBRD, 1996).

Supreme Rada refused to renew the broad powers given to Kuchma. This reassertion of power by the Supreme Rada did not bring greater fiscal responsibility, but rather a bout of populist transfer payments and massive institutional subsidies. The result was even greater inflation, leading to the resignation of both Kuchma and Pynzenyk. Kravchuk this time looked to the former Mayor of Donetsk, Yukhym Zviahilskyi, to be his new prime minister. Economic policies, however, remained dominated by what Oleh Havrylyshyn has defined as a

"Rentier capitalist" elite, whose profits depend on the economic system remaining highly dirigiste and regulated by the state . . . The so called "new" rentier capitalists are an amorphous and ill-defined group including directors of enterprises, kolhosps and radhosps, heads of trade groups and new private, "commercial" group entities formed as spins-offs from state enterprises . . . Illegal actions occur, of course, but they have been incidental or they have been built upon the main tendency of earning large "rents" from having a privileged position to obtain large credits and special licenses to trade or export.[41]

Ukraine's economic policies, while allowing the elite to retain its political and economic power, led to catastrophic economic decline.

Ukrainian institutions: building blocks of civil society?

The military

Of all the institutions that Ukraine inherited from the Soviet Union, the largest by far was the enormous military establishment. On the surface, the transition of the Soviet Army into a Ukrainian army has proceeded smoothly. The chaos that befell this institution of nearly 700,000 men after the dissolution of the USSR threatens to make the Ukrainian army an uncontrollable force within the country's politics. The Ukrainian army, grossly underfunded and top-heavy in officers, is being pulled by the same centrifugal forces affecting the rest of Ukrainian society. With the presence of large numbers of Russian officers, the army's loyalty to the new state and potential as a political player remain issues of serious concern to the Kiev government.

The Kravchuk administration attempted to Ukrainize the army by promoting ethnic Ukrainians and supporting the activities of the nationalist Union of Ukrainian Officers (UUO), which called for, among other things, a Ukrainian army with a strong preference given to ethnic Ukrainians for retention and promotions. This served to create tension among the many Russians within the officer corps. Some elements of the armed forces established close relationships with the extreme nationalist group UNA-UNSO, which tacitly supported Azerbaijan in its war with Armenia and assisted the government of Georgia in its effort to quell the rebellion in Abkhazia. Other factions joined assemblies of former Soviet officers calling for a common defense perimeter encompassing the former Soviet Union.

The chronic underfunding of the army prompted Kravchuk's second minister of defense, General Radetsky, to complain that two years after independence, the armed forces existed without a budget.[42] The collapse of financial support for the armed forces has resulted in several disturbing trends. These include an increase of crime within the army and of crimes committed by servicemen against civilians, the supply of weapons to criminals and paramilitary groups, and commercial speculation with military facilities and finances.[43]

The Ukrainian churches

The only Ukrainian independent institutions of any significance which might have become independent political players were the Greek Catholic Church, also known as the Uniate Church, centered in Lviv, and the Ukrainian Autocephalous Orthodox Church.

Greek Catholic Church. From the very start, the Greek Catholic Church, the embodiment of West Ukraine's distinct cultural heritage, saw as its function the defense of Ukrainian statehood. After the collapse of communism, it became embroiled in a battle with the Roman Catholic Church and the Ukrainian Autocephalous Church over properties in Western Ukraine and with the Vatican over the Pope's refusal to found new Greek Catholic parishes in central Ukraine. The Greek Catholic Church has come to rely increasingly on the state as its principal backer and refrains from any political activism which might have democratized Ukraine.

Ukrainian Autocephalous Orthodox Church. The sole body within Ukrainian Christian institutions with a strong democratic tradition is the Ukrainian Autocephalous Orthodox Church (UAOC), the leadership of which spent decades in exile. Perhaps because of its independent spirit and democratic values, President Kravchuk attempted to force a merger between the UAOC and the Ukrainian Orthodox Church-Kiev Patriarch (UOC-KP). The merger failed because of the Autocephalous disdain for Metropolitan Filaret, and the Ukrainian government responded by revoking the UAOC's registration. As a result, Ukraine lacks a national church to this day.

Ukrainian Orthodox Church. In summer 1995, nationalists attempted to use the Ukrainian Orthodox Church to confront the Russophone population when it tried to force the burial of Patriarch Volodymyr (Romaniuk) in St. Sophia Cathedral. The incident degenerated into violence, alienated most of the population, and succeeded in further eroding the possibility of the UOC becoming a building block of democracy and independence. The Orthodox Church might have had the potential to relieve the profound sense of anomie in Ukrainian society, but this would have meant freeing itself from its historical function as an agent of the state. The Orthodox church remains suspended between a discredited national church in Kiev and a denationalizing Russian Orthodox Church (ROC), which continues to perceive Ukrainian independence as a threat to the ROC's integrity as well as a canonal and historic anomaly. Many of the orthodox parishes in Ukraine have remained loyal to the ROC.

Ukrainian Orthodox Church-Kiev Patriarch. The attempt to establish an independent Ukrainian Orthodox Church met with near-failure. The Ukrainian Orthodox Church-Kiev Patriarch (UOC-KP), ostensibly established to uproot the Russian Orthodox Church, is seen as both autocratic and an agent of Moscow, and failed to establish itself as a credible democratic institution. President Kravchuk's support of Metropolitan Filaret to become the head of the Ukrainian Church guaranteed that the church would remain a state institution and a part of the existing power structure and extinguished any hope that a reinvigorated Ukrainian Church would become a force for democracy.[44] Filaret's decades as a KGB operative, along with his scandalous personal life, discredited the UOC-KP as either a spiritual or a democratic political institution.

The press

The predicament of the media reflects the state of viable political parties and the absence of economic pluralism in Ukraine. In a stable democracy, an effective media act as a restraint on the state, an unofficial fourth branch among those of the legislature, the executive, and the judiciary. While 46 percent of the media is owned by the state directly, the remaining 64 percent unfortunately remain highly dependent on the state for paper, access to printing presses, and financial support. President Kravchuk strengthened this dependency when he declared newsprint a strategic item which could not be privatized. While broad in its scope and diverse in points of view, the press suffers from financial poverty, small audiences and runs, and relatively low professional standards. Much of the Ukrainian media, both print and elec-tronic, continues to extol the virtues of Ukraine's independence and leadership in a sycophantic way reminiscent of the Soviet era, focusing on the President and his daily activities.[45]

Journalists who aggressively pursued investigative reporting were subject to searches and other forms of intimidation. On the other hand, acceptance of payment by journalists in exchange for favorable coverage is common-place. The author, in personal interviews with the managers of the indepen-dent news agency UNIAR and the editor of the independent journal *Politychna Dumka,* heard reports of harassment by tax authorities when politically sensitive issues appeared on their wire service or in their pages, respectively.

Government interference does not bear the sole blame for the slow development of an independent press. Two additional factors inhibit the Ukrainian press from being the public's watchdog. First, two-thirds of the country's press depends on regional power brokers. Thus, this segment of the press has little impact on national politics. Second, city dwellers tend to read publications originating in Russia. These readers, therefore, end up paying little attention to Ukrainian politics. A lukewarm public acceptance of the press has resulted, precluding its playing the vital role usually played by the press in a democratic society. This serves to curtail the power of the press and limits its political impact. The absence of a forceful independent press in Ukraine contributes to some of the arrogant and corrupt behavior of the nomenklatura. With the press cowed, the ruling elite feels immune and invulnerable. The elite knows that the press will not challenge its misconduct.

The 1994 parliamentary and presidential elections

In advance of the March 1994 elections, the Supreme Rada passed an electoral law that heavily favored incumbents and independents. Candidates

Table 8.6 *Results of the 1994 Ukrainian parliamentary elections and estimate of actual affiliations based on voting patterns of independents*

Left		Liberals		National Democrats		Radical Nationalists		Deputies with unconfirmed status	
Communist Party of Ukraine (CPU)	86	*Interregional Bloc for reforms:*		Ukrainian Republican Party (URP)	8	Congress of Ukrainian Nationalists (CUN)	5	*Interregional Bloc for reforms:*	
Socialist Party of Ukraine (SPU)	14	Labor Party of Ukraine (LPU)	4	Rukh	20	Ukrainian Conservative Republican Party (UCRP)	2	Party of Democratic Rebirth Ukraine (PDRU)	1
Peasant Party of Ukraine (PPU)	18	Social Democratic Party of Ukraine (SDPU)	1	Christian Democratic Party of Ukraine (CDPU)	1			Independents	170
		Unity Bloc:		Party of Democratic Rebirth of Ukraine (PDRU)	2				
		Civic Congress of Ukraine (CCU)	2	Democratic Party of Ukraine (DPU)	2				
		Party of Democratic Rebirth of Ukraine (PDRU)	1						
		Social Democratic Party of Ukraine (SDPU)	1						
Totals by official data	118 (34.9%)		9 (2.6%)		33 (9.7%)		7 (2%)		171 (50.2%)
Estimate of actual affiliations	147 (43.5%)		49 (14.5%)		80 (23.7%)		12 (3.5%)		48 (14.2%)

Source: Dominique Arel and Andrew Wilson, "The Ukrainian Parliamentary Elections," *RFE/RL Research Report* 3, no. 26 (July 1, 1994).

could be elected only after winning the support of a majority of at least 50 percent of registered voters in a given district. The electoral law also stated that candidates who failed to be elected in the first round had to win an outright majority of registered voters in the second round. The only other postcommunist states to adopt this hyper-majoritarian system have been in Central Asia.

To secure nomination, independent candidates need the support of only 300 citizens in a district, while candidates fielded by political parties have to receive the approval of both their national and their local organs. The registration of political parties requires permission from the Ministries of Justice, Economy, Foreign Economic Relations, and the Councils on Religion and Broadcasting, among others. Local authorities had to supervise and approve the nominating procedure of each party, and all registered groups had to keep the government appraised of their activities and open all of their meetings to the general public. They must be prepared to make all their documents and accounting books available to any government official. In Ukraine, this system has had two effects. First, it continued to retard the formation of political parties. Second, since local power brokers can easily get out the vote in the countryside, the system protects their own interests.

The results of the 1994 parliamentary elections contained only one major surprise – the poor showing of the Socialist Party of Ukraine (SPU). Founded by Oleksandr Moroz in late 1991 from the old CPU's rank and file, the SPU presented itself as the protector of the working man and deliberately avoided recruiting any leading figures from the old CPU. The strong pro-Russian position of the neo-communist SPU and its general disdain of Ukrainization manifested itself in calls for a federal Ukraine, legal status for the Russian language, and dual citizenship with the Russian Federation. Observers had expected that the SPU would do well. Instead a newly constituted Communist Party of Ukraine handily displaced Moroz's SPU and gave the Donbas considerable leverage in Ukrainian politics. While some analysts believe that the CPU owes its victory to a turnover in generations, Dominique Arel and Andrew Wilson attribute the victory of the new CPU to the social make-up of constituencies: "While the bulk of communist deputies come from the traditional triad of regional state officials, factory directors, and collective farm chairmen, most socialist deputies belong to what could be called the technical intelligentsia (people with advanced education not occupying leading administrative posts)."[46]

Still, the structure of the elections had assured that the "rentier capitalist – nomenklatura," often referred to by the public as the *partiya vlady* (party of power), remained in control. The largest bloc of votes went to independent candidates from whom the party of power draws its members.

Table 8.7 *Political parties with parliamentary representation in Ukraine after the elections of 1994*

Party/leader/membership	Platform/constituency
Christian Democratic Party of Ukraine (CDPU) Volodymyr Zhuravskyi (130,095)	Liberal reform & market economy Russian speakers from the Orthodox east
Civic Congress of Ukraine (CCU) Oleksander Bazyliuk (2,100)	Federalism; close links to Russia; opposition to market reforms Donetsk region
Communist Party of Ukraine (CPU) Petro Symonenko (122,560)	Anti-market; anti-nationalist; favors confederation w/ Russia Eastern & Southern Ukraine
Congress of Ukrainian Nationalists (CUN) Slava Stetsko (umbrella organization, no direct membership)	Ethnic nationalism; withdrawal from the CIS; pro-market reforms Lviv region, Donetsk
Democratic Party of Ukraine (DPU) Volodymyr Yavorivskyi (5,000)	Democratic nationalist party; against CIS membership Nationalist Ukrainian intelligentsia
Interregional Bloc for Reform (IBR) Leonid Kuchma/Volodymyr Hrynov (umbrella organization, no direct membership)	Advocates policies in support of Ukrainian heritage; more power to the regions; strategic alliance with Russia; controlled reform Eastern and Central Ukraine
Labor Party of Ukraine (LPU) Valentyn Landyk (n.a.)	Close links to Russia; several official languages; "state-regulated economic stabilization" East Ukrainian managers
Party of Democratic Rebirth of Ukraine (PDRU) Volodymyr Filenko (3,000)	Pro-market, social democracy Zaporizhzhia
Peasant Party of Ukraine (PtPU) Serhii Dovhan (65,970)	Support for agriculture Kolhosp chairmen
Rukh Viacheslav Chornovil (50,518)	Increasingly drifting toward nationalism; market reforms with territorial nationalism Kiev region & Western Ukraine
Social Democratic Party of Ukraine (SDPU) Yurii Zbitniev (1,300)	German-style social democracy
Socialist Party of Ukraine (SPU) Oleksandr Moroz (29,000)	Opposes nationalism & capitalism; favors "socially just privatization" and close links to CIS

Table 8.7 (cont.) *Political parties with parliamentary representation in Ukraine after the elections of 1994*

Party/leader/membership	Platform/constituency
Ukrainian Conservative Republican Party (UCRP) Stepan Khmara (1,000)	Nationalism; nuclear weapons; advocacy of Ukrainian rights outside Ukraine Lviv
Ukrainian National Assembly (UNA) Dmytro Korchynskyi (14,000)	Extreme nationalism; anti-capitalism Western Ukraine, Donbas
Ukrainian Republican Party (URP) Mykhailo Horyn (13,000)	Nationalism, ethnic tolerance; strong defense; unitary, presidential republic; supports "society of property owners", opposes "socially unjust privatization"

Sources: Alexander Ott, *Die politischen Parteien in der Ukraine* (Berichte des Bundesinstituts für ostwissenschaftliche und internationale Studien, January 1995); *The Europa World Year Book 1995*, vol. II (London: Europa Publications, 1995).

Many urban centers, especially Kiev, where a challenge to the party of power could have materialized, failed to meet the hyper-majoritarian requirements. The party of power could be pleased with the results. Even after some dozen runoff elections, the Kiev delegation to the Supreme Rada remains incomplete two years after the initial vote.

The March 1994 elections, held against the backdrop of the disappearance of Rukh political activist Mykhailo Boichyshyn in January 1994, deepened the sense of political nihilism across Ukraine. No political party enjoys widespread support among all Ukrainians (see table 8.7). Only 5.1 percent of the population professes any party affiliation, while only 6 percent believe that parties provide support for the people.

The presidential elections that followed in June and July 1994 relied on a similar majoritarian approach. Leonid Kravchuk, counting on growing popular apathy, banked on a low turnout during the first round which would enable him to annul the elections altogether. The electorate surprised both him and observers with a heavy turnout in the first round. In the runoff, Kuchma, running on a platform of closer links to Russia against Kravchuk's nationalist appeals, captured east Ukraine's demographic weight and unseated Kravchuk. With Kuchma's victory, Ukraine passed a crucial test of democracy. The so-called gray fox actually lost, and for the first time in Ukraine's history, a Ukrainian president left office as the result of the electoral process. Nonetheless, the contest between Kravchuk and Kuchma still represented an intra-clan feud within the party of power and not a contest between two political visions.

Table 8.8 *Presidential elections in Ukraine, 1994*

Candidate	Votes	% votes
First ballot:		
Leonid M. Kravchuk	9,997,766	37.68
Leonid D. Kuchma	8,274,806	31.25
Oleksandr O. Moroz	3,466,451	13.99
Volodymyr T. Lanovyi	2,483,986	9.38
Valerii H. Babych	644,236	2.43
Ivan S. Pliushch	321,686	1.22
Petro M. Talanchuk	143,361	0.54
Second ballot:		
Leonid D. Kuchma	14,017,684	52.14
Leonid M. Kravchuk	12,112,442	45.06

Source: *The Europa World Year Book 1995*, vol. II (London: Europa Publications, 1995), p. 3,104.

Ukraine under Kuchma

Unlike President Kravchuk, President Kuchma stressed the importance of economic recovery rather than state-building as the national priority. Kuchma, however, has thus far failed to introduce any fundamental economic reforms that would weaken, let alone break, the power of the nomenklatura. Although the budget deficit was trimmed, the policy of easy credit to politically reliable cronies continues. Ukrainian privatization has also failed to pick up significantly under Kuchma. Since 1994, the Supreme Rada repeatedly sought to limit privatization by classifying large groups of enterprises as objects of "national strategic importance" which cannot be privatized. In October 1995, Prime Minister Yevhen Marchuk declared that privatization is not "an end unto itself." While Ukraine has tamed inflation and made progress in carrying out small scale privatization, it remains one of the least free economies in the world. *The 1996 Index of Economic Freedom*, published by the Heritage Foundation, gave Ukraine a 4.0 on a scale of 1 (fully free) to 5 (repressive), placing it 126th in the world. Of the postcommunist states, only Azerbaijan did worse, coming in at 134th place.[47]

On the world stage, Kuchma has transformed Ukraine from an isolated quasi-rogue state to an important partner of the United States. The election of Kuchma has ushered in changes in Ukraine's relationship with Russia. START I and the NPT were ratified, and the Ukrainian government cut its budget deficits in exchange for aid from the United States and multinational organizations. Ukraine has become the third largest recipient of US foreign assistance, providing Kiev with the means to contain inflation and stabilize its currency without destabilizing the country.

President Kuchma has also tried to de-politicize the army and even appointed a civilian defense minister, an unprecedented move among the NIS. Fearing that the policy of his predecessor would lead to schisms in the army, President Kuchma curtailed the activities of the UUO, and the role of extreme-nationalist and pro-Russian elements within the armed forces has diminished recently. In February 1996, however, President Kuchma found it necessary to dismiss the chief of staff, General Anatolii Lopata, following the general's criticism of the government's defense policies.

The commercial activity of the armed forces also continues to grow. In the wake of reports of the Ukrainian army leasing military cargo planes to Colombian drug lords and exporting increasing amounts of sophisticated arms, apparently without any public discussion or political supervision, it appears that the military's commercial role is getting out of hand.[48] Although Ukraine's armed forces may not still pose a threat to the country's political leadership, the emergence of the army as an independent, unaccountable economic actor will make the transformation to a society based on the rule of law more difficult.

The situation of the media under Kuchma has not improved greatly, if at all. Recent restrictions on broadcasts from the Russian Federation and the canceling of an independently produced news program *Pisliamova* (Epilogue) are recent indications of a relapse into Soviet-style journalism and media policy.[49] President Kuchma has also exempted the state-owned press from the high value-added tax.

Independent trade unions, which in Poland especially played a key role in mass mobilization, remain in their infancy in Ukraine. As in the rest of the CIS, Soviet era trade unions, an integral part of the totalitarian power structure, did not succeed in transforming themselves into modern unions. With assistance from abroad, especially from the United States' AFL-CIO, independent trade unions have emerged; however, their impact on Ukrainian politics remains marginal. They are incapable of playing a major political role.

A stable, democratic society can boast vibrant and responsive links between the state and its citizens formed on the basis of voluntary formal and informal association. The most common and obvious examples of civil society are political parties. Parties, in the Western sense of the word, should mediate between the citizen and the state. As previously noted, Ukraine as yet has failed to develop mass political parties. It should be stressed that the parties that do exist lean towards regionalism, which consequently contributes to political polarization and the alienation of citizens.

In January 1991, 44 percent did not belong to any voluntary organization. By June 1993, the number had climbed to 86 percent.[50] The above figures may well exaggerate the decline, since prior to the collapse of the USSR, participation in many so-called voluntary organizations was quasi-compulsory. Nevertheless, the decline in the Ukrainian population's participation in public life is a visible political reality. Although Ukraine has been slow to develop a foundation for the emergence of a democratic civil society, the country does have different institutional actors which effect Ukraine's political development.

Ukraine's struggle for a constitution

Debates over a new Ukrainian constitution go back as far as 1990. After independence the struggle continued without any resolution. Just as Ukraine's elite prevented the reform of the economy and the liberation of the press, legal reforms were also slow and inconsistent. The old Brezhnev era constitution, never intended to be the basic law of a sovereign, democratic state, remained in place. Even with dozens of amendments, it failed to define either the separation of powers between the legislature and the executive branches or their responsibilities. In theory, this constitution vested most powers in the legislature, which was merely window dressing for the communist party apparatus.

Although disputes between the executive and the legislative did arise, given the nationalists' aversion to rocking the boat and the communists' preference for a weak executive, constitutional disputes did not at first provoke crises. Ukraine's position became particularly unfortunate and embarrassing, as it was soon the last of the Soviet successor states without a modern, or at least a post-Soviet, constitution. This relatively peaceful situation could not last indefinitely. As the economy continued to crumble, the legislature and the executive sought to pin the blame on one another and invest or win for themselves special powers.

Because the president and the Supreme Rada remain deadlocked over nominations, Ukraine failed to establish an independent judiciary and a functioning supreme court. Against this background of legal twilight, continued bickering among the elite and brazen corruption has deepened the sense of political alienation in the population.

Instability resulting from the lack of clear definitions of responsibilities between the legislature and the executive hampered President Kuchma's efforts to reform the economy. In the face of deepening political gridlock, in May 1995, President Kuchma threatened to call a referendum in order to force the issue of a constitution, bypassing the legislature altogether in the process. Kuchma's threat led to a constitutional crisis which was settled by an accord with the Supreme Rada. This agreement significantly broadened the powers of the President, granting him the power to nominate and dismiss the prime minister, as well as members of the cabinet, manage state properties, chair the national security council, and call referenda.

The special powers given the president did reduce the governmental paralysis, but the constitutional agreement left key issues essential for a modern democracy unresolved. Although the constitutional agreement mentioned the legality of "national, municipal, and private property," the exact meaning of these rights was not defined. This lack of clarity continued to block privatization and discouraged foreign investment. More importantly, the constitutional agreement failed to produce a functioning judiciary. Similarly, the Stalinist institution of the procurator was retained, but no mechanism to adjudicate disputes between the legislative and executive was established. Under the terms of the constitutional agreement, the executive and the legislature had to adopt a new constitution by June 1996. Since constitutional change would mean a reduction in the legislature's power in favor of the executive, the Supreme Rada kept up its resistance to change.

Finally, President Kuchma declared that the absence of a constitution posed a threat to the country's national security, implying that he might introduce emergency rule. The Supreme Rada retreated and in an all-night session, passed a constitution, article by article, on June 28, 1996. Although the passage of the constitution appears a personal victory for Mr. Kuchma, some key provisions will not become effective for several years to come. As a result, the full impact of the new document will not be seen for several years. At this writing, no official version of the constitution has been published, however a broad outline has emerged.

Ukraine will be governed by a three-branch government consisting of a single chamber legislative (Supreme Rada), an executive (President), and an eighteen-member Supreme Court. Although the ability of Ukraine to adopt a constitution without the violence that took place in Russia may well point up the peaceful disposition of the Ukrainian polity, preliminary reading of the published unofficial versions of the constitution indicate that key problems may not be fully resolved by the new document.

Although the legislature alone has the right to pass laws, the President's special power to issue decrees has been extended for three years. The constitution allows for the establishment of a normal judiciary system, but the procurator will continue to function for at least one year. While the constitution forbids foreign bases on Ukrainian soil; however, this article will not become effective for twenty years. On the vital issue of property rights, the Constitution, in deference to the communists, guarantees "the rights of all subjects in their rights to property and the use of property, and the rights to own land . . ."[51] The term "private property" appears to be omitted, however, leaving the issue of property rights not clearly settled. On the potentially divisive issue of language, the constitution recognizes Ukrainian as the sole official language but also makes provision to protect and nourish the Russian language as well. Although the constitution presents several potentially difficult and potentially paralyzing dilemmas, perhaps the most complicated problem facing Ukraine is one of implementation. Much like the economic reform, Ukrainian legislators agreed to institute the constitutional reform in a gradual fashion.

Serhii Holovatyi, Ukraine's capable and liberal justice minster, noted that the passage of the constitution was a major achievement for the country, but added, "As a citizen, I do not feel that democracy has finally been established in Ukraine." For Ukraine to become a real democracy, Holovatyi observed, it will have to undergo a major administrative and judicial reform,[52] a process which is far from certain. At this moment, the state alone has neither the means nor the tools to build a democratic civil society, a situation which allows other political actors to play a role unknown in scope among established democracies.[53]

Public opinion

Popular enthusiasm for moderate nationalism began to wane when Ukrainian independence failed to usher in economic wealth and brought with it instead a profound decline in the standard of living. Democracy and independence are becoming increasingly associated with economic decline.

An overwhelming Ukrainian majority feels that the country is moving in the wrong direction. When asked whether they can affect government decisions, 70 percent answered almost never, 15 percent answered "some of the time," and only 9 percent replied "always/mostly."

The Ukrainian people not only feel they have little to no effect on the actions of their government, they also have a very low level of confidence in the state's institutions. Fifty-three percent claim to have no confidence in the Supreme Rada, 66 percent in the judicial system, and 59 percent in the civil service.

The economic decline and simultaneous radicalization that has occurred on the political right also took place on the political left. Despite the trauma of Stalinism, when Ukrainians were asked whether they would be willing to trade their freedom for economic security, 22 percent strongly agreed, 19 percent somewhat agreed, 21 percent somewhat disagreed, and only 19 percent strongly disagreed.[54] In a 1993 survey, 79 percent of respondents felt that the most important value is equality of all citizens before the law and

Table 8.9 *Public views of the overall trend in Ukraine (% of adult population)*

Date	Right direction	Wrong direction
January 1992	43	35
October 1992	17	52
September 1993	7	78
October 1994	12	72

Source: "Public Opinion in Ukraine, 1992 to 1994," USIA Research Report, Washington, DC, March 1995.

70 percent felt that Ukraine must be a democratic state,[55] yet 58 percent of respondents to another poll one year later professed no interest in who is in power "so long as everything in all right."[56]

Ukraine's greatest asset in democratization may be its patient and tolerant people. Its people, despite Ukraine's bloody and tragic history, have thus far avoided embracing intolerant integral nationalism. In nationwide opinion polls, Ukrainians have consistently indicated a remarkable commitment to tolerance and freedom. A poll published by USIA in February 1995 revealed that 87 percent considered religious freedom important, and 83 percent supported the protection of ethnic minorities. Seventy-five percent viewed an uncensored press as vital.[57]

This stands in marked contrast to ugly events of Ukrainian history. During the late nineteenth and the first half of the twentieth centuries, Ukraine was the scene of numerous pogroms, leaving thousands dead and entire communities destroyed and dispossessed. Although popular belief holds that these pogroms reflected an instinctive intolerance on the part of the Ukrainians, such views are simplistic and inaccurate. For example, although the pogroms of the Civil War period were indeed savage, unlike the pogroms in Tsarist Russia, or the anti-semitic policies in interwar Central Europe, Ukrainian anti-Jewish violence lacked an ideology.[58] Ukrainian pogroms may best be typified by those committed by the anarchist Nestor Makhno, who led gangs of dissatisfied peasants in raids against so-called exploitation.

Another exception is the case of Galicia in the 1930s and 1940s. The Ukrainian population did adopt a racist and fascist integral nationalism (prevalent in much of interwar Central Europe). During World War II, adherents to this ideology participated in the German *Einsatzgruppen*, which conducted mass shootings of Jews in Eastern Poland and the Soviet Union, and, later, during the partisan war against both the Germans and the Soviets,

Table 8.10 *Public views of the influence of the Mafia in Ukraine (percent)*

Degree of influence	On government	On economy	On banking
A great deal	60	75	70
Fair amount	23	13	14
Little/none	5	2	3

Note: 77 percent of those polled believe that privatization has mainly benefited the Mafia.

Source: "In Ukraine, 'Mafia' Seen Active in Politics, Economics, Banking; Suspicion Limiting Support for Reforms," *Opinion Analysis*, US Information Agency, Washington, DC, January 4, 1995.

took part in ethnic cleansing of Poles in Western Ukraine.[59] Even in Galacia, however, prominent members of the Ukrainian community, most notably Greek Catholic Metropolitan Andrii Sheptytskyi, challenged extreme integral nationalist views and sheltered Jews during the German occupation. In the rest of Ukraine, the integralist ideology, to the dismay of its proponents, fell mostly on deaf ears and won over few supporters.[60] Across much of Soviet Ukraine, collaboration with the Germans was driven by the desire to decollectivize agriculture and establish a desirable concept of justice in the countryside, rather than the founding of an ethnically pure state.[61]

The desire for a strong, even if undemocratic, government could rise again. Many Ukrainians feel that Ukraine has fallen victim to organized crime. A public opinion poll published in January 1995 revealed just how strong that belief is.

Yet despite bitter disappointment in the country's economic performance, the plummeting trust that most Ukrainians have in their political leaders and institutions,[62] and declining support for independence, the Ukrainian people remain committed to democracy. As James Gibson demonstrated in a study going back to 1992, between two-thirds and three-fourths of the Ukrainian people favor democracy.[63] This finding was affirmed in a 1995 USIA study.[64] However, given the fact that 99 percent of the population identify the economy as the country's most pressing issue[65] and the widespread disdain toward political parties, politics, and politicians, the elite's incentive to bring about democratization remains weak. It is clear that the establishment of democracy, let alone its consolidation, is far from complete. If the Ukrainian economy continues to decline, the signs of a "rollback" of democracy must be taken seriously.

Conclusion

Ukraine's difficulties with democratic transformation have led to a radicalization of Ukrainian politics and a nostalgia for authoritarianism. The initial transformation of the left occurred during the 1994 elections when the electorate in Eastern Ukraine abandoned the Socialist Party and turned to the Communist Party. However, the communist goal of a return to Russia has been stymied by the unwillingness of the Russian elite to take on responsibility for the Ukrainian economy and resume transfers to Ukraine. Furthermore, the continuing war in Chechnya has dampened Ukrainian enthusiasm for a new union with Russia. The electoral defeat in Russia of the communist Gennadii Zyuganov with his promise to recreate the Soviet Union, sharply curtailed the Ukrainian communists' options. The economic failure of Ukrainian independence has made a profound impression on Ukraine's political landscape. Both the integral nationalist right and the Stalinist left remain small, yet vocal, fringes on the political scene. While there is no visible external threat to the country's security, there are some indications that internal stability may be in jeopardy.

Volodymyr Polokhalo, editor-in-chief of the Kiev-based journal *Politychna Dumka*, has observed that for the elite, Ukraine's independence was "a relatively painless, even organic, transition from a totalitarian communist nomenklatura to a neo-totalitarian postcommunist nomenklatura . . . Therefore, it is primarily the nomenklatura – and not the numerous social subjects of political life that the nomenklatura discriminated against – that received independence, as well as social and political *carte blanche*."[66] Polokhalo warns: "[The] low intellectual and cultural level of the current postcommunist nomenklatura (at all levels) and its current lack of professionalism and efficiency will diminish its capability for social and political maneuvering as well as its legitimacy. At the same time, it deepens the current alienation of political power from the majority of the population."[67] Given the growing discontent in Ukraine, Polokhalo fears that it is only a matter of time before a social explosion results in "violence against the majority of the population." The most serious obstacle to Ukraine's successful economic transformation and democratization remains the well-entrenched nomenklatura which derived enormous benefits from the economic distortions and political paralysis during the first five years of independence. However, it may happen that at some point, the nomenklatura itself will discover that the current situation is untenable and, now that they have already seized much of the country's wealth, they would actually stand to benefit from a reformed economy.

Ukraine, despite its seemingly endless economic and political crises, continues to be one of the most tolerant and violence-free societies within the

CIS. However, there are several disturbing signs that might tarnish President Kuchma's credentials as a committed reformer. Some view President Kuchma's decision to place 30,000 soldiers under his command as the first step towards the creation of a praetorian guard. It may be an exaggeration to say that Ukraine is on the verge of a return to dictatorship. Ukraine is not a police state and, indeed, remains one of the most peaceful, tolerant societies in the post-Soviet world.

During the last two years, President Kuchma has managed to create in Ukraine many of the vital ingredients for an economic rebound which would certainly help it reinforce its democracy and independence. Ukraine's small-scale privatization, however imperfect and corrupt, will, as in Russia and Central Europe, contribute to the rise of a middle class, a crucial element to any enduring democracy. The new constitution, while an imperfect document with many areas of potential deadlock and unclarity, is clearly a major step forward in Ukraine's transformation from a backwater Soviet province to a modern state. External developments, such as Yeltsin's re-election in Russia and the emergence of a US – Ukrainian partnership, help to create a climate conducive to foreign investment which will help to refloat Ukraine's economy. Finally, Ukraine's ability to resolve its internal quarrels peacefully is bound to raise the level of confidence of foreign, as well as domestic, investors who thus far either avoided the country or actually contributed to its capital flight.

All these positive omens provide Ukraine with no more than a window of opportunity between now and the end of President Kuchma's term of office in 1999. President Kuchma, the only Ukrainian politician who still commands the trust of a majority of his countrymen (54 percent), currently has the means to break with the past and transform the country's economy, enabling Ukraine to join the emerging markets of Central Europe and parts of Russia. Should President Kuchma succeed in reforming the economy and reigning in rampant corruption, Ukraine could become a thriving country and an integral part of a peaceful and stable Europe.

The failure to modernize Ukraine's economy and halt its decline will most likely threaten both Ukraine's democracy and its independence. The continuing impoverishment of the country could give credence to what the UNA-UNSO calls for: a right-wing, hyper-nationalist, and authoritarian solution and clashes within Ukraine as well as with Poland and Russia. Simultaneously, the communist left will call for an internationalist solution and a return to Russia. Either of the above scenarios will bring calamity to Ukraine, Europe, and the world.

President Kuchma and the Ukrainian people have thus far demonstrated an uncanny patience and creativity in avoiding numerous pitfalls in their quest to return to civilization. They could well seize the current opening afforded them and succeed where, following the collapse of the Tsarist empire, Hrushevskyi and the co-founders of a previous Ukrainian state failed.

Acronyms and political parties

CDPU   Christian Democratic Party of Ukraine (Khrystiiansko–demokratychna partiia Ukrainy – KhDPU)

CCU   Civic Congress of Ukraine (Grazhdanskii kongress Ukrainy)

CPC   Communist Party of Crimea (Kommunisticheskaia partiia Kryma – KPK)

CPU   Communist Party of Ukraine (Komunistychna partiia Ukrainy – KPU)

CNDF   Congress of National Democratic Forces (Kongres natsionalno–demokratychnykh syl – KNDS)

CUN   Congress of Ukrainian Nationalists (Kongres Ukrainskykh natsionalistiv – KUN)

DMD   Democratic Movement of Donbas (Demokraticheskoe dvizheniia Donbassa – DDD)

DPU   Democratic Party of Ukraine (Demokratychna partiia Ukrainy – DPU)

GPU   Green Party of Ukraine (Partiia zelenykh Ukrainy – PZU)

IBR   Interregional Bloc for Reform (Mizhrehionalnyi blok reformiv – MBR)

LCU   Labor Congress of Ukraine (Trudova kongres Ukrainy – TKU)

LPU   Labor Party of Ukraine (Partiia truda Ukrainy – PTU)

LDPU   Liberal Democratic Party of Ukraine (Liberalno–demokratychna partiia Ukrainy – LDPU)

LibPU   Liberal Party of Ukraine (Liberalna partiia Ukrainy – LibPU)

NMCT   National Movement of the Crimean Tatars (Natsionalnyi dvizheniia Krymskikh Tatar – NDKT)

NU   New Ukraine (Nova Ukraina)

NW   New Wave (Nova khvylia)

OUNvU   Organization of Ukrainian Nationalists in Ukraine (Orhanizatsiia Ukrainskykh natsionalistiv v Ukraini – OUNvU)

PCAU   Party of Civic Accord of Ukraine

PDRU   Party of Democratic Rebirth of Ukraine (Partiia demokratychna vidrodzhennia Ukrainy – PDVU)

PPU   People's Party of Ukraine (Narodna partiia Ukrainy – NPU)

PtPU   Peasant Party of Ukraine (Selianska partiia Ukrainy – SelPU)

Rukh   Rukh (formerly the Ukrainian Popular Movement for Restructuring)

SDPU   Social Democratic Party of Ukraine (Sotsial–demokratychna partiia
        Ukrainy – SDPU)

SNPU   Social National Party of Ukraine (Sotsial–natsionalna partiia Ukrainy –
        SNPU)

SPU   Socialist Party of Ukraine (Sotsialistychna partiia Ukrainy – SocPU)

SIU   Statehood and Independence for Ukraine (Derzhavna samostiinist
        Ukrainy – DSU)

UCDP   Ukrainian Christian Democratic Party (Ukrainska khrystiiansko–demo-
        kratychna partiia – UKhDP)

UCRP   Ukrainian Conservative Republican Party (Ukrainska konservatyvna
        respublikanska partiia – UKRP)

UNA   Ukrainian National Assembly (Ukrainska natsionalna assembleia – UNA)

URP   Ukrainian Republican Party (Ukrainska respublikanska partiia – URP)

Source: Andrew Wilson, "Ukraine," in *Political Parties of Eastern Europe, Russia
and the Successor States*, ed. Bogdan Szajkowski (Essex: Longman, 1994).

NOTES

1 See Roman Szporluk, "Urbanization in Ukraine Since the Second World War,"
   in *Rethinking Ukrainian History*, ed. Ivan L. Rudnytsky (Edmonton: Canadian
   Institute of Ukrainian Studies, 1981).
2 For a summary of Huntington's thesis, see Samuel P. Huntington, "Democracy's
   Third Wave," *Journal of Democracy* 2, no. 2 (Spring 1991).
3 The *szlachta* was the Polish gentry class which accounted for about 9 percent of
   Poland's population. From medieval times it enjoyed full political freedom.
   Although the influence of the *szlachta* declined after the collapse of the 1863
   uprising, the social and political values of the *szlachta* were substantially adopted
   by Poland's educated class by the mid-nineteenth century.
4 Ivan L. Rudnytsky, "The Role of Ukraine in Modern History," *Slavic Review* 22,
   no. 2 (June 1963).
5 Mykola Rabchuk, "Between Civil Society and the New Etatism: Democracy in
   the Making and State Building in Ukraine," in *Envisioning Eastern Europe*, ed.
   Michael Kennedy (Ann Arbor, MI: University of Michigan Press, 1995), p. 127.
6 See Serge Cipko, "The Second Revival: Ukrainian Minority as an Emerging
   Factor in Eurasian Politics," unpublished paper presented at the Harriman
   Institute, Columbia University, September 1995.
7 V. Tkachenko and O. Rient, *Ukraina: Na Mekhi Tsivilizatsii* (Kiev: Institut Istorii
   Ukrainy, 1995); also Andrii Derkatch, Sergei Veretennikov, and Andrei
   Yarmolaev, *Beskonechno dliashchecia nastoiashchee Ukraina: chetyre goda puti*
   (Kiev: Libid', 1995), p. 13.
8 See George S. N. Luckyj, *The Young Ukraine: The Brotherhood of Saints Cyril
   and Methodius, 1845-1847* (Ottawa & Paris: University of Ottawa Press, 1991);

also Basil Dmytryshyn, *Imperial Russia: A Source Book* (Orlando: Harcourt Brace & Jovanovich, 1990).

9 Dmytro Doroshenko, "The Survey of Ukrainian Historiography," *The Annals of the Ukrainian Academy of Arts and Science in the United States* 5-6, no. 4 (1957), 270.

10 Robert Conquest, *The Harvest of Sorrow: Soviet Collectivization and Terror Famine* (New York: Oxford University Press, 1986).

11 According to a 1995 public opinion poll, 89.6 percent of the respondents believed that government should guarantee employment. See Volodymyr Zviglyanich, "Public Perceptions of Reform," *Transition* 1, no. 13 (28 July 1995), 36.

12 Alexander J. Motyl, *The Turn to the Right: The Ideological Origins and Development of Ukrainian Nationalism, 1919-1929* (New York: East European Monographs, 1980).

13 See John A. Armstrong, *Ukrainian Nationalism*, 3d ed. (Englewood, CO: Ukrainian Academic Press, 1993).

14 Levko Lukianenko, a dissident from the Soviet era who spent nearly twenty-four years in Soviet labor camps, supported legislation for a mandatory seven-year prison term for anyone questioning Ukraine's current frontiers.

15 US State Department, "Ukraine Human Rights Practice."

16 See D. Shakhai, "Our Tactics with Regard to the Russian People," in *Political Thought of the Ukrainian Underground, 1943-1951*, ed. Peter J. Potichnyj and Yevhen Shtendera (Edmonton, Alberta: Canadian Institute of Ukrainian Studies, University of Alberta, 1986); also Mykhailo Dobriansk'yi, *Ukraïna i Rosiia* (Lviv, Krakow and Paris: Prosvita, 1993).

17 See Taras Kuzio and Andrew Wilson, *Ukraine: Perestroika to Independence* (New York: St. Martin's Press, 1994), p. 51.

18 See Jaroslaw Bilocerkowycz, *Soviet Ukrainian Dissent: A Study in Alienation* (Boulder, CO: Westview Press, 1988).

19 See Ivan L. Rudnytsky, "The Political Thought of Soviet Ukrainian Dissidents," in *Essays in Modern Ukrainian History*, ed. Ivan L. Rudnytsky (Edmonton, Alberta: Canadian Institute of Ukrainian Studies, University of Alberta, 1987); "Declaration of Principles of the Ukrainian Helsinki Union – 7 July 1988," in *Perestroika in the Soviet Union: Documents on the National Question*, ed. Charles F. Furtado, Jr., and Andrea Chandler (Boulder, CO: Westview Press, 1992), p. 221.

20 Although during most of the Brezhnev era there was anxiety about declining investments in the Donbas coal fields, it is noteworthy that in reality subsidies to the Donbas went unabated, leaving Ukraine's 1.2 million miners producing less coal than Russia's 800,000.

21 Alexander J. Motyl, *Dilemmas of Independence: Ukraine After Totalitarianism* (New York: Council on Foreign Relations Press, 1993), p. 163.

22 Kuzio and Wilson, *Ukraine: Perestroika to Independence*, p. 81.

23 Draft Program of the People's Movement of Ukraine for Restructuring (Rukh), February 1989.

24 See E. Mikhailovskaia, *Ukraina: Politicheskiye partii i organizatsii* (Moscow: Panorama, 1992), p. 56.

25 See Julian Birch, "The Nature and Sources of Dissidence in Ukraine," in *Ukraine in the Seventies*, ed. Peter J. Potichnyj (Oakville, Ontario: Mosaic Press, 1974).

26 Its official "Concept of State Building," published at its Fourth Congress in December 1992, declared Ukraine a "national state" along with special rights for Ukrainians living outside Ukraine. "The IV All-Ukrainian Congress of the Popular Movement Rukh" (Kiev, 4-6 December 1992).

27 Kuzio and Wilson, *Ukraine: Perestroika to Independence*, p. 150.

28 *Nations in Transit: Civil Society, Democracy and Markets in East Central Europe and the Newly Independent States* (New York: Freedom House, 1995), p. 139.

29 It may well be that Ukraine's state of political atomization is most succinctly reflected in the Ukrainian folk expression: "Moia khata s kraiu nicheho ne zanaiu" [My home is on the outskirts, I do not know a thing].

30 Kuzio and Wilson, *Ukraine: Perestroika to Independence,* p. 203.

31 Motyl, *Dilemmas of Independence*, p. 49.

32 Oleh Bilyi, "Nihilism and Political Phantoms of the Post Communist Period," *Political Thought* 5 (Kiev) (1994), 114-15.

33 Viktor Stepanenko, "Ukrainian Independence: First Results and Lessons," *The Ukrainian Review* 40 (Summer 1993), 40.

34 *Pravda Ukrainiy,* 5 June 1992.

35 Roman Solchanyk, "Ukraine: A Year of Transition," *RFE/RL Research Report* 2, no. 2 (1 January 1993).

36 After the short tenure of Valentyn Symoneneko as prime minister.

37 In late 1992, Ukraine was still paying only 10-20 percent of the world energy prices levels. See Oleh Havrylyshyn, "Ukraine's Economic Crisis and Western Economic Assistance," *Political Thought* (Kiev) 3 (1993), 163.

38 "Where the Oil River Flows," *Delovoi mir*, no. 9, p. 4.

39 *Izvestia*, 15 May 1993.

40 See F. Sizy, *Komsomolskaia Pravda,* 15 January 1995.

41 Havrylyshyn, "Ukraine's Economic Crisis," p. 163.

42 See John Jaworsky, *Ukraine: Stability and Instability*, Institute of National Strategic Studies, National Defense University, Washington, DC, McNair Paper 42, August 1995, p. 59.

43 Oleg Strekal, *The Ukrainian Military: Instruments of Defense or Domestic Challenge?* Institute for National Security Studies, US Air Force Academy, Colorado, November 1994, p. 28.

44 See Bohdan Bociurkiw, "Orthodox and Catholics in Ukraine," in *The Politics of Religion in Russia and the New States of Eurasia*, ed. Michael Bourdeaux (Armonk, NY: M. E. Sharpe, 1995).

45 Chrystyna Lapychak, "Media Independence Is Still Alien to Ukraine's Political Culture," *Transition*, 18 October 1995.

46 Dominique Arel and Andrew Wilson, "The Ukrainian Parliamentary Elections," *RFE/RL Research Report*, 1 July 1994, p. 13-14.

47 Bryan T. Johnson and Thomas P. Sheehey, *1996 Index of Economic Freedom* (Washington, DC: The Heritage Foundation, 1996).

48 "Ukraine Exporting Millions' Worth of Advanced Weapons," *New Europe*, 12-18 May 1996, p. 11.

49 Matthew Kaminski, "Ukraine's Old Guard Kills off TV News," *Financial Times*, 15 February 1996.

50 I.E. Bekeshkina, *Konfliktolochinyi pidkhid do suchasnoi sytatsii v Ukraini* (Kiev: Arbys, 1994), p. 35 quoted in Jaworsky, *Ukraine: Stability and Instability*.

51 UNIAN (Kiev), 27 June 1996.
52 UNIAN, 2 July 1996.
53 US State Department, "Ukraine Human Rights Practice."
54 See, *Benchmark in Democracy Building: Public Opinion and Global Democratization, A Case Study of Four Countries: Ukraine Romania, Panama and El Salvador*, Report R-2-95 (Washington, DC: US Agency for International Development, 1995), pp. 7, 11, 12.
55 Iu. N. Pakhomonov and E.I. Golovakha, *Politicheskaia Kul'tura Naseleniia Ukrainy* (Kiev: Nukova Dumka, 1993), p. 9.
56 Evhen I. Golovakha and Nataliya Panina, "The Development of a Democratic Political Identity in Contemporary Ukrainian Political Culture," in *Nationalism, Ethnicity and Identity: Cross National and Comparative Perspectives*, ed. Russell F. Farnen (New Brunswick and London: Transaction Publishers, 1994), p. 405.
57 Ibid.
58 Henry Abramson, "The Scattering of Amalek: A Model for Understanding the Ukrainian–Jewish Conflict," *East European Jewish Affairs* 24, no. 1 (1994), 39–47.
59 Armstrong, *Ukrainian Nationalism*.
60 Ibid.
61 Note that although the German-sponsored military unit "SS Halychyna" did fight alongside the German Wehrmacht, it was cleared of any participation in war crimes (that is, the liquidation of the Jews) by the Canadian Commission of Enquiry on War Crimes. See *Deschenes Commission Report* (Canadian Communication Group, 1986), pp. 2-57.
62 See Zenovia A. Sochor, "Political Culture and Foreign Policy: Elections in Ukraine, 1994," in *Political Culture and Civil Society in Russia and the New States of Eurasia*, ed. Vladimir Tismaneanu (Armonk, NY: M. E. Sharpe, 1995), p. 214.
63 James Gibson, "Resilience of Mass Support for Democratic Institutions and Processes in the Nascent Russian and Ukrainian Democracies," in ibid., pp. 53-111.
64 See *Benchmark in Democracy Building*.
65 "Economic Concerns Dominate Ukraine Opinion," USIA, 14 March 1996.
66 Ibid., p. 16.
67 Volodymyr Polokhalo, "The Neo-Totalitarian Transformation of Post Communist Power in Ukraine," *Political Thought* (Kiev) 3 (1994), p. 134.

Appendix

<hr />

Research guidelines for country-studies

Factors influencing the formation of political groups and parties

1. What are the key elements of the precommunist historical legacy of each country? Did the country have any precommunist experience of democracy, and have any elements of the postcommunist polity, such as particular government structures, intermediary associations, and political parties, been modeled on precommunist patterns?

2. What are the key elements of the legacy of the communist era? How has the political and social evolution of each country in the late communist era (e.g., the emergence or nonemergence of a significant dissent movement) affected the postcommunist formation of societal interest groups and parties?

3. How did the nature of the transition from communism (e.g., gradual versus abrupt; peaceful versus violent; internally – versus externally – precipitated) affect the formation of intermediary associations and parties in the early postcommunist period?

4. In the postcommunist selection of government leaders, what has been the importance of competitive elections and other forms of citizen political participation compared with threats of violence and the use of violence? Have military officers or the political police played a significant role in the selection process?

5. What political forces and calculations shaped the late-communist and especially the postcommunist electoral legislation and the timing of elections?

6. In brief, what are the main social and ethnic cleavages in postcommunist society?

<hr />

7. In brief, what have been the pattern and pace of postcommunist economic change, and which social groups have been the winners and losers?

8. How has the presence or absence of violent conflict inside the country or with other states affected the inclination and ability of political parties or other organizations with political agendas to mobilize social groups in support of internal democratization?

The political evolution of society

9. Which types of political associations or actors have become most prominent in each country's political life? (For example, political parties, state sector managerial lobbies, trade unions, business organizations, professional associations, religious organizations, clans, paramilitary units, criminal groups, etc.) How has the public perception of political parties and what they claim to represent affected citizens' attitudes toward the political system? What is the relative importance of parties as vehicles for new elites intent on accumulating political power and wealth? What alternative vehicles have been used or preferred?

10. How have attempted marketization and privatization affected the political strength and behavior of business and managerial groups? Have labor groups formed or formally affiliated themselves with political parties, and what role have they assumed in the financing of elections and the control of the media?

11. How have attempted marketization and privatization affected the political strength and behavior of agricultural groups? Have these groups formed or formally affiliated themselves with political parties, and what role have they played in elections?

12. How have attempted marketization and privatization affected the political strength and behavior of organized industrial labor? Have labor unions sponsored or become affiliated with political parties? In their political programs and behavior (e.g., strikes), what is the relative importance of preserving democracy versus improving economic welfare?

13. What has been the political impact of organized criminal groups? Are associations or political parties linked with organized crime? How has the public perception of the role of organized crime affected citizens' attitudes toward the political system?

14. What do existing survey data show about the level of public support within the country for democratization? Do attitudes toward democratic governmental institutions, political compromise, participation in elections,

and membership in political parties and intermediary associations differ significantly between younger and older citizens? Do attitudes on these matters differ substantially between major ethnic groups? Similarly, are there significant attitudinal differences between men and women over democracy and the various forms of political participation? How has the performance of the postcommunist economy affected public attitudes toward democracy?

15. Have the media become a channel for the expression of a range of societal interests independent of the preferences of the government? How has control of the media affected the conduct of elections and other forms of political participation?

Political parties and the party system

16. How strong are the country's political parties and party system? Since the end of communism, has the country's party system been characterized only by the creation of ephemeral parties, or do patterns of leadership, electoral results, and survey data indicate that some stable parties have emerged?

17. How have the structure and durability of political parties been affected by the electoral law(s) and by laws – if any – on campaign finance? How have parties been affected by the timing of elections – including regional versus countrywide elections?

18. How have the cohesion and durability of political parties been affected by the structure of government – in particular, the existence of a parliamentary versus a presidential system, of a unitary versus a federal state, and the amount of discretionary power in the hands of a state bureaucracy independent of the top governmental authorities?

19. To what extent have the renamed communist parties actually changed (a) their attitudes toward liberal democracy (b) their political leadership, and (c) the interests that they represent? What role has been played by electoral competition in any changes that have occurred?

20. Apart from communist successor-parties, have anti-democratic parties or social movements based on clericalism, fascist traditions, or radical nationalism developed?

21. Among the major parties, what proportion consists of parties that are: a) disloyal or loyal to democratic procedures b) ethnically or religiously based c) based primarily in one geographic region d) willing to endorse political violence, and e) linked with paramilitary forces?

22. Has the party system facilitated or obstructed the creation of governments able to formulate and carry through reasonably coherent policies? How has the capacity of postcommunist regimes to formulate and implement policies affected citizen support of democratization and marketization processes?

Index

Adamovich, Ales' 236, 239
age distribution of population
  Belarus 234
  Moldova 287
Agolets, Valentin 258
Agrarian Democratic Party (Moldova)
    307, 309, 310, 311, 312, 313,
    315–17, 319
  attitude to property and minorities 313,
    314, 315, 316
  and privatization 318
Agrarian Party (Belarus) 245–6
Agrarian Party of Russia (APR) 72, 84,
    102–3, 104, 143, 160
  and the 1995 elections 204–5
  and the Fifth State Duma 193, 195,
    198, 199
agriculture, in the Russian Federation 92
  see also rural population
Aksyuchits, Viktor 179–80, 188
Albania 4, 21
Albats, Evgeniia 95
Almond, Gabriel 50, 51
Andreeva, Nina 240
Andrews, Josephine 141
Andropov, Yuri 98
Anpilov, Viktor 189
Antonchyk, Syarhei 243, 266
APPE (Association of Privatized and
    Privatizing Enterprises) 192
APR *see* Agrarian Party of Russia
Arel, Dominque 353
armed forces *see* military
Armenia 4, 10
Astaf'ev, Mikhail 180, 188
authoritarianism/authoritarian regimes 6,
    7–8, 43
  Belarus 6, 7, 14, 19, 224, 256–9

and political culture 22, 24
and political participation 12–13, 14
and political parties 18–19, 21, 57
Russian Federation 69, 119, 132–3,
    150–1, 210
Ukraine 330, 363
Azerbaijan 8, 9, 10, 356

Baburin, Sergei 188, 204
Bahdankevich, Stanislau 245, 268, 271,
    274
Bahry, Donna 143
Bahusevich, Francishak 229
Baltic states 10, 20
  and Russian oil 273–4
Bauer, Vladimir 196
Belarus 9, 10, 25, 223–77
  authoritarian regime in 6, 7, 14, 19,
    224, 256–9
  constitution 254–5, 272
  Constitutional Court 266, 267, 272
  demographic trends 232, 233–4
  economic performance/reforms 234–5,
    250, 251–2, 268–70
  education 232, 234, 235, 259
  elections 247, 250, 253–4
    failed parliamentary 262–5
  electoral system 16
  ethnic composition 232, 243
  historical roots and dilemmas 225–8
  Hramada-Nasha Niva group 231, 244
  Kurapaty forest killings 232–3, 238
  labor force 233–4
  language and culture 226–7, 229–30,
    232, 235–6
  media 255–6, 263
  military 250, 252

and the Fifth State Duma 193, 194,
    199–200
Soviet Union (former)
  banning of 186, 188
  in Belarus 225
  and political party development
      180–2, 208
  and regional politics 132–3, 134, 136,
      138, 143, 144
  and Stalinism 150
  Ukraine (CPU) 336, 337–8, 339,
      342–3
  and the 1994 elections 352, 353, 354
communist regimes 4, 5
  and civil society 23
  economic performance 47–8
  legacy of 46–8
  political participation in 12–13
  and political parties 17
competitive elections 3, 4, 15
  and communist regimes 12
  and democratic consolidation 5–6, 43,
      44
  and the political evolution of society
      52, 53
  in postcommunist societies 5
  see also elections; electoral systems
Conciliation legislators (Moldova), atti-
    tude to property and minorities 313,
    314, 315, 316
conflict, violent political action 14–15
Congress of Russian Communities 72
Congress of Ukrainian Nationalists
    (CUN) 352, 354
consolidation of democracy see demo-
    cratic consolidation
constitutional democracies 4, 5, 7
Constitutional Democratic Party, Russia
    (CDP) 179, 180, 188
Cooper, Julian 100, 104
corruption 25–6, 53
  Moldova 286–7
  Russian Federation 70, 112–13
Cossacks 228
Council of Europe 224, 265, 272, 273
CPB see communist parties, Belarus
CPRF see under communist parties
CPSU see under communist parties
CPU see communist parties, Ukraine
Crawford, Beverly 45, 48
crime see organized crime
Croatia 5, 9, 10, 11, 16, 23
CUN (Congress of Ukrainian National-
    ists) 352, 354
Czech Republic 2, 5, 6, 10, 11, 17–18,
    25, 26

Czechoslovakia 9, 11, 344

Dabija, Nikolai 289
Dabravolskii, Alyaksandr 244
Dahl, Robert 49
Daniels, Robert V. 150
DCR (Democratic Choice of Russia)
    195–6, 202, 203, 205, 207
delegative democracy 6–7
democracy
  defining 4–5, 40–2, 330
  states with prior experience of 11–12,
      46
  transition to 5, 41, 43, 130, 131, 223
  see also liberal democracy
Democratic Choice of Russia (DCR)
    195–6
democratic consolidation 5–6, 130
  measuring 42–4
  Moldova 317–20, 320
  Russian Federation 119
  and regional politics 141–51, 162
Democratic Party of Russia see DPR
Democratic Party of the Soviet Union
    184
Democratic Party of Ukraine (DPU) 352,
    354
Democratic Russia movement 71–2, 139,
    182–4, 190, 192
Democratic Union (Russia) 183
democratization
  and democracy 42
  and establishing national identity 45–6
  failed 2
  and marketization 53
  paradigms of 2
  and political parties 17–19, 58
  and postcommunist political culture 24
  and prior experience of democracy
      11–12
diasporas
  internal ethnic 10
  Ukrainian 332–3
dictatorships 7, 24
  Belarus 224, 268–72
  in communist regimes 13
  and violent political action 14
direct democracy 12
direct military rule 7–8
dissidents 13–14, 23
  in Belarus 236–7
DPR (Democratic Party of Russia)
    181–2, 190, 191, 193, 194, 198
DPU (Democratic Party of Ukraine) 352,
    354
Drach, Ivan 341